Office of the
Deputy Prime Minister
Creating sustainable communities

D1796714

State of the English Cities

A Research Study

Volume 1

March 2006
Office of the Deputy Prime Minister: London

Photographic Acknowledgements:
Images reproduced by kind permission of:
Top left: Trams in Nottingham, Nottingham City Council
Centre right: Couple on sofa, Newcastle Gateway Initiative
Bottom left: Manchester Millennium Quarter, Manchester City Centre Management Co. Ltd

The findings and recommendations in this report are those of the authors
and do not necessarily represent the views of proposed policies of
the Office of the Deputy Prime Minister

The Office of the Deputy Prime Minister
Eland House
Bressenden Place
London SW1E 5DU
Telephone 020 7944 4400
Web site www.odpm.gov.uk

Further copies of this publication are available from:

ODPM Publications
PO Box 236
Wetherby
West Yorkshire
LS23 7NB
Tel: 0870 1226 236
Fax: 0870 1226 237
Textphone: 0870 120 7405
E-mail: odpm@twoten.press.net

This document is also available on the ODPM website.

Printed in the UK March 2006 on material containing no less than 75% post-consumer waste.

ISBN: 10 1-851128-45-X
        13 978185112845-7

Reference No: 05 HC 03595/1

Contents

Volume 1

Volume 2

Acknowledgements

This project would not have been possible without the sustained help and support from a wide range of colleagues. In particular we would like to acknowledge the invaluable contributions made by the following:

The members of our research teams: Jay Karecha, Richard Meegan, Jean Parry (European Institute for Urban Affairs, Liverpool John Moores University), Juliet Carpenter, Andrew Chadwick (Oxford Brookes University), Dimitris Ballas, John Pritchard, Bethan Thomas (University of Sheffield), Joanne Abbots, Dave Fitch, John Flint, Carol McKenzie (University of Glasgow), Mark Johnson, Miranda Phillips (National Centre for Social Research), Peter O'Brien (Llewellyn Davies)

Colleagues in the SOCR project team at the ODPM: Greg Clark, Rachel Conner, Joanna Disson, Sarah Fielder, Christine Gough, Mark Kleinman, David Lunts, Angela Ruotolo, Keith Thorpe.

The members of the SOCR Project Advisory Group: Joan Bailey, Jon Bright, Greg Clark, Sarah Fielder, Christine Gough, Paul Hildreth, Michael Kell, Mark Kleinman, Jacky Moran, Keith Thorpe (ODPM), Jacob Nell, Simon Ridley (HMT), Maria Kenyon (DTI, Small Business Service), Peter Bunn, Paul Steeples (DTI), Angelina Cannizzaro (DWP), James Shaw, John Shaw (DfES), Vanessa Brand (DCMS), Sue Woddington (DfID), Barbara Noble (DfT), David Lunts (Greater London Authority), Robin Benn (Scottish Executive), Bob Kerslake (Sheffield City Council), Lin Homer (Birmingham City Council), Alan Clarke (One North East), Eamonn Boylan (Manchester City Council), Richard Williamson (GOSW), Manny Lewis (LDA), Graham Garbutt (GOWM), Hazel Baird (CRE), Chris Brown (AMEC/Igloo), Roger Madelin (Argent), Tony Hawkhead (Groundwork), Trevor Beattie (English Partnerships), Joanna Averley (CABE), Derek Long (Housing Corporation), Geoff Mulgan (Institute of Community Studies), Lesley Chalmers (English Cities Fund), Alistair Parker (Cushman & Wakefield Healey & Baker), Rosemary Feenan (Jones Lang LaSalle), Dermot Finch (IPPR).

The very many colleagues across the country who gave us their time and views from a range of institutions, especially in the cities of: Birmingham, Bristol, Burnley, Cambridge, Derby, Leeds, Leicester, London, Manchester, Medway, Sheffield, Sunderland.

We are immensely grateful to all of them.

Foreword

This independent report to Government fulfils our commitment to publish a detailed update on the urban renaissance, 5 years after the Urban White Paper.

Since then, there's been remarkable progress in creating sustainable communities in our major towns and cities.

We do not underestimate the scale of the challenges which remain. But the clear message of this Report is that our cities are very much back in business as more successful places to live, work and enjoy. They are engines of growth once again.

After years of industrial change, our cities are competing more effectively in a rapidly changing global economy in which capital, goods and knowledge travel faster than ever before.

Old industrial assets like the canals and waterways have been transformed into attractive places to live and work.

People and jobs are coming back into our city centres – in many ways thanks to our planning policies which require retailers and developers to use brownfield sites before green fields.

Overall, a combination of sustained economic growth, increased investment through public private partnerships, and entrepreneurial local leadership means that our cities are better placed than at any time for a century or more.

After 8 years of economic growth, sustained investment, and local leadership, our cities are more confident than they've been for decades. But we recognise the need to continue to develop and improve. The economic and social gains of urban renewal need to be shared and sustained.

This Report provides an analysis – unprecedented in its scope and detail – of how our cities stand and they could improve. It offers detailed ideas for change to which the Government will respond.

The Government is determined to work with local people, businesses, local government and other stakeholders to seize the best opportunities for cities they have enjoyed for 100 years.

John Prescott
Deputy Prime Minister

Rt Hon David Miliband
Minister of Communities and
Local Government

Chapter 1: Towards a new urban agenda

1.   Introduction

1.1.1   In its Urban White Paper of 2000, *Towards an Urban Renaissance*, the Government made a commitment to commission a report on the progress and performance of English cities in the last five years. This State of the Cities report to government by a consortium of research organisations fulfils that commitment. It provides a comprehensive assessment of urban conditions and drivers of urban change in England. It reviews the impact of government policies upon cities, explores how they contribute to local, regional and national success and identifies key policy messages. Its four main themes, which reflect current government policy ambitions as well as much academic analysis of urban performance are – social cohesion; economic competitiveness and performance; liveability and governance.

1.1.2   This report is based on a series of reports prepared by the team, which contain a much richer mix of evidence, opinions and analysis than can be contained here. The study draws upon many sources – extensive academic and consultancy literature; case studies in 12 cities; interviews with over 250 policy makers; a review of international experience; analysis of public attitudes to cities and a review of demographic trends. It is underpinned by a new, large set of key indicators of urban performance specifically created for the project – the State of the Cities Database. The report is intended to be an authoritative statement of the state of English cities, the opportunities and challenges they face in an international context and the policy steps that need to be taken to build upon the progress that has been made in recent years.

1.2   Cities matter globally

1.2.1   These are exciting – if challenging – times for cities. During the past decade many cities in many countries have emerged from a period of decline to find new economic, political and cultural niches. There has been a sea change in how cities are regarded. Governments, the private sector and researchers increasingly see them as the dynamos of national and regional economies rather than economic liabilities. Cities are becoming again 'the wealth of nations'. (Boddy & Parkinson, 2004; Buck, Gordon, Harding & Turok, 2005)

1.2.2   In Europe and North America there is renewed investment in cities, growing urban cultural development and an increased appetite for urban lifestyles. The quality of urban life, culture and environment are increasingly recognised as one of the hallmarks of a successful society. Many cities have many assets which make them more – not less – significant in an increasingly globalised world. Many are centres of strategic decision-making, exchange and communication. Many have concentrations of intellectual resources in universities and research institutions, which encourage high levels of innovation. Many cities have achieved substantial physical regeneration especially of their centres, which offer impressive commercial, residential and retail facilities. Many have substantial cultural resources, which are increasingly the source of economic growth and job creation.

1.2.3 Cities are not only economic assets – not merely marketplaces. They have great capacity to promote community development, social cohesion, and civic and cultural identity. However, despite this potential, recent disturbances in some English and French cities have underlined that the pursuit of economic success has not led to the elimination of social problems, across countries with very different institutional, economic and social arrangements and policies. Achieving economic success with social justice in sustainable cities remains a challenge to many governments and organisations – local, regional, national and international.

Winds of policy change

1.2.4 For all these reasons, across Europe, north America and beyond, cities are moving up the political agenda and have become the focus of many policy initiatives. In Europe there has been particular focus upon cities and in recent years Ministers from the 25 EU member states and the European Commission have produced collective commitments to improve urban performance (EU 2005; ODPM 2005). At national level in Europe there have been three broad policy trends. First, the balance between national, regional and local institutions has been redrawn with many countries reducing the role of the national government and providing greater responsibilities – although not always resources – to cities. Second, many European governments have recognised the contribution that cities can make to national economies and have made more coherent attempts to boost their economic performance. Third, many have developed explicit national urban polices which specifically address the opportunities and challenges facing cities, their communities and residents.

1.2.5 The development of explicit national policies is most developed in the United Kingdom, France, the Netherlands, Denmark and Belgium. Others, including Germany, Finland, Sweden, Italy, and Portugal have placed urban issues on their national agendas, although not with the same critical mass. Some national governments have given greater powers and more scope for manoeuvre to cities. In some countries, cities have generated initiatives that have shaped the national urban agenda. Along with a continuing commitment to promote social cohesion in cities, governments in several countries have shifted their policy emphasis from social, problem-led policies to economic, opportunity-led policies. Many governments are developing policies to improve the international competitive position of their major cities. (Van den Berg et el 2006 forthcoming)

1.2.6 Much of this attention has been generated by concerns about national prosperity in the face of growing internationalisation of the world economy and competition from the newly industrialising countries, particularly in labour intensive, mass production manufacturing industries. In response to these competitive pressures many first world economies are trying to stay ahead of the game by developing activities based on high levels of knowledge where they still have the competitive edge in world markets. The Lisbon Strategy[1],

---

1 At its meeting in Lisbon in March 2000, the European Council launched its new mid-term strategic goal: to make the European Union by 2010 "the most competitive and dynamic knowledge-based economy in the world, capable of sustainable growth with more and better jobs and greater social cohesion". EU leaders also agreed a detailed strategy for achieving this goal – the Lisbon Strategy – aimed at:
 • Preparing the transition to the knowledge-based economy;
 • Promoting economic reforms for competitiveness and innovation;
 • Renewing the European social model by investing in people and combating social exclusion; and
 • Keeping up with a macro-economic policy mix for sustainable growth.

which hopes to make Europe the most dynamic knowledge economy in the world by 2010, is symptomatic of this effort. It is increasingly realised, however, that such actions do not take place on the head of the proverbial pin, but in real places – often cities.

1.2.7   Initially, the policy focus was upon regions. More recently it has shifted towards the relationships between cities and regions. In the USA, much research has shown strong relationships between city and regional economic performance (CCWG 2004). European evidence also shows that the most successful regions typically have an economically successful city at their core (ODPM 2004). As a result there is a growing recognition that the characteristics of cities – and the ways policies affect them – are crucial determinants of regional and national economic performance (Begg 1999, Pyke and Sengenberger 1992, Amin and Tomaney 1995).

1.3   Some key messages from the report

1.3.1   This long report has many detailed messages. To provide a route map for the reader we have outlined below some of the key messages.

Successful economic recovery in our cities – which needs to be expanded and sustained

1.3.2   A key message is that many English cities have been continuously economically successful during recent decades. Many others that have endured serious economic problems have begun a process of economic restructuring and are finding new niches. In particular, many former industrial cities have seen the worst of economic restructuring and have begun to exploit the advantages and successes associated with the service economy. It is important not to underestimate the achievements that have been made, as well as recognising the challenges which remain. In 2006, English cities look and are different from the 1970s and 80s when, at the height of their economic decline, many larger cities rapidly lost tens of thousands of manufacturing jobs and virtually their whole economic rationale. Since then such cities have dramatically improved their economic performance. The process of urban renaissance, especially in city centres, is well entrenched as many cities have dramatically improved the quality of their cultural, leisure and retail facilities. Substantial private sector investment is taking place. More generally, many cities have begun to develop post-industrial niches. They are beginning to expand and attract the economic sectors that underpin the more successful cities in the south and east. Many are developing the qualities and assets which underpin successful urban economies, – innovation, diversity, a skilled labour force, communications, quality of life and leadership capacity.

1.3.3   The process of urban regeneration is well developed – especially in many city centres – but it needs to be sustained and widened. The Government's policies will continue to have a significant influence on this. There is a need to ensure that the economic success of the cities is spread more widely, within the cities themselves and also across the country. There remain great social and economic differences within many English cities, whether or not they are successful economically. The process is uneven across England. London and the cities in the south and east typically have economies based more upon high value added, knowledge-based industries and are often better connected to the capital and the international economy. They are performing better than cities in the north and west of the country, which originally had industrial bases and fewer of the advantages of those in the south and east.

1.3.4   Closing the gap across the country remains a large challenge and is not quickly achieved. National policies will need to increase the connectedness of the national urban system and change the scale or direction of the flows of people and resources across it. For example, while levels of graduate creation are similar across urban areas, levels of retention differ as graduates flow from universities in cities in the north and west to the economic opportunities presented by London and cities in the south and east. In part, the challenge will also be to increase the physical connectivity across the system. The ambition must be to encourage the cities of the north and west to perform more effectively themselves and also help to reduce the pressures that growth brings to the south and east, which could limit their cities' long term sustainability. The recent Northern Way[2] initiative should help this process.

We need to learn from successful cities abroad

1.3.5   There is real evidence than many English cities are picking up in terms of their recent economic performance. But many English cities, with the notable exception of the global player of London, are not performing as well as their competitors in Europe and beyond. In this context the framework set by national government matters a great deal. Although there are differences, the trend in continental Europe is to decentralise and regionalise decision-making, placing powers at the lowest level. The evidence suggests that where cities are given more freedom and resources they have responded by being more proactive, entrepreneurial and successful. Decentralisation in France has invigorated provincial cities during the past 20 years. The most successful cities in Europe have been German, which is the most decentralised country in Europe. The renaissance of Barcelona in part stems from the move towards regionalisation and the lessening of the grip of the capital city, Madrid. In addition, some European governments have been moving towards more long-term contractual relationships between national and local government to deliver improved urban economic performance.

We need to encourage local leadership

1.3.6   Local leadership is important. Many of the advances of recent years have been as a consequence of the sustained national economic recovery, which has provided a more supportive environment in which cities have flourished. But they are also the result of engaged and successful local leadership, in both the

2 The Northern Way is a long-term strategy focused on closing the £30 billion productivity gap between the North and the UK average. It is being taken forward by the three northern Regional Development Agencies under the leadership of an independently chaired Steering Group. Further information can be found on their website at www.thenorthernway.co.uk

public and private sectors, exploiting favourable national economic performance. There is much evidence that local leadership is crucial in helping to find new economic futures for cities, their businesses and residents. This report provides many examples of entrepreneurial local leadership, often by local government.

1.3.7   Cities are critical in many ways to the successful delivery of national government ambitions. There is much support within them for the key principles which increasingly shape government policy for cities. These include: greater investment of public resources in the mainstream programmes which impact upon cities; greater recognition and focus upon the economic potential of cities and the policy levers to encourage it; greater willingness to address regional imbalances; recognition of the importance of sustainable communities; greater focus upon City-Regions and collaboration across regions; and growing willingness to simplify and reduce national demands and constraints upon local and regional players.

1.3.8   This report also shows that the policy climate for cities in the past was not sufficiently helpful to city leaders and their partners. Government needs to ensure that all departments and mainstream policies continue to focus on cities. The ODPM needs sufficient internal capacity to carry through its agenda. Urban policy must continue to encourage the efforts of local and regional players who have to make national policies work. The geographical boundaries within which cities have to operate must encourage their economic success. The balance of powers and resources between national, regional and local governments should allow English cities to benefit from the freedoms, resources and responsibilities found in the more successful European and North American cities.

1.3.9   There is plenty of evidence in this report that many English cities have the qualities, assets and leadership skills to make a growing contribution to national welfare and prosperity. More cities could contribute more in future. Previous policies have not always helped that cause. However, there is evidence that government today values the contribution of cities and wants to sustain the right support and right context for successful City-Regions. But an even greater commitment to that cause by all of government could deliver local, regional and national economic and social benefits. Later chapters of this report provide the detailed evidence for this assessment. They also provide more detailed policy messages.

1.3.10   The really key message of this report is that England's cities are now better placed than at any time since the end of the nineteenth century to become motors of national advance. The combination of sustained macro-economic growth, rising public investment in education, policing, health and transport, partnership with the private sector, growing higher education and a dynamic social and cultural scene is uniquely positive. The years of decline and decay have been overcome. There is now an opportunity to create centres of economic and social progress that will shape the country for a generation. There are big challenges ahead. Only the right policy decisions will deliver that positive future. But the opportunity is clear, present and exciting.

Chapter 2: Evaluating policy for English cities

2.1 Introduction

2.1.1 This chapter does two things. First it outlines the thrust of government policy for cities since 1997, identifying its key principles and the actions it has undertaken. Second it identifies, in some detail, the methodology we use in this report to evaluate that rapidly changing set of policies.

2.2 The changing landscape of policy for English cities

2.2.1 Our introduction argued that in recent years cities have become more significant economically and politically at a global level. Where does the UK fit into this increased international concern for cities? It has had a policy for cities for much longer than many other countries. A national policy has existed in some form since the late 1960s. However, during this period its scope, nature and resources have expanded enormously as different governments have produced different answers to an enduring set of questions about policy for cities. Those questions include:

- What is the target of policy – inner city problems or wider urban opportunities?

- Should policy focus on economic, social, physical or environmental factors – or some combination of all four?

- Should social need or economic opportunity determine priorities and the flow of national resources to cities?

- Are competition and partnership mutually reinforcing or exclusive ways of delivering urban policy?

- What is the best mix of public, private and community intervention?

- What is the best method of improving the delivery of urban policies – structural changes or improved processes?

- What is the right relationship and balance of powers and resources between national and local government?

- What is the best spatial level to address urban issues – neighbourhood, city, City-Region or region?

- What is the best mix of special policy initiatives and mainstream programmes?

- How can government develop an integrated approach to cities?

2.2.2   During the 1980s and much of the 1990s the previous governments had particular answers to those questions. It wanted to reduce the role of the public sector and increase that of the private sector in relation to cities. It reduced many of local authorities' powers and resources. Many local services were privatised or opened up to competitive tendering. Local control over revenue and capital spending was reduced, as was national financial support to local authorities. New actors from the private and community sectors became involved in delivering urban services and urban regeneration. The result was: declining public expenditure for cities; highly fragmented local service provision; a reduced role for local government; greater role for the private sector and public-private partnerships; an explicit national urban policy although not linked to mainstream programmes; and the allocation of resources on the basis of competition rather than need.

2.2.3   These developments had led to concerns in many cities, including: that although resources for the narrow urban programme had increased, expenditure on mainstream programmes for cities was reduced; not all government departments were equally committed to supporting cities; the impact of resources was diluted by being spread across too many initiatives; and competition was an inappropriate way of allocating resources to cities.

Government policies for cities 1997-2006

2.2.4   When the current government took office in 1997 it identified four main challenges of urban policy and governance. Policymaking had become too centralised, bureaucratic and remote from local people. The gap between poorer and richer urban neighbourhoods and regions was rapidly widening. The creation of large numbers of quangos required new ways of working between local, regional and national partners. Declining local voting demonstrated the need for democratic renewal, modernisation of local government and new forms of citizen engagement.

What has been done?

2.2.5   There has been an enormous amount of activity and change in urban policy in England during the past seven years. There has been a large number of independent and government reports assessing the conditions and prospects of English cities. The most notable include: *Lord Rogers Task Force on Urban Renaissance* (DETR, 1999), the government's own White Paper in 2000, *Better Towns and Cities: Delivering an Urban Renaissance*; the *National Neighbourhood Renewal Strategy* in 2001 (SEU, 2001) and The Sustainable Communities Plan in 2003 (ODPM, 2003)[3]. There have been white papers, green papers and legislation on housing, planning, regional government and local government.

3 *Sustainable Communities: building for the future*, ODPM 2003.

2.2.6   The government has introduced a range of measures designed to:

- devolve responsibility by giving regional and local organisations greater discretion in return for good performance;

- promote greater collaboration between local, regional and national partners and more strategic, 'joined up' governance;

- modernise local government by creating stronger, visible, civic leadership and reward achievement;

- improve the quality, value for money of local services and their responsiveness to communities;

- encourage greater citizen engagement in decision-making.

2.2.7   The measures have been underpinned by the following principles.

Recognising cities are economic drivers not liabilities

2.2.8   The government increasingly regards cities as economic opportunities rather than liabilities, although achieving social cohesion and encouraging liveability and sustainability remain important goals.

Changing the balance of power between nation, region, city and neighbourhoods

2.2.9   There have been efforts to improve working relationships and reduce conflicts between national government and cities. National resources to cities have increased. Competition between cities for resources has been reduced. Controls over local authorities have been reduced, combined with attempts to improve urban mainstream services with agreed targets. There has been increased regionalisation with new institutions like Regional Development Agencies and Regional Assemblies. City-regions have been developed. Efforts have been made to improve deprived neighbourhoods. The importance of mainstream programmes, which provide the bulk of public expenditure for cities, have been clearly recognised.

Reducing sprawl and encouraging sustainability

2.2.10   There have been changes in planning policies and legislation in relation to housing, retail and transport to discourage suburbanisation and encourage the use of brownfield rather than greenfield land.

Developing sustainable communities and managing housing markets

2.2.11   Government has recognised the different housing pressures in different regions of the country with a new policy for Sustainable Communities and new initiatives, like Growth Areas and Housing Market Renewal Pathfinders created to address over and under-supply of housing in the north and west and south and east.

Improving joined up policy delivery

2.2.12 The government has recognised the need to integrate different departments by giving them joint targets for improved urban performance.

2.2.13 Table 2.1 identifies some of the key actions government has taken to implement these principles since 1997. It established a Social Exclusion Unit to address the problems of deprived neighbourhoods. It launched a range of new area-based initiatives, like New Deal for Communities, Educational Action Zones, Health Action Zones, Sure Start and Employment Zones. It set up business-led Regional Development Agencies to improve the co-ordination of regional economic strategies and to provide a strategic framework for local regeneration programmes.

2.2.14 In 2000, the White Paper on Towns and Cities rehearsed the country's principal urban challenges, set out a new vision for urban living and accepted the need for long-term policies that jointly addressed economic, social and environmental issues. It agreed to monitor the progress of cities closely and recommended the formation of an Urban Policy Unit within the Office of the Deputy Prime Minister and a Cabinet Committee to review the collective impact of national policies on cities.

2.2.15 Government introduced a series of measures to improve service provision in urban areas. A comprehensive spending review led to three-year departmental budgets to promote longer-term planning and cross-departmental working. It introduced a new framework for local government to achieve greater accountability, innovation and democratic renewal. This set clearer targets for service improvement and tightened inspection regimes, allowed for directly elected mayors and cabinet style administrations. Councils were required to draw up Community Strategies with partners and to obtain 'Best Value' for services in place of compulsory competitive tendering. A strategic authority headed by a directly elected mayor was created for London with responsibility for transport, police, fire services and economic development.

2.2.16 Government appointed the Egan review on the nature and quality of sustainable communities skills, which led to the creation of Regional Centres for Excellence and the Academy for Sustainable Communities in 2005 to improve the supply of skills. There are continuing experiments to create closer working between central and local partners and greater local freedoms and flexibilities through Local Area Agreements. RDA responsibilities in enterprise support, business-university links, innovation, research and development, inter-regional strategies and regional skills planning have been increased.

2.2.17 In 2004, to counterbalance continued growth in the south, government and the three northern Regional Development Agencies, launched the Northern Way Strategy. This is intended to increase investment in the north's eight major City-Regions and boost prosperity, jobs and create sustainable communities. An additional £100m was provided to fund projects. Similar inter-regional strategies for the midlands and south west have since been prepared, though they differ in strategy and content.

Table 2.1: Major developments in urban policy and governance since 1997

Event	Details/significance
Social Exclusion Unit established (1997)	Set up to tackle the problems of marginalised groups and areas
Education/Health/Employment Action Zones & New Deal for Communities programmes launched (1998)	Shift away from competitive bidding to resource allocation based on need
Regional Development Agencies created (1998)	To promote economic development within regions and co-ordinate regional regeneration plans
Commission for Architecture and the Built Environment established (1998)	To champion better architecture, urban design and parks and open spaces and also perform a design review role
Urban Task Force appointed to identify how to tackle urban decline (1999)	Recommended better designed and maintained buildings and spaces, higher density of development and related encouragement of public transport, walking and cycling, incentives to promote more urban rather than green field development
Urban White Paper (2000)	Endorsed most of UTF recommendations except VAT equalisation
Local Government Act (2000)	Introduced new power of well-being, requiring community strategies for localities and new political structures – mayors and cabinets with scrutiny committees and area committees
Neighbourhood Renewal Unit established (2001)	Created to implement National Strategy for Neighbourhood Renewal. To narrow gap between most deprived neighbourhoods and the rest through realignment and reshaping of mainstream funding programmes.
Urban Policy Unit created within ODPM (2001)	Brief to create framework for urban revival with responsibility for improving urban design standards, creating play areas and greenspaces and co-ordinating 'cleaner, safer, green' agenda and promoting inter-regional growth plans
Local Strategic Partnerships launched (2001)	Designed to encourage public, private, community and voluntary sectors to work together in a more integrated way
Sustainable Communities Plan (2003)	Sets out growth plans for South East, measures for tackling low housing demand and to create sustainable communities that minimise resource use, environmental impact and social polarisation
Making it Happen: The Northern Way (2004)	A growth strategy and action plan for the North, designed to narrow the £29bn prosperity gap between the North and the rest of the UK in the eight constituent 'City-Regions'
Planning and Compulsory Purchase Act (2004)	New planning system replaces Unitary Development Plans with Local Development Frameworks which must incorporate community strategy provisions and introduces regional spatial strategies
Egan Review (2004)	Reviewed skills needed to deliver sustainable communities agenda and recommended the creation of a national centre for sustainable community skills

Table 2.1: Major developments in urban policy and governance since 1997 *(continued)*

Event	Details/significance
Local Area Agreements pilots launched (2004)	Mechanisms to improve local services through better joint working between central and local partners and more locally tailored policymaking
Sustainable Communities: Homes for All (2005)	Government's five year plan for delivering new homes, enhancing residential environments, promoting market renewal in low demand areas, making housing more affordable and extending choice
Sustainable Communities: People, Places and Prosperity (2005)	Government's five year plan to give people more say in how places are run, working with local authorities to deliver excellent services and provide leadership, tackling neighbourhood disadvantage and increasing regional prosperity

Source: Audit Commission, 2004; Paskell & Power, 2005

2.2.18 In recent years, government has placed increased emphasis on mainstream programmes as research revealed that these programmes sometimes perpetuated neighbourhood inequalities and undermined area-based programmes (SEU, 1998). The National Strategy for Neighbourhood Renewal (SEU, 2001) stressed the need to integrate both. It required local authorities in the 88 most deprived areas to set up Local Strategic Partnerships (LSPs) involving public, private, voluntary and community bodies to promote joint working and draw up Local Neighbourhood Renewal Strategies to improve deprived neighbourhoods. It set up a Neighbourhood Renewal Fund to support improvements in mainstream service delivery in those areas and appointed Neighbourhood Managers. It established the Community Empowerment Fund and Community Chests to encourage and support financially community involvement in LSPs.

2.2.19 Government established a set of floor targets to improve economic and social conditions in the poorest neighbourhoods and convergence targets to close the gap between them and the average. It accepted its mainstream programmes should make a major contribution to the NSNR. Although it has continued to introduce area-based initiatives, government has increasingly allocated funding on the basis of need not competitive bidding (Table 2.2).

Table 2.2: Main elements of the Neighbourhood Renewal Strategy

Worklessness • New Deal • Work-related tax and benefit changes • Action Team for Jobs	• Additional childcare funding • Additional RDA funding • Phoenix Fund for business start-ups
Community Safety • More drug treatment funding • Additional funding for Police • New National Drug Treatment Agency	• Additional responsibilities for Crime & Disorder Reduction Partnerships (anti-social behaviour and racist crime) • Neighbourhood Wardens schemes
Education and Skills • Extension of Sure Start • Extension of Excellence for Cities • Entitlement to out-of-hours study support for secondary pupils • Children's fund for work with vulnerable 5-13 year olds	• Connexions • New online centres for adults • Adult Basic Skills strategy
Health • Primary care staff recruitment incentives in deprived areas • Additional Personal Medical Service schemes	• More help for smokers • Healthy eating schemes for children
Housing and physical environment • More funding for housing investment and management • More stock transfers	• Clarification of local authority role in preventing abandonment • Housing Corporation pilot on funding demolition.

Source: Lutpon, 2003

The Sustainable Communities Plan

2.2.20   In 2003, spiralling house and land prices and a shortage of affordable homes in London and the south east, which contrasted with depressed housing markets and low demand in the north and midlands, led the government to produce its Sustainable Communities Plan (SCP). This three year £22bn investment package was designed to increase housing supply in growth areas, provide more affordable housing for low income households and key workers, address low demand problems, regenerate deprived areas, bring social and private rented homes to a decent standard, introduce a regional approach to housing policy and measures to increase supply of regeneration skills. The SCP is a key policy ambition for government in relation to urban areas.

2.2.21   The government's definition of its sustainable communities is that they are places where people 'want to live and work, now and in the future.' They should be: active, inclusive and safe; well run; environmentally sensitive; well designed and built; well connected; thriving; well served and fair for everyone.

How will sustainable communities be achieved?

2.2.22 Those ambitions for sustainable communities translate into a set of five strategic priorities for the Office of the Deputy Prime Minister, with 8 performance targets or Public Service Agreements (PSAs). They are the specific policy ambitions and targets against which current government policy for urban areas must be assessed.

Table 2.3 ODPM Strategic Priorities and PSA Targets

Strategic Priority I Tackling disadvantage by reviving the most deprived neighbourhoods, reducing social exclusion and supporting society's most vulnerable groups.	**PSA 1.** Tackle social exclusion and deliver neighbourhood renewal, working with departments to help them meet their PSA floor targets, in particular narrowing the gap in health, education and crime, worklessness, housing and liveability outcomes between the most deprived areas and the rest of England, with measurable improvement by 2010.
Strategic Priority II Promoting the development of the English regions by improving their economic performance so that all are able to reach their full potential, and developing an effective framework for regional governance taking account of the public's view of what's best for their area.	**PSA 2.** Make sustainable improvements in the economic performance of all English regions by 2008, and over the long term reduce the persistent gap in growth rates between the regions, demonstrating progress by 2006. This PSA is owned jointly with the Department of Trade and Industry and HM Treasury.
Strategic Priority III Delivering better services, by devolving decision making to the most effective level – regional, local or neighbourhood. Promoting high quality, customer-focused local services and ensuring that adequate, stable resources are available to local government. Clarifying the roles and functions of local government, its relationship with central and regional government and the arrangements for neighbourhood engagement, in the context of a shared strategy for local government.	**PSA 3.** By 2010, reduce the number of accidental fire-related deaths in the home by 20% and the number of deliberate fires by 10%. **PSA4.** By 2008, improve the effectiveness and efficiency of local government in leading and delivering services to all communities.

Table 2.3 ODPM Strategic Priorities and PSA Targets *(continued)*

Strategic Priority IV Delivering a better balance between housing supply and demand by supporting sustainable growth, reviving markets and tackling abandonment.	**PSA 5.** Achieve a better balance between housing availability and the demand for housing, including improving affordability, in all English regions while protecting valuable countryside around our towns, cities and in the green belt and the sustainability of towns and cities. **PSA6.** The planning system to deliver sustainable development outcomes at national, regional and local levels through efficient and high quality planning and development management processes, including through achievement of best value standards for planning by 2008.
Strategic Priority V Ensuring people have decent places to live by improving the quality and sustainability of local environments and neighbourhoods, reviving brownfield land, and improving the quality of housing.	**PSA7.** By 2010, bring all social housing into a decent condition with most of this improvement taking place in deprived areas, and for vulnerable households in the private sector, including families with children, increase the proportion who live in homes that are in decent condition. **PSA8.** Lead the delivery of cleaner, safer and greener public spaces and improvement of the quality of the built environment in deprived areas and across the country, with measurable improvement by 2008.

2.3 The Methodology of the State of the English Cities Report

2.3.1 The remainder of this chapter discusses how we undertook the work. First it discusses methodological issues – the database and the case studies. Next it discusses our substantive work, grouping them around two broad themes. The first theme is processes, places and people. It asks the question – what is going on in English cities? The second theme is policies. It asks the question – are policies helping or hindering cities?

The State of the Cities Database (SOCD)

2.3.2 The SOCD provides extensive quantitative data which shows how different urban areas in England have been performing and changing in recent years at different spatial levels. It is flexible enough to incorporate new data in future about different indicators, policies, and spatial levels. The database will be publicly accessible and will allow users to conduct more detailed analyses of places or themes than we are able to do in this report. Since government will sustain it after the State of the Cities Report has been published, it also provides a baseline against which to measure change in the future.

2.3.3   The SOCD has a set of 60 key indicators that draw upon the analytical framework and drivers of urban success developed in earlier work for the ODPM, *Competitive European Cities: Where Do the Core Cities Stand?* (ODPM, 2004). These are: economic diversity, skilled workforce, connectivity, innovation in firms and organisations, quality of life and strategic capacity to deliver long term development strategies. The indicators of these drivers are grouped under four broad headings: social cohesion, economic competitiveness, liveability and governance.

2.3.4   The SOCD collected, where available, data for the following time points: the most recent available period – e.g. 2001, 2002, 2003; the position in the middle 90s and at the beginning of the 1990's. Where data was readily available for more time points, for example the Census, the database tracks trends over a longer time period. The indicators are listed in Annex 1.

For which areas are indicators being collected?

2.3.5   The point of departure for our definition was the official set of Urban Areas definitions based on 2001 built-up areas. Hence we identify major cities in terms of their physical extent and not in terms of local authority areas or administrative boundaries. We created a set of Primary Urban Areas (PUAs) which have a minimum size cut-off 125,000 in terms of their 2001 population. This definition produces the list of 56 cities (PUAs) shown in Map 2.1. They contain 58% of the population of England and 63% of its employment. It is important to remember throughout this report, that PUAs are not coterminous with local government boundaries, even though the names are sometimes the same. PUAs are larger than local authorities and frequently contain several of them. Annex 2 specifies which individual local authorities are grouped into the 56 PUAs. The SOCD does have data about individual local authorities which can be accessed in future. However, the spatial unit for our statistical analysis of cities in this report is not local authorities.

Map 2.1

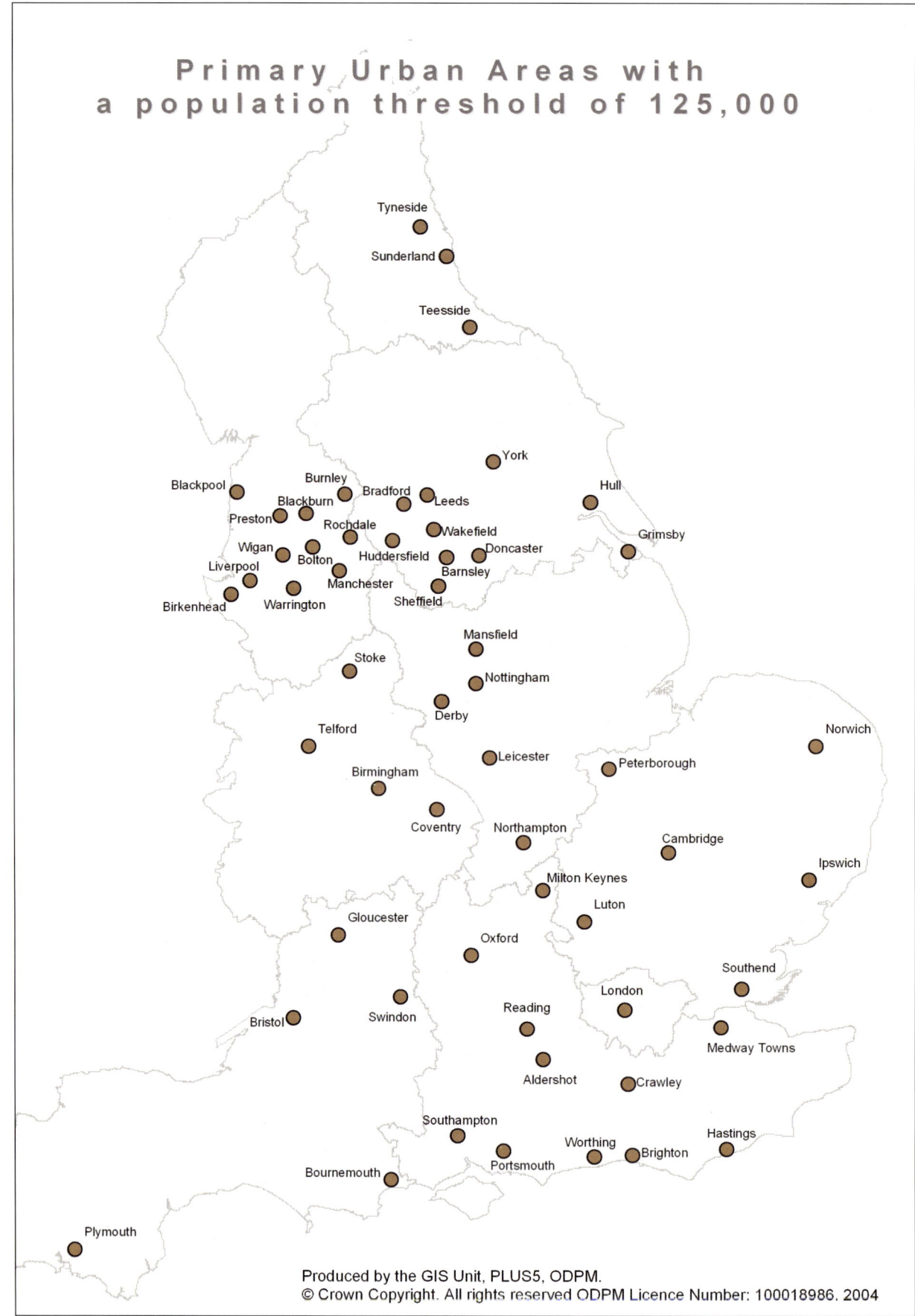

Primary Urban Areas with
a population threshold of 125,000

Tyneside

Sunderland

Teesside

York

Blackpool
Burnley
Blackburn
Bradford
Leeds
Hull
Preston
Rochdale
Wakefield
Grimsby
Wigan
Doncaster
Liverpool
Bolton
Huddersfield
Barnsley
Manchester
Birkenhead
Warrington
Sheffield

Mansfield

Stoke
Nottingham

Derby

Telford
Norwich
Leicester
Peterborough

Birmingham

Coventry
Northampton
Cambridge
Ipswich

Milton Keynes
Luton

Gloucester
Oxford

Southend

Bristol
Swindon
Reading
London
Medway Towns

Aldershot
Crawley

Southampton
Worthing
Hastings
Portsmouth
Brighton
Bournemouth

Plymouth

Produced by the GIS Unit, PLUS5, ODPM.
© Crown Copyright. All rights reserved ODPM Licence Number: 100018986. 2004

For which spatial levels does the SOCD produce data?

2.3.6   The project explores differences between as well as within urban areas. The SOCD contains data which places the PUAs in their wider national, regional and City-Regional context. For the regional level we use the Government Office in the Regions boundaries. For the City-Regions we worked with Travel to Work Area (TTWA) boundaries. For differences within the PUAs we provide data for all local authorities, all wards and other neighbourhood tracts created for this project.

2.3.7   Hence the SOCD provides data for seven different spatial levels:

1. the 56 Primary Urban Areas

2. the 56 Travel to Work Areas

3. the individual local authorities

4. each Government Office Region

5. all of England

6. all wards

7. a set of neighbourhood 'tracts' averaging 35,000 residents

Typology

2.3.8   In this report we explore the trends affecting different types of urban areas. There are a wide variety of classifications currently in use. Our classification uses two criteria – regional location and city size. There is no perfect way of dividing the country on a regional basis. We use the boundaries of Government Offices in the Regions to define the regions. All areas falling in the boundaries of the Government Offices for the North West, North East, Yorkshire and the Humber and West Midlands we categorise as in the north and west. All other areas in the remaining Government Offices we place in the south and east. We treat the capital London a separate case. We also examine the six metropolitan areas of the north and west as a separate category. We define large cities as those with a resident population of over 275,000 in 2001. Small cities are between 125,000 and 275,000. Large towns are between 50,000 and 125,000. Small towns are below 50,000 population. Therefore, this report typically analyses and presents data for the following types of places:

- London

- Six metropolitan centres in the north and west – Birmingham, Leeds, Liverpool, Manchester, Newcastle, Sheffield

- Large cities in the north and west

- Small cities in the north and west

- Large cities in the south and east

- Small cities in the south and east

- Large towns in the north and west

- Large towns in the south and east

- Small towns and rural areas in the north and west

- Small towns and rural areas in the south and east

Case studies – why, how, where and what?

2.3.9   We undertook 12 case studies to fill gaps in the evaluation literature, provide qualitative material to complement the quantitative data analysis, explore different types of urban area, explore differences within urban areas, explore policy effects and identify emerging trends and future challenges. They involved quantitative data collection, review of key documents and interviews with key actors in the public, private and community sectors. Each case study explored the following range of questions:

The State of the City/City-Region

- Had the area improved in the past decade in terms of its economic competitiveness, levels of social exclusion, governance, and liveability?

- Which people and places had been the winners and losers in the process of change?

- What were the main challenges facing the area?

The Impact of Government Policy

- What had been the relative importance of central government policy in change?

- Did the impact of government policy upon different parts of the area vary?

- What was the relative importance of mainstream and area-based policies?

- How well integrated was policy horizontally, vertically and sectorally?

- Had local governance influenced the recent trajectory of the city?

- What were the potential effects of new national policy agendas on the area?

Policy lessons

- Which government policies had been most successful in improving the area's performance?

- What principles characterised the more successful government policies?

- What policy pitfalls should be avoided in future?

Where?

2.3.10 The case studies were chosen to illustrate the diversity of urban areas in England in terms of size, geographical location, economic performance, social challenges and range of policy interventions. We selected representatives from: the capital city, from the eight Core Cities with a range of economic and social performance, smaller cities facing significant economic and social challenges in the north and west and south and east; and smaller, more economically successful cities in the north and west and the south and east. The exact choice is:

- London
- Manchester
- Birmingham
- Bristol
- Cambridge
- Derby

- Burnley
- Leicester
- Leeds
- Sunderland
- Sheffield
- Medway

2.4 The structure of the report

Section 1: Processes, places and people

Chapter 3: The demographic shape of urban England

2.4.1 This chapter explores key demographic trends in urban England in recent years. It assesses the extent to which they represent a continuation of or break with previous trends. It addresses four questions: what are demographic megatrends affecting England and how do they impact on its cities? How far are cities performing in terms of population and employment growth? What are the drivers of change in terms of components of change and cities' characteristics? What issues do they raise for policy?

Chapter 4: The competitive economic performance of English cities

2.4.2   This chapter explores urban competitiveness defined as the ability of cities to continually upgrade their business environment, skill base, and physical, social and cultural infrastructures, to attract and retain high-growth, innovative and profitable firms, and an educated, creative and entrepreneurial workforce, to thereby enable it achieve a high rate of productivity, high employment rate, high wages, high GVA per capita, and low levels of income inequality and social exclusion. It does this by analysing SOCD data on the performance of the 56 largest City-Regions and by exploring the economic performance of and the impact of policies on four cities – Sheffield, Derby Cambridge and London.

Chapter 5: Social cohesion in English cities

2.4.3   This chapter assesses the current state of social cohesion in English cities, comparing the position of different cities and types of city, exploring whether policy has made a difference to social conditions. It uses data from the SOCD as well as original analyses of a variety of survey-based data on less tangible aspects of cohesion. It explores issues of social cohesion and the role of policy in five cities which face different challenges and have had different experiences – Sunderland, Leeds, Burnley, Leicester and Medway.

Chapter 6: Liveability in English cities

2.4.4   This chapter explores whether our cities and towns are beginning to look, feel and work better in what ways and why. It focuses on environmental quality, place quality in physical and functional terms and safety and security of place. It combines statistical data on the state of some components of the built environment, using the SOCD, national Best Value Performance Indicators data and local Quality of Life surveys and qualitative data in two of our case study cities – Manchester and Leicester.

Chapter 7: Public attitudes in English cities

2.4.5   This chapter explores public attitudes to urban life and conditions, drawing primarily on the British Social Attitudes Survey. It contrasts the attitudes of urban and non-urban residents and explores the attitudes of city-dwellers to the following themes explored in this report: cohesion, connectivity, services and governance.

Chapter 8: English cities in an international context

2.4.6   This chapter provides a comparative perspective to the English SOCR. The review of the North American experience focuses on trends in and policy responses to demographic change, immigration and diversity, marketing restructuring, employment decentralisation and the geography of poverty. The review of European experience focuses upon urban trends, challenges and policy responses drawing upon a variety of literature and statistical databases including the European Urban Audit. It identifies potential policy lessons for English cities.

Section 2: Policies – helping or hindering?

2.4.7   This section reviews an extensive range of academic, consultancy and government publications and forms a bridge to Section 1, which drew primarily upon the SOCD and fieldwork. It uses a wide range of evaluations to assess the extent to which policies have helped or hindered the development of urban England. This section reviews the nature and role of government policies and their impact upon urban areas examining how policies interact at different spatial levels – neighbourhoods, local authority, City-Region and region. It identifies what has worked best in encouraging competitiveness, liveability and governance and identifies key messages about what to build upon and what to avoid in future. The section has four chapters.

Chapter 9 Have policies made cities more socially cohesive and liveable?

Chapter 10 Have policies made cities more competitive?

Chapter 11 Have policies made cities better governed?

Chapter 12 Policies on the ground

This chapter moves beyond literature to explore the views of key policy makers and interviews with policy makers and recipients at national and regional level and case studies in Manchester, Birmingham and Bristol.

Section 3: Positions and prospects

Chapter 13: English cities: picking up, catching up, staying up?

2.4.8   This chapter marshals the key data and trends presented in earlier chapters. It shows whether cities are improving their performance and to what extent cities in the north and west are catching up with cities in the south and east and internationally.

Chapter 14: Policy for Cities: What's Next

2.4.9   This chapter draws together the key messages about the impact of policies upon cities in the past decade. It identifies the features which have made policies more or less successful and choices that government needs to address to sustain the gains that cities have made in recent years.

Chapter 3: The demographic shape of urban England

3.1   Introduction

3.1.1   The chapter argues that several megatrends now provide a more promising context for 'urban renaissance' than in the past. However, it also suggests that cities generally have relatively greater potential for population and employment growth. It shows that there remain powerful forces behind the migration of people from cities to towns and more rural areas, including the continued strong national preference for living in the 'countryside'. But it also emphasises the variation between cities' performance in terms of their size and regional location; the distinctiveness and dominance of London and the recent improved performance of some large cities in the north and west.

3.1.2   The chapter focuses on the changing size, distribution and composition of population as well as the broad pattern of employment change. For each of these issues, it looks at variation across the settlement system using the ten-fold classification based on regional location and urban status outlined in Chapter 2. In terms of the 56 Primary Urban Areas which are the primary focus of this study, it pays particular attention to the 24 cities with over 275,000 residents. In particular, it explores the experience of the seven big cities of London and the six 'Mets' – the cities of the former metropolitan counties – Birmingham, Leeds, Liverpool, Manchester, Newcastle and Sheffield. In interpreting the results in this and many subsequent chapters, it is important to remember that – as outlined in Chapter 2 – each of the 56 cities is defined on the basis of its 'Primary Urban Area'. This means that the data for a city refer not to the narrower local authority area but to its continuously built-up area including the more suburban areas surrounding it.

3.2   The wider context of population and employment change

3.2.1   A number of major, social developments are taking place which affect England's cities directly or indirectly. The majority are shared with many other countries, though their importance varies in scale, timing and peculiarities of history and geography. The most significant are the following:

- The population of England is now growing more rapidly than at any time since the early 1970s, providing a demographic driver for city growth.

- England is now a country of net immigration, with particularly high gains in recent years for London and a number of other cities, especially in the Greater South East.

- Through a combination of continued net immigration and strong natural increase, England's Black and ethnic minority population has been growing in size and becoming more diverse, although remains concentrated in certain areas.

- Fertility rates, while higher than for some European countries, remain well below the level needed for long-term population replacement. However, the rate of natural increase is high in certain cities including London.

- Life expectancy is continuing to rise, with a particularly marked fall in mortality rates of older males in recent years, suggesting a reversal of long-term increase in the proportion of elderly people living alone.

- The population is ageing markedly and will continue to do so despite the substantial net immigration of young adults, with England's more rural areas generally leading on this process.

- Patterns of partnering and household formation have become more fluid, with rising rates of marriages ending in divorce and of unmarried cohabitation and separation.

- Average household size continues to decline, and especially the proportion of 'home aloners' to rise, because of lower fertility, more older people, more household fission and more people 'living apart together'.

- The proportion of younger adults without children has risen, constituting a potentially favourable trend for cities since these seem to be more favourably disposed to city living than families with children.

- Aspirations for, and the achievement of, home ownership continue to remain high, as the social composition of households has moved increasingly into white-collar and more skilled occupations and as female participation in the labour force has grown.

- The quest for the 'rural idyll' appears just as strong nationally as in the past, according to opinion polls (see Chapter 7) and as evidenced by continued high levels of net out-migration from England's larger cities.

- Economic restructuring has involved a major long-term reduction in the number of manufacturing jobs. But it has also brought high rates of increase in jobs in financial services, other private services and – in recent years – in public services, though not necessarily in the places with traditional concentrations of declining sectors.

- The broad regional disparities in population and employment growth show little sign of having narrowed in the long term, though relative performance across the country varies over time, most notably in correspondence with the national economic cycle.

- The proportion of school leavers going to university has been growing steadily since the early 1990s, with the vast majority of the additional student places being city-based.

3.2.2   These trends provide a mixed picture for the prospects of England's cities providing some opportunities as well as threats. Some suggest that government policy is pushing at a more open door than in the past. National population growth, the strong net immigration from overseas, the rapid growth of the ethnic minority population, the increasing proportion of younger adults without children, the growth in the financial services sector and rising participation in higher education all suggest bright demographic prospects for urban England, especially its larger cities.

3.2.3   But some trends point in the opposite direction for cities. These include the ageing of the population and the preference of older people for living in seaside locations, more rural areas or the Mediterranean sunshine. Rising home ownership encourages suburbanisation. Even for those not engaged in child rearing, the lure of the countryside is very strong, while those experiencing divorce and separation tend to stay put rather than return to the 'city lights'. Finally, the fall in average household size, especially the rising number of one-person households, is also problematic for cities at least in the immediate future, given the low rate of housing replacement and the dominance of standard family houses.

3.3   Population change

National and regional contexts

3.3.1   In 2003 England's population was 49.8 million compared with 49.4 million in 2001, 47.8 million in 1991 and 46.8 million in 1981. There has been an increase of 3 million during the past 22 years. This increase was concentrated in the south and east of England which is now home to 30.2 million or roughly 3 in 5 of the national total in 2003. North and west England's population actually declined in this period and was 8,700 smaller in 2003 than in 1981. But there have been fluctuations over time in both the national rate of population change and the differential between the south and east and the north and west (Figure 3.1). For the country as a whole, the broad picture is of the growth rate rising over most of this 22-year period with short-lived downturns, in the mid 1980s and early 1990s. The annual rate of 0.4 per cent in recent years is the highest since the early 1970s.

3.3.2   The regional trends fluctuate much more than this, following trajectories that are more or less a mirror image of each other (Figure 3.1). The gap between the north and west and south and east was at its widest in the mid 1980s and again in the latter part of the 1990s, but was much narrower in 1988-93. It became similarly narrow again by 2002. Above all, this reflects the timing and geography of the national economic cycle, with recovery from recession being led by London.

3.3.3   These patterns are reflected in the population trends of cities as follows:

1981-1986: national upturn in population growth, faster in the south and east but with some recovery of rates in the north and west;

1986-1991: reduction in population growth of south and east along with marked upward shift for north and west;

1991-1997: rise in the south and east's growth rate while the north and west's falls, leading to sharply widening gap between the two;

1997-2003: further rise in the south and east's rate to produce the widest regional differential of the 22-year period before the two rates move together again, as happened in 1986-91.

3.3.4   Table 3.1 clearly shows the acceleration in national growth rate over the period, together with the initial narrowing and subsequent widening of the growth-rate differential between the south and east and the north and west.

Figure 3.1: Annual population change rate (%), 1981–82 to 2002–03

Table 3.1: Population change, 1981-2003, for England and its two broad regions, selected periods

Area	1981–2003	1981–1986	1986–1991	1991–1997	1997–2003
Thousands					
England	3035.3	366.8	687.5	789.0	1192.0
South and east	3044.0	558.2	582.1	802.6	1101.1
North and west	-8.7	-191.4	105.4	-13.6	90.9
% per year					
England	0.30	0.16	0.29	0.28	0.41
South and east	0.51	0.41	0.42	0.47	0.63
North and west -	0.00		0.11	-0.01	0.07
% point gap between regions					
Gap	0.51	0.60	0.31	0.49	0.55

Note: % change rates have been rounded, so may not sum exactly.

Using the typology

3.3.5   The typology used in this study emphasises two key dimensions of England's urban system, size and regional location. The next three figures show how powerful and consistent these are in terms of population change. In brief, the smaller the settlement size, the stronger is its rate of population growth – apart from London. The growth rate for each of the five size groups in the south and east of England is higher than for their counterparts in the north and west.

3.3.6   Figure 3.2 shows that, while the proportion of England's population living in London has grown at an increasing rate, elsewhere the picture is overall population deconcentration, with higher growth rates as one moves down the urban hierarchy from large to small cities and to towns and rural areas. This happened during all four periods, though the strength of this relationship weakened somewhat during the 1980s. Then the large cities staged a recovery that paralleled London's, although they subsequently stalled.

Figure 3.2: Population change rate (% per year), 1981–1986 to 1997–2003

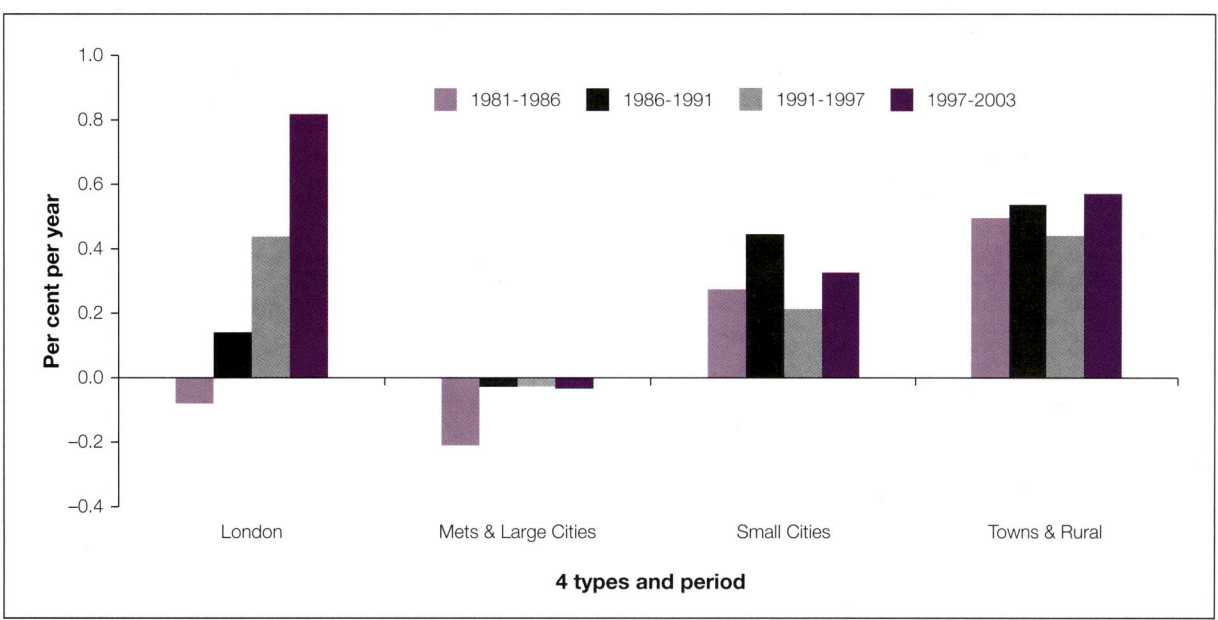

3.3.7   Figure 3.3 focuses upon the regional dimension. It shows the extent of the gap in city population growth rate between the two parts of England. Even leaving London out of the equation, the cities of the south and east grew faster than those of the north and west in each of the four periods. However, some convergence has taken place. While their growth rate in the south and east has reduced over time, the decline in the north and west is now much smaller than it was in the early 1980s. Even so, there was still a significant gap between them in 1997-2003.

3.3.8   Finally, the importance of the regional dimension of population growth is underlined in Figure 3.4. Almost all the observations for north and west England are below the zero line, signifying underperformance relative to the England rate. 1986-91 provide the only substantial departures. For south and east England, almost all are above the England line, with only five departures, two of them for 1980s London.

Figure 3.3: Population change rate (% per year), 1981–1986 to 1997–2003

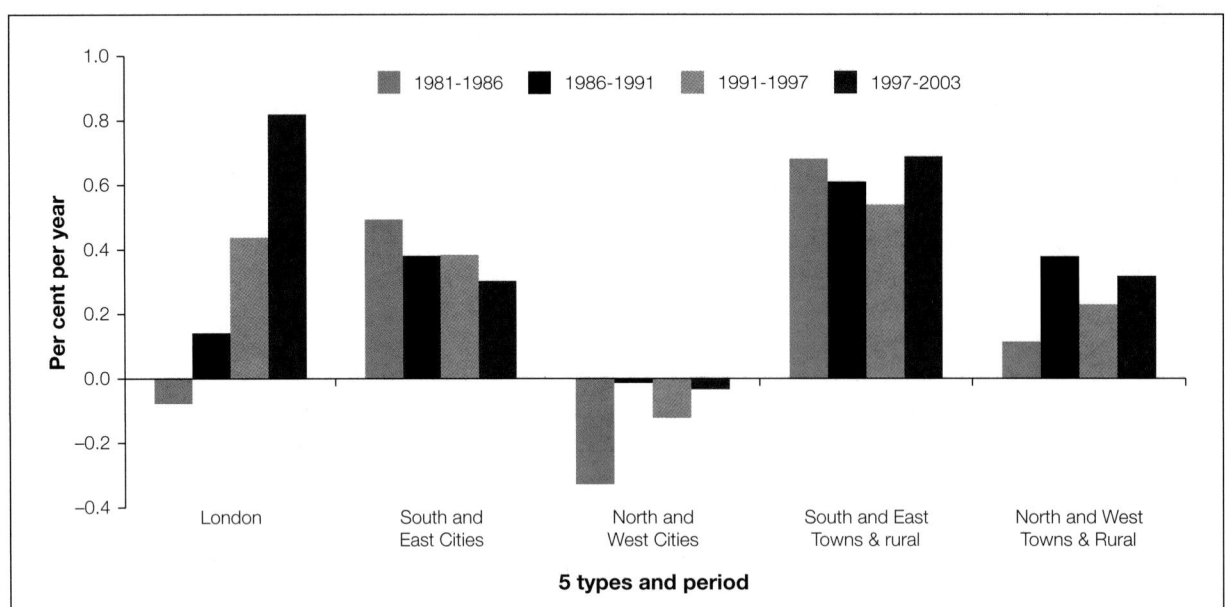

Figure 3.4: Population change rate, 1981-1986 to 1997-2003: % point differential from England's annual average

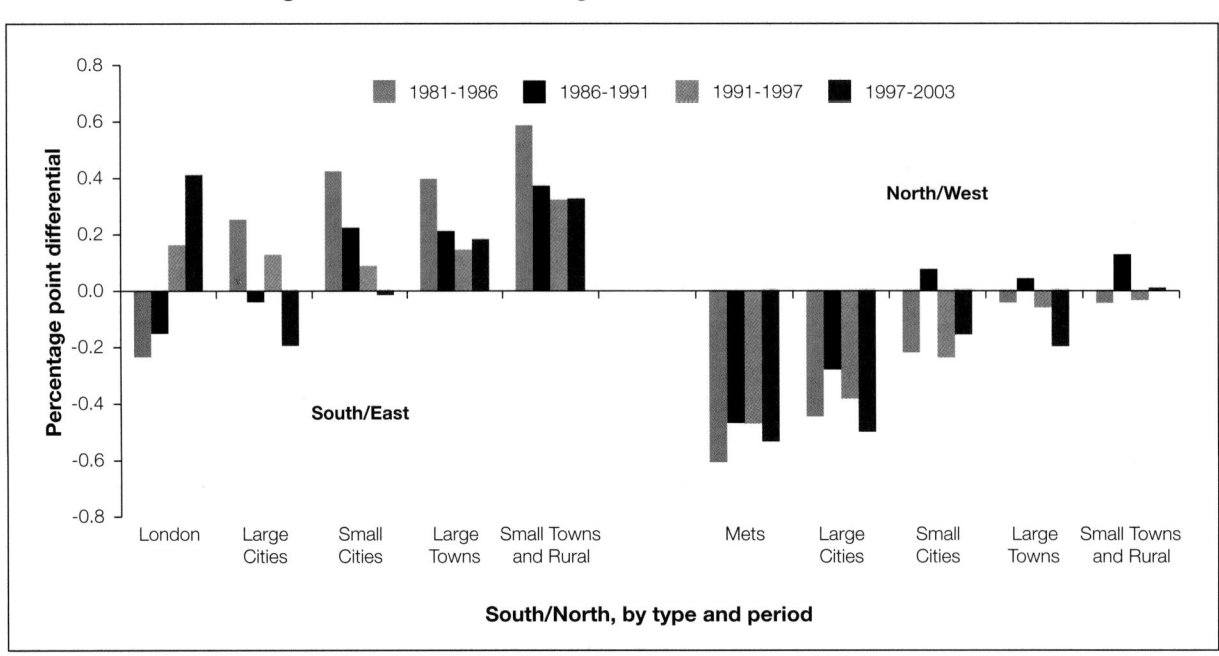

The individual performance of the 56 cities

3.3.9   Tables 3.2 and 3.3 provide rankings of the highest and lowest ten cities on the basis of annual average population growth rate over time.

Table 3.2: Highest and lowest ten population change rates among the 56 cities, 1981-1991, 1991-2001, and shift between the two periods

Rank	1981-1991	%/year	1991-2001	%/year	Shift	% point
Top 10						
1	Milton Keynes (5)	4.16	Milton Keynes (5)	1.93	London (1)	0.65
2	Northampton (5)	1.58	Telford (6)	1.22	Oxford (5)	0.63
3	Peterborough (5)	1.53	Crawley (5)	0.99	Crawley (5)	0.61
4	Swindon (5)	1.31	Reading (3)	0.82	Southampton (3)	0.50
5	Telford (6)	1.26	Southampton (3)	0.78	Coventry (4)	0.45
6	Reading (3)	1.03	Luton (5)	0.70	Blackburn (6)	0.44
7	Bournemouth (3)	1.02	London (1)	0.68	Rochdale(6)	0.33
8	Hastings (5)	0.94	Gloucester (5)	0.62	Gloucester (5)	0.29
9	Warrington (6)	0.88	Northampton (5)	0.57	Liverpool (2)	0.29
10	Cambridge (5)	0.57	York (6)	0.52	Leeds (2)	0.28
Bottom 10						
56	Liverpool (2)	-0.80	Hull (4)	-0.51	Milton Keynes (5)	-2.23
55	Coventry (4)	-0.49	Liverpool (2)	-0.50	Peterborough (5)	-1.32
54	Hull (4)	-0.38	Birkenhead (4)	-0.46	Northampton (5)	-1.02
53	Blackburn (6)	-0.36	Plymouth (5)	-0.41	Swindon (5)	-0.81
52	Newcastle (2)	-0.35	Sunderland (4)	-0.38	Hastings (5)	-0.63
51	Sheffield (2)	-0.33	Newcastle (2)	-0.31	Bournemouth (3)	-0.59
50	Manchester (2)	-0.30	Barnsley (6)	-0.23	Warrington (5)	-0.52
49	Rochdale (6)	-0.21	Birmingham (2)	-0.22	Worthing (5)	-0.46
48	Middlesbrough (4)	-0.20	Stoke (4)	-0.21	Sunderland (4)	-0.33
47	Birkenhead (4)	-0.18	Manchester (2)	-0.20	Plymouth (5)	-0.32

Note: Figures in brackets denote Type (1 London, 2 Mets, 3 South and east large city, 4 North and west large city, 5 South and east small city, 6 North and west small city). Change rate is calculated from the % change for the period divided by the number of years.

Table 3.3: Highest and lowest ten population change rates among the 56 cities, 1991-1997, 1997-2003, and shift between the two periods

Rank	1981-1991	%/year	1991-2001	%/year	Shift	% point
Top 10						
1	Milton Keynes (5)	4.16	Milton Keynes (5)	1.93	London (1)	0.65
2	Northampton (5)	1.58	Telford (6)	1.22	Oxford (5)	0.63
3	Peterborough (5)	1.5	Crawley (5)	0.99	Crawley (5)	0.61
4	Swindon (5)	1.3	Reading (3)	0.82	Southampton (3)	0.50
5	Telford (6)	1.26	Southampton (3)	0.78	Coventry (4)	0.45
6	Reading (3)	1.03	Luton (5)	0.70	Blackburn (6)	0.44
7	Bournemouth (3)	1.02	London (1)	0.68	Rochdale(6)	0.33
8	Hastings (5)	0.94	Gloucester (5)	0.62	Gloucester (5)	0.29
9	Warrington (6)	0.88	Northampton (5)	0.57	Liverpool (2)	0.29
10	Cambridge (5)	0.57	York (6)	0.52	Leeds (2)	0.28
Bottom 10						
56	Ipswich (5)	-0.55	Hull (4)	-0.89	Northampton (5)	-0.80
55	Birkenhead (4)	-0.54	Sunderland (4)	-0.44	Hull (4)	-0.80
54	Liverpool (2)	-0.51	Newcastle (2)	-0.40	Reading (3)	-0.73
53	Plymouth (5)	-0.35	Stoke (4)	-0.38	Milton Keynes (5)	-0.67
52	Sunderland (4)	-0.29	Liverpool (2)	-0.37	Luton (5)	-0.54
51	Barnsley (6)	-0.26	Plymouth (5)	-0.31	Crawley (5)	-0.52
50	Manchester (2)	-0.25	Birkenhead (4)	-0.30	Leicester (3)	-0.51
49	Grimsby (6)	-0.25	Grimsby (6)	-0.13	Derby (5)	-0.37
48	Birmingham (2)	-0.20	Birmingham (2)	-0.10	Bournemouth (3)	-0.36
47	Wigan (4)	-0.19	Sheffield (2)	-0.08	Stoke (4)	-0.33

Note: Figures in brackets denote Type (1 London, 2 Mets, 3 South and east large city, 4 North and west large city, 5 South and east small city, 6 North and west small city). Change rate is calculated from the % change for the period divided by the number of years.

3.3.10 The following patterns emerge:

- The highest growth rates are found in small cities in the south and east. Telford, Warrington and York are the only representatives of north and west England.

- New Towns head the rankings in both decades. Milton Keynes is in a class of its own, although its distinctiveness was less in 1991-2001.

- London's performance is truly remarkable. It heads the list of upward shift in rate – amazing for a city of its huge size. Reading and Southampton also impress by being large cities in the top 10 in 1991-2001.

- Five of the 10 largest upward shifts in rate are for north and west cities. Liverpool and Leeds are impressive because of their large size, Coventry too as a large city, plus Blackburn and Rochdale.

- Despite the upward shift of some north and west cities, several remain in the bottom 10 in 1991-2001, including four of the Mets – Liverpool, Newcastle, Birmingham and Manchester.

- Plymouth is the sole representative of the south and east in the bottom 10 in 1991-2001. None were in the bottom 10 in the previous decade.

- Warrington and Sunderland are the only north and west cities in the list of biggest downward shifts, both reflecting the rundown of the New Towns programme

3.3.11   Table 3.3 shows the results for 1991-2003. There are some quite strong similarities but some significant differences:

- Milton Keynes still heads the list of high-fliers in 1997-2003, but its distinctiveness has been further eroded. The New Towns have faded further, with only two remaining in the top 10.

- London continues to impress by reaching 5th place in 1997-2003. Although it does not rank quite as high in terms of shift between the two periods, since its upward trajectory had already begun by 1991-97.

- Southampton is also continuing to grow strongly for a large city, but Reading recorded one of the largest downward shifts between periods.

- Some small cities with universities are among the strongest in 1997-2003 – Oxford, Cambridge and York. They also feature among the cities with the highest upward shift between the two periods.

- Hull, Leicester and Stoke are the other large cities in the list of large downward shifts between 1991-97 and 1997-2003.

- Unlike between the 1980s and 1990s, there are no large cities in the list of cities with the largest upward shifts. Compared to 1991-97, Liverpool and Birmingham continue to feature in the bottom 10 on growth rate. They were joined in 1997-2003 by Newcastle and Sheffield, although by then Manchester has moved out of this list.

- Among the large cities of the north and west, Hull, Sunderland, Stoke and Birkenhead were the weakest in 1997-2003, with Hull and Stoke having the greatest downward shift compared to their performance in 1991-97.

- Among the north and west's small cities, only Telford and York make it into the top 10 on 1997-2003 growth. But there are three among the top 10 of 'improvers' between 1991-97 and 1997-2003 – York, Wakefield and Bolton.

3.3.12   Table 3.4 shows trends after 1991 for the 24 largest cities. The main feature is that London outshines all the others. In 1991-97 the only other major cities that grew faster were Reading, Southampton, Leicester and Bournemouth. In 1997-2003 London's 0.82 per cent rate was second to none. It registered the highest upward shift in growth rate between these two periods. On the other hand, as shown in Figure 3.5, London's growth peaked early in the second period and had fallen back markedly by 2002-03.

Table 3.4: Population change, 1991-97 and 1997-2003, for London, the six Mets and the large cities

City by type	Thousands (for period)		% change per year		% point shift in rate
	1991–1997	1997–2003	1991–1997	1997–2003	
England	789.0	1192.0	0.28	0.41	0.13
London (type 1)	210.1	402.8	0.44	0.82	0.38
Mets (type 2)					
Birmingham	-28.2	-13.3	-0.20	-0.10	0.11
Leeds	9.6	-1.1	0.23	-0.03	-0.25
Liverpool	24.8	-17.3	-0.51	-0.37	0.14
Manchester	-26.6	0.6	-0.25	0.01	0.25
Newcastle	-8.3	-19.6	-0.17	-0.40	-0.23
Sheffield	-6.2	-3.6	-0.13	-0.08	0.06
South and east large cities (type 3)					
Bournemouth	10.3	3.3	0.52	0.16	-0.36
Brighton	4.3	7.7	0.24	0.42	0.18
Bristol	11.1	12.8	0.30	0.34	0.04
Leicester	13.4	0.7	0.54	0.03	-0.51
Nottingham	1.4	-2.8	0.04	-0.08	-0.12
Portsmouth	5.7	3.0	0.20	0.10	-0.09
Reading	23.7	7.7	1.06	0.32	-0.73
Southampton	13.3	12.3	0.71	0.63	-0.08
North and west large cities (type 4)					
Birkenhead	-13.4	-7.3	-0.54	-0.30	0.23
Bradford	0.4	8.6	0.01	0.31	0.29
Coventry	0.8	0.3	0.04	0.02	-0.03
Huddersfield	4.9	7.5	0.22	0.33	0.11
Hull	-1.4	-14.0	-0.09	-0.89	-0.80
Middlesbrough	-2.6	1.2	-0.09	0.04	0.14
Stoke	-1.1	-8.5	-0.05	-0.38	-0.33
Sunderland	-5.1	-7.7	-0.29	-0.44	-0.15
Wigan	-3.5	1.7	-0.19	0.09	0.28

3.3.13   For the six Mets, the overall picture is one of decline in both decades, with only Leeds bucking the trend in 1991-97 and only Manchester in 1997-2003. On the other hand, four of the six registered upward shifts in rate between the two periods, led by Manchester. Moreover, all six experienced upturn towards the end of the second period (Figure 3.5). Compared with the opposite experience of London, this reflects the northward shift of the 'national' economic recovery from the south east of England since the late 1990s.

Figure 3.5: Annual population change rate (%), 1991-92 to 2002-03, London and the Mets

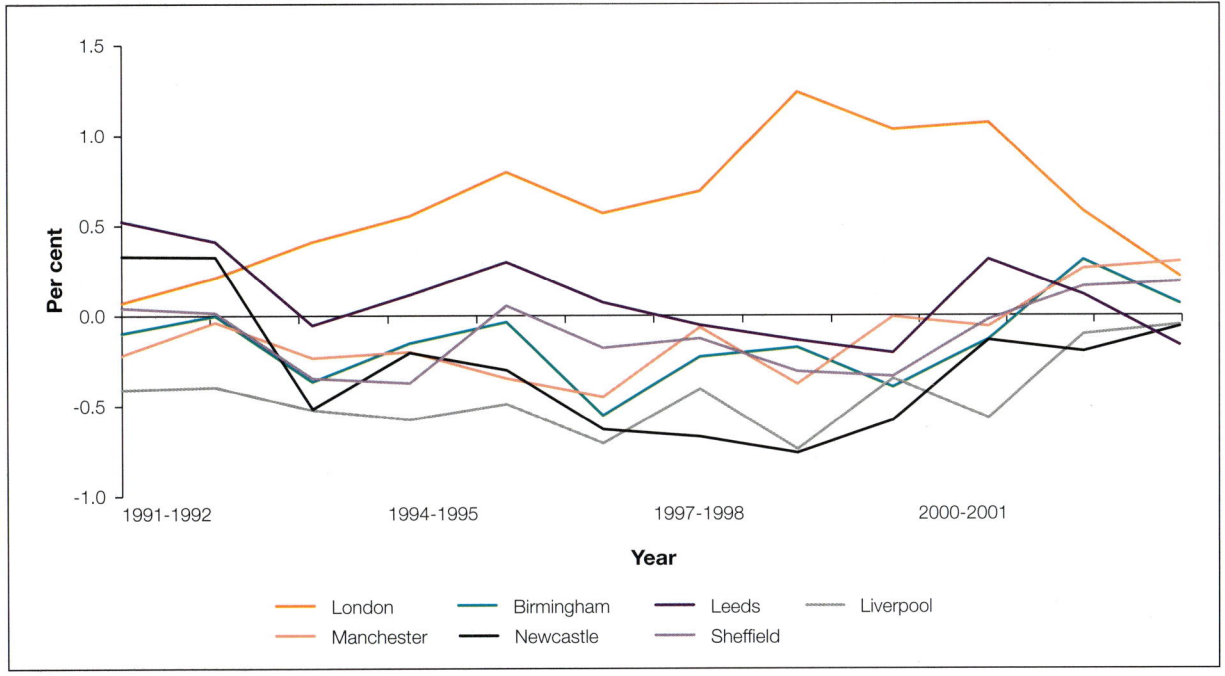

3.3.14   For the large cities, the dominant pattern in the south and east is one of growth, with Southampton and Bristol as the most consistently strong performers and Nottingham and Portsmouth as the least strong. Reading, Leicester and Bournemouth registered the biggest downturns between the two periods, and only Brighton and Bristol saw an upturn in rate. In the north and west, there was, roughly, an even split between growth and decline in both periods, but none of the nine cities surpassed the England rate in either period.

3.3.15   In sum, the single most impressive feature of population change over the past two decades has been London's upward trajectory from decline to its position in the late-1990s of accounting for over one third of national growth. Elsewhere across England, the prevailing patterns continue to be the faster growth of the south and east and the relative shift of population down the size hierarchy of settlements. As a result, the list of fastest-growing cities is dominated by the smaller cities of the south and east, but the towns and rural areas there have been gaining even more strongly. The last few years, however, have seen some changes, including the maturing of new towns, the accelerated growth of university cities and the recovery of the Mets.

3.4 Components of population change – birth, deaths and migration

3.4.1 In explaining patterns of population growth, a crucial step is to separate out the direct causes in terms of the components of change. Currently most attention is given to migration. This is not surprising now that this is such an important issue in relation to both immigration and the urban exodus. It is also partly because a place's migratory growth tends to be used as an indicator of its dynamism. Nevertheless, natural change should not be ignored, because it is still responsible for around half the country's population growth.

The balance between natural change and migration

3.4.2 For England as a whole, the surplus of births over deaths totalled 1.06 million between 1991 and 2003, contributing just over half the country's overall population growth of 1.98 million (Table 3.5). Its distribution was highly skewed across the 10 types. London alone contributed 544 thousand or over half the national total. At the other extreme, the small towns and rural type of the north and west registered natural decrease and their counterpart in the south and east barely managed an overall surplus. In terms of migration, by contrast, these latter two types accounted for the lion's share of growth, while the Mets and large cities of the north and west were net losers.

Table 3.5: Components of population change, 1991-2003, England, by SOCR type

| | Population (000s) | | 1991–2003 change (000s) | | | Change rate (% per year) | | |
	1991	2003	Overall	Natural	Migration and other	Overall	Natural	Migration and other
England	47,875.1	49,856.1	1,981.0	1,060.1	920.9	0.34	0.18	0.16
South and east	*28,279.5*	*30,183.2*	*1,903.7*	*812.4*	*1,091.3*	*0.56*	*0.24*	*0.32*
London	7,996.8	8,609.7	612.9	544.0	68.9	0.64	0.57	0.07
Large cities	3,436.4	3,564.3	127.9	83.9	44.0	0.31	0.20	0.11
Small cities	3,353.0	3,506.8	153.8	116.5	37.3	0.38	0.29	0.09
Large towns	4,509.8	4,787.0	277.2	63.0	214.2	0.51	0.12	0.40
Small towns & rural	8,983.5	9,715.4	731.9	5.0	726.9	0.68	0.00	0.67
North and west	*19,595.6*	*19672.9*	*77.3*	*247.7*	*-170.4*	*0.04*	*0.11*	*-0.07*
Mets	7,217.0	7,078.2	-138.8	142.1	-280.9	-0.16	0.16	-0.32
Large cities	3,268.0	3,228.8	-39.2	72.7	-111.9	-0.10	0.19	-0.29
Small cities	2,921.2	2,972.2	51.0	41.0	10.0	0.15	0.12	0.03
Large towns	2,994.8	3,071.8	77.0	17.6	59.4	0.2	0.05	0.17
Small towns & rural	3,194.6	3,321.9	127.3	-25.7	153.0	0.33	-0.07	0.40

Note: data may not sum exactly due to rounding.

3.4.3　In this way, there is a pretty clear reverse relationship between rates of natural change and migration across the five size groups in both parts of the country (Figure 3.6). The rate of population growth caused by natural change tends to fall with smaller settlement size, while that of migration rises. On balance, however, it is the migration component that is the stronger force, hence the prevailing pattern of net overall population shift down the urban hierarchy in both parts of the country bar London.

Figure 3.6: Annual rates of natural and other changes, 1991-2003, by SOCR type

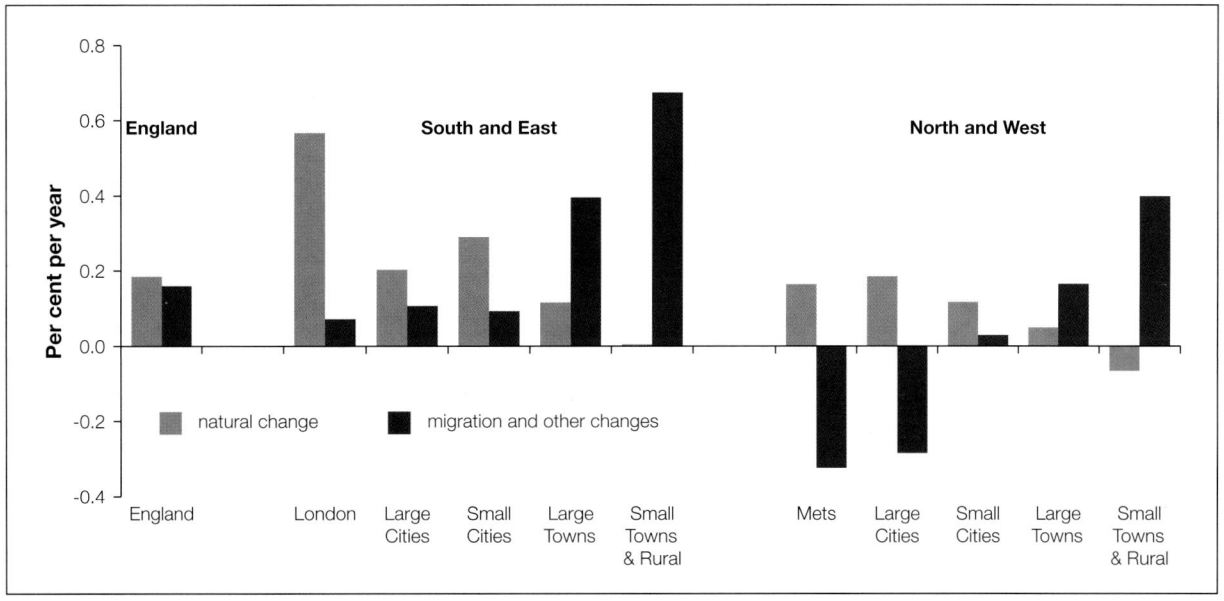

3.4.4　These patterns are pretty durable and, if anything, have become more entrenched since 1991 (Figures 3.7 and 3.8.) Nationally, migration's contribution to population growth has increased, while that of natural change has diminished. The latter has affected all of the 10 types apart from London. Yet, even for London, it is migration that was responsible for the surge in overall growth during the 1990s and, equally, for its cutback since the turn of the century.

3.4.5　Elsewhere in the south and east, there is a contrast between the two city types and the rest. The former have had much lower rates of migratory growth, so their growth is primarily due to natural change. By contrast, for the region's small towns and rural areas, migration is responsible for virtually all the growth since 1991.

3.4.6　Across the north and west, the recovery in overall growth rate in recent years has been entirely due to the upward shift in migration rates. The latter was achieved by all five types of place there, even including the already strongly-gaining small towns and rural category (Figure 3.8). Perhaps most impressive here is the shrinkage of the net migration losses of the Mets and large cities in the final three-year period.

Figure 3.7: Annual rate of natural change, 1991-2003 in four 3-year periods, by SOCR type

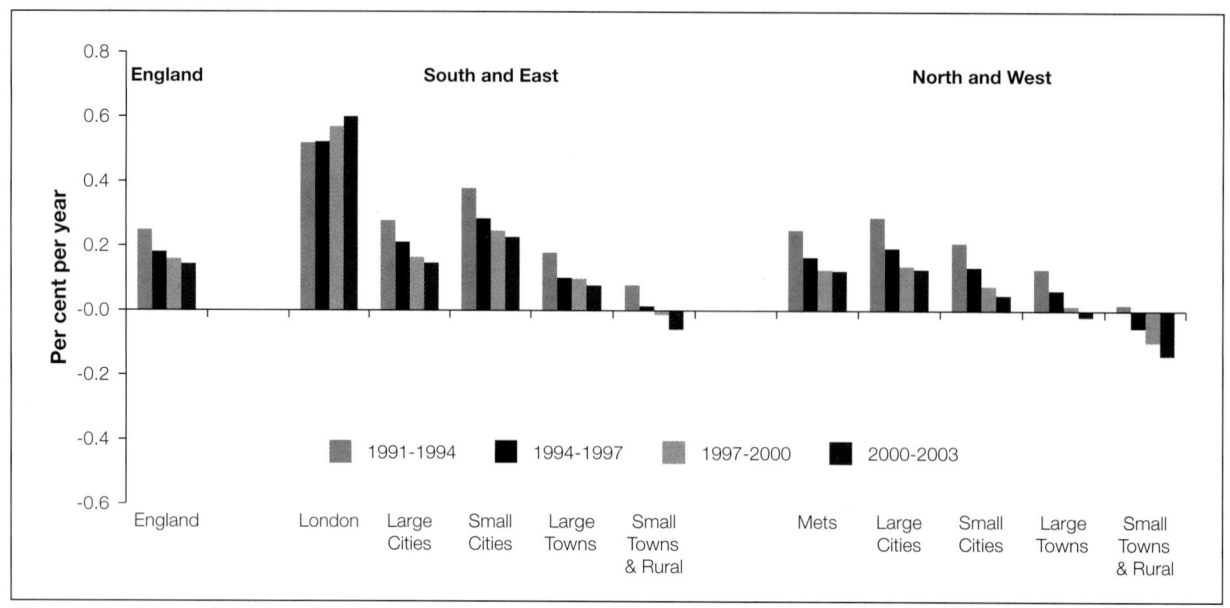

Figure 3.8: Annual rate of migration and other changes, 1991-2003 in four 3-year periods, by SOCR type

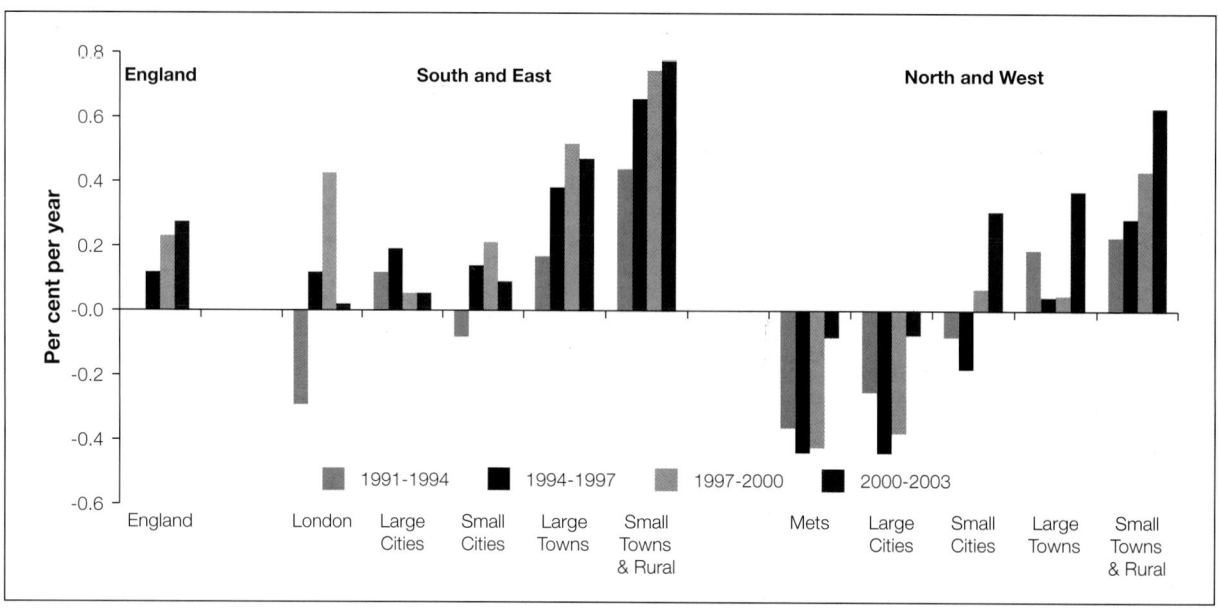

3.4.7   Figure 3.9 provides an overview of the role of these two basic demographic drivers of change for all 56 cities. In plotting their average rates of natural increase and migratory change against each other for the period 1991-2003, the graph's four quadrants provide a simple classification. In the bottom-left quadrant, characterised by a combination of natural decrease and migration loss, lie just two cities, Newcastle and Birkenhead. In the top left-hand quadrant is a distinctive group of cities with net migration growth but natural decrease, all traditional seaside retirement places.

Figure 3.9: 56 cities: relationship between rates of natural change and migration and other changes, 1991-2003

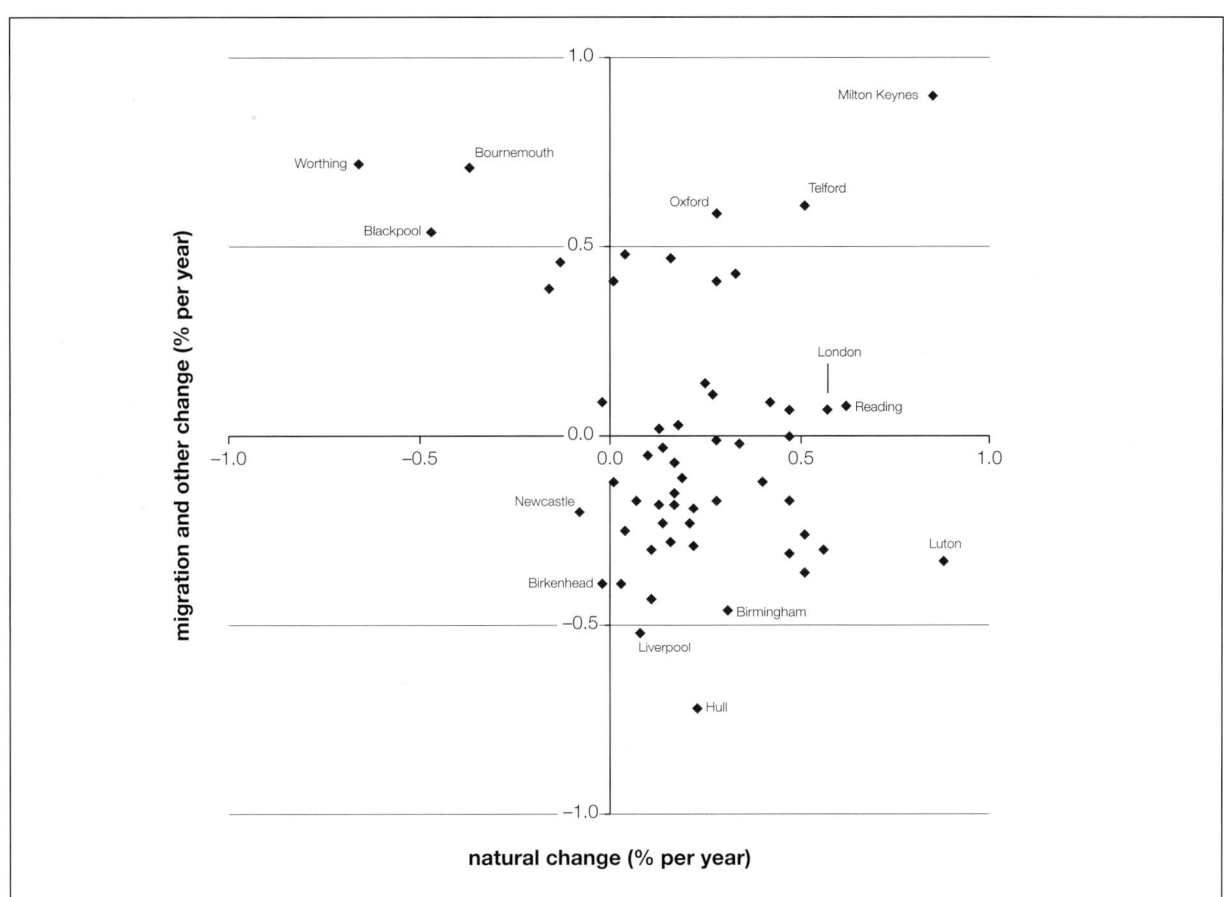

3.4.8　In the top-right corner of Figure 3.9 lies Milton Keynes, with strong growth due equally to natural increase and migration, followed by Telford, Oxford, York, Cambridge, Crawley, Norwich and Southampton. London and Reading group together by combining strong natural increase with an overall positive migration balance for the 12-year period. Warrington, Derby, Northampton, Gloucester, Preston, Portsmouth and Swindon also grew on both components.

3.4.9　The majority of cities, 31 in all, lie in the bottom-right quadrant, where a surplus of births over deaths is matched against net migration loss. Below a diagonal line drawn from top-left to bottom-right lie cities registering overall population decline because the net migration losses outweigh the natural increase. Hull, Liverpool and Birmingham are the most extreme cases on the migration measure. Above the diagonal is where natural increase exceeds migration loss, giving overall population growth. Here Luton is the most distinctive city, having the same high level of natural increase as Milton Keynes but, in contrast to the latter, experiencing migration loss.

Within UK and international components of migration

3.4.10　England's migration is made up of several different elements. The most fundamental distinction is that between moves taking place within the UK and those involving migration between England and the rest of the world beyond the UK, the latter including asylum-seekers and an estimate of the number of illegal migrants. Data for 2002-2003 (Table 3.6) reveals that these two components have a completely different incidence across England. International migration is highly skewed towards the cities, especially the larger ones. London itself accounts for over half of England's net gain from overseas. By contrast, migration within the UK is exactly the opposite, with the largest gains made by the small towns and rural types.

Table 3.6: Within UK and international components of total net migration, 2002–2003, by SOCR type

SOCR type	Net flows			Rate (% population 2002)		
	Within-UK	Inter-national	Total	Within-UK	Inter-national	Total
England	-22542	145668	123126	-0.05	0.29	0.25
South and east						
London	-112521	77226	-35295	-1.31	0.90	-0.41
Large cities	-10543	13605	3062	-0.30	0.38	0.09
Small cities	-4642	10760	6118	-0.13	0.31	0.18
Large towns	16477	5902	22379	0.35	0.12	0.47
Small towns and rural	82378	3825	86203	0.86	0.04	0.90
North and west						
Mets	-28165	23822	-4343	-0.40	0.34	-0.06
Large cities	-7452	7064	-388	-0.23	0.22	-0.01
Small cities	5749	3977	9726	0.19	0.13	0.33
Large towns	11598	1768	13366	0.38	0.06	0.44
Small towns and rural	24579	-2281	22298	0.74	-0.07	0.67

3.4.11 The relationship between these two components of migration is rather more complicated when examined for the 56 cities individually (Figure 3.10). In particular, two cities – Cambridge and Oxford – stand out as extreme cases on the basis of their very high rate of net gain from international migration, because of students from overseas. The broad pattern is that the higher the rate of net immigration from overseas, the more negative is a city's migration with the rest of the UK.

3.4.12 At the same time, the dynamics are complex. The factors prompting cities' net losses to the rest of the UK include all the normal reasons for migration that for decades have powered suburbanisation. They include the search for cheaper housing, better quality of environment and services, less pressurised pace of life and the 'rural idyll' more generally. Even so, international migration gains may well be encouraging this urban exodus by stimulating the housing markets within cities.

3.4.13   In sum, this analysis of the components of population change reveals the importance of distinguishing between natural change, international migration and within-UK movements. All three contribute towards the difference in overall growth rate between the south and east and the north and west.

Figure 3.10: 56 cities: relationship between rates of international and within-UK migration, 2002-2003

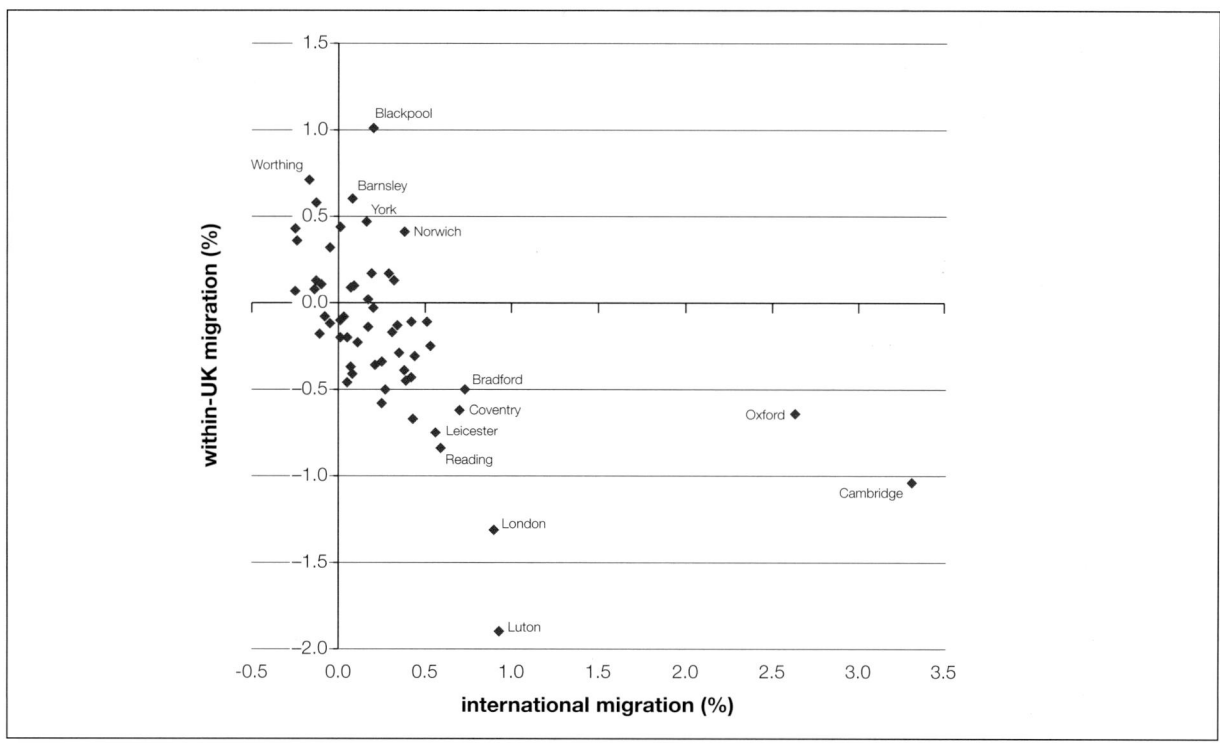

3.5   Changing population composition

Age structure

3.5.1   The age profile of places is important for several reasons. First a more youthful place will normally have a higher rate of population growth. Second, a below-average representation of a particular age group can be interpreted as a lack of attractiveness and sign of weakness. In addition, some age groups are seen as more valuable to city economies than others, namely people of working age and especially younger adults.

3.5.2   The best diagnostic indicator is the proportion aged under 45. Data for 2003 shows London has the largest proportion, at 67 per cent, with a particularly high representation of 30-44 year olds. Next come the large and small cities of the south and east and the Mets, all with 62 per cent. At the other extreme lie the small towns and rural categories of both the south and east and the north and west, with 55 per cent. In fact, across England, there is a close correspondence between settlement size and age structure, with the proportion of older people becoming progressively larger down the urban hierarchy.

3.5.3   Impressively, even in the full list of 56 cities, London has one of the four most youthful age structures (Table 3.7). Only Luton and the university cities of Oxford and Cambridge had a smaller proportion of people aged 45 and over in 2003. Even Milton Keynes, despite its very rapid growth through both natural increase and migration, had a larger share.

Table 3.7: Highest and lowest 10 Cities for proportion of residents aged 45 and over, 2003

Rank	Highest	%	Rank	Lowest	%
1	Blackpool (6)	47.3	56	Oxford (5)	29.6
2	Worthing (5)	46.1	55	Cambridge (5)	30.5
3	Bournemouth (3)	45.7	54	Luton (5)	33.2
4	Southend (5)	44.1	53	London (1)	33.2
5	Birkenhead (4)	43.7	52	Milton Keynes (5)	33.8
6	Hastings (5)	42.5	51	Reading (3)	34.5
7	Norwich (5)	42.1	50	Blackburn (6)	34.5
8	Doncaster (6)	41.6	49	Leicester (3)	36.0
9	Barnsley (6)	41.6	48	Bradford (4)	36.1
10	Mansfield (5)	41.3	47	Coventry (4)	36.3

Note: Figures in brackets denote Type (1 London, 2 Mets, 3 South and east large city, 4 North and west large city, 5 South and east small city, 6 North and west small city).

3.5.4   The urban-rural gradient of ageing is not of recent origin, but is becoming more pronounced. There was a very clear relationship between higher growth rate of old people and smaller settlement size (Figure 3.11). The most conspicuous features are the very strong growth of the under 45s age group in London and its substantial contraction in all five types of the north and west.

Figure 3.11: Change in numbers aged under 45 and 45+, 1993-2003, by 10 SOCR types

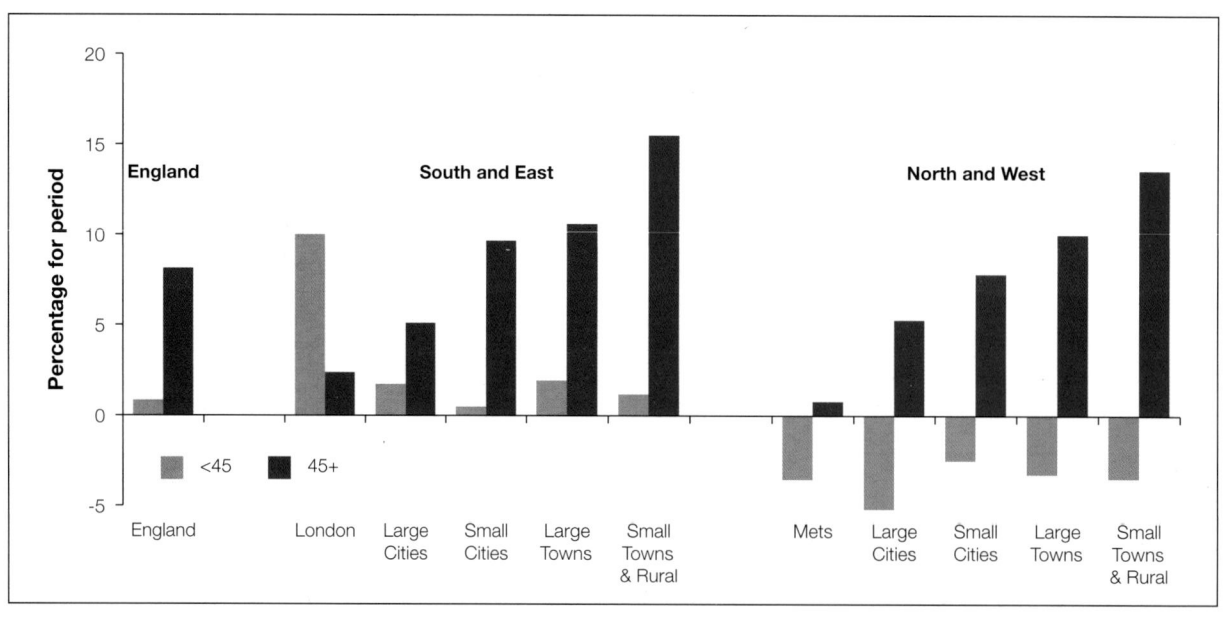

3.5.5   As a result, between 1993 and 2003 London saw a literal rejuvenation of its population, with a 1.6 percentage point drop in its proportion of people aged 45 and over. In this, it was one of only six cities moving against the national ageing trend, the others being the university cities of Oxford and Cambridge, the traditional resorts of Brighton and Worthing, and Coventry. At the other extreme, Milton Keynes' proportion grew by 5.2 percentage points, as its large cohorts of 1970s and 1980s newcomers aged.

3.6   Ethnicity

3.6.1   This section examines the importance of ethnic groups other than White in places' overall population change and looks at changes in the distribution of ethnic groups between places. In 2001 there were 4.46 million people in England who were members of ethnic groups other than White (referred to as 'Non-Whites' below). This compares with a figure of 3.06 million for 1991, a rise of 1.4 million or 46 per cent. On the same basis, the total population increased by 932,000, a 1.9 per cent rise, with the White population reducing by 470,000.

3.6.2   The picture for the 10 SOCR types is shown in Figure 3.12. All 10 types contributed to the growth of England's Non-White population. But the volume of increase ranged from London's 693,000 – almost exactly half of England's total gain – to just over 11,000 for the north and west's small towns and rural category. In seven of the 10 types the volume of Non-White growth was greater than that of the White population. All six city types registered a reduction in number of White residents, with the losses being especially substantial for the six Mets and London.

Figure 3.12: Change in numbers of all, White and Non-White residents, 1991-2001, by SOCR type

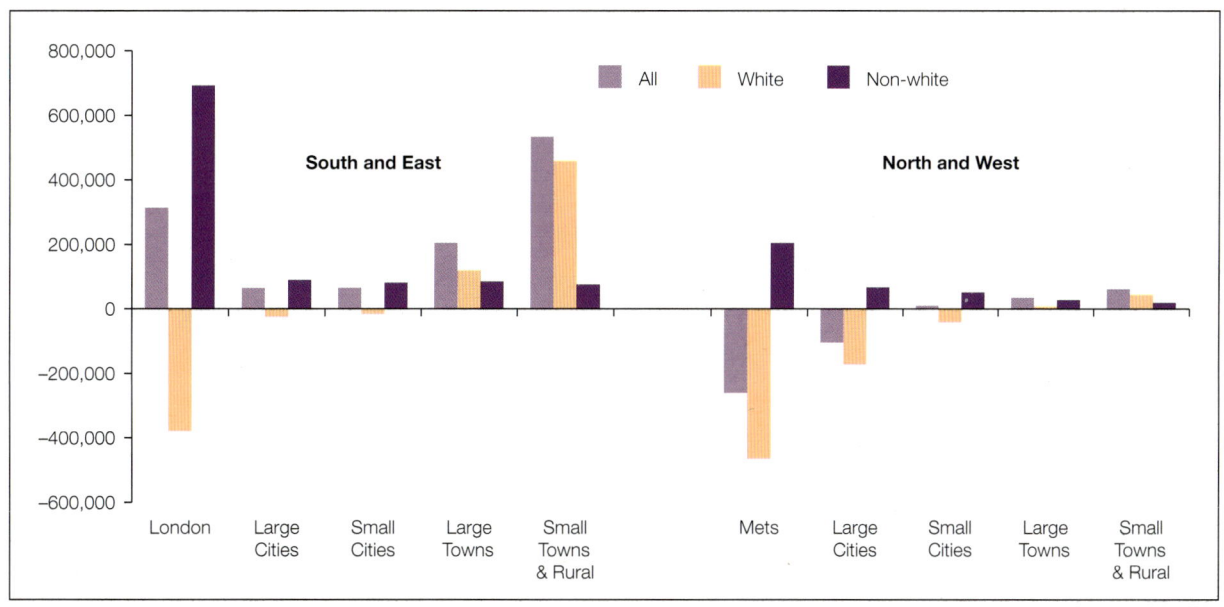

3.6.3   How has this affected the distribution of the Non-White population between the SOCR types? Hardly at all. Figure 3.13 shows that each of the types increased its level very much in line with its initial level in 1991. The highest increase was for London up by 7.6 percentage points and the lowest being for the north and west's small towns and rural up by 0.6 percentage points.

3.6.4   The main dimensions of the geography of the Non-White population across England are clear. There is a clear urban-rural gradient in the representation of Non-Whites in the population. And for each size of city the proportion of Non-White is higher in the south and east.

3.6.5   The distribution of ethnic groups varies widely across cities. For instance, the seven Non-White groups shown in Figure 3.14 vary greatly in the extent to which they are concentrated in London. At one extreme, in 2001 four out of five of England's Black Africans were living there. By contrast, London accounts for barely one in five Pakistanis, for whom the six Mets are the modal type.

Figure 3.13: Non-White residents as a proportion of all residents, 1991 and 2001, for 10 SOCR types

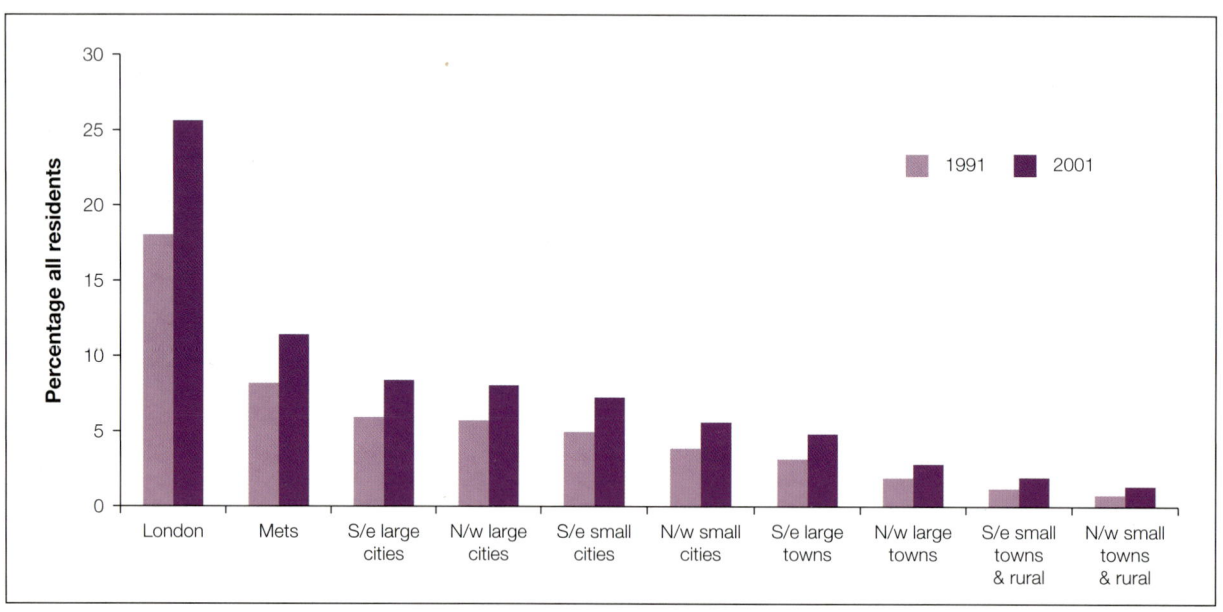

Figure 3.14: Distribution of individual ethnic groups across 10 SOCR types, 2001

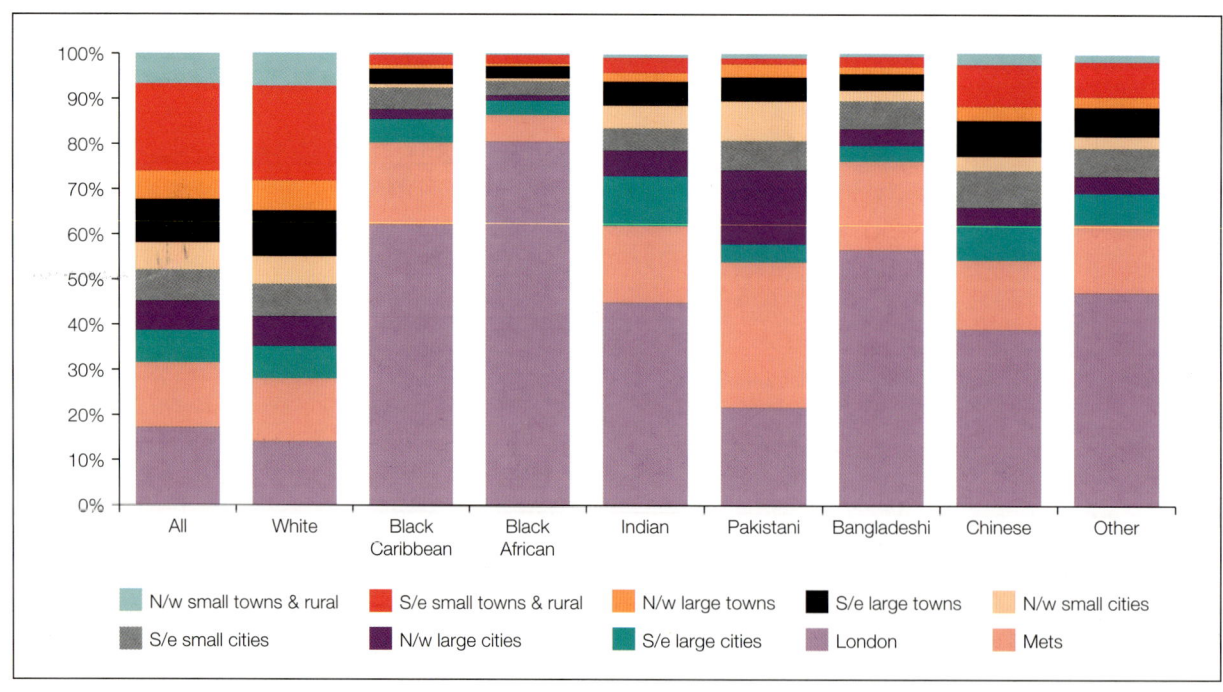

3.6.6   There is also great variation between the 56 cities, as the following indicators show. In 2001 the Non-White share of residents ranged from 27.4 per cent in Bradford to 0.9 per cent in Barnsley. Over the previous decade, all 56 had registered an increase in their Non-White share, but this ranged from one of 7.7 percentage points for London to just 0.3 for Barnsley. All 56 also saw growth in their number of Non-Whites. But the rate of increase varied from a more than doubling for Bournemouth, York and Blackpool to a rise of just under one quarter for Doncaster and Derby.

3.6.7   Moreover, just as for the SOCR types, the cities vary greatly in their Non-White ethnic make-up. Concentrating on the 15 cities with the highest proportion of Non-Whites in 2001, Figure 3.15 shows that some appear to be almost one-group cities (apart from their White populations), notably Bradford, Burnley and Rochdale in terms of Pakistanis, and Leicester, Coventry, Bolton and Preston in terms of Indians. Some cities have two large Non-White groups, notably the Indians and Pakistanis in Blackburn and the same groups to a more limited extent in Birmingham, Huddersfield, and Derby. Other places are more mixed in their Non-Whites groups, including London, Luton and especially Oxford.

Figure 3.15: Top 15 cities for Non-White share of population, 2001: % composition by seven Non-White ethnic groups

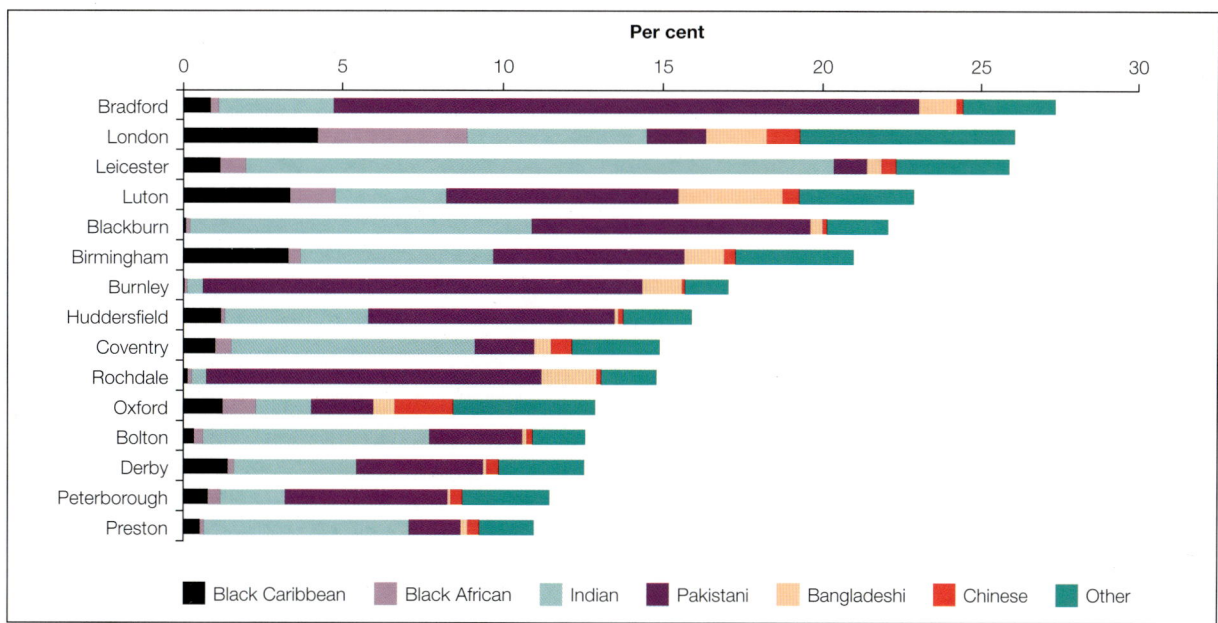

3.6.8   To an even greater extent, it is commonly a single group that dominates the Non-White population growth of individual cities. Figure 3.16 lists the top 15 of the 56 cities in terms of the increase in Non-White share of population between 1991 and 2001, i.e. where the White share declined most in percentage of all residents. Virtually all of Bradford's increased Non-White presence was due to the growth in the Pakistani proportion, as it was for Burnley and Rochdale and to a somewhat lesser extent for Luton, Birmingham, Huddersfield and Sheffield. For Blackburn the strong growth in the Non-White proportion was accounted for largely by Pakistanis and Indians in equal measure, while Indians dominated the Non-White growth of Preston and Leicester. London's Non-White growth was dominated by Black Africans.

By contrast, some cities saw a much more mixed pattern of ethnicities represented in the rapid growth of their Non-White share, notably Cambridge, Milton Keynes, Coventry and Crawley.

Figure 3.16: Top cities for increase in Non-White share of population, 1991-2001: % point contribution of seven Non-White ethnic groups

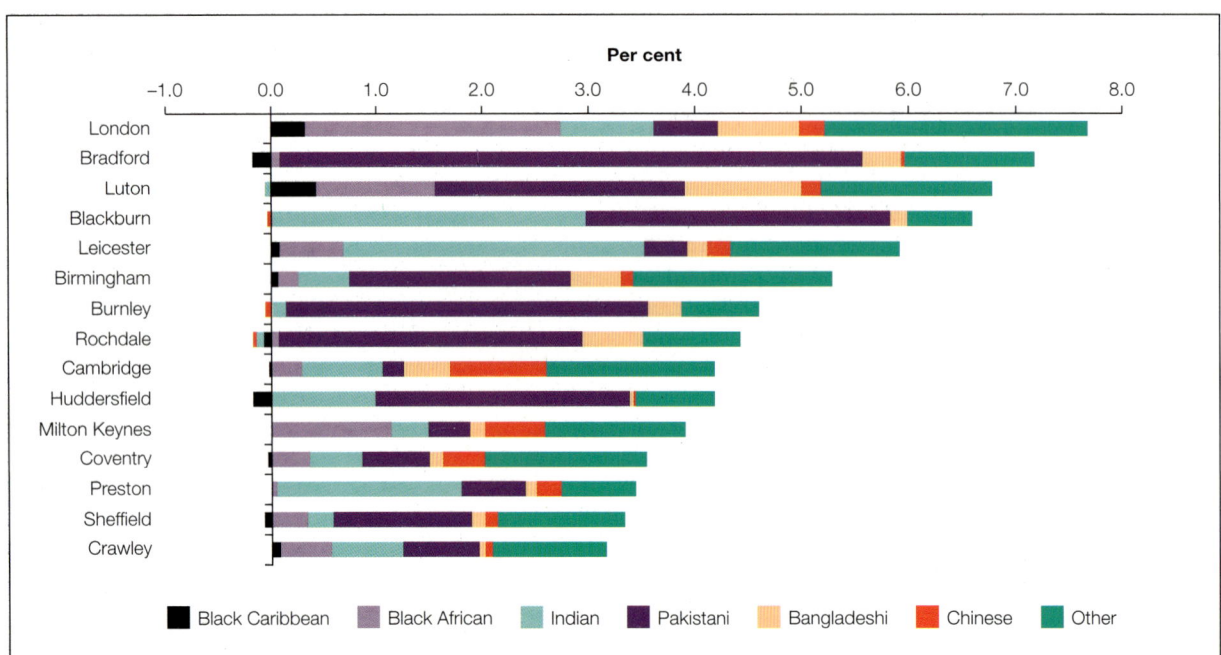

3.7 Household composition

3.7.1 A focus on households adds two related dimensions to our understanding of urban change in England that are relevant to policy, especially in terms of planning for housing. One concerns change in the number of households. The other is change in the types of households.

3.7.2 The most important long-term trend is the decline in the average size of household, almost halving over the past century from around 4.5 persons to under 2.5 now. This means that nationally the number of households has consistently been increasing at a faster rate than the size of the population. Even at times when nationally England's population has been in decline, as in the 1970s, the number of households has continued to increase. This also may happen for regions, cities and towns that experience population loss.

3.7.3 Figure 3.17 shows that all 56 cities saw some increase in their number of households between 1991 and 2001, according to the census. This included several cities with shrinking populations. The vast majority of the cities recording the highest rates of household growth lie in the south and east. But four do not. Of these, York is one of England's fast-growing cathedral cities, while Telford, Warrington and Preston owe this high-ranking position to their previous new town status and the resultant high rate of household formation in their generally young populations.

Figure 3.17: Growth in household numbers 1991-2001 for 56 cities

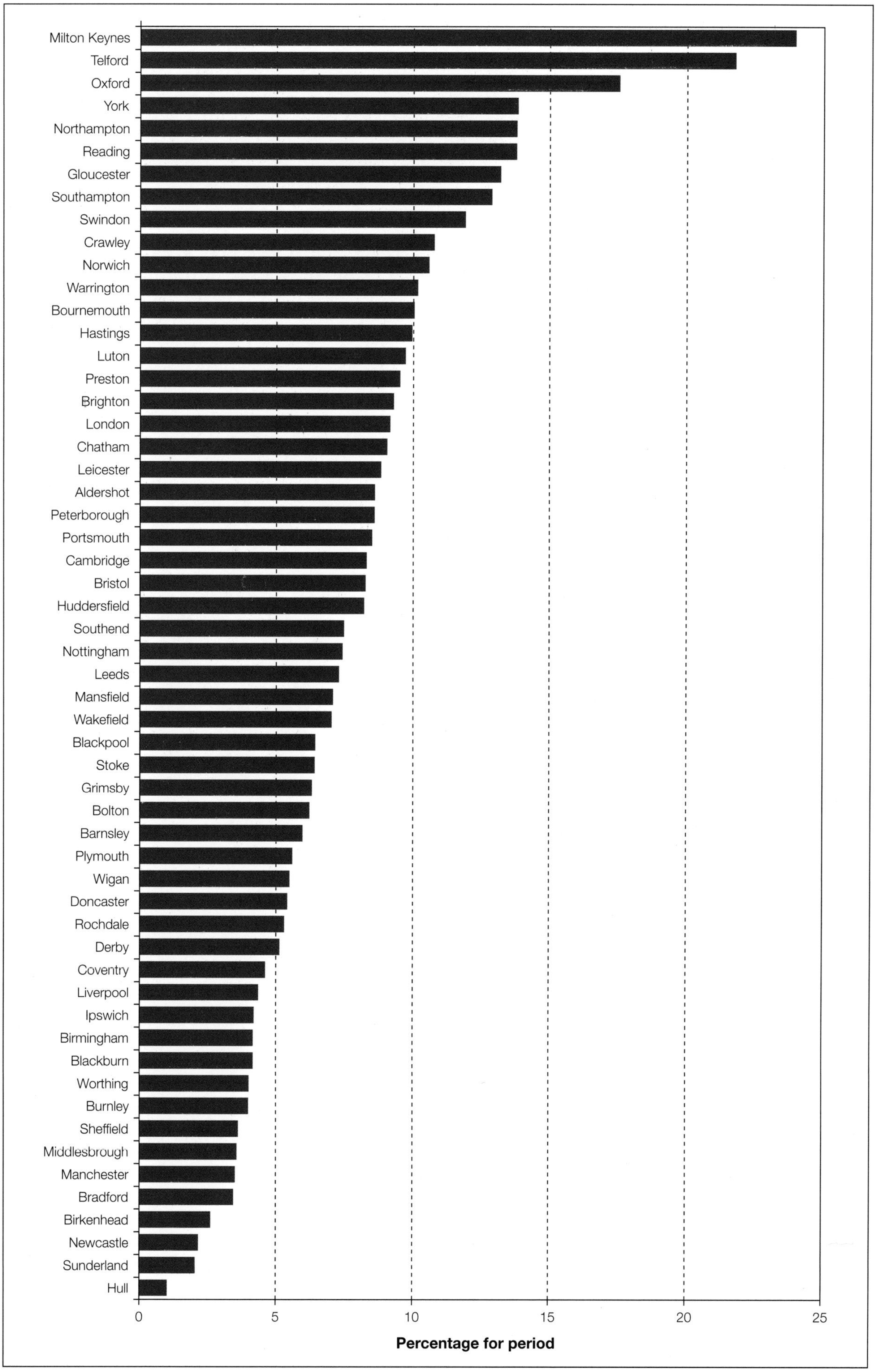

3.7.4   Nationally, the number of households rose by 1.7 million between 1991 and 2001. The largest single contribution was made by the small towns and rural districts of the south and east, with some 460,000 additional households by 2001. London's was next, at just under 300,000, followed by that of the large towns of the south and east, up by 200,000. Around 100,000 extra households were accounted for by each of the other SOCR types, apart from the barely 50,000 of the north and west's large cities.

3.7.5   Figure 3.18 shows the proportionate increases that these absolute changes involved. England's 1.7 million rise represents an increase of 9 per cent on the 18.8 million in 1991, taking its total to 20.5 million in 2001. The rates of increase for the 10 SOCR types display a familiar 'counter-urbanisation' pattern, rising down the scale of settlement size.

Figure 3.18: 1991-2001 change in household numbers, for England and 10 SOCR types

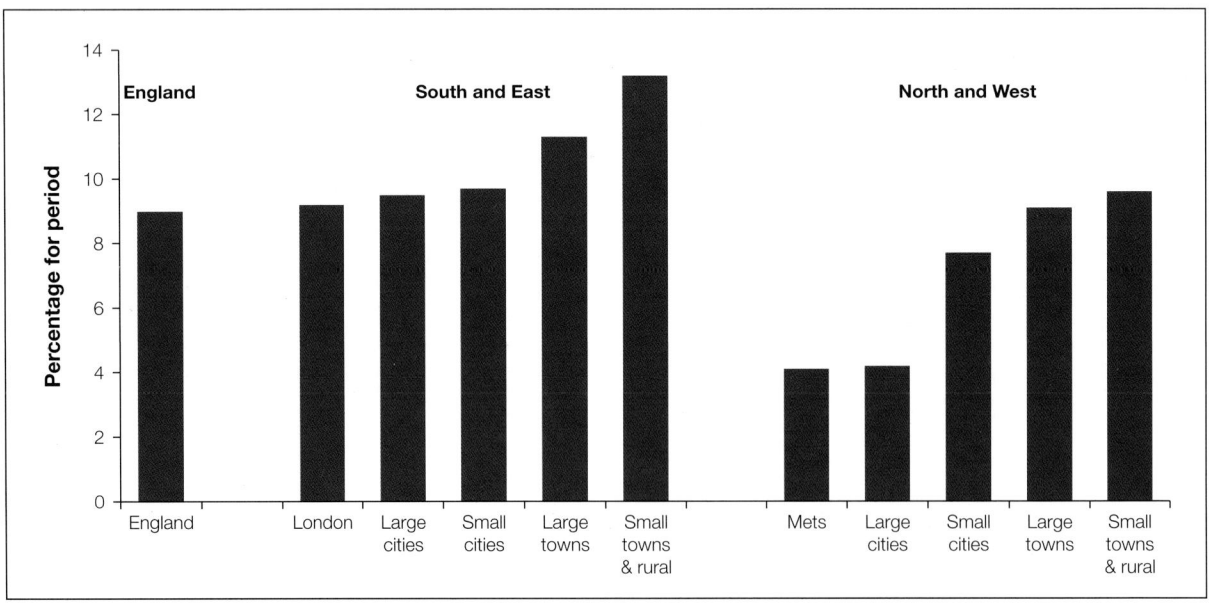

3.8   Employment Trends

Self-employment

3.8.1   The number of self-employed people rose from 2.77 million in 1991 to 2.95 million in 2001, an increase of 6.8 per cent for the decade. As Figure 3.19 shows, all 10 SOCR types registered some growth, but the rate varied considerably. In both parts of England, self-employment rose progressively as the size of place declined, apart from the largest cities. In this respect, London's 14 per cent growth over the decade – a rise of almost 70,000 self-employed people – is outstanding. If similar drivers were also operating in the Mets, then they were working in a much more muted form. Overall the growth rates for each of the five types in the north and west are consistently lower than for their counterparts in the south and east.

3.8.2 In terms of the 56 individual cities, London's 14 per cent growth put it in fourth place behind Milton Keynes (23 per cent), Warrington and Crawley. Reading and Telford also saw increases of over 10 per cent. Clearly, there is a 'new town' factor in this list of high-fliers, making the presence of London and Reading in the top five all the more impressive. At the other extreme, Plymouth saw the largest dip in self-employed numbers, down by just over 10 per cent according to the census. The next largest reductions were recorded by Hull, Blackpool, Grimsby, Wigan, Burnley and Leicester, all with falls of 2.5 per cent or more.

Figure 3.19: Change in number of self-employed, 1991-2001, %

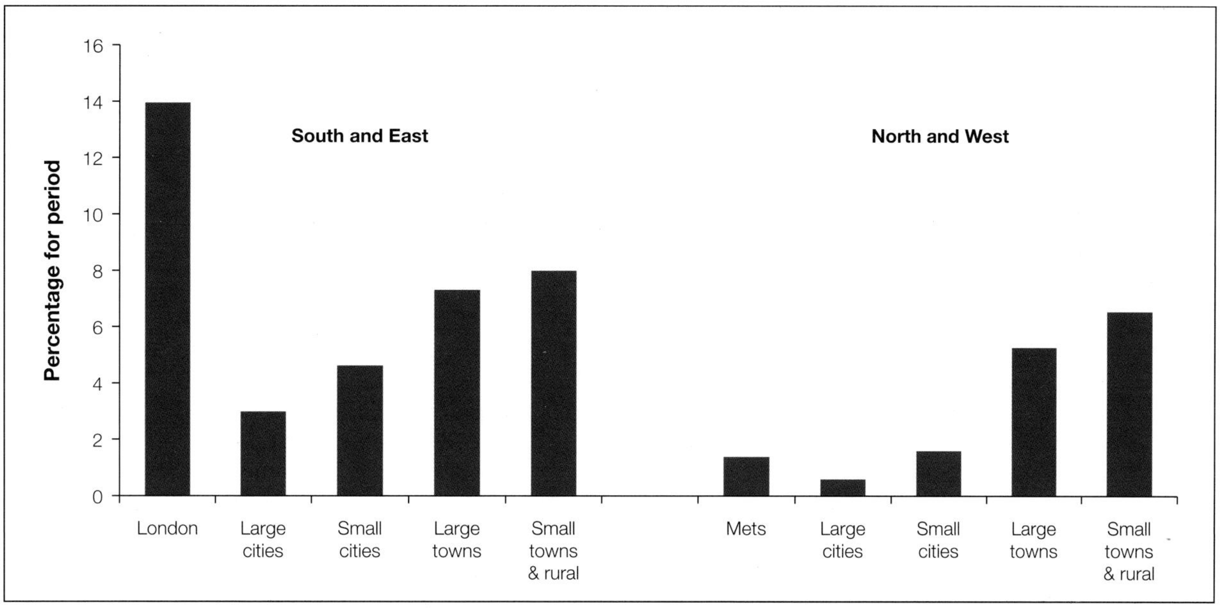

Employees

3.8.3 This section looks at the changes taking place between 1991 and 2003. This period captures the major part of the longest economic upturn experienced for some decades, as reflected in an estimated 15.7 per cent increase in total employment for England. This recovery began in London and did not take off in a substantial way in the northern half of the country until the latter half of the decade. The result was that, while over this 12-year period the estimated number of jobs in the south and east rose by 19.2 per cent, in the north and west the increase was not much more than half this, at 10.4 per cent.

3.8.4 Table 3.9 emphasises this regional divide. None of the five types in the north and west achieved a growth rate as high as the lowest in the south and east. In the north and west of England, the low growth rate for the large cities is the most distinctive feature.

Table 3.9: Estimated percentage change in employment (excluding agriculture), 1991-2003, by SOCR type

SOCR type	Total jobs	Full-time jobs	Part-time jobs
England	15.7	10.9	28.0
South and east			
London	16.9	7.5	53.4
Large cities	15.4	9.7	29.4
Small cities	15.8	10.9	27.1
Large towns	17.8	14.7	24.7
Small towns and rural	26.8	27.0	25.2
North and west			
Mets	10.7	5.6	24.7
Large cities	4.7	-0.5	17.4
Small cities	11.5	8.8	17.8
Large towns	12.4	9.1	19.8
Small towns and rural	13.2	12.3	14.4

3.8.5 Nationally the 1991-2003 growth rate is weighted much more strongly in favour of part-time jobs, taking their share of all jobs to 32 per cent by 2003. This driver of job growth has been particularly important in London. In the north and west the Mets outpaced the other four types over this period. For full-time jobs, by contrast, growth rates are higher the smaller the city, apart from the Mets in the north and west.

3.8.6 Table 3.10 disaggregates change into three broad economic sectors and a residual category which includes construction and a wide range of non-public services besides finance and business services (Table 3.10).

Table 3.10: Estimated percentage employment change, 1991–2003, for broad sectors, by SOCR type

	All sectors (excl farming)	Manu-facturing	Public services	Financial services	Other (excl farming)
England	15.7	-20.8	18.2	43.2	21.0
South and east					
London	16.9	-30.0	6.8	41.6	20.0
Large cities	15.4	-25.7	22.9	37.1	19.7
Small cities	15.8	-24.1	14.3	43.6	23.9
Large towns	17.8	-21.1	20.5	36.5	26.3
Small towns and rural	26.8	-5.9	21.6	73.7	34.1
North and west					
Mets	10.7	-26.1	22.2	44.0	11.6
Large cities	4.7	-24.6	17.7	25.4	10.3
Small cities	11.5	-23.3	26.5	47.3	14.8
Large towns	12.4	-20.2	17.7	39.2	19.8
Small towns and rural	13.2	-12.4	24.9	15.1	20.7

3.8.7   For manufacturing, between 1991-2003 there was a one in five job loss nationally. There is a clear urban/rural dimension. The rate of job loss falls progressively with degree of 'urbanness'. The gradient is steeper for the south and east, led by London's 30 per cent reduction. Moreover, except for the small towns and rural category, the rate of decline was, type for type, higher in the south and east than in the north and west. For public services, there is no clearly discernable pattern either between the two halves of the country or across the urban/rural dimension within them. However, London is quite distinctive in its low rate of increase in this sector, up by under 7 per cent – not much more than one-third of the national rate. For financial services, the main feature is the impressive scale of growth nationally, with estimated job growth of 43 per cent.

3.8.8   Table 3.11 presents the same information for the 24 largest cities. Focusing first on London and the six Mets:

- Leeds appears as the star performer for total employment growth between 1991 and 2003. London also impressed because of its large size as did Manchester lying in third place. Liverpool and Birmingham appear to be the least dynamic, but have seen some growth over this period.

- Leeds, Newcastle and Sheffield appear to have done best in surviving the shrinkage of manufacturing jobs. London and Liverpool have registered the greatest proportionate losses.

- Leeds saw the fastest percentage growth in public services jobs, London and Manchester the slowest.

- Newcastle scored by far the worst on growth in financial services. However Liverpool – so often grouped with Newcastle as the weakest of the Mets – was a high-flier, along with Leeds and Manchester.

- London, Leeds and Manchester saw fastest growth in terms of all other sectors combined. Liverpool was the only one of the seven to experience decline.

Table 3.11: Estimated employment change, 1991–2003, for London, Mets and large cities, (%)

City by type	Total employment (excl farming)	Manu-facturing jobs	Public services jobs	Financial services jobs	Other jobs (excl farming)
England	15.7	-20.8	18.2	43.2	21.0
London (type 1)	16.9	-32.0	6.8	41.6	20.7
Mets (type 2)					
Birmingham	6.1	-27.5	23.2	33.3	10.7
Leeds	22.9	-19.6	33.8	61.3	19.8
Liverpool	5.8	-34.8	25.8	62.9	-4.4
Manchester	14.1	-30.9	12.8	59.5	20.3
Newcastle	8.5	-14.9	23.1	7.5	5.3
Sheffield	11.2	-16.9	27.6	42.2	7.1
S & E Large City (type 3)					
Bournemouth	23.2	-12.5	23.4	39.7	28.2
Brighton	28.1	-9.6	25.4	42.7	30.8
Bristol	20.0	-19.8	32.6	21.2	29.4
Leicester	-2.2	-33.4	5.7	47.5	-1.7
Nottingham	4.6	-30.1	15.6	32.7	6.6
Portsmouth	14.4	-25.1	25.1	7.9	30.7
Reading	38.1	-24.9	53.5	91.1	23.4
Southampton	10.3	-27.5	8.6	22.9	19.1
N & W Large City (type 4)					
Birkenhead	-1.6	-28.3	10.3	9.0	4.7
Bradford	3.1	-20.0	17.0	16.6	3.6
Coventry	3.8	-30.9	4.3	27.7	26.2
Huddersfield	10.3	-22.0	21.2	49.6	25.6
Hull	7.0	5.9	11.7	27.7	-1.0
Middlesbrough	8.8	-36.9	27.7	38.4	19.5
Stoke	-7.1	-38.0	38.1	-15.9	-3.9
Sunderland	14.3	-4.1	20.9	49.5	10.4
Wigan	10.4	-19.2	9.5	71.6	16.5

3.8.9   In terms of the two categories of large cities (types 3 and 4), the main features are:

- The four strongest performers overall are all in the south and east – Reading, Brighton, Bournemouth and Bristol. Leicester and Nottingham are the weakest of the large cities here.

- All but one of the 17 large cities saw decline in their number of manufacturing jobs, the exception being Hull.

- Reading led the way for the 17 large cities in terms of growth rate for public services jobs, followed by Stoke and Bristol. Least dynamic in this sector were Coventry, Leicester, Southampton and Wigan.

- All but Stoke gained financial jobs. But the growth rates for Portsmouth and Birkenhead were also far below the national figure. The highest percentage growth was for Reading and Wigan.

3.8.10 Finally, we break down the 12-year period into two parts in order to gauge the effect of the economic boom working its way across the country. This confirms the rippling out of the recovery from London in recent years. For example, while south and east England's overall rate of job growth fell from 1.7 per cent a year in 1991-1998 to 1.1 per cent in 1998-2003, in the north and west it rose from 0.6 to 1.1 per cent. In other words, during this most recent 5 year period the north and west's growth rate moved from being barely one third of the south and east's to matching it.

3.8.11 Figure 3.20 shows how the 10 SOCR types contributed to this regional shift. The key features are the more than halving of London's growth rate between the two periods and the very marked resurgence of the Mets. They moved up to a level that is double London's rate for 1998-2003. The north and west's large and small cities also saw their rate move upward, but very much more modestly. In the south and east, only the small cities bucked the regional trend of slowing job growth. Even so, comparing the two parts of England, the general pattern since 1998 has been the continuing stronger growth of the south and east, with all types except London outpacing their counterparts in the north and west.

Figure 3.20: Annualised change in total jobs (excluding agriculture), 1991-1998 and 1998-2003, for ten SOCR types

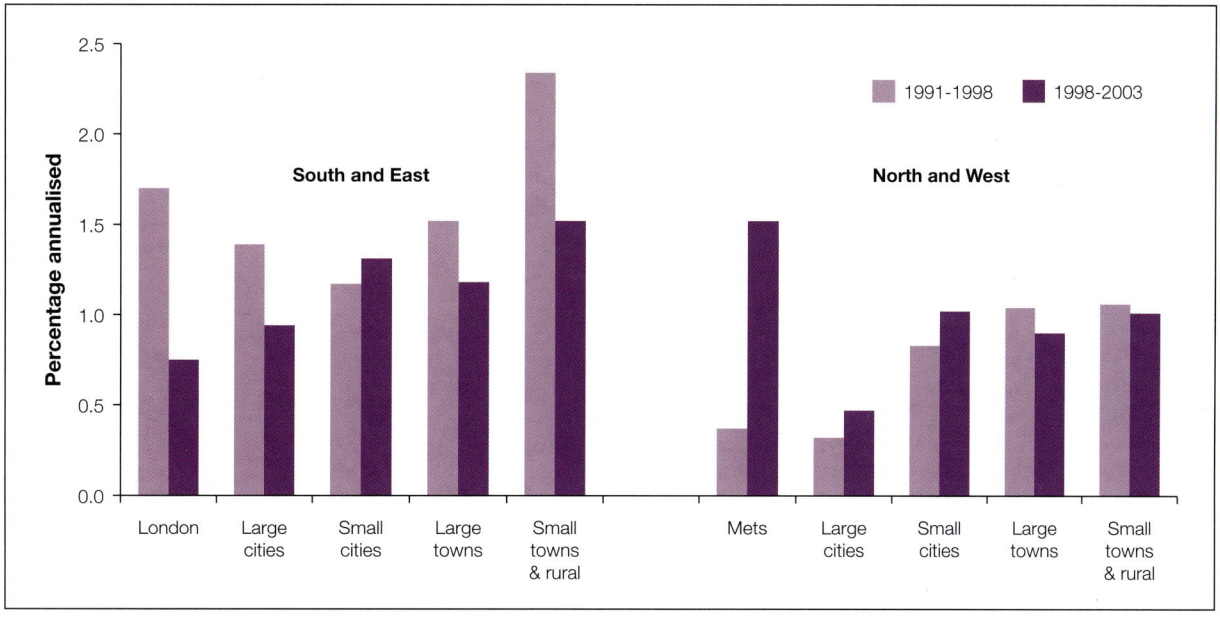

3.9 Population shifts within cities

3.9.1 So far this chapter has looked at trends between cities. We now look at trends within. First we look at patterns of centralisation and decentralisation, examining the relative growth of their inner and outer areas. We then look at the degree of variability across cities at 'tract' level. This throws light on the debates about fragmentation and polarisation within cities, in which some parts of cities have become increasingly attractive with surging house prices, while others have become 'low demand' areas. Our analysis is restricted to the largest cities and to overall population change.

Comparing the inner and outer parts of five cities

3.9.2   Figure 3.21 shows a mixed pattern in terms of the population trend for the inner districts of England's five largest cities. For Inner London the record is one of pretty consistent upward shift in growth rate, largely paralleling the trend for the whole of the London urban area. Liverpool and Manchester/Salford follow the same pattern. The latter's recovery after 1997 is much more like London's than Liverpool's, that is of general recovery over the full period interrupted by slight setback in 1991-97. Meanwhile, Birmingham's recovery did not begin until the later 1990s. Newcastle is distinctive in its combination of growth in 1991-97 and subsequent slippage.

Figure 3.21: Population change for inner districts of five large cities, 1981-1986 to 1997-2003 (annualised rates)

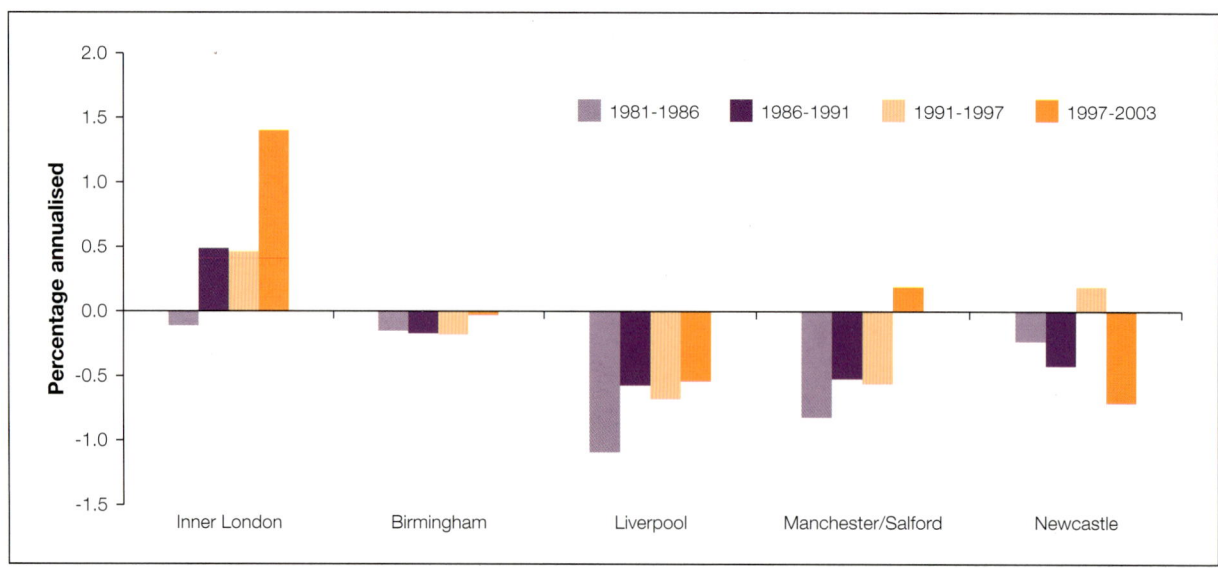

3.9.3   Comparing these inner-area population growth rates with those for these cities' outer districts (Figure 3.22), London is again exceptional. In the final period, its inner districts grew at an annual rate 0.9 percentage points higher than its outer area, though considerable volatility is apparent over time with both parts being quite evenly matched in 1981-86 and 1991-97. Newcastle presents a mirror image of London's pattern, with its central city being outperformed by its outer areas in the late 1980s and since 1997. Liverpool has been in Newcastle's current situation since 1991, following a period of relative balance between its inner and outer areas. By contrast, the Manchester/Salford core has grown away from the rest of the Manchester urban area in the last few years. So too has Birmingham's, although to a much smaller extent.

Figure 3.22: Population growth differential between inner and outer parts of five large cities, 1981-1986 to 1997-2003 (annualised rates)

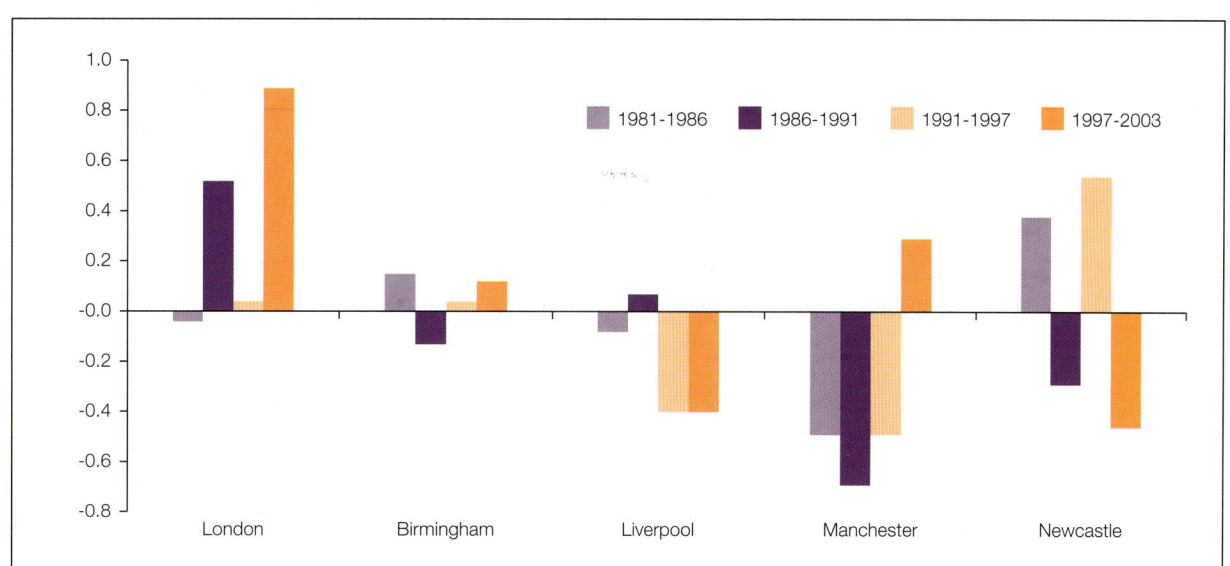

Population change at the tract level for nine cities

3.9.4   The tracts, averaging some 35,000 residents, which we developed for State of the Cities Database, provide a useful way of showing the way in which cities are altering internally. Tract level data can show whether better-off tracts are growing faster or slower than the poorer ones. We addressed this question by classifying tracts into 'quarters', which distinguishes a 'rich' quarter of the tracts, a 'poor' quarter and the remaining half that lie in between that can be termed 'middle'. We carry out the analysis for the nine cities. Their population change rates are shown in Table 3.12.

Table 3.12: Population change, for rich, middle and poor quarters of nine cities, (%)

Primary Urban Area	1991-2001			Rich minus Poor		
	Rich	Middle	Poor	1991-2001	1981-1991	shift
London	5.0	2.2	6.3	-1.3	-0.7	-0.7
Birmingham	-1.9	-3.9	-3.0	1.0	4.9	-3.8
Manchester	-1.1	-2.5	-11.0	9.8	1.6	8.3
Liverpool	-3.0	-5.3	-10.9	8.0	4.5	3.5
Newcastle	-2.6	-5.3	-9.3	6.7	7.3	-0.6
Nottingham	-1.5	0.4	-7.4	5.9	5.3	0.6
Sheffield	0.2	-3.1	-8.5	8.7	12.4	-3.7
Leeds	5.3	-0.5	-8.0	13.2	5.5	7.7
Leicester	4.2	-2.1	-0.5	4.6	6.0	-1.4

3.9.5   For London, the picture is one of increasing population polarisation. The rich and more deprived tracts are both growing considerably faster than the ones in between. A similar pattern is found in Birmingham, although there are slower population decreases of the two extremes. In Leicester, too, the two extremes are more buoyant than the middle group. Nottingham is the reverse of this pattern – the middle tracts are the most buoyant, suggesting some rebalancing of population away from the extremes and with a particularly large decline in the population of its less well off tracts.

3.9.6   The other five cities are characterised by positive progression in growth rates from poor to rich. Leeds provides the clearest example of this, with its more deprived tracts seeing an 8 per cent decrease between 1991 and 2001. The middle tracts are quite stable in size and the richer ones grew by 5 per cent. Manchester, Liverpool, Newcastle and Sheffield share this pattern. Although none is as dynamic as Leeds in terms of population change for their rich and middle tracts.

3.9.7   The right-hand panel of Table 3.12 summarises the 1990s experience by comparing the growth rates of the more and less deprived quarters of the nine cities and then contrasting this with their performance in the previous decade. The 1991-2001 column emphasises the dynamic situation of Leeds, with its strong population flow out of more deprived tracts into the rich ones. London lies at the other extreme. Indeed it is the only one of the nine cities where the less well off tracts grew faster than the less deprived ones. The same was true in the 1980s, though in this period it was Sheffield rather than Leeds that exhibited the largest growth differential between its areas of more and less deprivation.

3.10   So can English cities do more?

3.10.1   England's cities are important to national success, because they represent such a large part of the nation in terms of both population and economic activity. Until recently the rest of England was doing better in terms of growth in numbers of people and jobs. The cities' contribution has been growing more recently – their 42 per cent contribution to national population growth in 1997-2003 was a clear and impressive improvement on previous experience. London alone grew by 403,000 (34 per cent of England's total), so was pulling almost twice its weight over this period. By contrast, the 55 other cities contributed 8 per cent of the national growth, compared to their 40 per cent share of total population. However, London's growth dropped sharply after the turn of the century with the performance of the big six cities of Birmingham, Leeds, Sheffield, Manchester, Liverpool and Newcastle moving up steadily from their high losses of the early 1990s.

3.10.2   Cities are even more important for employment than for population. In 2003 the 56 combined accounted for 63 per cent of England's total jobs, 5 percentage points more than their population. Although they account for barely half of its self-employed population, their overall contribution to national growth has been greater in recent years than in the mid 1990s. Also the number of cities contributing to growth in jobs has grown and as London's dominance has been challenged with the rippling out of the economic recovery further west and north.

3.10.3   Finally, it is important to remember that the position is still fluid. In particular, London's population growth rate began to plummet around the year 2000, while the population growth rates of the six Mets moved upwards. By 2003, relatively little separated the population growth rates of these seven cities. Historically, this is not unexpected. At key points of the national economic cycle in the past, as the economy of London has overheated, the combination of tight labour market and inflated house prices has led to the rippling out of stronger job and migratory growth into the north and west. Nevertheless, this stage provides renewed life for the previously lagging cities in this part of England. It represents a particularly opportune time for policy intervention to build on the market trend and make an extra difference that could last beyond the end of the recovery cycle and lead to a 'virtuous circle' of future investment and growth.

Chapter 4: The competitive economic performance of English cities

4.1   Introduction

4.1.1   This chapter explores the competitive economic performance of English cities. It argues that since much economic activity takes place in cities, their success is critical to that of our regional and national economies. The chapter presents a range of theoretical, analytical and empirical material. It begins with a review of different theoretical explanations and the range of factors which they identify as critical for cities' economic success. It then draws upon that analysis to explore and explain the economic changes taking place in the 56 English cities in this study. It examines the differences between the more successful cities primarily, although not exclusively, located in the south and east and those elsewhere in England. It illustrates the dynamics at work by looking at the economies of four cities in different regions of the country which face different opportunities and challenges – London, Cambridge, Derby and Sheffield. The chapter ends with a discussion of the implications for government policies and funding, underlining their need to have a more explicit urban focus in future.

Defining competitive economic performance

4.1.2   There has been a surge of academic and policy attention devoted to the idea of urban competitiveness recently. We define it as:

> *'the ability of cities to continually upgrade their business environment, skill base, and physical, social and cultural infrastructures, so as to attract and retain high-growth, innovative and profitable firms, and an educated, creative and entrepreneurial workforce, thereby enabling them to achieve a high rate of productivity, high employment rate, high wages, high GDP per capita, and low levels of income inequality and social exclusion'.*

The new conventional wisdom is that nations, regions and cities have to be more competitive to survive in the new marketplace being forged by globalisation and the new information technologies. Within government, interest has grown in the regional foundations of national competitiveness. The government has focused on the competitiveness of the country's regions, cities and more recently, city-regions, as part of its aim to improve the productive and innovative performance of the national economy (HM Treasury, 2001, 2003, 2004; ODPM, 2003, 2004). Similarly, the European Commission argues that the improvement of the competitiveness of cities in Europe's lagging regions is vital to the pursuit of social cohesion (European Commission, 2004).

4.1.3   At the same time, cities and regions have become increasingly concerned with local competitiveness and with devising policy strategies to move their areas up the competitiveness league table. However, this new focus on place – or territorial-competitiveness – raises a host of questions as to what, precisely, is meant by the notion of regional and urban competitiveness. In what sense do regions and cities compete? How can regional and urban competitiveness be measured? What are the implications for public policy? There is no single theoretical framework for analysing the economic competitiveness of cities. But there are a number of recurring themes in the literature. For example, the export base of a city has a key influence on the performance of its economy. Competitive advantage depends on creating and attracting a highly educated and skilled labour force. High rates of innovation and entrepreneurship help ensure high productivity, high wages and high employment and enable a city to adjust to economic and technological change. The socio-cultural assets of a city are an important source of urban competitive advantage, shaping its attractiveness to educated and creative people. The quality of the communications infrastructure – road, rail, air and telecommunications – and hence its internal and external connectivity, has a direct influence on a city's economic performance. The strategic decision-making capacity of a city also affects its competitiveness, particularly through its mechanisms of economic governance. The next section shows how we use these factors in our model of urban competitiveness.

Our analytic approach

4.1.4   We have incorporated these factors into an urban competitive performance pyramid (Figure 4.1). This shows that the analysis of urban economic competitiveness consists of several different levels. The most aggregate measures of urban competitive advantage concern a city's standard of living, conventionally captured by GDP per capita. Underpinning aggregate performance are revealed measures of urban competitive advantage – namely productivity, the employment rate, wage levels and profit rates. These are in turn the outcome of the key 'drivers' of urban competitive performance – innovation, investment, human capital, economic structure, connectivity, quality of life and the structures of decision making. The drivers are themselves the outcome of more basic underlying determinants – a city's business environment, educational base, urban social and cultural infrastructure and governance structures and organisation.

4.1.5   Competitiveness is a dynamic process. The critical issue is how a city maintains its competitive and absolute advantages over time, how it adjusts to shifts in technology, demand, external competition and policy regime. Cities are complex, self-organising market driven systems of economic, social, technological and social relationships. They differ in their economic, social and institutional structures. Each is the product of a unique history of development. These differences persist over time, so there are strong tendencies making for 'path dependence' in the patterns of size, function, and specialisation among cities. There are corresponding differences between cities in their capacity to adapt to changing technological, economic and market conditions and opportunities. However, path dependence is not the only feature of economic development. It is also driven by the emergence of new sectors, technologies and institutions that replace the old. Dynamic urban competitiveness therefore also depends on the ability of cities to generate novelty and innovation.

4.1.6   In terms of the 'competitiveness pyramid' in Figure 4.1 we must understand how a city responds to changes in its technological, competitive, market and regulatory environment. These changes set off complex processes of change and adaptation, in which some existing technologies and institutions survive, while other new ones emerge. The outcome of this complex process reshapes the determinants and drivers of a city's competitive advantage (Figure 4.2). Therefore each city follows its own distinctive historical trajectory. In principle, policies to alter or accelerate those individual trajectories must also be tailored to the specific histories and circumstances of each city. A key policy dilemma is therefore that while urban economic growth requires effective, long-term policies that are built from the bottom upwards, English cities compared to successful cities abroad have weaker powers and more limited finance with which to develop and implement such policies.

Figure 4.1: Conceptualising Urban Competitive Performance

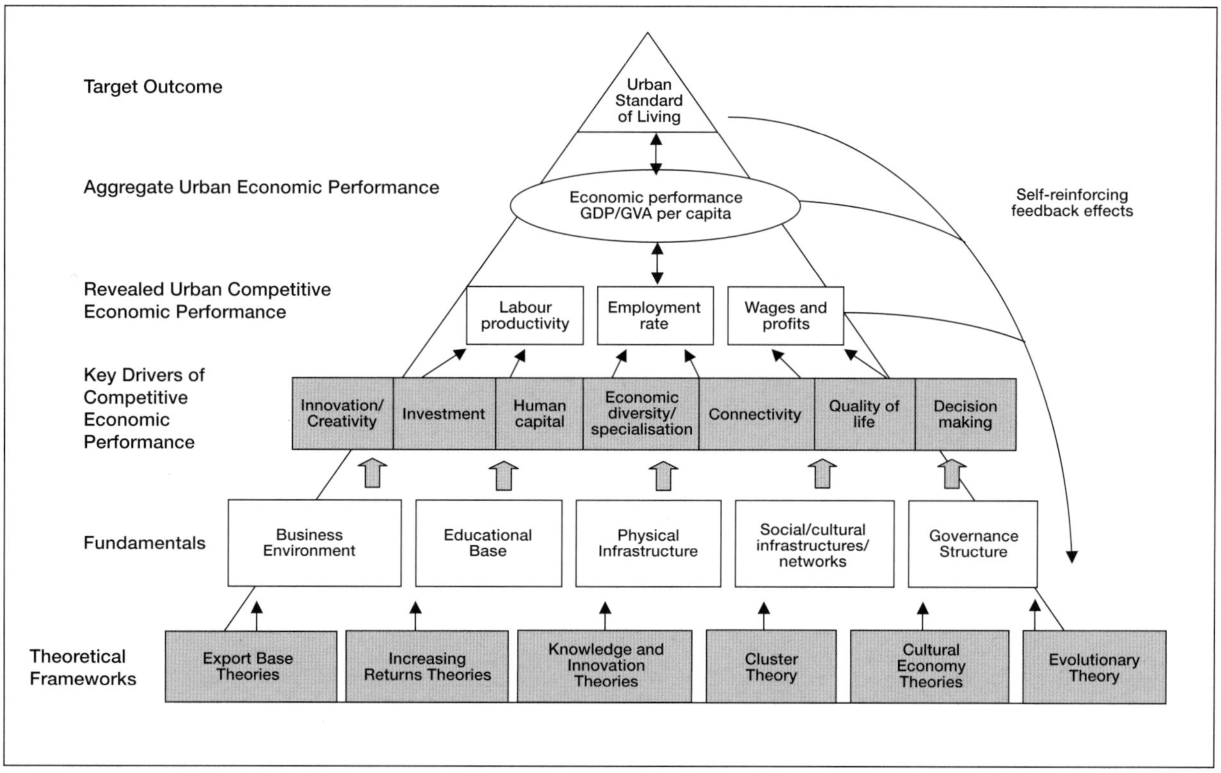

Figure 4.2: Dynamic Urban Competitiveness as an Evolutionary Process

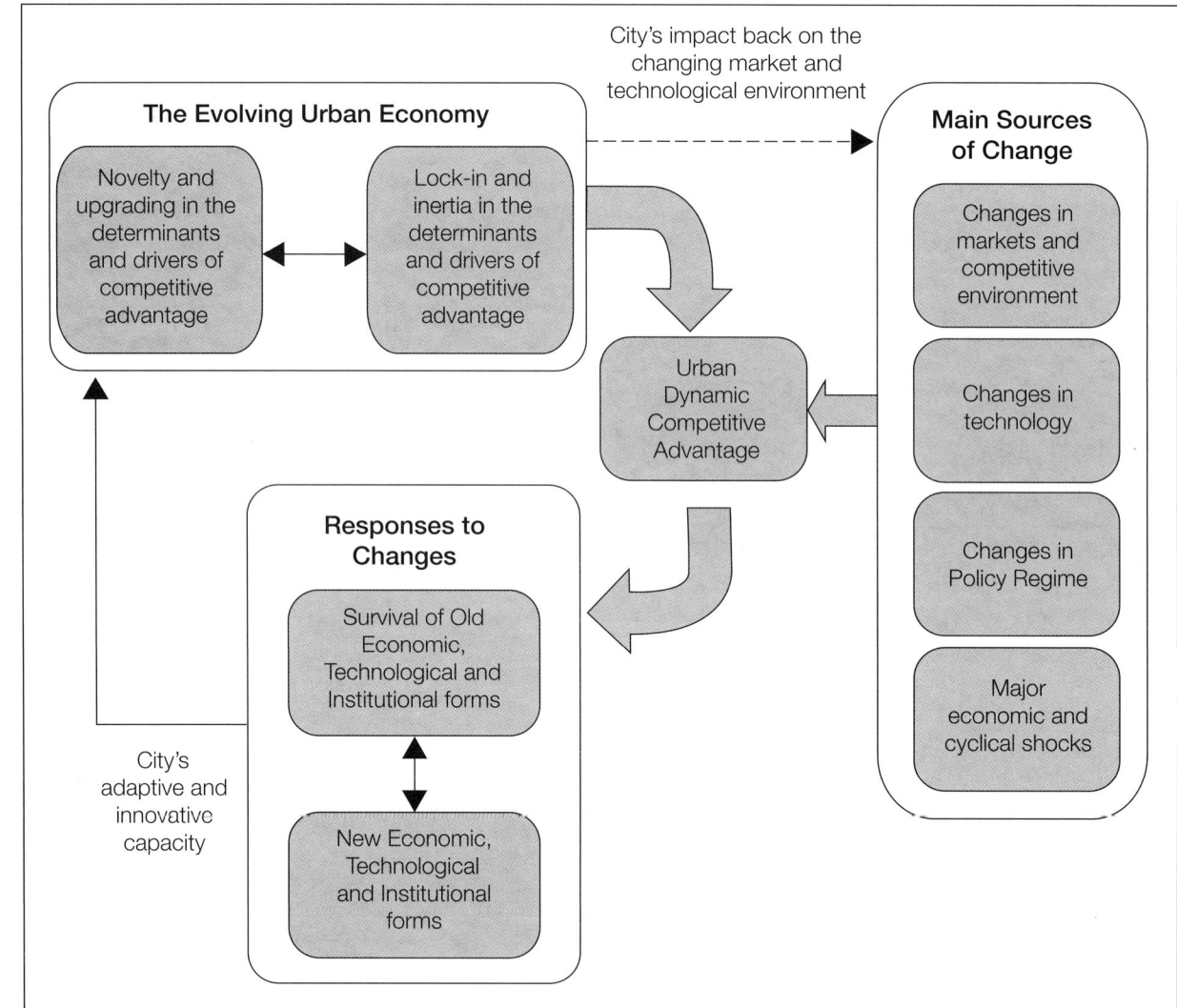

4.2. Measures and indicators of urban competitive economic performance

4.2.1 We use this evolutionary approach to the analysis of urban competitiveness in the following empirical analysis of English cities. We analyse secondary data on the changes taking place in the economic performance of the 56 largest English cities during the 1990s and early years of this century. We argue that the ability to meet all of the criteria of urban competitiveness outlined above simultaneously is revealed by indicators which show rising productivity, full employment and rising wages. We analyse the key drivers of this performance together with their underlying basic determinants.

4.2.2 It is important to define the most appropriate geography of urban economies, therefore we require a consistent and comparable basis for data collection. We think that the City-Region is the most appropriate geographical level at which to analyse economic performance. Therefore in keeping with the typology of this study we have used data from Travel to Work Areas (TTWAs) to approximate that boundary. We have analysed data from the largest 56. Their boundaries and locations are shown in Map 4.1.

Map 4.1: Index map of the 56 TTWAs used in this study

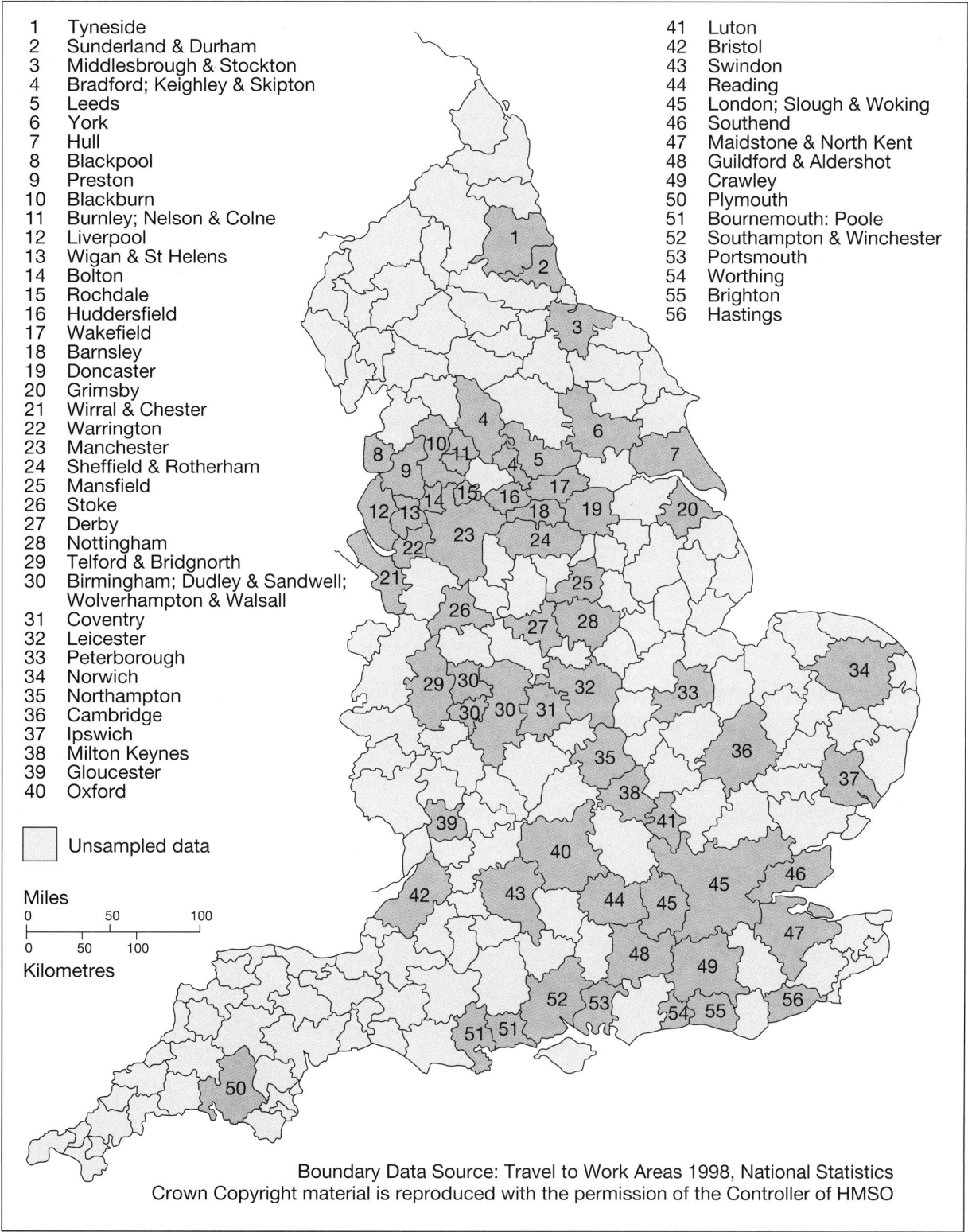

1 Tyneside
2 Sunderland & Durham
3 Middlesbrough & Stockton
4 Bradford; Keighley & Skipton
5 Leeds
6 York
7 Hull
8 Blackpool
9 Preston
10 Blackburn
11 Burnley; Nelson & Colne
12 Liverpool
13 Wigan & St Helens
14 Bolton
15 Rochdale
16 Huddersfield
17 Wakefield
18 Barnsley
19 Doncaster
20 Grimsby
21 Wirral & Chester
22 Warrington
23 Manchester
24 Sheffield & Rotherham
25 Mansfield
26 Stoke
27 Derby
28 Nottingham
29 Telford & Bridgnorth
30 Birmingham; Dudley & Sandwell;
   Wolverhampton & Walsall
31 Coventry
32 Leicester
33 Peterborough
34 Norwich
35 Northampton
36 Cambridge
37 Ipswich
38 Milton Keynes
39 Gloucester
40 Oxford

41 Luton
42 Bristol
43 Swindon
44 Reading
45 London; Slough & Woking
46 Southend
47 Maidstone & North Kent
48 Guildford & Aldershot
49 Crawley
50 Plymouth
51 Bournemouth: Poole
52 Southampton & Winchester
53 Portsmouth
54 Worthing
55 Brighton
56 Hastings

Unsampled data

Miles
0   50   100

0   50   100
Kilometres

Boundary Data Source: Travel to Work Areas 1998, National Statistics
Crown Copyright material is reproduced with the permission of the Controller of HMSO

4.2.3   The main advantage of using TTWAs is that they are constructed on a consistent basis according to two main economic criteria. The first is that at least 75 per cent, of the resident economically active population actually work in the area. Second, of everyone working in the area, at least 75 per cent actually live in the area. They capture a significant proportion of both local economic activities and the residential areas in which the employees of those activities live. Therefore to capture economic performance of the wider City-Region, we use this larger TTWA level, which is one step higher up in our typology, than the Primary Urban Areas which we typically use in other sections of this report.

4.2.4   We examine the use of Gross Disposable Household Income (GDHI), exports and GVA per capita, productivity, employment and wages and profits, as indicators of the economic performance of the 56 cities in the SOCR. We show the contribution to national economic performance by comparing their performance with that of the average for England, using mean weighted data. Those cities that fall below the English average are considered to lag the national economic performance. Those that outperform the English average are considered to lead the national performance. On this simple criterion a majority of large English cities lag the national economic performance on all three main measures.

Gross Disposable Household Income

4.2.5   Turning first to GDHI, Map 4.2 shows the geography of GDHI in 1998. Blue colours represent those cities with above average GDHI and which led the national economic performance. Red colours are those that performed below the average for England. Most of the blue areas were concentrated in the south and east. Most of the red areas were in and around the north and west of England.

Map 4.2: Average disposable weekly household income, equivalised after housing costs, 1998

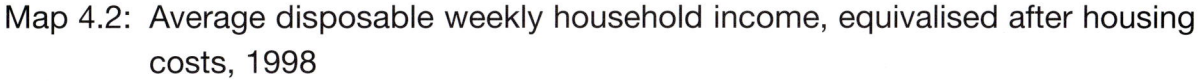

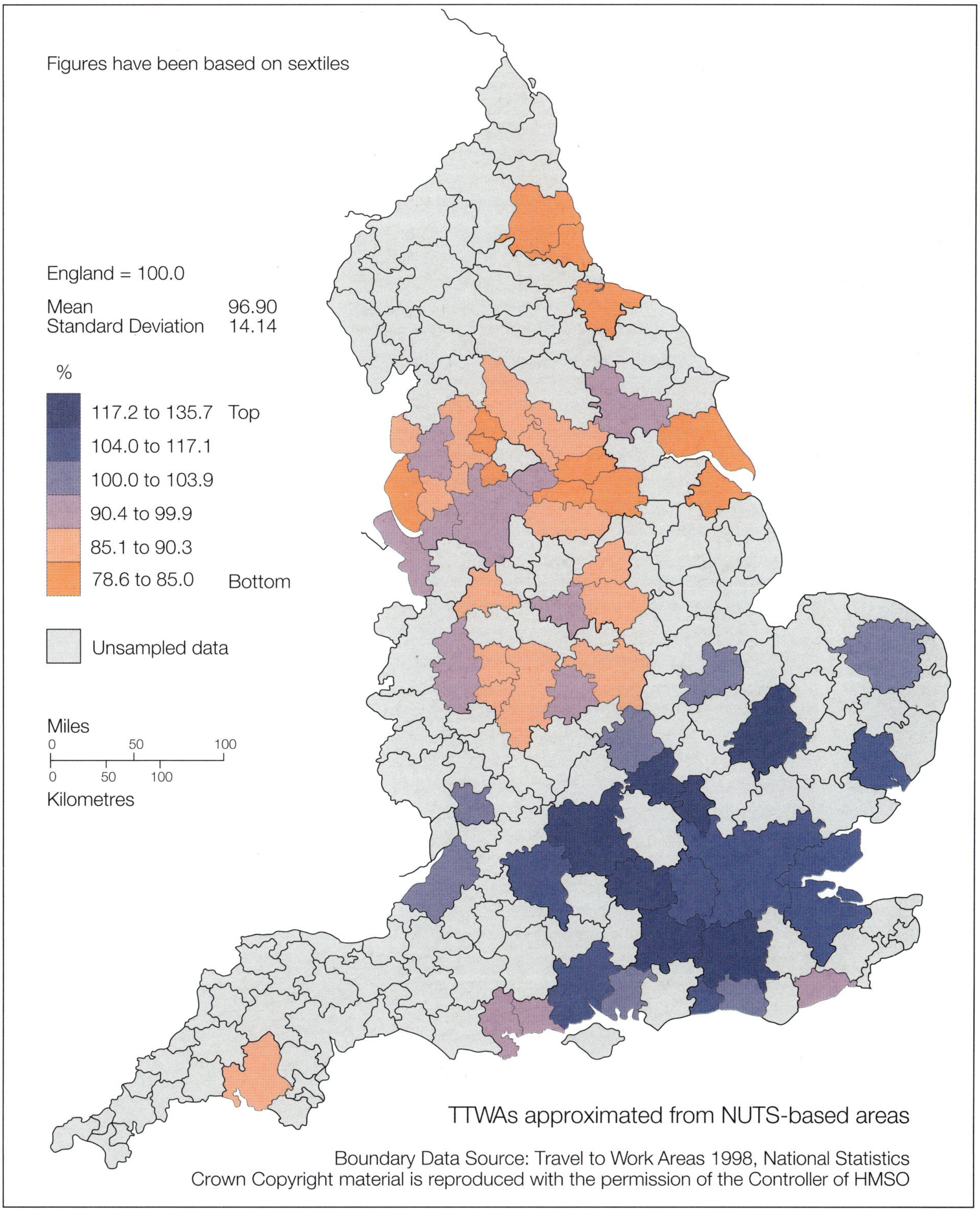

Figures have been based on sextiles

England = 100.0

Mean   96.90
Standard Deviation   14.14

%

- 117.2 to 135.7   Top
- 104.0 to 117.1
- 100.0 to 103.9
- 90.4 to 99.9
- 85.1 to 90.3
- 78.6 to 85.0   Bottom

Unsampled data

Miles
0   50   100
0   50   100
Kilometres

TTWAs approximated from NUTS-based areas

Boundary Data Source: Travel to Work Areas 1998, National Statistics
Crown Copyright material is reproduced with the permission of the Controller of HMSO

4.2.6   Figure 4.3 shows the levels for each city for 1995 and 2003 as an index of the average for England. The majority of all the 56 cities were below the average for England in 1995 and have remained so. Twelve of the 56 cities show GDHI above the English average in both years.

Figure 4.3: Gross Disposable Household Income 1995 and 2003

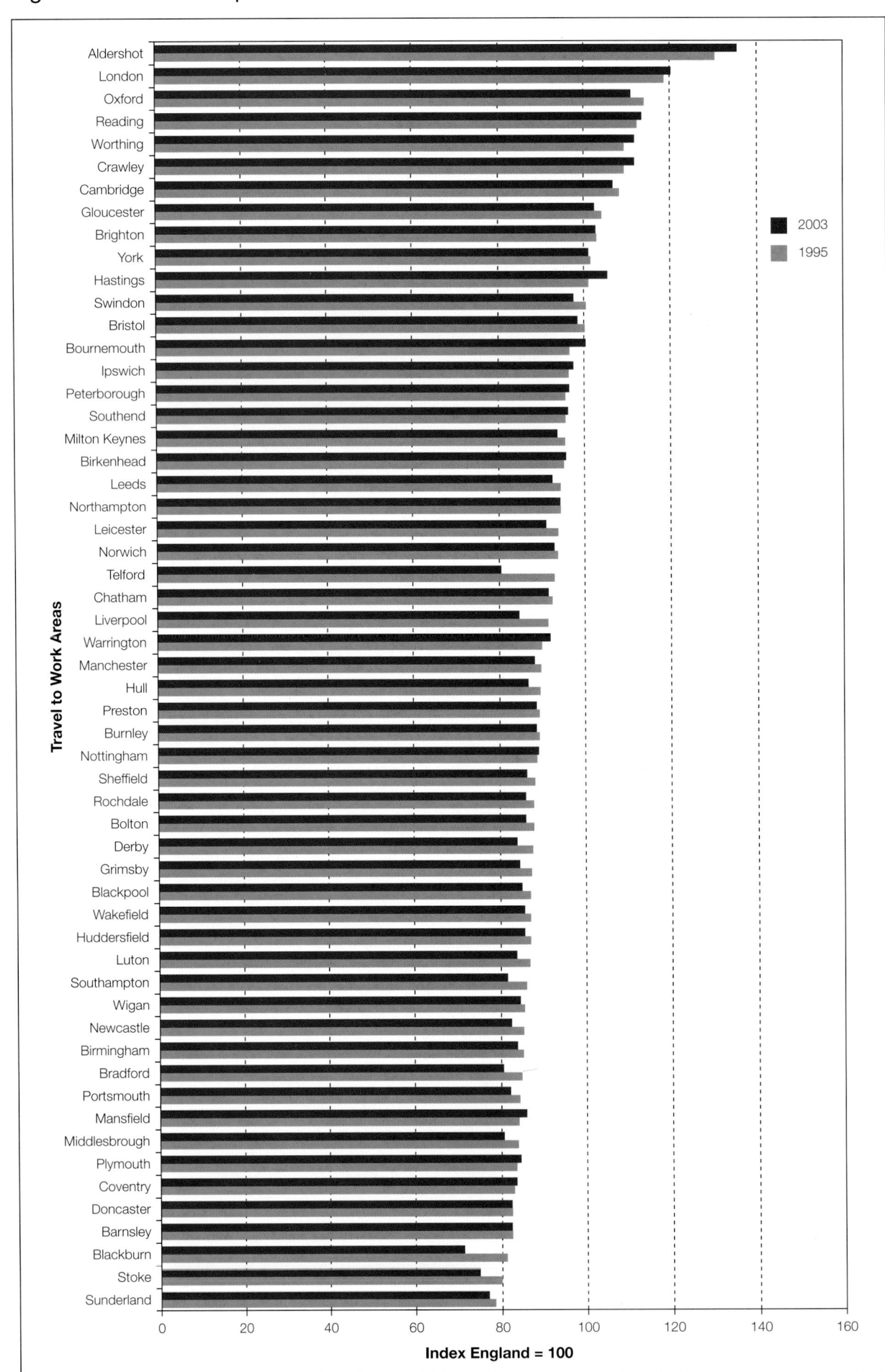

Exports

4.2.7 Export base theories emphasise the significance of exports in the economic performance of different cities. The bulk of any city's trade will be with other cities in the same country. As a result, its competitive success will reflect how well it does relative to other cities in its own national urban system as well as its ability to compete in international markets. Even the most successful urban economies seldom export more than around 20-30 per cent of their outputs of goods and services.

4.2.8 We would have liked to be able to use total exports as a key indicator of urban economic output performance. Unfortunately the data available are for visible exports only. However, these constitute a significant proportion, sometimes a majority of exports in cities that depend on manufacturing but are also an important part of London's exports. They are not perfect but remain a robust measure of export capacity. Map 4.3 shows the absolute levels of visible exports in 2002 indexed to the average for England as a whole. Those cities leading the national average are shown in dark blue. Those lagging the average are shown in pink and red. Despite being primarily a services based city, London was among the leading exporters of goods in 2002. It was joined by a contiguous club of leading exporters including Reading, Oxford, Swindon, Luton and Milton Keynes. Outside this area other leading exporters included Peterborough, Derby and Nottingham, Stoke and Telford, Warrington, and Grimsby.

4.2.9 Figure 4.4 shows visible exports per capita for the years 1996 and 2002. Ten cities performed above the English average. These included London, where some of the minority of manufacturing that remains in the city is internationally competitive. In addition a further six of these form part of a networked club of high performing cities in the south and east including Swindon, Milton Keynes, Reading, Aldershot/Guildford and Northampton. However, 23 out of the 56 cities declined in their visible exports over this period.

Map 4.3: Visible exports per capita, 2002

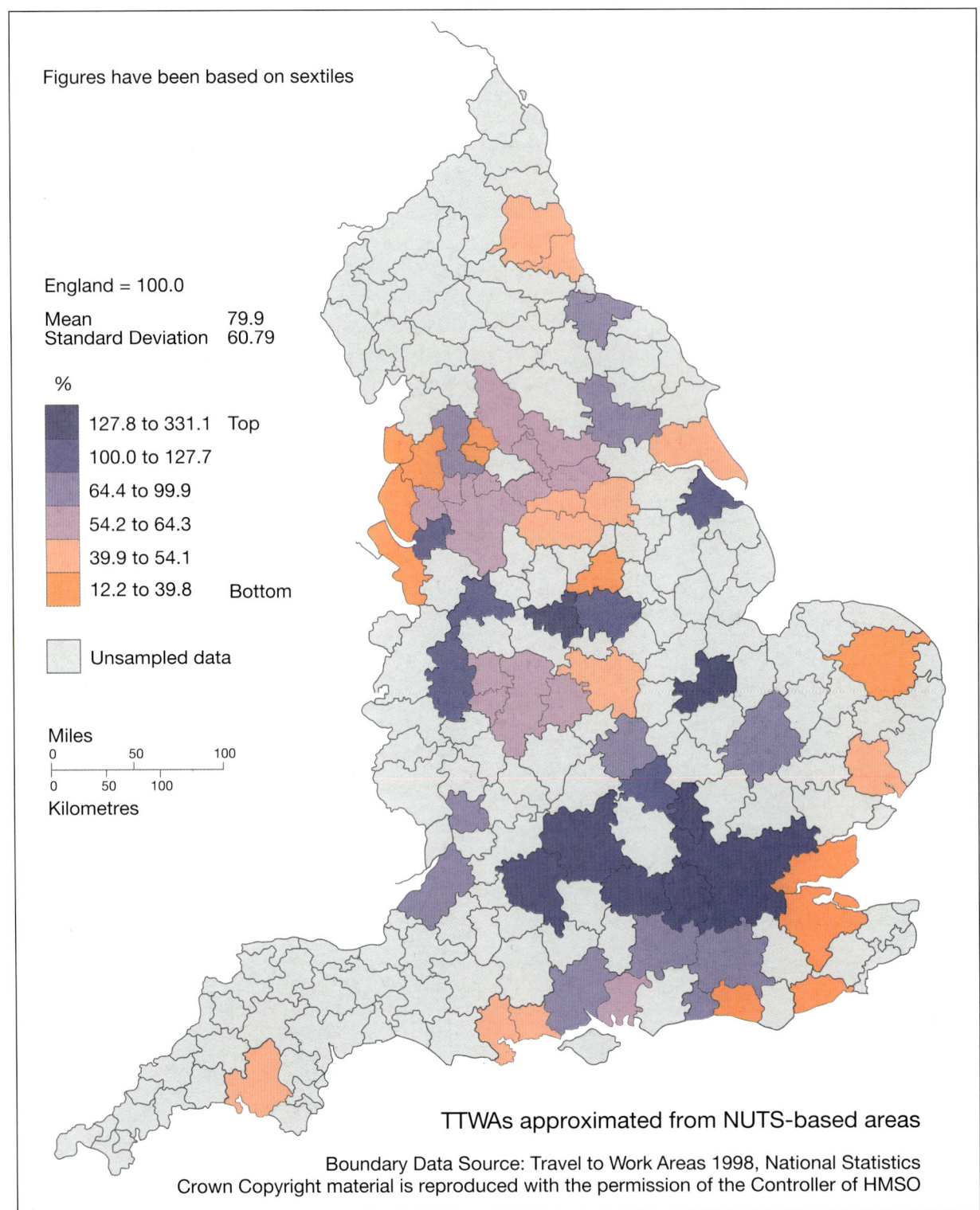

Figures have been based on sextiles

England = 100.0

Mean 79.9
Standard Deviation 60.79

%

127.8 to 331.1	Top
100.0 to 127.7	
64.4 to 99.9	
54.2 to 64.3	
39.9 to 54.1	
12.2 to 39.8	Bottom

Unsampled data

Miles
0 — 50 — 100
0 — 50 — 100
Kilometres

TTWAs approximated from NUTS-based areas

Boundary Data Source: Travel to Work Areas 1998, National Statistics
Crown Copyright material is reproduced with the permission of the Controller of HMSO

Figure 4.4: Visible exports per capita 1996 and 2002

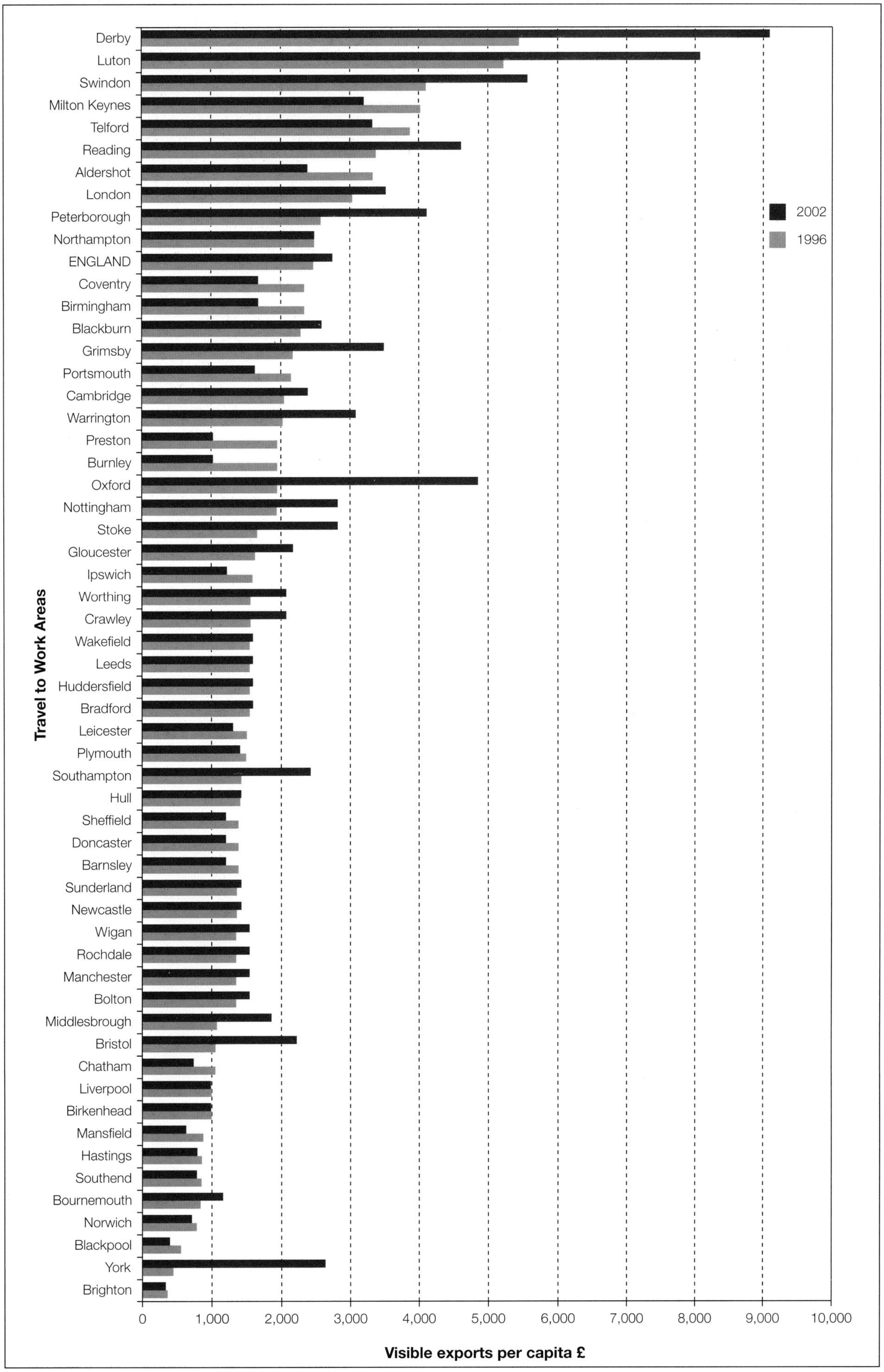

Travel to Work Areas (y-axis)

Legend:
- 2002 (black)
- 1996 (grey)

Categories (top to bottom): Derby, Luton, Swindon, Milton Keynes, Telford, Reading, Aldershot, London, Peterborough, Northampton, ENGLAND, Coventry, Birmingham, Blackburn, Grimsby, Portsmouth, Cambridge, Warrington, Preston, Burnley, Oxford, Nottingham, Stoke, Gloucester, Ipswich, Worthing, Crawley, Wakefield, Leeds, Huddersfield, Bradford, Leicester, Plymouth, Southampton, Hull, Sheffield, Doncaster, Barnsley, Sunderland, Newcastle, Wigan, Rochdale, Manchester, Bolton, Middlesbrough, Bristol, Chatham, Liverpool, Birkenhead, Mansfield, Hastings, Southend, Bournemouth, Norwich, Blackpool, York, Brighton

x-axis: Visible exports per capita £ (0 to 10,000)

Gross Value Added

4.2.10 Map 4.4 shows the geographic distribution of GVA per head in 2002. Most of the best performing cities that led the national average were located in and around the south and east. Outside that area, the main cities leading the national economy were Bristol, Leeds, York, Manchester, Leicester and Peterborough. Most of the cities in the north and on or near the east coast lagged behind the national economic performance.

Map 4.4: Gross Value Added (GVA) per head, 2002

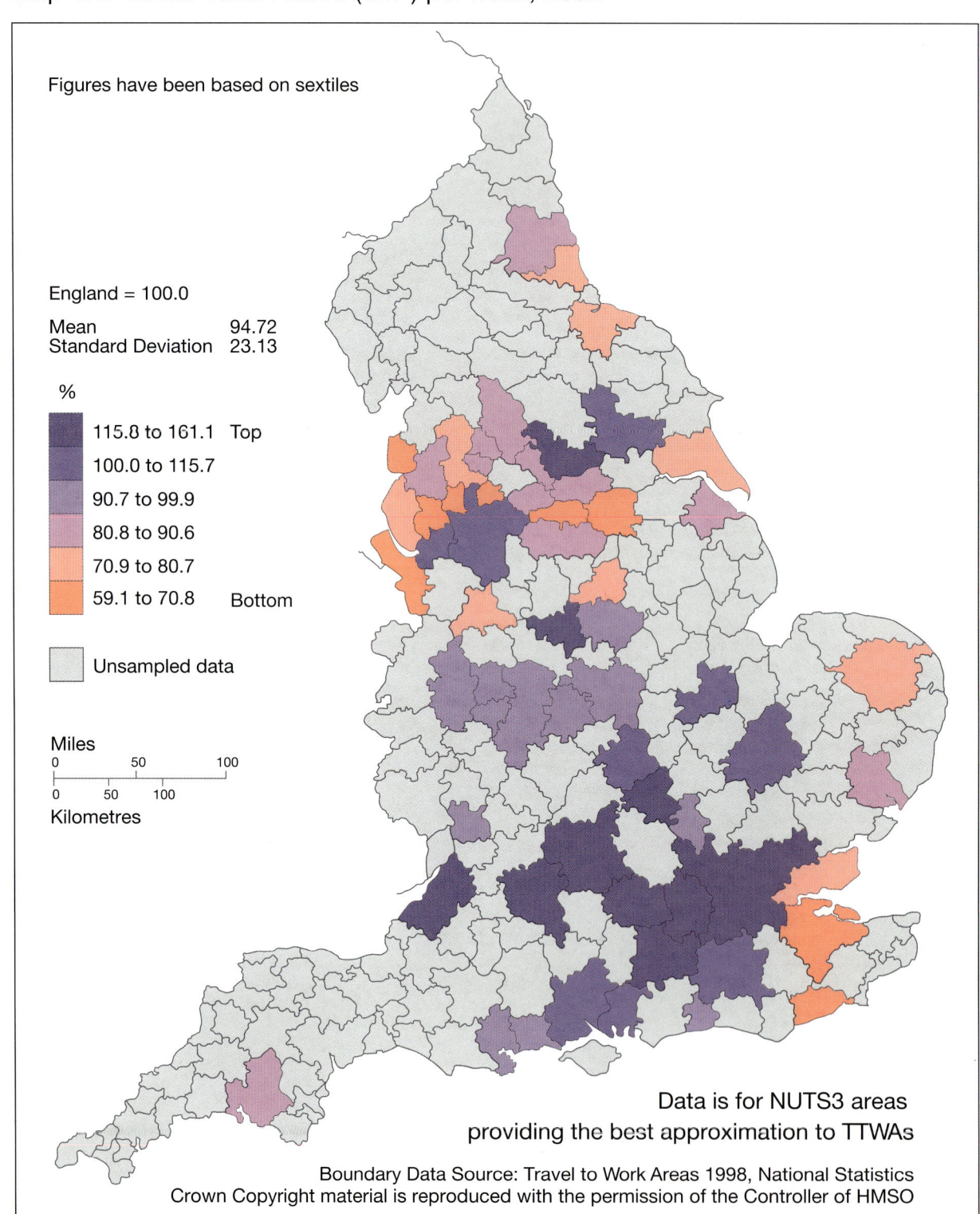

Figures have been based on sextiles

England = 100.0
Mean   94.72
Standard Deviation   23.13

%

- 115.8 to 161.1 Top
- 100.0 to 115.7
- 90.7 to 99.9
- 80.8 to 90.6
- 70.9 to 80.7
- 59.1 to 70.8 Bottom

Unsampled data

Miles
0   50   100

0   50   100
Kilometres

Data is for NUTS3 areas
providing the best approximation to TTWAs

Boundary Data Source: Travel to Work Areas 1998, National Statistics
Crown Copyright material is reproduced with the permission of the Controller of HMSO

4.2.11 Figure 4.5 shows the dynamic changes taking place in GVA per capita between 1995 and 2002. This reveals some recent progress by cities in the north and west. The average growth for England as a whole was 42.7 per cent. Twenty-five cities grew faster than that, of which 12 were in the north and west, including all of the Core Cities in the region. Nine cities achieved growth rates of 10 per cent or more than the English average. Most were in the south and east of England, but Manchester and Derby were in that most successful group. The places which form the City-Regions of the Northern Way had mixed fortunes. Leeds, Newcastle, Liverpool, Sheffield, and York posted the best performances. The least good performances were in Bradford, Burnley Blackpool, Wigan, Hull, Rochdale, Bolton, Grimsby, Middlesbrough and Blackburn.

Figure 4.5: Change in Gross Value Added per capita 1995–2002

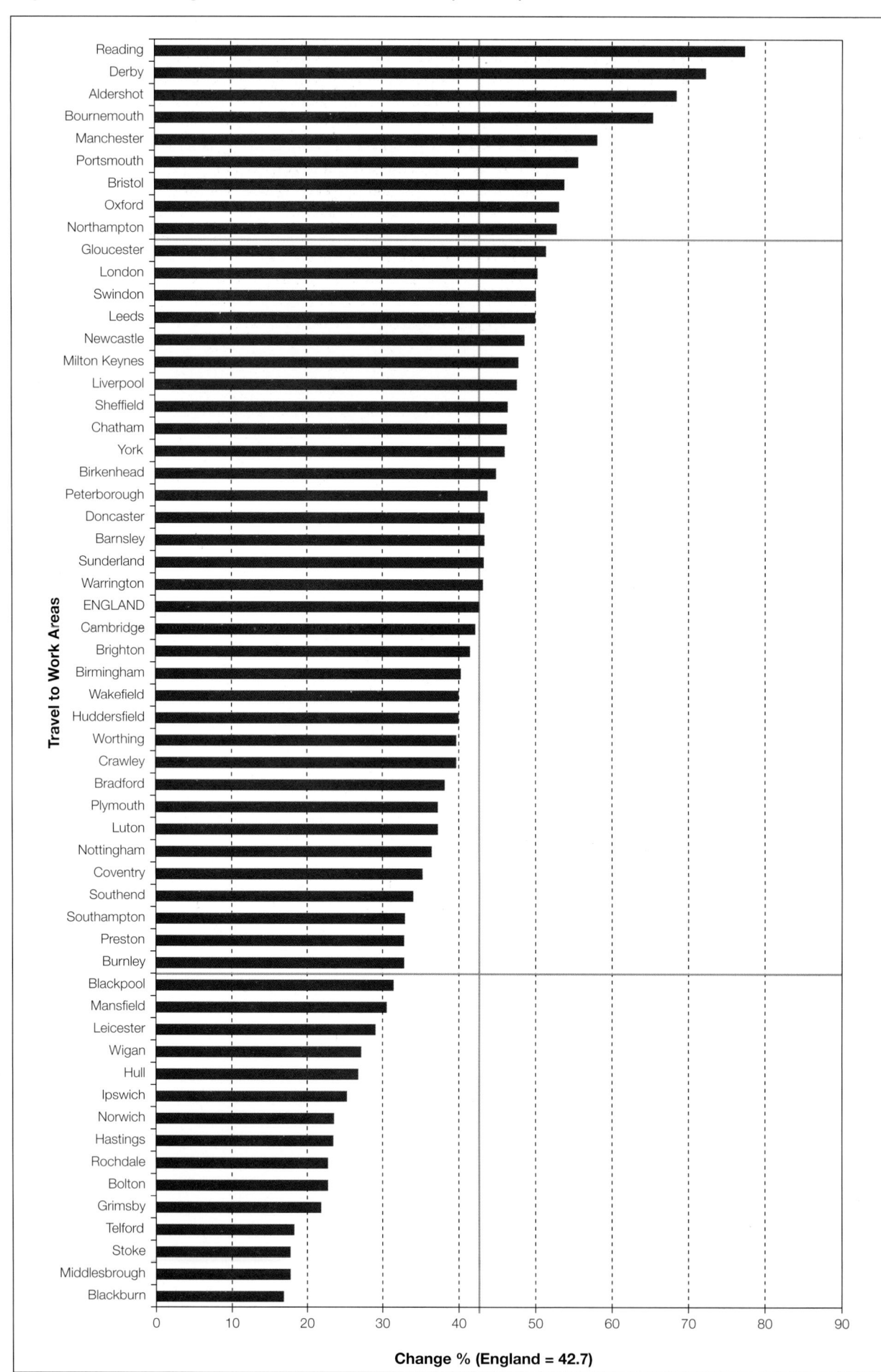

Change % (England = 42.7)

Productivity

4.2.12   The overall performance of urban economies is mainly shaped by the competitive performance of the firms located in them. Three critical indicators reveal the competitive performance of urban economies – labour productivity, employment rates, wages and profits. These factors are interrelated. Truly competitive economies will be characterised by a combination of rising productivity, full employment and rising wages. The level of output in an economy, for example, is a function of both the efficiency or productivity of labour and the amount of labour being used.

4.2.13   Figure 4.6 shows the rate of change in productivity in our sample of high and low performing cities. Not surprisingly most of the top performing economies in terms of GVA per employee also exceed the English average change between 1996 and 2001 of 13.7 per cent. Portsmouth is the exception to this rule. Productivity actually appears to have declined over the period in Blackpool, Blackburn and Hastings. Among our case study cities, productivity improved by more than the English average in Derby, Cambridge and London. Sheffield came close to achieving the national average improvement in productivity.

Figure 4.6: Rate of change in productivity (GVA per employee) selected Travel to Work Areas 1996–2001

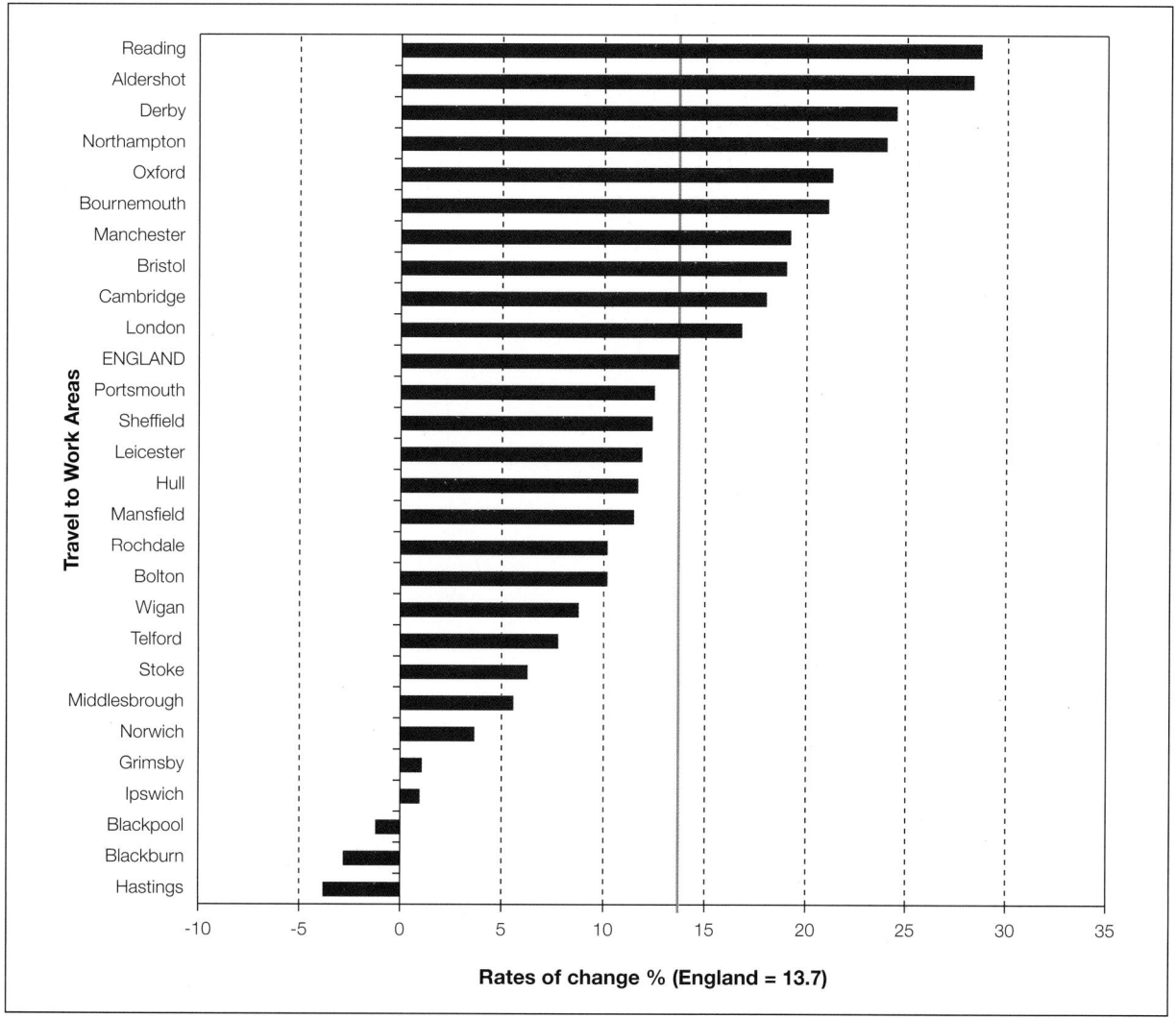

4.2.14 Map 4.5 shows the geographic scale of the productivity deficit in the national economy as at 2001. Most of the cities that lead productivity in England are located in the south and east. The only city with above average productivity outside this area in 2001 was Derby. Since productivity plays such a critical role in competitiveness and economic performance, these data show the scale of the challenges facing many of England's cities in leading rather than lagging the national economic performance.

Map 4.5: Gross Value Added (GVA) per employee job, 2001

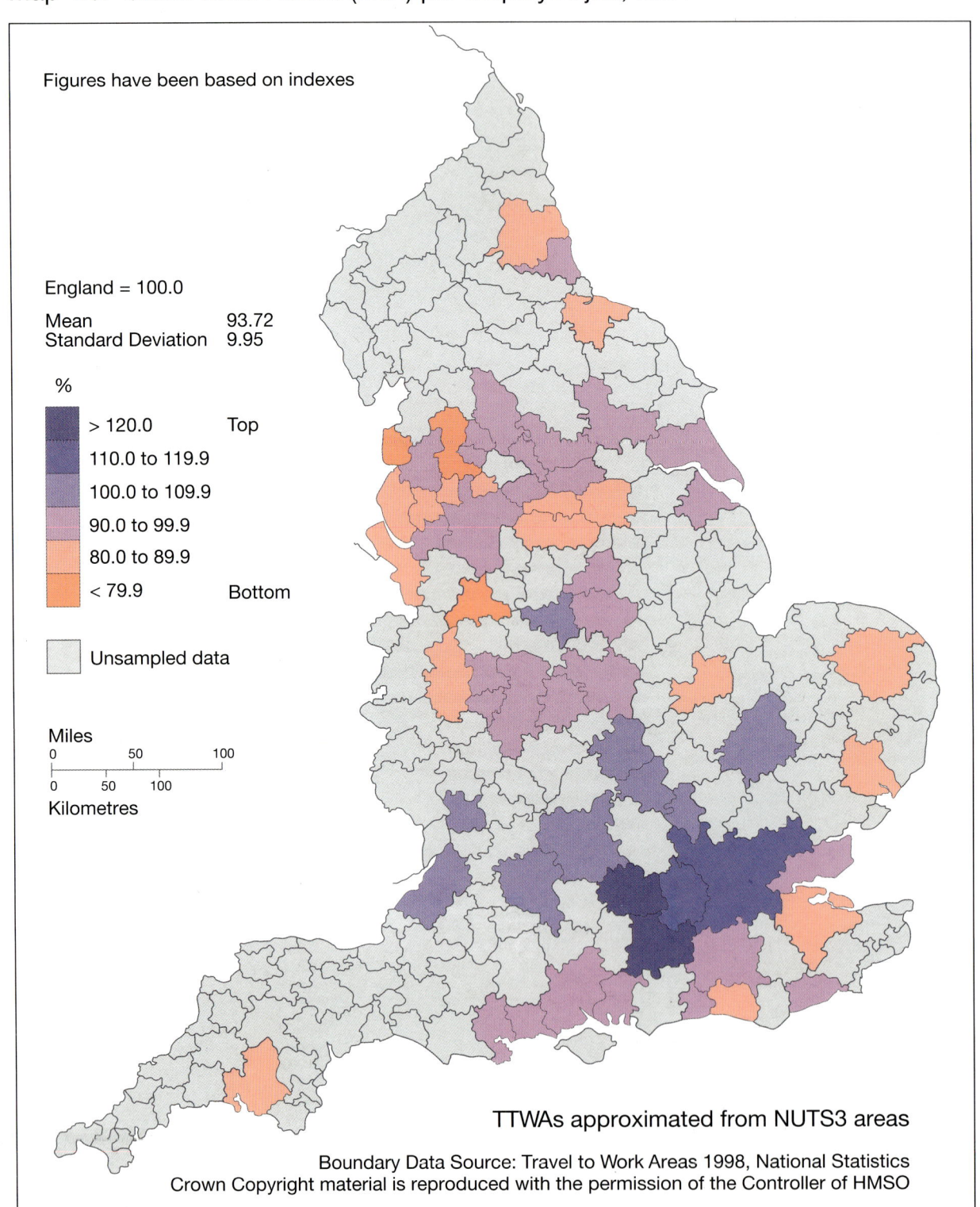

Figures have been based on indexes

England = 100.0

Mean 93.72
Standard Deviation 9.95

%

> 120.0 — Top
110.0 to 119.9
100.0 to 109.9
90.0 to 99.9
80.0 to 89.9
< 79.9 — Bottom

Unsampled data

Miles
0 50 100
0 50 100
Kilometres

TTWAs approximated from NUTS3 areas

Boundary Data Source: Travel to Work Areas 1998, National Statistics
Crown Copyright material is reproduced with the permission of the Controller of HMSO

Employment

4.2.15 Employment rates are our second main indicator of the revealed competitive performance of urban economies. Here there was good news. During the 1990s rates of employment improved in most English cities. Figure 4.7 shows that they improved in our entire sample of high and low performing cities with the most notable exception of Cambridge, which was already at a very high level. Some of the highest rates of improvement were experienced in those cities that started with the lowest employment rates at the beginning of the decade. These include Wigan, Grimsby, Middlesbrough, Sheffield and Hull.

Figure 4.7: Change in employment rate selected TTWAs 1991-2001

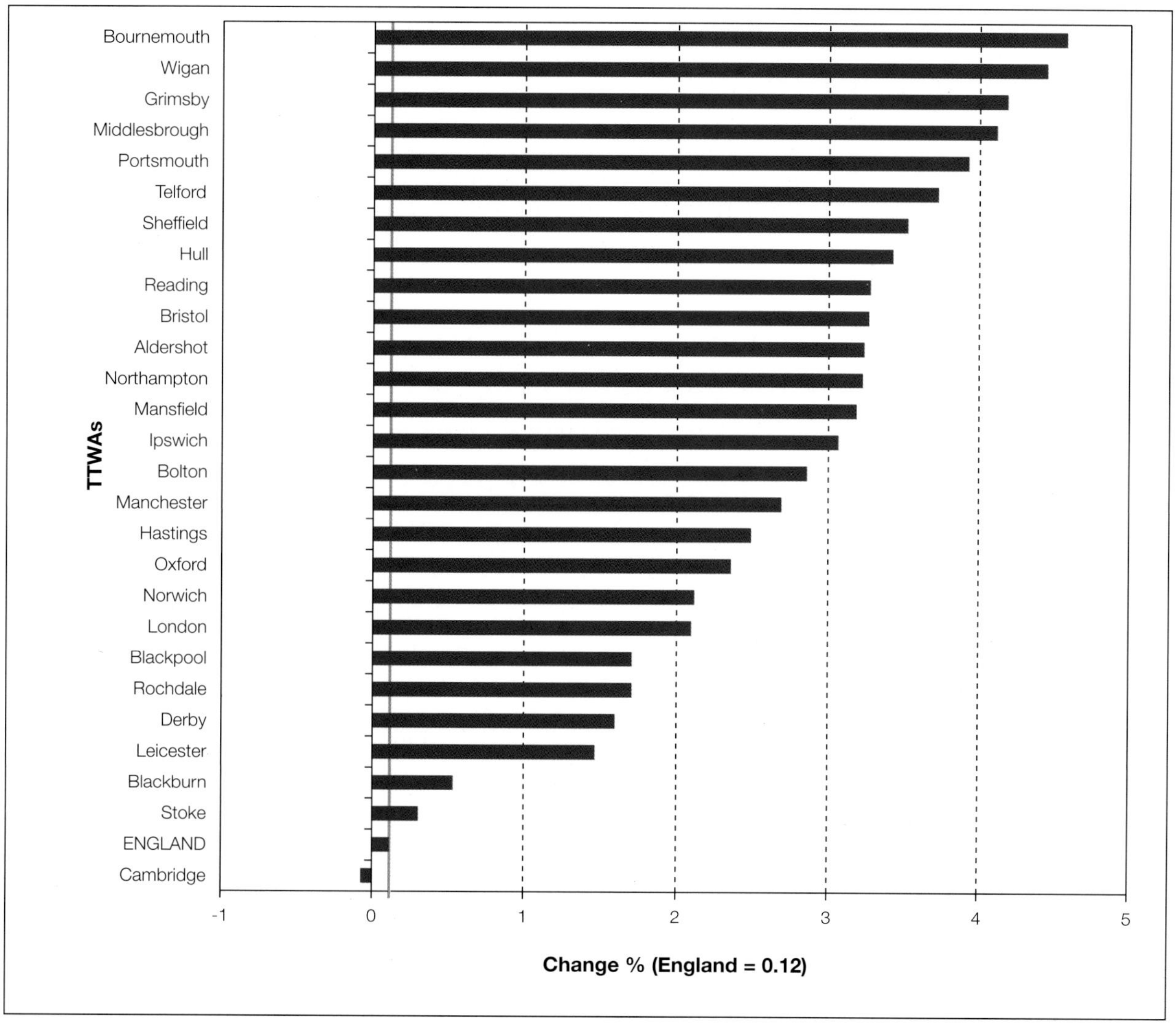

4.2.16 The distinctive characteristic of the English economy in achieving performance growth with a combination of relatively high levels of employment with a lower level of productivity than most of our European partners and international rivals means that there is a weak link between employment and productivity growth. Figure 4.8 shows that the correlation between productivity and employment growth during the 1990s in our sample of both high and low performing cities was very weak indeed. It was even weaker among all 56 cities.

4.2.17 Many of the low performing cities did quite well in terms of employment growth. However, none of them matched the best urban economies in terms of productivity growth. In some English cities, it has been possible to have increasing employment, lowered productivity and low rates of growth in GVA even during a period of national economic growth.

Figure 4.8: Change in rate of employment by change in productivity in selected Travel to Work Areas

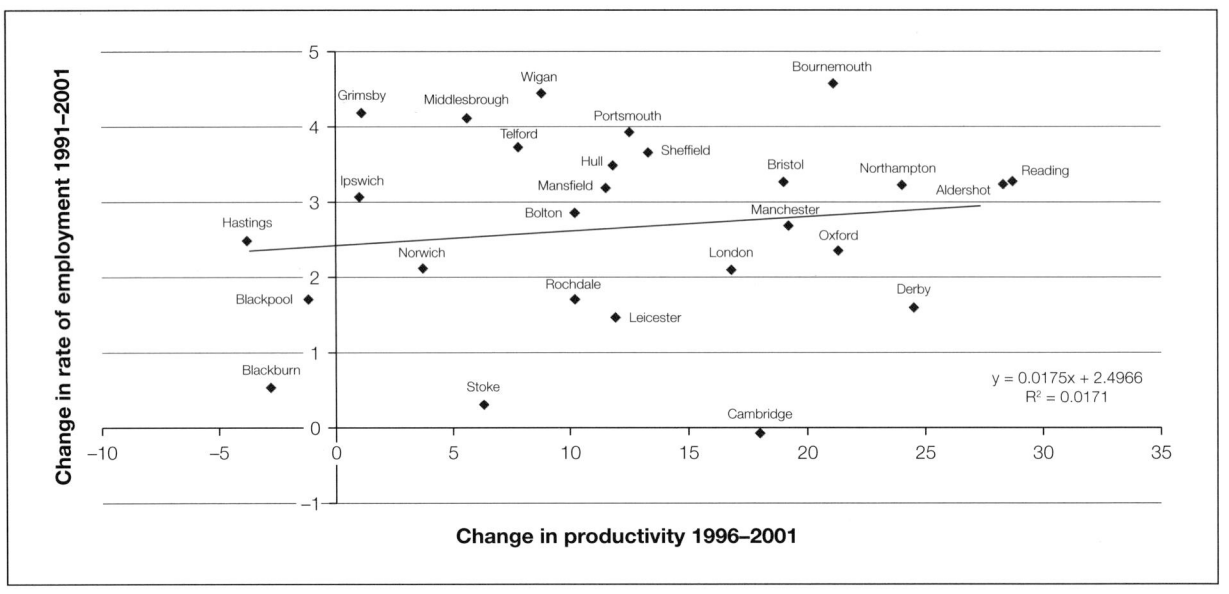

Wages and profits

4.2.18 The third main available indicator of the revealed competitive economic performance of urban economies is average weekly earnings. For this we use workplace as opposed to residence based data. Fig 4.9 shows the change taking place in average weekly earnings in our selection of high and low performing cities. Again there is progress. Among the cities with the highest rates of earnings growth are those that started with relatively low absolute levels in 1998. These include Blackburn, Blackpool, Hastings and Mansfield.

Figure 4.9: Change in weekly earnings in selected Travel to Work Areas 1998–2004

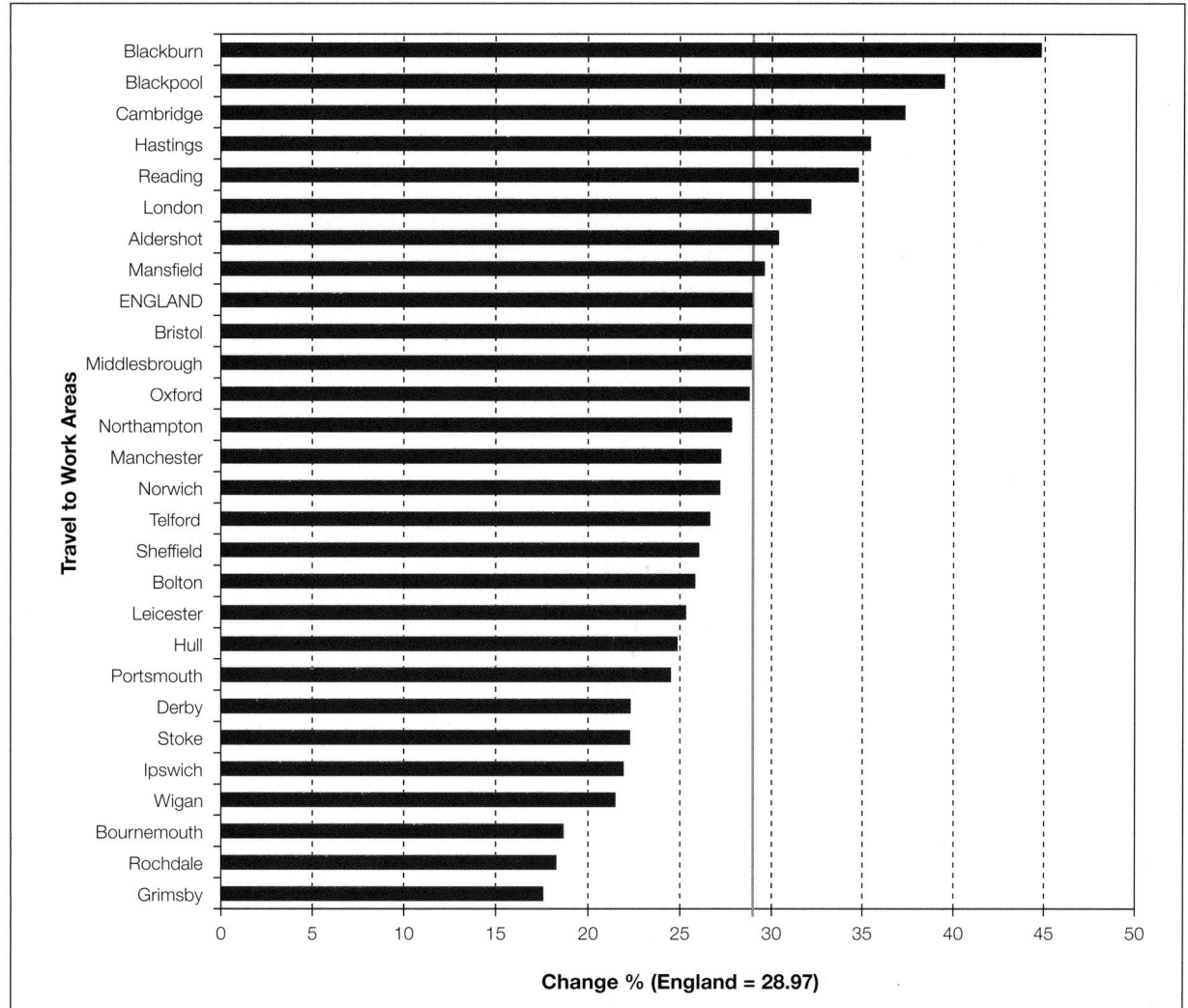

4.3   Drivers of competitive economic performance

4.3.1   Our model identifies the six key drivers of competitive performance – innovation, investment, human capital, diversity, connectivity and strategic decision-making capacity. In this section we explore data about the 56 cities to determine how important each driver is and how the position varies across English cities.

Innovation

4.3.2   The most significant driving forces of knowledge driven economies are ideas, innovation, highly educated people and risk investment. For the practical purposes of this research we define innovation and creativity to include new products, processes and services, entrepreneurship and new firm formation. The data available on innovation at the level of TTWAs is limited. We use two main indicators. Each has its limitations but they are the best available indicators of innovation for cities. The first indicator is applications to the European Patents Office derived from the data in the third Community Innovation Survey (CIS 3). This has been conducted across Europe every four years. It offers the best national and regional data on technological product and process innovation. Its limitations with respect to cities are that at this geographic level the sample size is very small and so all results at the urban level should be regarded with extreme caution. Second, like the available data for exports, service firms are mainly excluded from the sample. It does sample a few private sector technological services but all other service sectors are excluded.

4.3.3   Figure 4.10 shows patent applications to the European Patents Office for our selection of cities for the beginning and end of the 1990s. It shows that again almost all of the high performing cities produced more patent applications than almost all of the low performing cities.

Figure 4.10: Patent applications to the European Patents Office 1990–92 and 1999–01

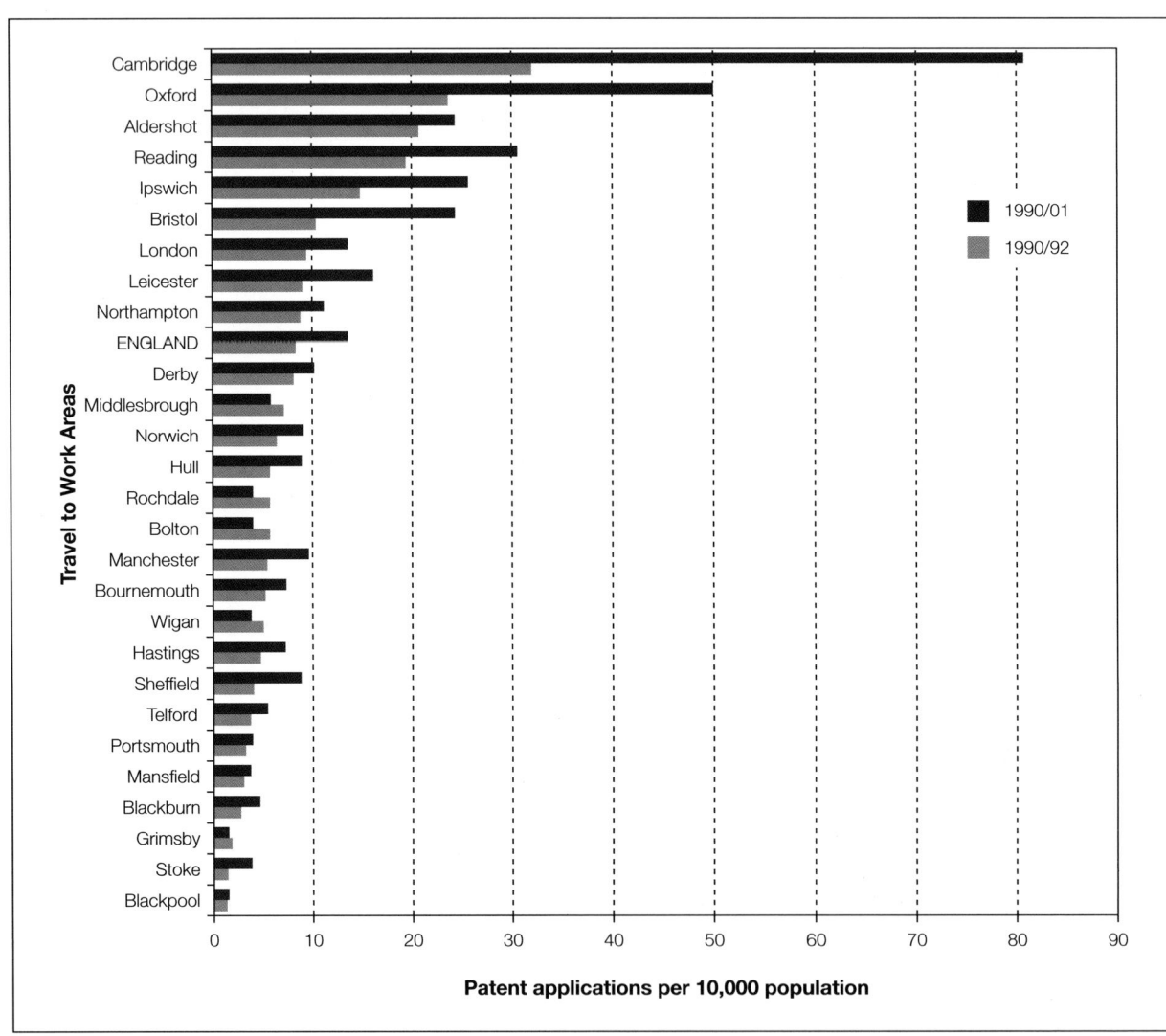

4.3.4   Some indication of the significance of the diffusion of innovation in our sample of high and low performing economies is shown in Figure 4.11. This shows the proportions of turnover accounted for by new and novel products. The sampled firms in most of the high performing economies had higher proportions of their total turnover accounted for by the adoption of new products than most of the low performing economies. These data sets do not provide the most ideal information on innovation and should be regarded with caution. Nevertheless, they are consistent with the argument that adaptive capacity and the diffusion of innovation are critical to the economic performance of modern urban economies.

Figure 4.11: Turnover accounted for by new and novel products 2000

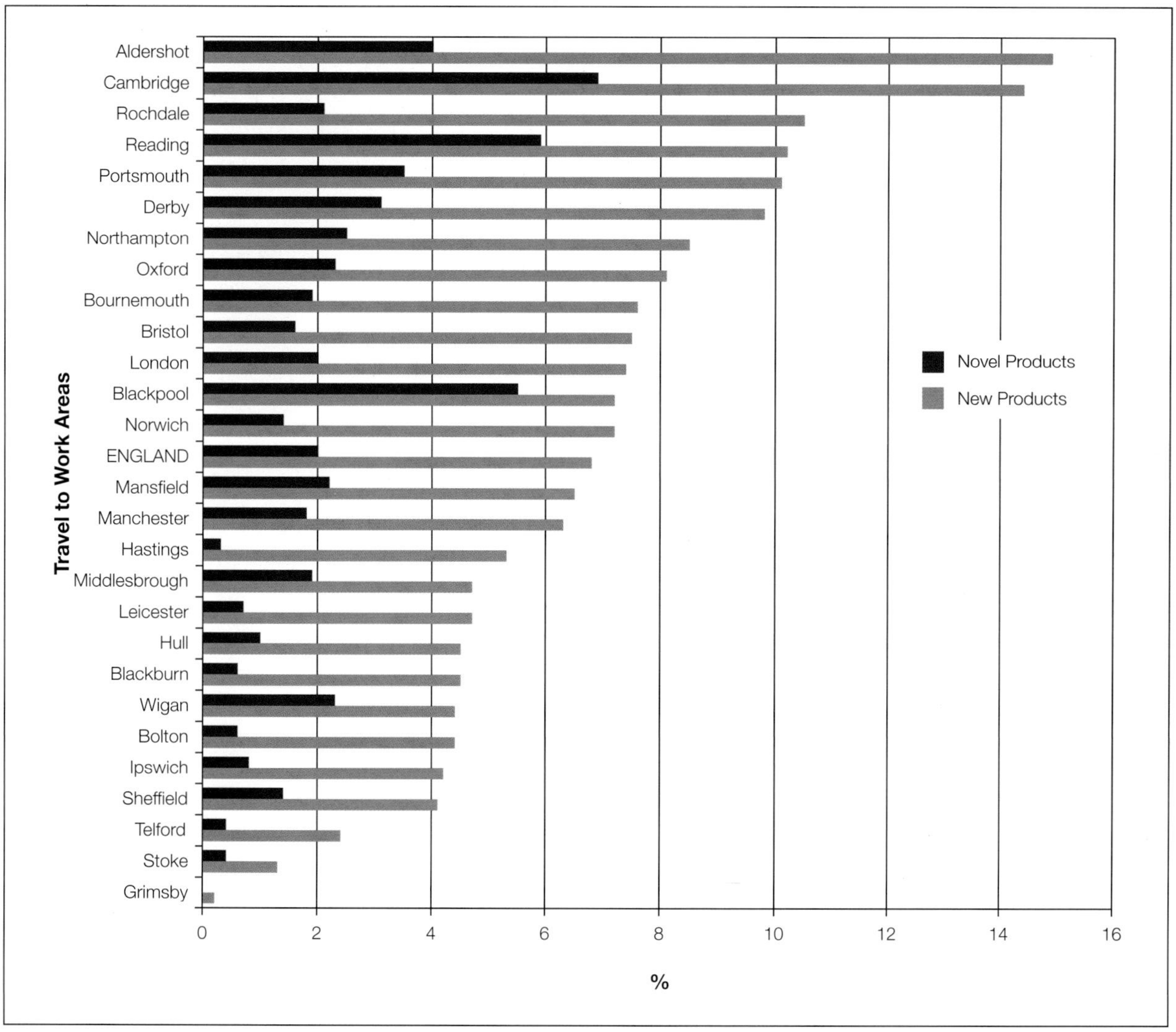

Investment and venture capital

4.3.5   Innovation requires investment. Large firms are often able to provide internal funding for research and development (R&D) to develop their own inventions into innovations or to license the use of patents produced elsewhere. But small and medium sized enterprises (SMEs) are much more reliant on external sources of funding. Venture capital is the main type of risk funds potentially available to them. Like the UK's financial system more generally, the venture capital industry is highly concentrated in and around London, both in term of the location of venture capital firms themselves, and in terms of investment activity. Figure 4.12 shows that London contains by far the largest number of venture capital firms. Some 243 of the 263 head-office members of the British Venture Capital Association are located there. The other metropolitan centres have few independent companies and are mainly locations for branches of London-based firms. Of these only Manchester, Leeds and Birmingham have significant clusters – 42, 36 and 35 firms respectively.

Figure 4.12: Private equity firms located in cities 2005

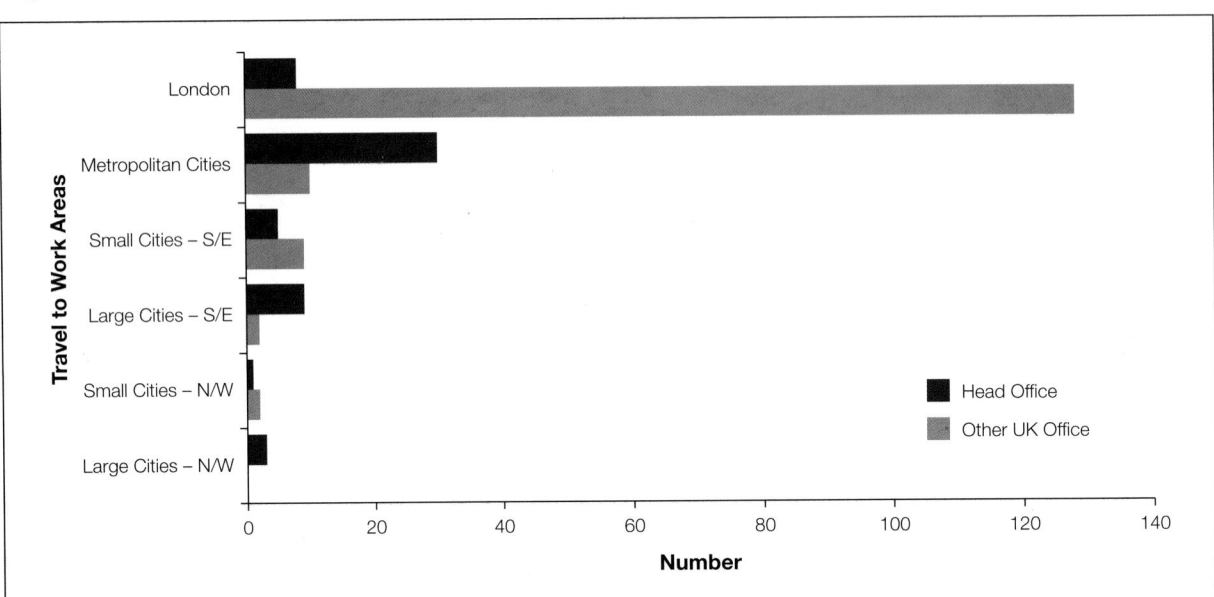

4.3.6   Particularly since the publication of the Lambert (2003) review of business and university collaboration, much is expected of the universities in contributing to innovation. Figure 4.13 shows the main locations of the Higher Education Funding Council (HEFC) research funds. It suggests that the distribution of research funding tends to reinforce the effects of the location of venture capital firms and the resulting higher performance of cities.

Figure 4.13: Higher Education Funding Council research funds per capita 2005–06

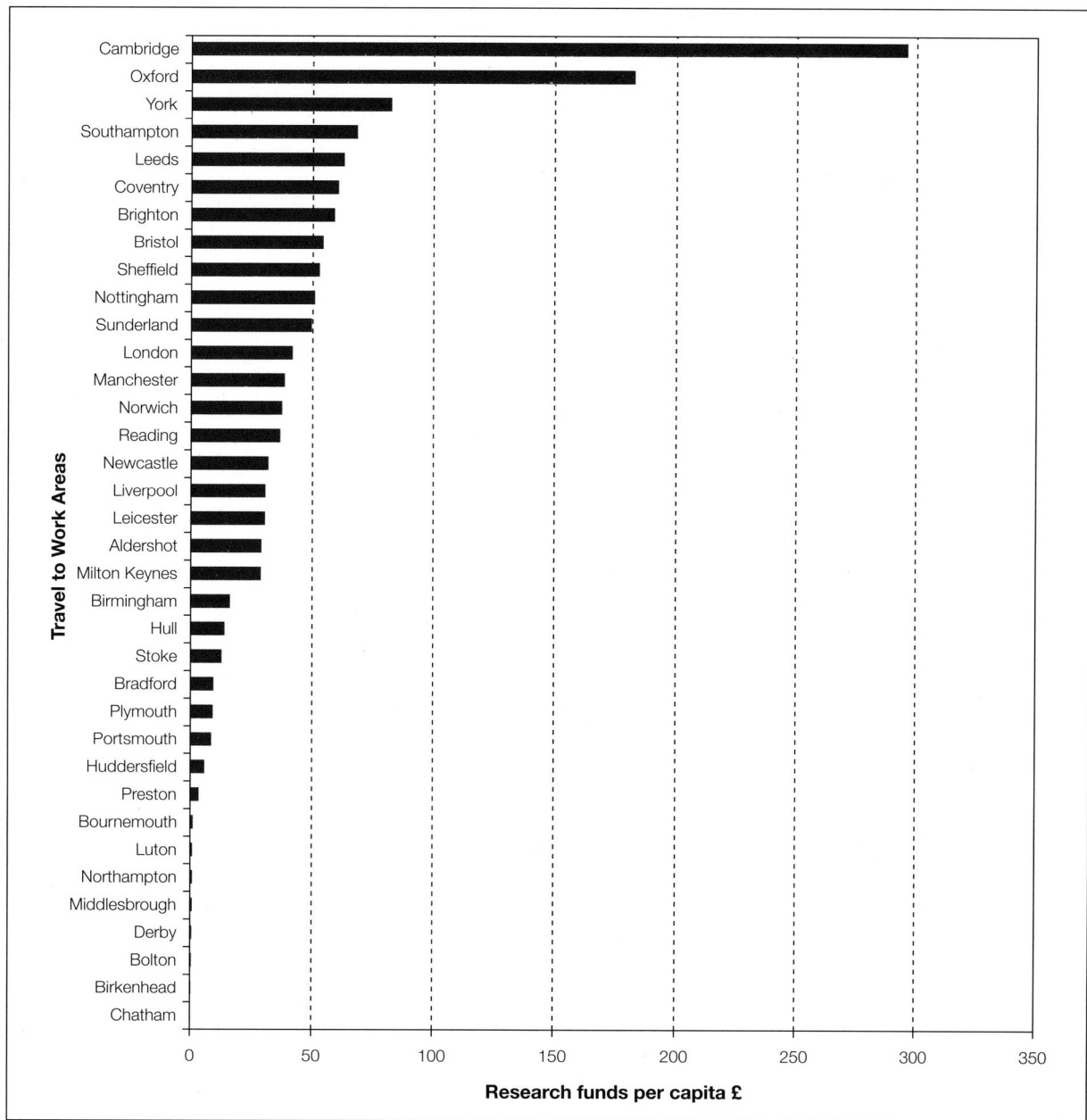

Human capital

4.3.7   Variations in human capital lead to differences in invention, innovation and ultimately productivity in different urban and regional economies. Cities that have traditionally specialised in sectors where the returns to education are low suffer cumulative disadvantage in comparison with dynamic cities that value high skill levels. Figure 4.14 shows that, among our sample of the highest and lowest performing cities, all of the lowest performers increased the proportion of graduates in their workforces by less than the English average. Even some of the higher performing economies such as Aldershot/Guildford, Manchester, Derby and Bournemouth had lower rates of increase than England as a whole.

Figure 4.14: Change in % of working age population with degree level qualifications 1991–2001

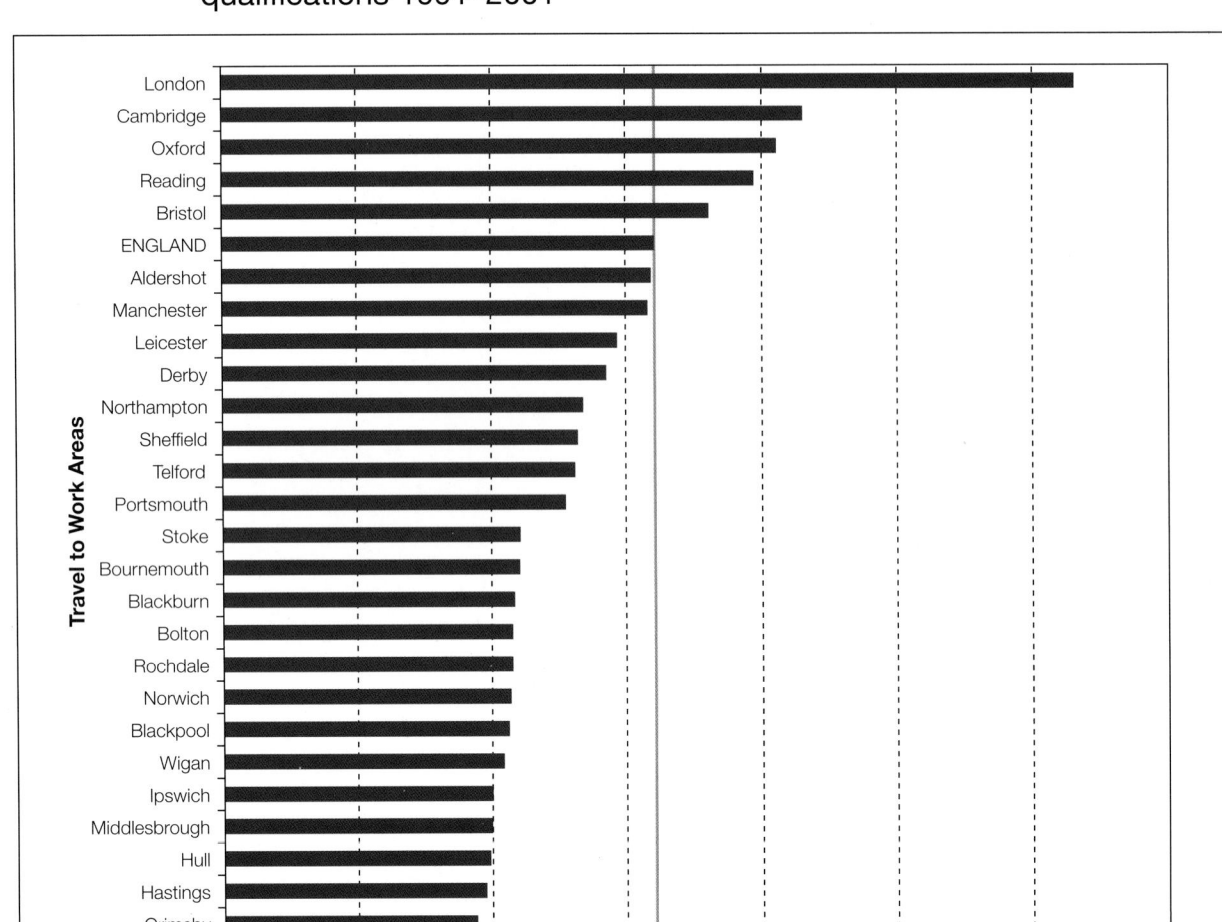

4.3.8   The importance of highly qualified labour in knowledge driven economies is shown in Figure 4.15. This shows the correlation between degree level qualifications in our sample of cities and patent applications per 10,000 population to the EPO around 2001. This supports the general proposition that dynamic knowledge driven economies that rely on ideas, innovation, institutional and organisational change and adaptability need high calibre human capital.

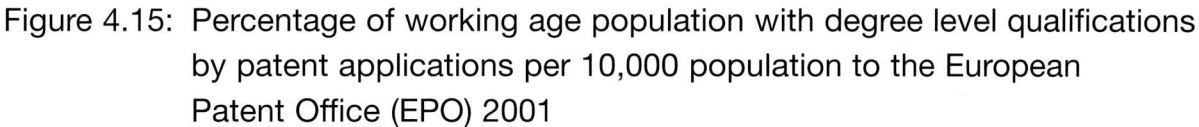

Figure 4.15: Percentage of working age population with degree level qualifications by patent applications per 10,000 population to the European Patent Office (EPO) 2001

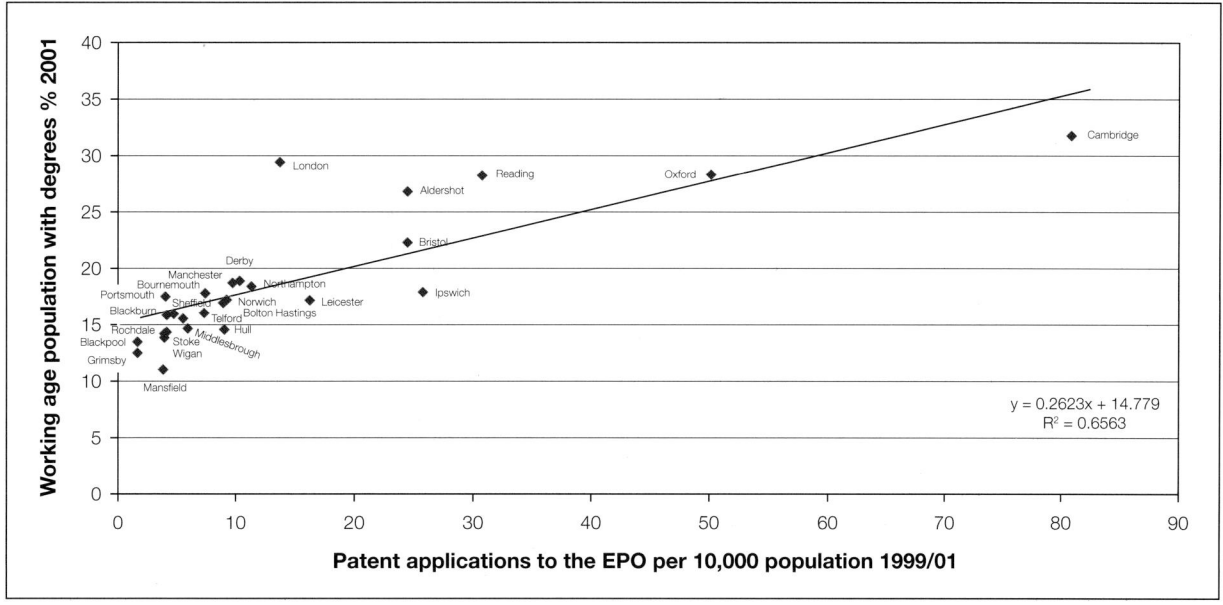

4.3.9   There is a distinctive geography in terms of the location of R&D employment. Map 4.6 shows the changes taking place in the location of such employees during the 1990s. The highest rates of increase were experienced to the west of London in Oxford, Aldershot/Guildford, Swindon and Southampton. Cambridge, and more surprisingly Hastings, also had among the highest rates of increase. Only Middlesbrough and Sheffield outside the south experienced some of the higher rates of increase of R&D employees. The presence and growth of R&D workers in these localities provided their local business environments with possibilities for improving their competitive advantages in the production of new ideas.

4.3.10   Technological product and process innovations are not the only form of innovation in knowledge driven economies. Indeed, they may form a minority of all innovations, since all modern economies are primarily based on services. Thus, innovation in services are likely to be even more significant than those in manufacturing. Again there is a distinctive geography to the changes taking place in the location of knowledge intensive business services (KIBS) during the 1990s. Map 4.7 shows that the highest rates of growth were experienced in and around London in Reading, Oxford, Cambridge, Crawley and Aldershot/Guildford. Outside these, significant growth also took place in Telford, Preston and Burnley.

4.3.11   The kinds of business environment that underlie knowledge economy activities are themselves unevenly distributed across the English urban system. The highest rates of growth in R&D employment have been mainly concentrated to the west of London and in Cambridge. The highest rates of growth in KIBS have also been concentrated in these areas and London itself. There are no other clubs of multiple cities that experienced similar rates of growth in these key idea generating sectors during the 1990s.

Map 4.6: Percentage change of employees in research and development per 1,000 employees between 1991 and 2001

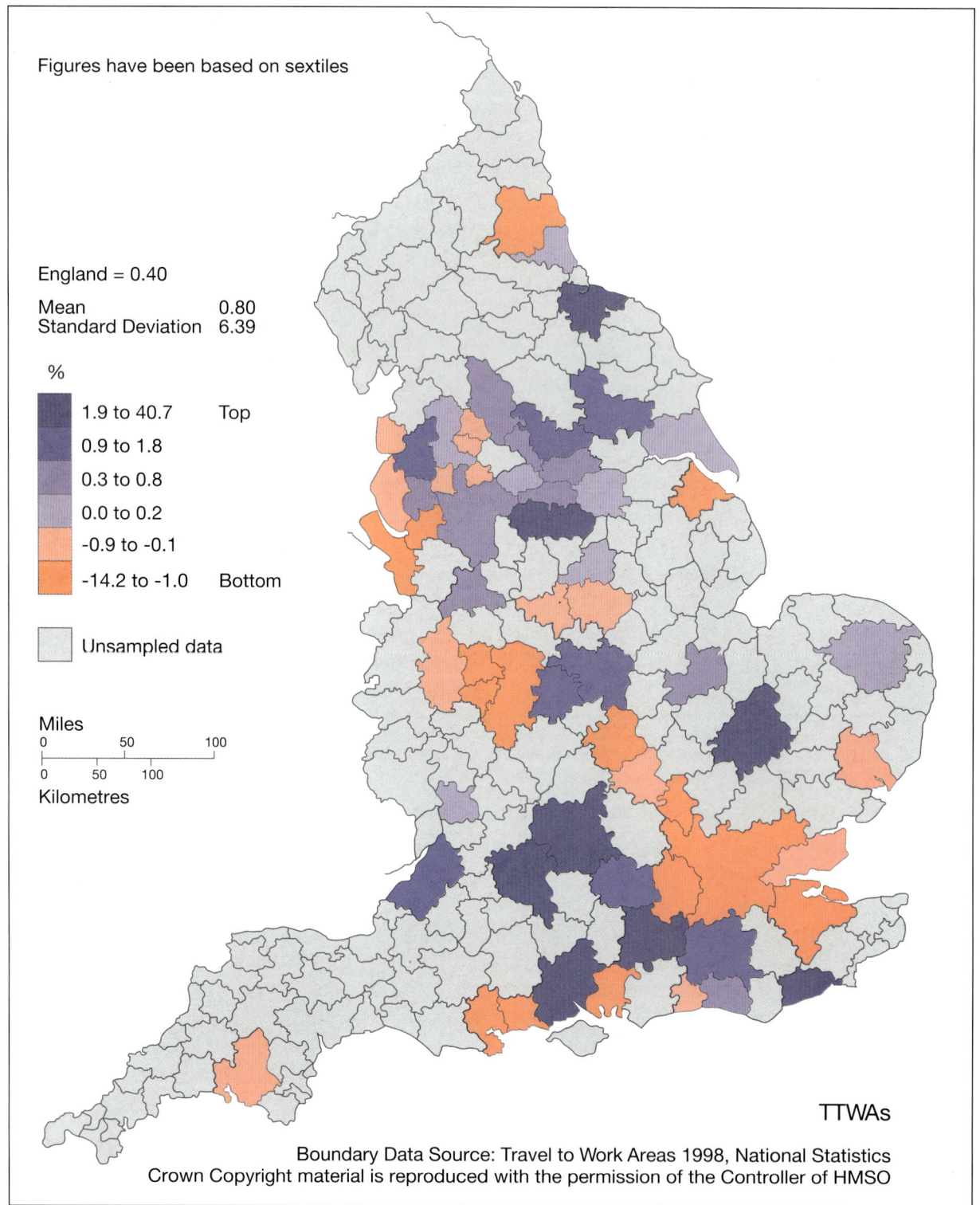

Figures have been based on sextiles

England = 0.40

Mean   0.80
Standard Deviation   6.39

%

1.9 to 40.7   Top
0.9 to 1.8
0.3 to 0.8
0.0 to 0.2
-0.9 to -0.1
-14.2 to -1.0   Bottom

Unsampled data

Miles
0   50   100
0   50   100
Kilometres

TTWAs

Boundary Data Source: Travel to Work Areas 1998, National Statistics
Crown Copyright material is reproduced with the permission of the Controller of HMSO

Map 4.7: Percentage change of employees in knowledge intensive business service between 1991 and 2001

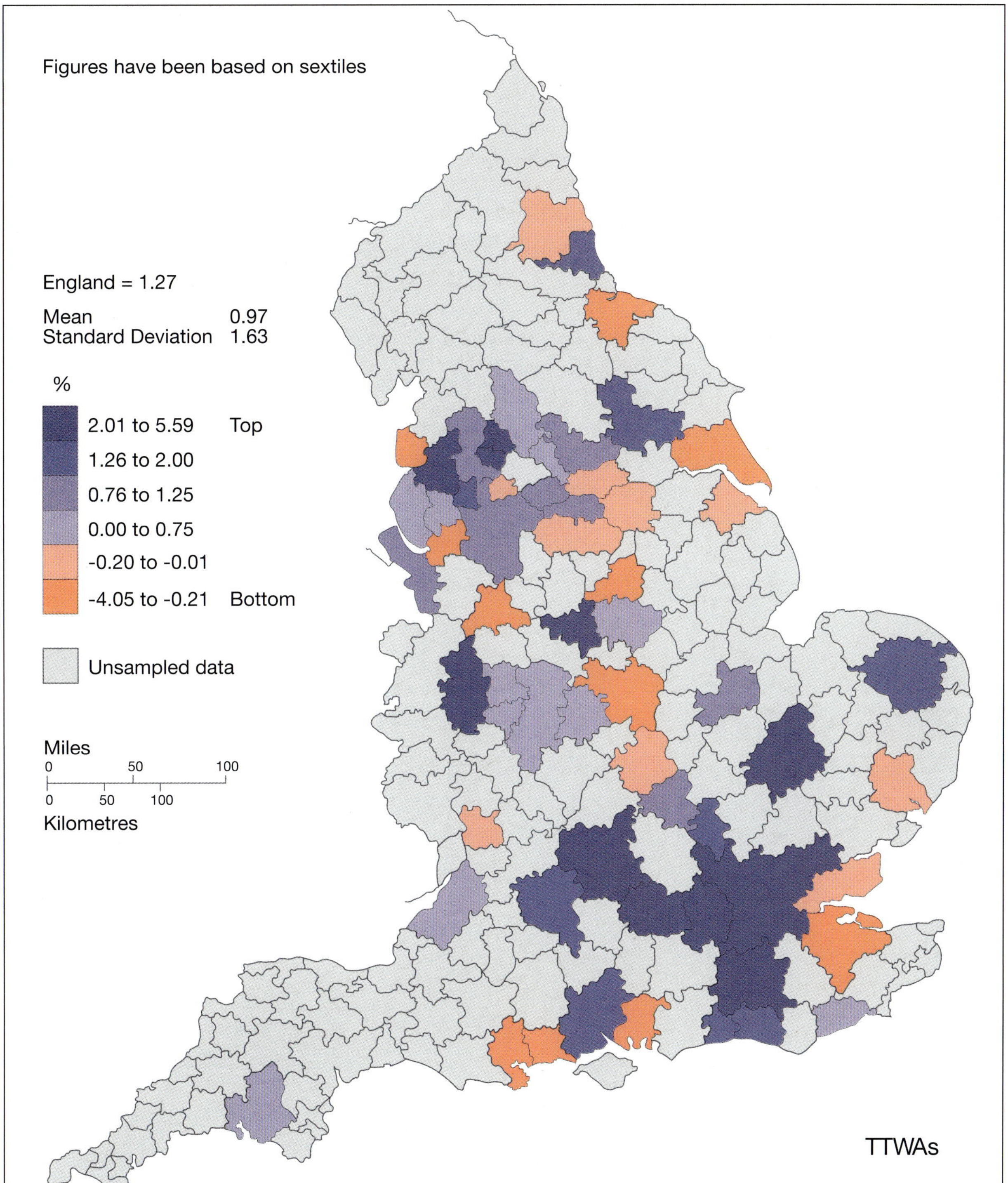

Figures have been based on sextiles

England = 1.27

Mean   0.97
Standard Deviation   1.63

%

■ 2.01 to 5.59	Top
■ 1.26 to 2.00	
■ 0.76 to 1.25	
■ 0.00 to 0.75	
■ -0.20 to -0.01	
■ -4.05 to -0.21	Bottom

Unsampled data

Miles
0   50   100

0   50   100
Kilometres

TTWAs

Boundary Data Source: Travel to Work Areas 1998, National Statistics
Crown Copyright material is reproduced with the permission of the Controller of HMSO

4.3.12   There is much discussion of the concept of the creative class (Florida 2002). This is a somewhat disparate group of occupations that have been linked with economic success. They are seen as particularly important for urban economies because they tend to be concentrated in cities and particularly their core areas. They therefore provide vital new job opportunities in those localities. Map 4.8 shows the changes taking place in the creative and cultural industries in the 56 cities of this study. Surprisingly only 18 cities exceeded the English average change of 0.89 per cent. The majority of these are located in the south and east. They include Cambridge, Reading, Oxford, London, Brighton, Luton, Aldershot/Guildford, Crawley and Milton Keynes. Outside this area cities like Telford, Preston and Derby experienced the highest rates of growth albeit from low bases. The geography of change in the creative and cultural industries shows a by now familiar pattern. There is a club of cities in the south and east that have experienced the highest rates of increase in creative and cultural industry employees. Outside this club there are other isolated cities that have had positive rates of change above the average for England. There are also some cities where the proportion of creative and cultural employees declined during the 1990s.

Map 4.8: Percentage change of employees in creative industries between 1998 and 2001

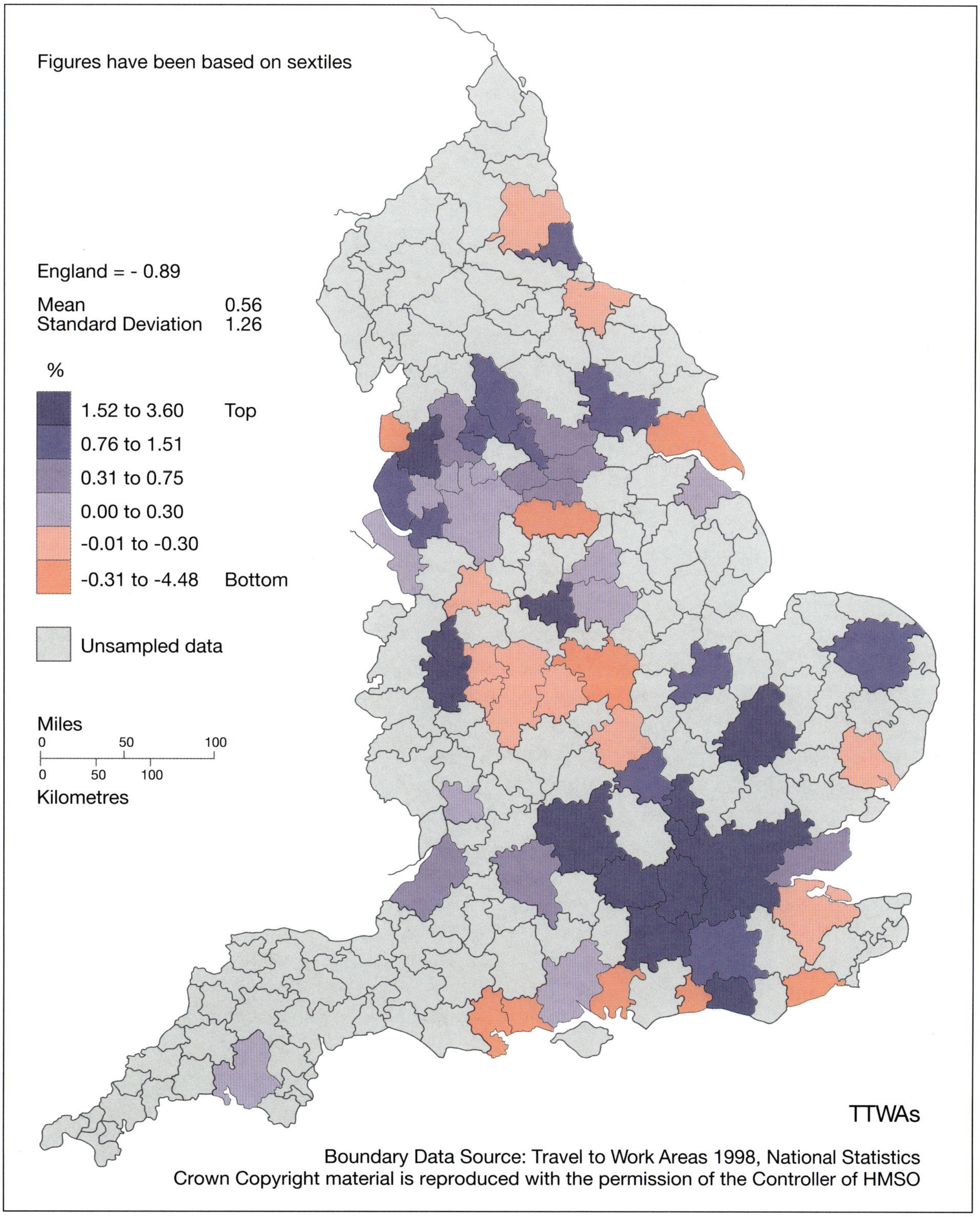

Figures have been based on sextiles

England = - 0.89

Mean   0.56
Standard Deviation   1.26

%

	1.52 to 3.60	Top
	0.76 to 1.51	
	0.31 to 0.75	
	0.00 to 0.30	
	-0.01 to -0.30	
	-0.31 to -4.48	Bottom

Unsampled data

Miles
0   50   100
0   50   100
Kilometres

TTWAs

Boundary Data Source: Travel to Work Areas 1998, National Statistics
Crown Copyright material is reproduced with the permission of the Controller of HMSO

4.3.13   Figure 4.16 shows that there is a positive correlation between the presence of employees in creative industries and productivity in all 56 cities. Reading, London and Aldershot/Guildford stand out in this respect.

Figure 4.16: Percentage of employees in creative industries by Gross Value Added (GVA) per employee 2001

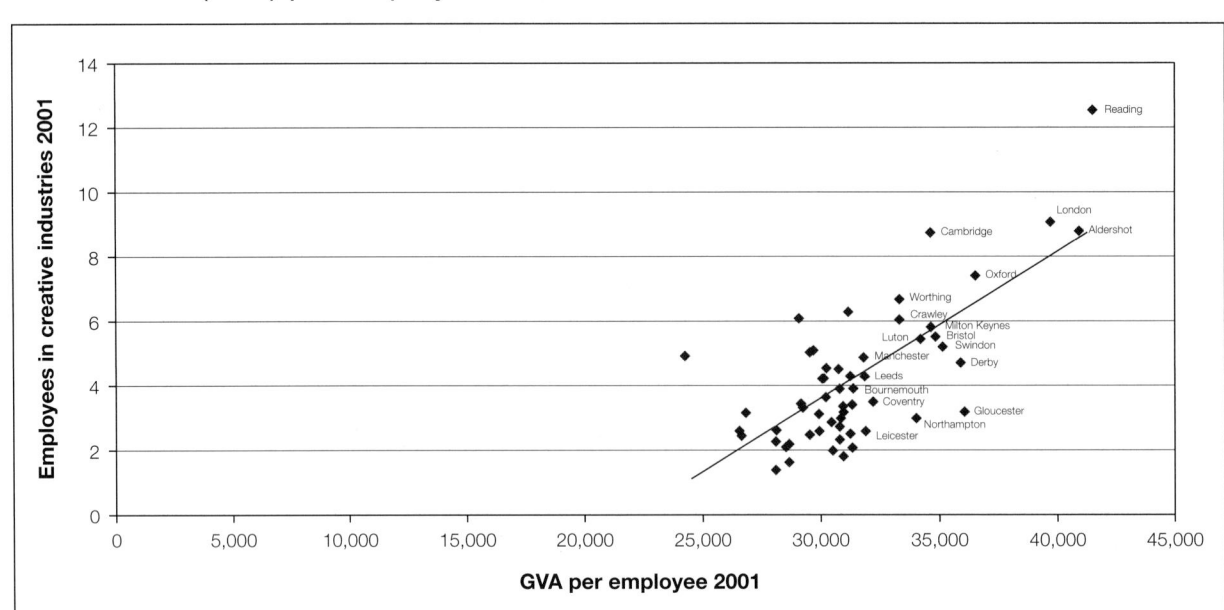

Economic diversity or specialisation?

4.3.14   There has been a long running debate about whether high economic performance in urban economies is driven by diversity or specialisation. The question is which is more conducive to the external economies associated with the localised spill-over of technology and the promotion of local innovation. Our analysis suggests that localised industrial specialisation possibly makes a greater contribution to economic performance than diversity. This reflects the need for highly sophisticated knowledge and competence in modern goods and services. However it is clearly possible that highly specialised urban economies can become stuck in particular structural and technological trajectories that make them very vulnerable to shifts in competition, trade and technology. This has certainly happened to some English cities that continued to specialise in such industries as ship building and steel making long after those industries were in decline. The best combination is specialisation and diversity, 'clustered diversity', combined with adaptive capacity.

Connectivity

4.3.15   For practical purposes we define connectivity in terms of national and international road, rail, air, telecommunications and business networks, although this barely does justice to the complexity and significance of the idea. An indication of physical connectivity is given by the fastest available journey times to London by rail. Figure 4.17 shows that the main club of high performing and interconnected cities in the south and east are mostly within 50 minutes of London by train. The ability to move between cities on fast and reliable rail networks is greater in countries like France and Germany than it is in the UK. We show some data on this in Chapter 8. Thus the development of networked cities, for example in the Northern Way area, must depend partly on the development of rail networks that match the best in Europe.

Figure 4.17: Fastest post 06.00 rail weekday journey time to London 2005

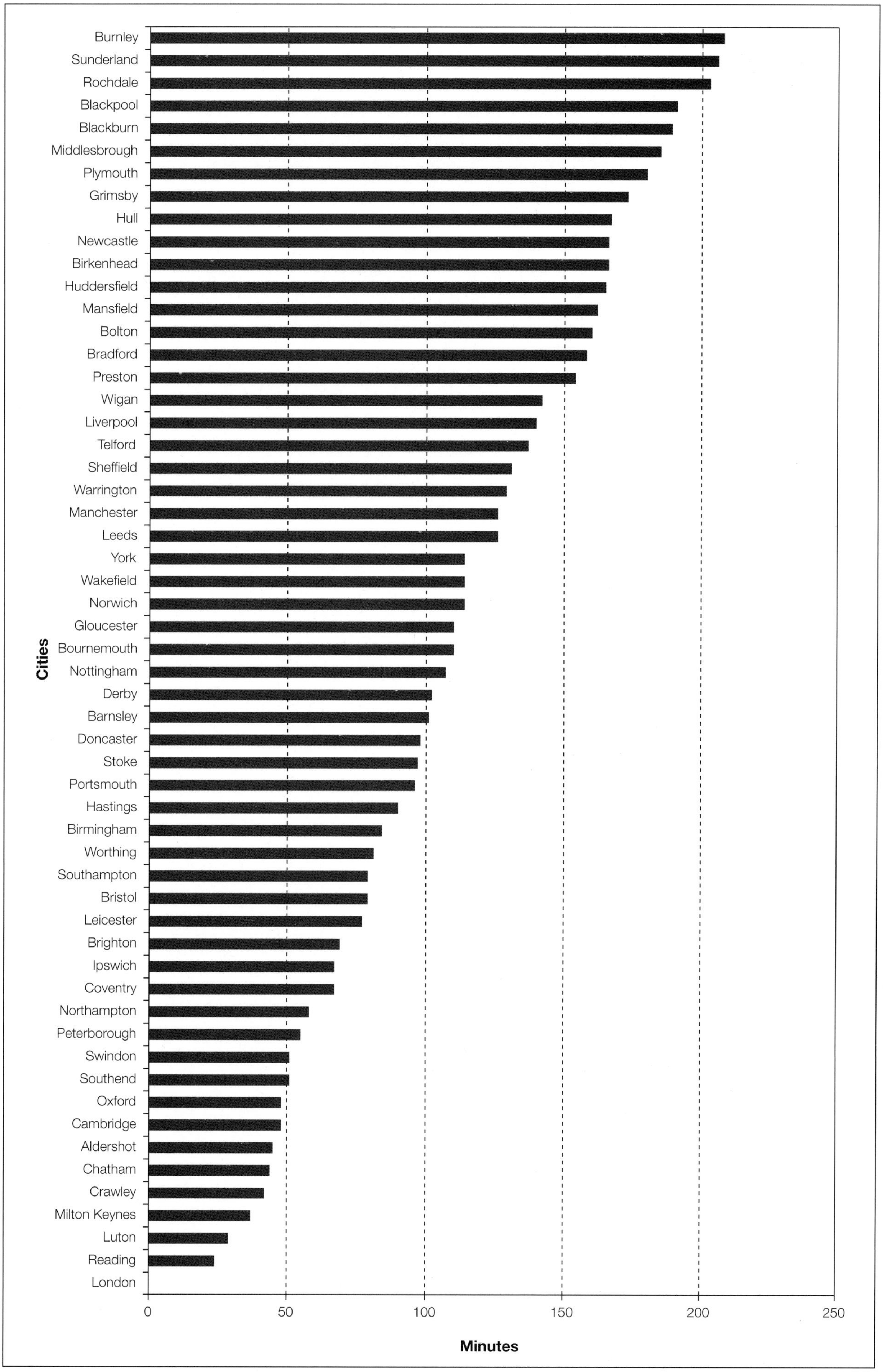

4.3.16   The growing importance of the international economy and the need for face-to-face communications when making significant decisions, means that air travel makes a critical contribution to the connectivity of international nodes in knowledge based economies. Here the cities outside the south and east are at a disadvantage. The airports there dominate both the regular flights to business destinations and the passenger numbers using them. Fig 4.18 shows that the numbers of frequently served international scheduled destinations served by the regional airports outside the south and east is small but growing. Manchester, Birmingham, Bristol, Nottingham, Newcastle and Liverpool have all increased their international connectivity during the 1990s. Even collectively, however, they still have some way to go before the balance between the regional airports and those that serve the London region is more appropriate to their needs. Chapter 8 again provides evidence about the links between air travel and city competitiveness.

Figure 4.18: Number of frequently served international scheduled destinations 1990 and 2004

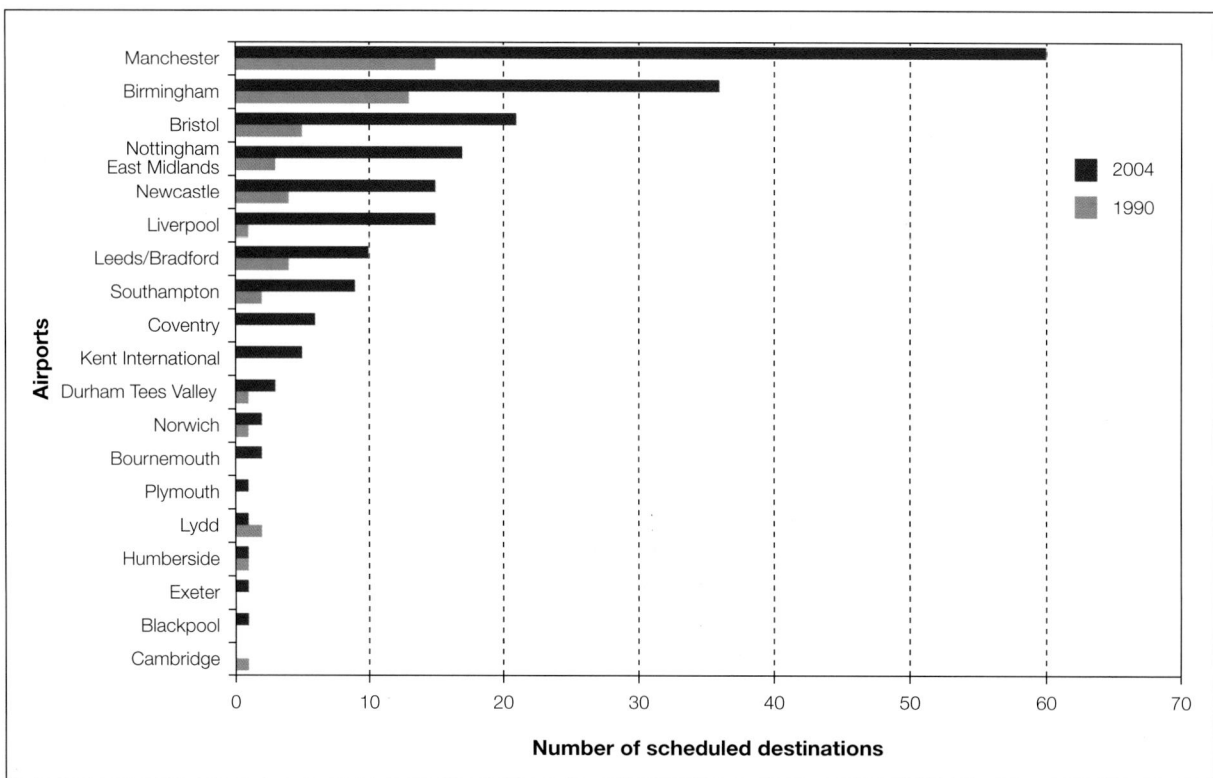

Strategic decision making capacity

4.3.17   The degree of autonomy over strategic decision making is one of the most significant distinguishing features between high performing continental European cities and their English counterparts. The differences can be seen in the different levels of control that cities have over local expenditure. Local governments in England control only 25 per cent of public sector expenditure. This is below that found in most other OECD countries. In Germany the figure is 35 per cent. Even in the US it is 42 per cent. In both countries cities benefit from economic development by receiving either local sales or enterprise taxes. There are no such incentives attached to economic development in English cities. Local authorities no longer receive the business rates generated within their areas.

4.3.18   In England the majority of strategic decisions are taken for cities by central government rather than by cities themselves. This is particularly true about the main economic drivers of competitiveness. In most cases central government departments – notably ODPM, DTI and the Treasury – take and fund the key decisions that affect city competitiveness. Figure 4.19 shows an approximation of the relative degrees of responsibility by different levels of government for the key drivers of urban competitiveness. Local authorities overall have limited influence as do regional agencies. Local authorities retain more strength in planning, amenity, recreation, consumption, public spaces and to a lesser degree over local transport. These have indirect and weak links to competitiveness. Regional agencies are strongest in the areas of innovation and economic diversity and skills. Central departments are overwhelmingly the prime influence on policies for all the drivers, whether through policy framing, steering or funding. English cities are highly reliant on weak governance arrangements such as voluntary collaborations and partnerships to develop and implement strategies for maintaining or improving the competitiveness of their local economies.

4.3.19   Figure 4.19 also illustrates the large number of departments and other agencies involved in taking decisions affecting the competitiveness of cities. This structure of responsibilities provides multiple opportunities for disjointed policy making rather than joined up thinking and ensuring the consistent targeting of mainstream funding on the key drivers of competitiveness in cities.

Figure 4.19: Degrees of influence of different levels of governance on drivers of local economic competitiveness.

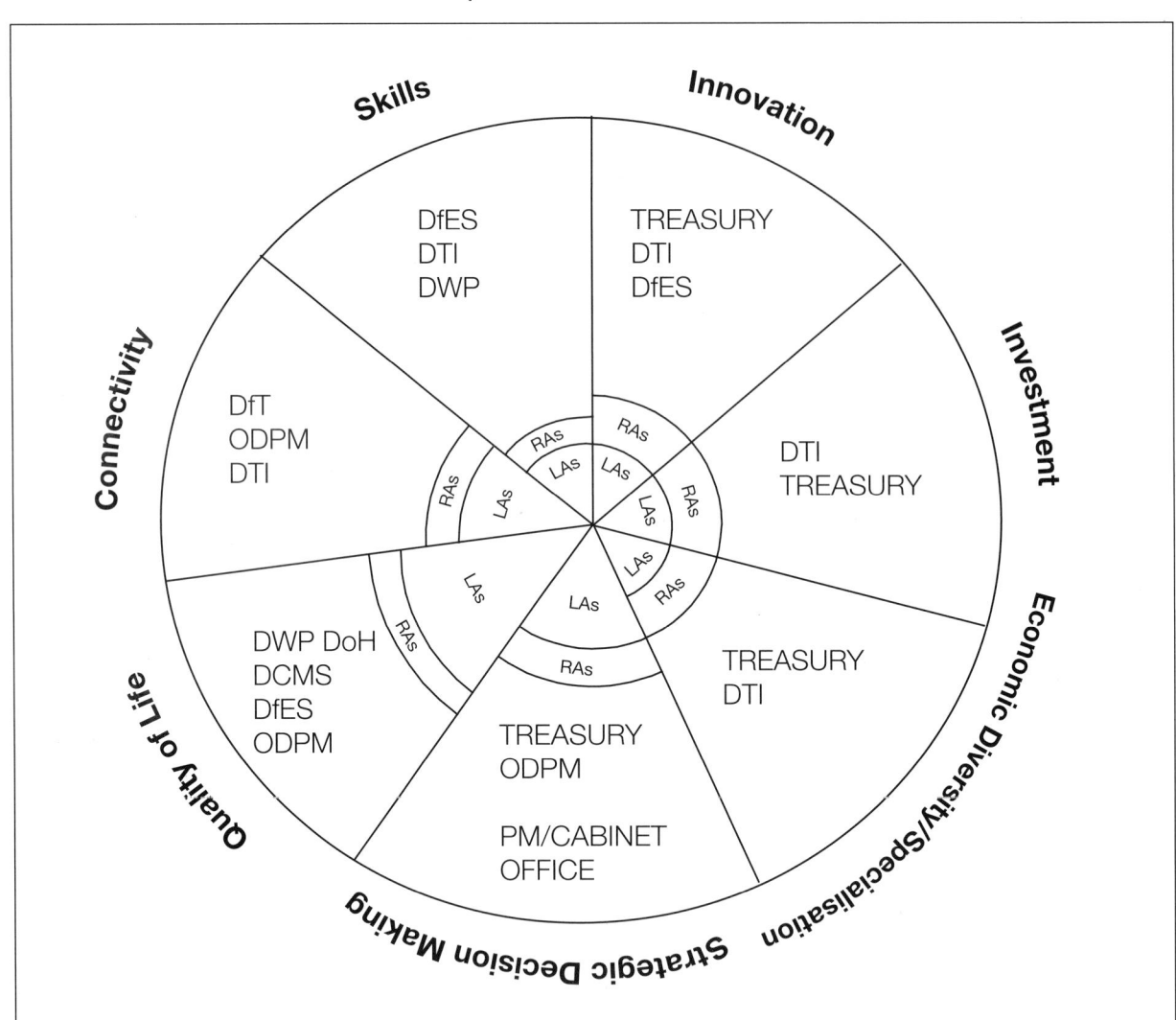

Economic performance and social cohesion

4.3.20 There is a great deal of discussion of the extent to which the pursuit of economic competitiveness leads to social success. Our evidence shows there is no necessary connection between the standard of living of the residents of a city and the economic performance of its economy. The correlation between GDHI and GVA per capita among the 56 cities is low. Figure 4.20 shows our selection of high and low performing cities ranked by GVA per capita in 2002. Their economic performance is compared with their standard of living as indicated by the proportions of low income households in the Index of Multiple Deprivation (IMD). There were 10 cities with GVA per capita above the average for England in 2002. Among those 10, six also had higher than average levels of household income deprivation. Most notable among these were London, Oxford and Manchester. Among the 14 cities that had lower than average GVA per capita, eight had higher than average levels of household income deprivation.

4.3.21 Economic performance and social cohesion are therefore not necessarily linked in urban economies. Nevertheless, the figure shows the chances of being income deprived in cities where the economy is generating less than the English average GVA per capita are generally higher than in those cities with more successful economies. What are needed are multiple specialised and high performing sectors on the one hand, combined with institutional arrangements that qualify local residents to either work in those sectors themselves, or benefit from the demands they generate for other local activities such as services.

Figure 4.20: Gross Value Added per capita 2002 and low income households 2001

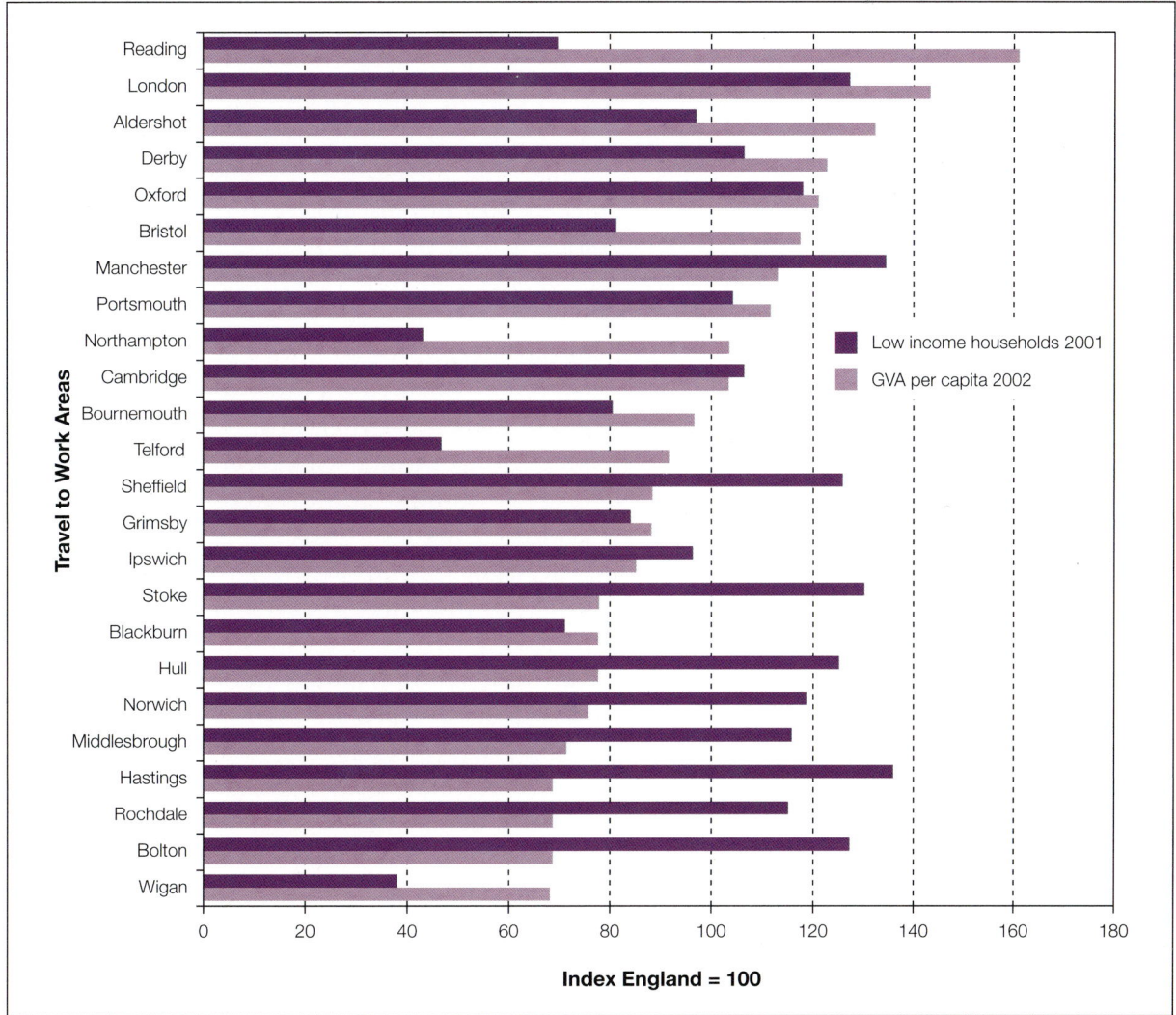

4.4 Competitiveness, continuity and change in four cities

4.4.1 This section illustrates the analyses in previous sections by exploring the forces making for economic continuity and change in four very different cities – London, Cambridge, Derby and Sheffield. It illustrates the range and diversity of economic trajectories in English cities during the past decade. London illustrates the process of dynamic adaptation. Cambridge is the iconic model of the long-term development of a knowledge-based economy. Derby shows that it is possible to maintain a successful advanced manufacturing based economy outside the club of high performing cities in the south and east. Sheffield illustrates the wider experience of English cities that have experienced industrial restructuring, are developing new economic niches, but which still face large challenges which require national policy support.

London – dynamic urban adaptation

4.4.2 London is unique among English cities. Its scale and reach is so large that in recent years it has been a crucial component of national economic performance. London's economy illustrates dynamic adaptation, particularly over the last decade or so. Its competitive success is primarily based on a range of specialist knowledge-intensive labour functions, whether offered by innovative service or manufacturing institutions. London has a distinctive and unique long term economic trajectory, which has adapted as a response to external forces. The effective market adaptation of new technologies has been an important force for change, and also an outcome, of this success.

4.4.3 London ranks very highly on several national measures of competitiveness in our study. Its GVA per resident was over 40 per cent above the England average in 2002, ranked 3rd of 56 cities. It has been growing faster than the national average since 1995. GVA per workplace job was 14 per cent above average, also 3rd in national city rankings. The same is true for standard of living measures, such as gross household income (4th) and, even taking account of house prices, disposable income (8th). Competitiveness was also revealed in resident (3rd) and workplace earnings (3rd), and the quality of human capital, measured by the proportion of adults with degrees (2nd). The potential quality of London's business environment is indicated by the high share of employment in KIBS (5th) and the creative industries (2nd), as well as the rate of new company VAT registrations (1st), and the city's cultural diversity (1st). Gross fixed capital formation rates in Greater London were 48 per cent above England in 2000 and the city possessed 136 out of the 213 national venture capital firms. Despite the loss of so much manufacturing in London itself, visible exports per capita from London's TTWA were still ranked 7th among the English cities.

4.4.4 It is important to understand that London's economic success is a recent phenomenon. Until the early 1990s its output growth lagged behind other regions, even in northern England, as the impact of deindustrialisation and the collapse of the old port continued to wreak its effects. Growth began to exceed national, and even southern England, rates only after 1994. Also the 2002-2003 recession was a reminder of the continuing volatility of international service markets. The importance of London is what it tells us about the dynamic, adaptive characteristics of the city's business environment that could support economic revival in such a relatively short period. These include its workforce quality, and changing physical, social, cultural and governance infrastructures, and the sorts of innovativeness and creativity required. The city's economy has been able to support new forms of activity, the application of new technologies, and new institutional arrangements, all taking advantage of national and international growth opportunities.

4.4.5   Several important characteristics of innovation and creativity in London underpin its competitiveness. First, its export success is service-based, with important consequences for the types of innovativeness required to be competitive. Technological innovation is important, but perhaps most significant is the range of specialist knowledge intensive service expertise, supporting non-technological, as well as technological, adaptability to changing business and consumer markets. Various opportunities have arisen to exploit such adaptability over the past twenty years, including market internationalisation, UK business liberalisation, and an encouraging land development regime in London itself.

4.4.6   Second, although in a sectoral sense it is a specialised economy, London supports great potential diversity of functional interaction, across its host of expert labour functions. This diversity partly arises from the scale of its labour markets. However, it also requires institutional variety and flexibility to promote the assembling of skills serving many creative, including technology-based business and public sector projects. Innovative and creative processes need to be the focus for a significant proportion of large firm functions, a variety of dynamic SMEs and flexible networks of interaction between these. In London, this pattern is augmented by the city's symbiotic relationship with its hinterland region, especially in innovative manufacturing and international transportation infrastructure. Adaptability should also extend to the public sector and labour market institutions.

4.4.7   Finally, even London is not big enough for some activities, especially functions with global scope and impact, such as in the financial services or cutting-edge scientific research. Its ability to support international cooperation and exchange, sometimes as the focus for national endeavours, is critical to its continuing success.

Cambridge – building a knowledge based economy

4.4.8   Cambridge illustrates the long-term development of an iconic knowledge based economy starting as long ago as 1960 with the formation of Cambridge Consultants and the important Mott Report of 1969. Both of these represent important forces for change. Even so it took a further ten years to get the Cambridge Science Park up and running in 1970, and later still the St John's Innovation Centre in 1987 followed by the Peterhouse Science Park. There are now some 900 high tech firms in the Cambridge area. The environment is also characterised by business and social networks so that knowledge is in the air.

4.4.9   Cambridge is one of UK's most dynamic and successful cities. It has a high GDP per capita, one of the highest rates of employment growth in recent years and high average earnings. Its success is founded largely on its cluster of very innovative high tech industries, and other knowledge-based activities, especially its world-renowned university. It has the highest innovation rate of any city in the UK. This, combined with the highly-educated students its main university generates, means the city makes a major contribution to Britain's knowledge-driven economy. The city's high-tech growth – the much celebrated 'Cambridge Phenomenon' – has not happened overnight, but has taken some forty years or so to develop.

4.4.10   That development was shaped by some highly specific circumstances. These include the lack of an old industrial past; the reputation of the university as a centre of world-class scientific research; the land-holdings and foresight of some of the Cambridge colleges; and the attractiveness of the city as a place in which to live and work. This high-tech led development has since become self-reinforcing. A key component of this growth has been the formation of a highly educated workforce, produced both locally and attracted to the city from elsewhere. The city's high-tech economy throws interesting light on the economic diversity versus specialisation debate. In one sense it can be viewed as specialised in high-tech. But the city's high-tech economy has continuously evolved over the past forty years, becoming more diverse in the process. Arguably this protects the city from specific high-tech downturns such as the Internet economy recession in 2000-2001.

4.4.11   The growth and expansion of Cambridge has not been without its strains and problems seen in other successful, rapidly growing high-tech cities and regions across the world – rising land and housing costs, traffic and commuting problems, pressure on the environment. As a result, Cambridge's growth and its competitive advantage have been threatened by its lack of housing, its very high housing costs and what most inhabitants regard as an erosion of the quality of life in the city. Cambridge still scores well in terms of quality of life and environment, but both are seen as under considerable strain

4.4.12   The city's growth has also outstripped its physical and transport infrastructure. Although well connected to London by road and rail and reasonably well connected to the Midlands by road, in recent years mounting congestion on the major trunk roads around the city together with large commuter flows from surrounding villages and market towns, have produced negative externalities for workers, residents and businesses. Although relatively close to Stansted airport, the lack of air flights to the USA and Far East is a significant disadvantage for the business community

4.4.13   The city's social and cultural infrastructure and facilities have also not kept pace with its expansion nor its image as a high-tech centre. There has therefore been increasing tension between the city's growth and its historic character, and increasingly over the sustainability of its expansion. Over the past decade considerable public enquiry and debate have addressed Cambridge's growing problems of housing supply, inadequate connectivity and accessibility, and infrastructural deficit, and there has been a wave of institution building aimed at maintaining the city's success whilst attempting to protect its environment and quality of life. A more strategic sense of purpose has crystallised amongst the local authorities and other institutions concerned with Cambridge's development in recent years.

Derby – a high performer outside the south east

4.4.14   Derby tells a different story of a city's responses to change. It is a successful manufacturing city outside the shadow of London and the south east. The city is performing well with strong GVA per capita, high GVA per employee, and the highest visible exports per capita of all 56 cities in the study. These strong economic indicators, in particular visible exports, are explained by the important presence of high value export manufacturing firms Rolls Royce,

Bombardier and Toyota. During the last decade, Derby's position in terms of these economic indicators has improved considerably in comparison with the other 56 cities. However, Derby performs less well on indicators of quality of life related to social inclusion. The employment rate is relatively low, education attainment levels are below average and health indicators show underlying deprivation. There have been absolute improvements in recent years in levels of unemployment and deprivation. Nevertheless, their position has worsened in comparison relative to the other 56 cities.

4.4.15   There may also be economic challenges ahead that will test the city's ability to adapt. The economy is dominated by a highly specialised manufacturing sector. This is one of Derby's strengths. However, it was also recognised that the city needs to diversify within manufacturing and expand the services sector to provide a more diverse economic profile and guard against shifts in the future. It was argued that a tradition of family employment in large manufacturing companies had not encouraged an entrepreneurial culture within the workforce. This is also reflected in relatively low figures for new business creation, well below the English average. Data on investment in Derby show a relatively weak position, with low Gross Fixed Capital Formation and no private equity firms located within the city, suggesting that venture capital and finance for new initiatives are hard to come by.

4.4.16   One of the key drivers of competitiveness, innovation, is closely linked to the city's history. There is a strong engineering heritage and tradition in the city that goes back some 100 years, to the location of Rolls Royce in the city at the turn of the 20th century. Firms in Derby are significantly more innovative than their English counterparts, and high-tech engineering companies such as Rolls Royce and Toyota invest heavily in R&D and innovation, developing new technological forms to respond to changing markets and competitive environments. While private sector firms are constantly looking to upgrade and innovate in a fiercely competitive global market, it has been suggested that because the city has never faced the major economic crisis as some other cities have, the public sector may not yet have developed a sufficiently entrepreneurial strategy to cope with potential economic challenges. The way in which the city has responded in the past to change in markets, technologies, policies and cyclical shocks showed some potential barriers to change in the future. There were a number of concerns expressed about the range and variety of decision-making bodies and the lack of coordination between them. The city may need to adapt and change its economic, technological and institutional forms to hold onto its competitive economic position in a shifting global context.

Sheffield – responding to industrial change

4.4.17   Sheffield is an example of a traditional manufacturing based economy that is responding to rapid industrial change. There have been a variety of economic, social and political improvements during the last ten years. The south Yorkshire region improved its GDP figures to move out of EU Objective 1 status. There has been significant investment in and restructuring of the city centre led by the Urban Regeneration Company. The local authority has significantly improved its performance. There is a well-developed set of local partnerships. However, Sheffield leaders recognise that, despite those achievements, like similar cities, it still has some distance to travel to recreate competitive advantage. The local economy has traditionally been dominated by manufacturing industry, specialised in a restricted number of sectors, primarily related to the steel industry. However, recently there has been greater diversification in the city economy, which should increase with the "Creative Sheffield" initiative. There is a shared understanding between the local, regional and national levels of the need to diversify the city economy. This has been masterminded around key clusters in the city.

4.4.18 The universities provide two of the main possibilities for change. They are seen as the key to innovation in the city, with both institutions being active in research and collaboration efforts to develop new technological forms. The recent Creative Sheffield initiative is designed to promote innovation within the economic strategy for the city as a force for change. However, it is recognised that the city still needs to encourage the development of more entrepreneurs, to expand the markets served by the city and to further diversify its economy. Local strategic decision-makers are developing new institutional and economic forms. There are real gains to build upon. The city has come a long way from the economic decline in recent decades, Sheffield leaders, however, recognise that the fortunes of the city cannot be turned around overnight. The experience does underline the significance and impact of national policies – in terms of supporting innovation, research and development, connectivity and workforce skills – in supporting the city's future competitiveness.

Conclusions from the four cities

4.4.19 Each of these four case studies tells a different story of economic development and change over several decades. Rapid change such as that seen in London in the 1990s is the exception rather than the norm. Nevertheless, it underlines the vital importance of a city's adaptive capacity to deal with external change and a constantly changing business environment. It is also important to appreciate how each city has followed its own distinctive economic trajectory. Policy makers should exercise caution when seeking to copy a policy that appears to have been successful in one city in a different location. The complex and distinctive combinations of circumstances and actors in any given city are highly likely to be different in another place. No two cities that will have exactly the same economic histories. The key message is to take a set of principles, not all of which will be relevant in all cities, and apply them in developing locally appropriate strategies tailored to the particular economic strengths and weaknesses of individual cities. These strategies should be designed to ensure that the forces for change in a city outweigh those for continuity and that the adaptive capacity of a city's economy is increased.

4.5 Conclusion – what is the balance sheet on the economic performance of cities?

4.5.1 This chapter has stressed that those local economies that start with more of the most desirable factors of production are likely to accumulate more of them as the economic forces of cumulative causation work themselves out. The result will be divergence rather than convergence towards an equilibrium position. Our data on economic performance and competitiveness do indicate some divergence between the economies of the 56 cities over the 1990s and early 2000s. Figure 4.21 shows that GDHI, GVA per capita, visible exports, productivity and average earnings all diverged over the periods for which we have time series data. This suggests that the PSA convergence target for English regions will require some dramatic local urban economic policies if real and measurable progress in that direction is to be made before 2010.

Figure 4.21: Change in convergence/divergence 1991–2004

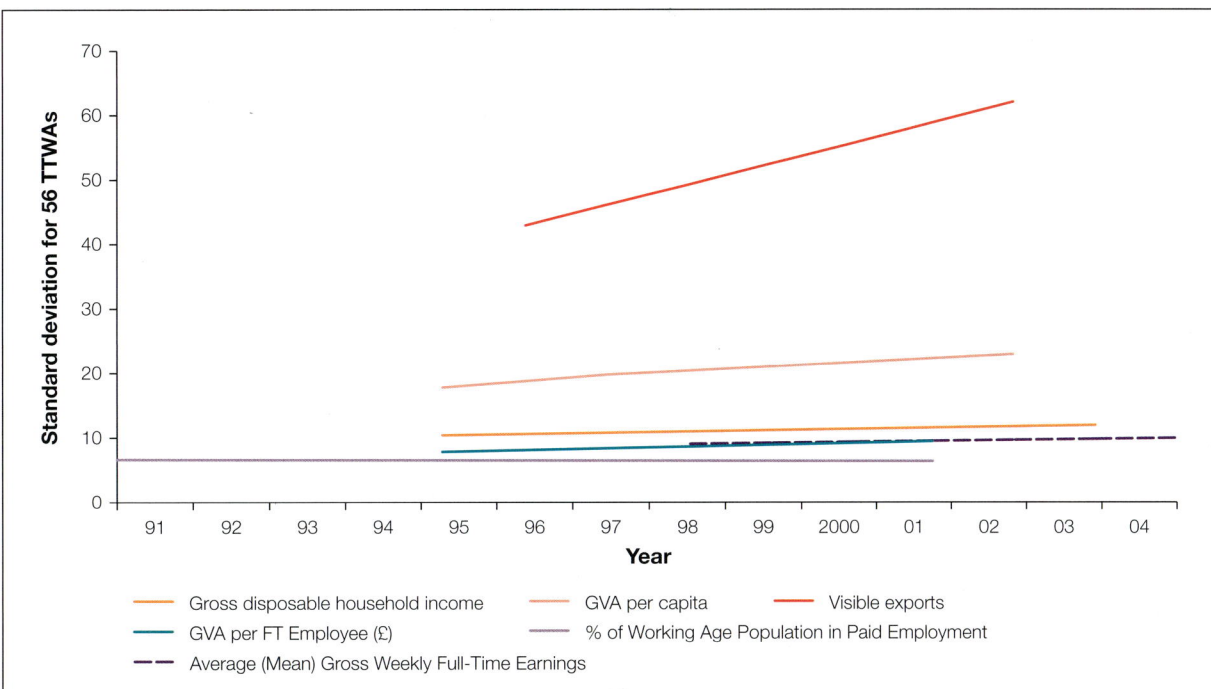

4.5.2   The overall economic performance of the 56 cities showed that there were nine where growth led that for England as a whole by 10 per cent or more. There were also 15 economies that lagged the English average by more than 10 per cent during the same period. Most of the best performing TTWAs were located in the GSE around London. The least well performing cities were almost all located around the north of England. The main exceptions to this rule were Ipswich, Norwich and Hastings in the south. One of the key features of the club of best performing economies located around London is their connectivity especially in terms of business services networks. There is a great deal of evidence to suggest that local and international networking is a significant feature of successful knowledge driven economies. Policy makers therefore need to analyse and facilitate the development of this kind of soft infrastructure at least as much as physical infrastructures.

4.5.3   Our evidence showed that it is possible to have good overall economic performance without social cohesion. Cities like Derby and Manchester, for example, performed well overall in purely economic terms, but still retained above average levels of social deprivation. Part of the explanation for this appears to be connected with the proportions of firms and sectors in the local economy that are responsible for the high overall economic performance. Derby, for example, has Rolls Royce, Toyota and a much slimmed down rail industry. The productivity and output of this minority of firms is high enough to affect the overall figures for the city. On the other hand there are not enough such high wage firms to raise the overall levels of wages and reduce the levels of deprivation in the economy. Policy makers should not therefore expect that economic growth will necessarily lead to greater social cohesion. There will normally be a need for two different broad types of policy – one to facilitate economic growth and another to enable more local residents to participate directly or indirectly in the benefits created.

4.5.4   England has a particular combination of relatively high levels of employment with lower levels of productivity. Nevertheless, employment rates improved in most cities during the 1990s. Much of the increase in rates of employment was a reflection of the upturn in the business cycle. It should not, therefore, necessarily be regarded as an indication of increasing competitiveness. What is required from the point of view of long-term policy in these circumstances is not just an emphasis on job creation, but attention to the quality and productivity of those jobs.

4.5.5   Innovative capacity is the most significant basis of productivity and competitiveness – the critical factor in the ability of an urban economy to compete is its adaptive capacity and how easily innovations are diffused around the relevant firms and sectors in the locality. The evidence suggests that innovation diffusion is a key requirement for overall competitiveness rather than major breakthroughs. Most of the high performing cities had higher rates of the adoption and diffusion of technological product and process innovations than the low performing cities. The former also produced more patent applications to the EPO.

4.5.6   There is an equity gap between large companies and SMEs and between the availability of venture capital in the south and north of England. Despite the fact that the venture capital industry in the UK is the largest in Europe, it is highly concentrated in London. It is also concentrated on services and information technology. There are therefore problems especially for SMEs in the north and west or those not engaged in services or IT in accessing venture capital. The availability and relevant use of venture capital outside London and the south and east remains a significant policy problem.

4.5.7   Human capital is the third essential ingredient of successful knowledge driven economies. The changes taking place in the proportions of the working age population with degree level qualifications favoured London, Brighton, Cambridge, Oxford, Reading, Bristol and Southampton in and around the south and east. Outside this area the only cities that exceeded the average English growth rate were York, Nottingham and Leeds. The importance of a highly qualified workforce as a prerequisite to compete among the knowledge driven economies can hardly be over-emphasised. While many of the largest English cities have one or more universities and produce their own graduates, some have difficulties in recruiting and retaining them in their own local economies.

4.5.8   In terms of diversity, our evidence suggests that specialisation and diversity are important in driving the performance of local economies. It remains probable, however, that the more specialised sectors there are in any given local economy the better. Locally tailored policies could seek both to encourage specialisation and branching into or the development of new specialisations. However, given the external forces that impact upon all cities, a reliance on too few specialised sectors is clearly a risky strategy. Clustered specialisation combined with diversity has been the basis of the comparative economic success of many of the top performing cities, as the examples of London and Cambridge illustrated.

4.5.9   Connectivity is critically important for successful cities. This takes many forms including physical road, rail and air connections, electronic telecommunications, and possibly even more important, business networks. We found some correlation between connectivity indicated by the fastest rail journey times to London and patenting. In many respects road and rail connections between English cities are not up to the standards of the best in Europe, which puts them at a competitive disadvantage particularly in the context of the continuing development of the European common market. This now provides the largest market for English exports. Air connectivity is dominated by airports located in and around London. This presents some hurdles for northern businesses wishing to access even some European markets on a regular basis. Despite a regulatory and competitive environment that makes increasing scheduled flights from regional airports to Europe, North America and the Far East difficult, these are essential to facilitate international connectivity.

4.5.10 Another critical underlying factor is the educational base. Indigenous educational strengths are important. But urban economies also need sectors that provide returns to education. For example, the poorest economic performers like Stoke, Chatham, Ipswich, Middlesbrough, Wigan and Blackpool all moved up the rankings of educational deprivation between 1998/99 and 2001. This emphasises the need to encourage high quality, productive and knowledge based employment. In too many cases these types of employment are mainly provided by the public sector in northern cities. Policies to relocate more public sector employment away from the south east can help to create new demands for graduate labour but will also reinforce this public sector bias. Some effort therefore needs to be devoted to using existing public and private sectors to create employment that provides greater returns to education. This could encourage cultural and aspirational shifts in local attitudes towards education.

4.5.11 English cities face two big hurdles in developing policies to improve their economic competitiveness. The first is that many of the factors that contribute most to competitiveness are part of the self-organising and market driven private sector. Traditionally, English local authorities have had few ways of intervening in such systems other than by collaboration and persuasion. Second, English cities have generally weak powers over strategic decision making and finance. Central ministries, especially through mainstream as opposed to spatially targeted programmes, make and fund more of the key decisions concerning urban economies than do local authorities.

4.5.12 In future more powers and funding should be devolved to City-Regions to improve their economic strategic decision making capacities for five related reasons. First, a centralised system makes decisions on behalf of the whole country. This can be inefficient in circumstances where the needs and interests of City-Regions are significantly different. It is clear that this is the case among the 56 cities studied here. The second reason is that decentralisation can be a source of policy innovations. Where City-Regions are given more responsibility for their own welfare this can give rise to creative attempts to improve their own local economies. Third, decentralisation in decision making can lead to greater transparency and accountability. Elected City-Regional authorities could make economic decision making more accountable than it is at the moment under the direction of central government appointed RDAs (Rodriguez-Pose and Gill 2005). Fourth, central government simply cannot know, understand or process enough information on the individual economic trajectories of all the cities within its national territory to make relevant decisions tailored to their needs. Even our limited case studies show the widely differing economic trajectories among only a small number of cities. Finally, a more decentralised decision making and funding system could improve upon some of the anomalies that arise in centrally directed mainstream funding. As the new experimental accounts data for sub-regions have shown, even formula driven identifiable mainstream funding is not consistently distributed according to need. In addition, unidentifiable expenditures such as defence R&D and procurement are both much greater and distributed disproportionately in London and the south east than regional assistance is to other areas (Gripaios and Bishop 2005).

4.5.13   Economic success is not confined to cities in the south and east. Leeds, York and Manchester in the north are in the top quartile of overall economic performance. But there are many across the north and down the eastern coast of England that are in the bottom quartiles. Bringing their real performance up to the average for England as a whole, even in the long term, will require some dramatic policy initiatives combined with favourable external conditions. Such policies would have to be large scale with major funding implications. The scale of change required will need vision, long-term strategies, large scale funding and some luck with external circumstances.

4.5.14   Finally our evolutionary approach to the analysis of city economies has emphasised the significance of their long-term historical trajectories. They have arrived where they are today as a result of the long-term interactions between their particular circumstances and the external forces that have impacted on them. This approach shows not only that history matters, but that it takes a long time to develop along a particular path. It also shows that policy-makers and policies need similarly long-term perspectives to achieve changes in those paths. There are no quick fixes that will turn around lagging city economies.

Chapter 5: Social cohesion in English cities

5.1   Introduction

5.1.1   This chapter assesses the state of social cohesion in English cities. It draws upon a wide range of data sources to examine key patterns, trends, processes and policies. Social cohesion is a multi-faceted notion covering many different kinds of social phenomena. The different dimensions of cohesion have an important bearing upon each other but they are not synonymous. Figure 5.1 conveys its essential features in a simple framework.

5.1.2   Starting at the base of the pyramid, material conditions are fundamental to social cohesion, particularly employment, income, health, education and housing. Relations between and within communities suffer when people lack work and endure hardship, debt, anxiety, low self-esteem, ill-health, poor skills and bad living conditions. These basic necessities of life are the foundations of a strong social fabric and important indicators of social progress. The second basic tenet of cohesion is social order, safety and freedom from fear, or 'passive social relationships'. Tolerance and respect for other people, along with peace and security, are hallmarks of a stable and harmonious urban society. The opposite is lack of acceptance of social and cultural differences, along with conflict and crime, hence stress, insecurity and instability.

5.1.3   The third dimension refers to positive interactions, exchanges and networks between individuals and communities, or 'active social relationships'. Such contacts and connections are potential resources for places since they offer people and organisations mutual support, information, trust and credit of various kinds. The opposite is misunderstanding, suspicion, mistrust and resentment, which undermine social well-being. The fourth dimension is about the extent of 'social inclusion' or integration of people into the mainstream institutions of civil society. It also includes people's sense of belonging to a city and the strength of shared experiences, identities and values between those from different backgrounds – do they have a genuine stake in local society and pull together? The opposite is social or residential segregation, social exclusion, disaffection and isolation.

5.1.4   Lastly, 'social equality' refers to the level of fairness or disparity in access to opportunities or material circumstances, such as income, health or quality of life, or in future life chances. The opposite is a high level of inequality in living standards or very unequal prospects for upward social mobility. This may be associated with frustration, envy and resentment experienced by those lower down the scale, which can damage overall social welfare in a variety of ways.

5.1.5   One of the complications associated with the concept is that the state of social cohesion differs depending on whether one is referring to cities, neighbourhoods or particular social groups. Tight-knit communities may exist within a fractured city if they involve self-centred behaviour and discrimination against other groups. In other words, one group's coherence may come at the expense of another's exclusion. Conversely, tolerance and trust between different communities can obscure conflicts within them, for example, between young and old, or rich and poor. Clearly, groups and communities can be defined on different bases – socio-economic, religious, ethnic, age, disability, gender. It is important to be specific about what one is referring to when considering the state of cohesion in a city.

Figure 5.1: Different dimensions of social cohesion

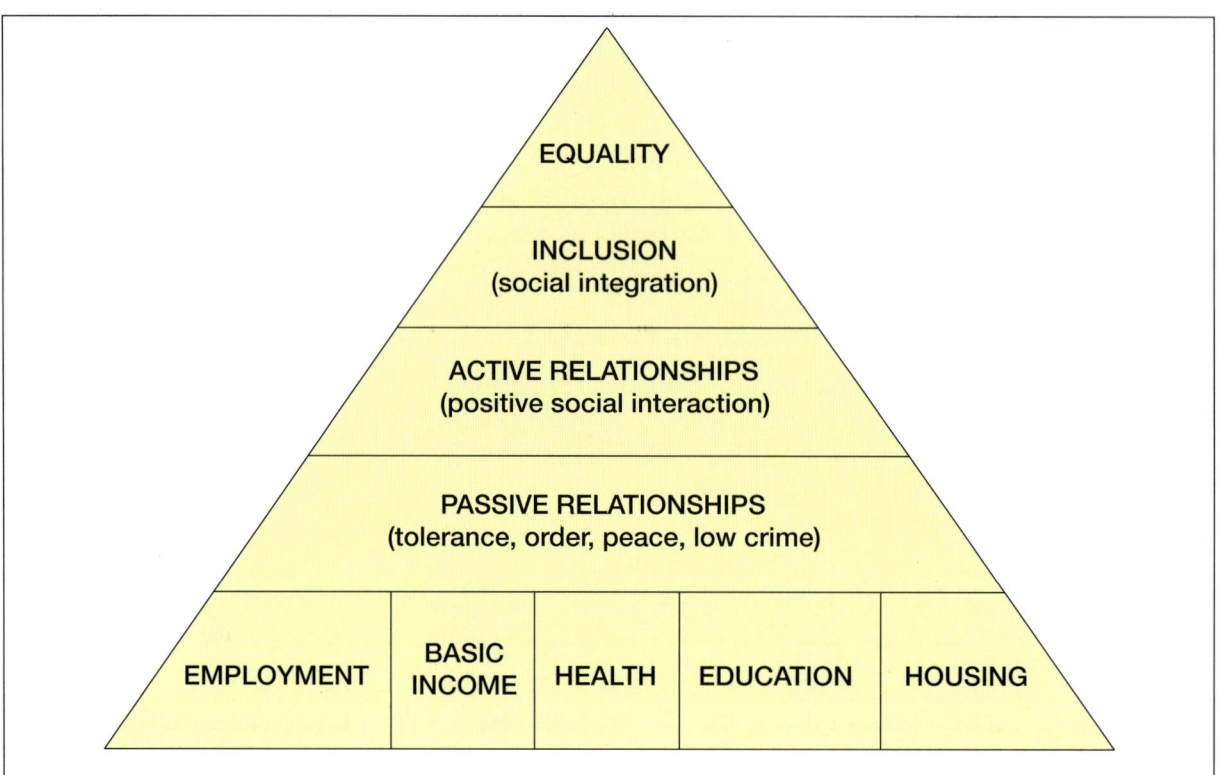

5.2 Patterns and trends in social cohesion

5.2.1 This chapter provides a quantitative assessment of contemporary social conditions in English cities. It addresses three overriding themes:

- current patterns: differences in conditions between and within cities, and between cities and the rest of the country;

- recent trends: whether conditions have been getting better or worse; and

- what lies behind these trends: the analysis is based on a wide range of secondary data sources, including the SOCD, the Population Census, the Labour Force Survey (LFS), the Index of Multiple Deprivation (IMD), official statistics on educational attainment, the Health Survey for England, recorded crime statistics and data on welfare benefits.

5.2.2 The structure follows the underlying conditions or drivers of social cohesion: income and deprivation; employment; education and skills; crime and community safety, health and well-being and housing and neighbourhood dynamics. We analyse individual cities and neighbourhoods within them, and groups of cities in order to compare different settlement types. We also analyse patterns and trends for different socio-economic, demographic and ethnic groups, where the data permits this level of subdivision. Emerging patterns and trends provide clues to the underlying dynamics and processes of change.

5.3 Income and Deprivation

5.3.1   Low income and deprivation are key elements of poverty and social exclusion. These are of course fundamental to the level of social cohesion or lack of cohesion in cities and neighbourhoods. Household poverty and neighbourhood deprivation are often associated with personal hardship, high levels of debt, stress and anxiety, chronic illness, drug and alcohol addictions, crime, family breakdown and awkward neighbours.

5.3.2   The key questions are:

- What is the level of deprivation in English cities and towns?

- What is the gap between the most and least deprived neighbourhoods?

- Where are the most and least deprived neighbourhoods?

- How does the level of child poverty vary between cities and towns?

- Is the Non-White population more likely to live in the poorest neighbourhoods?

- Have conditions been getting better or worse in different cities?

5.3.3   Figure 5.2 shows wide disparities in the level of deprivation between different types of area. Deprivation is generally a much bigger problem in the cities than in the towns and rural areas. Metropolitan centres and large cities in the north and west have by far the highest levels of deprivation, and towns and rural areas in the south and east have the lowest. Looked at more closely, both settlement size and region seem to matter, although the regional dimension clearly matters more than urban size. Most types of area in the north and west do worse than most types of area in the south and east. London's position is consistent with its size and region.

Figure 5.2: Level of deprivation by city type, 2004

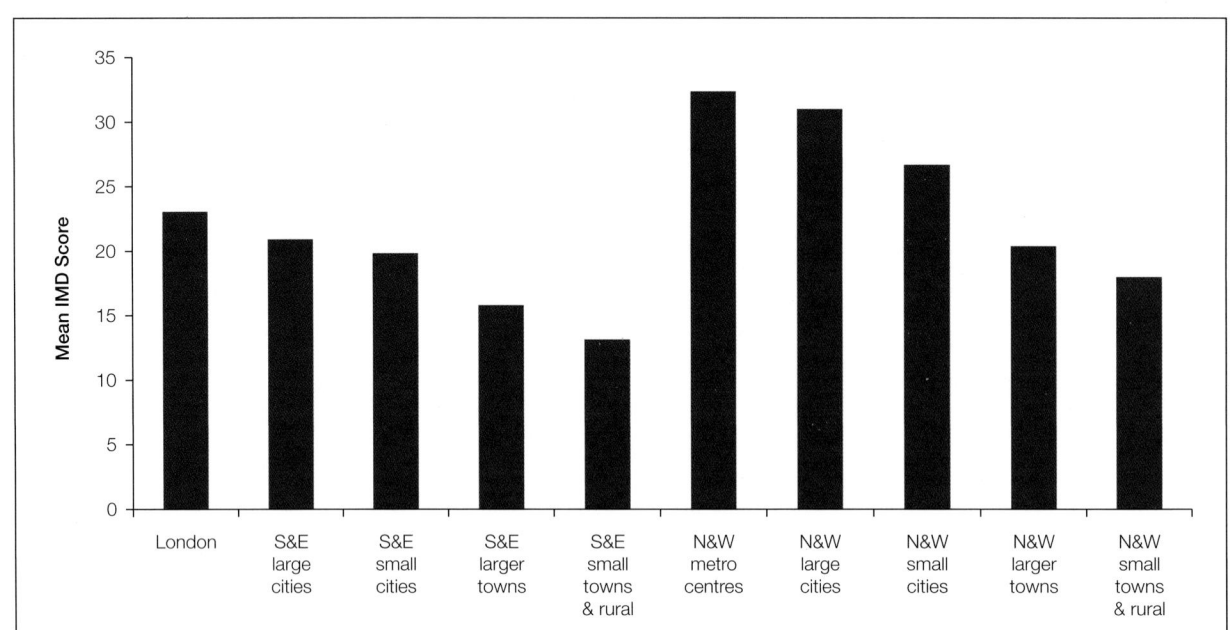

5.3.4   Figure 5.3 shows the level of deprivation for the 56 individual cities. The disparities are naturally much wider than between different categories of city. Liverpool has by far the highest level of deprivation, followed by Hull. Aldershot has the lowest level of deprivation, followed by Reading and Crawley. The metropolitan centres have similar levels of deprivation. Nottingham stands slightly apart from the other large cities in the south and east with more deprivation. Similarly, Hastings and Mansfield stand apart from the other small cities in the south and east. York stands apart from small cities in the north and west with relatively low deprivation. London is in the middle of the spectrum with a lower level of deprivation than most cities in the north and west, but higher than most cities in the south and east.

Figure 5.3: Level of deprivation by individual city, 2004

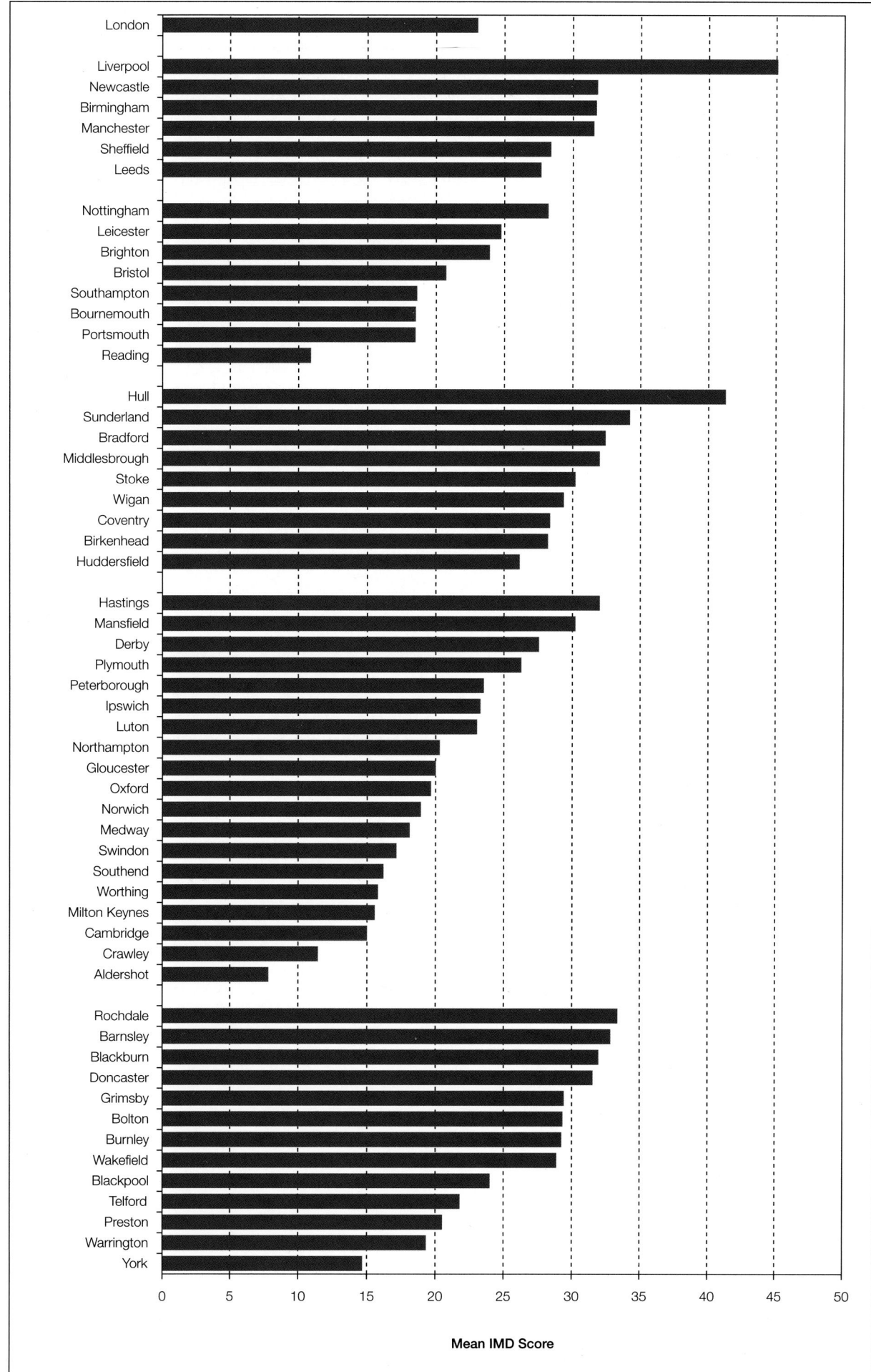

Mean IMD Score

The location of the most and least deprived neighbourhoods

5.3.5   The overall level of deprivation and the gap between the most and least deprived neighbourhoods are both highest in major cities in the north and west. How are the poorest neighbourhoods actually distributed across England? How many more of the country's poorest neighbourhoods are located in cities in the north and west compared with the south and east? How many more of the country's least deprived neighbourhoods are located in towns and rural areas in the south and east? These questions are addressed by looking at the incidence of England's most and least deprived 10 per cent of neighbourhoods.

5.3.6   Figure 5.4 shows the proportion of neighbourhoods in each type of city that fall within the country's most and least deprived 10 per cent of neighbourhoods. Every bar in the graph would be 10 per cent if these places had their proportionate share of England's poorest and least deprived areas. In fact, the metropolitan centres have more than two and a half times their share of the poorest neighbourhoods and less than half their share of the least deprived areas. Towns and rural areas everywhere have less than their share of the poorest areas. Every category of city or town in the south and east has less than its share of the poorest areas. So region seems to matter most to the location of deprived neighbourhoods. Settlement size also matters, particularly in the north and west, in that larger cities have more of the most deprived areas than smaller cities and towns. Once again, London's pattern is consistent with its size and regional location.

5.3.7   The incidence of least deprived neighbourhoods is essentially the inverse of the most deprived neighbourhoods. For instance, towns and rural areas in the south and east have far more than their proportionate share, whereas metropolitan centres have far less. An important implication of the offsetting effect of most and least deprived neighbourhoods is that cities do not appear from this to be much more strongly polarised than towns and rural areas. They certainly have far more poor neighbourhoods, but they also appear to have far fewer prosperous neighbourhoods. The main difference is that cities generally have more deprivation than towns and rural areas, not that they have more of both poor and well-off neighbourhoods.

Figure 5.4: Incidence of the most and least deprived neighbourhoods by city type, 2004

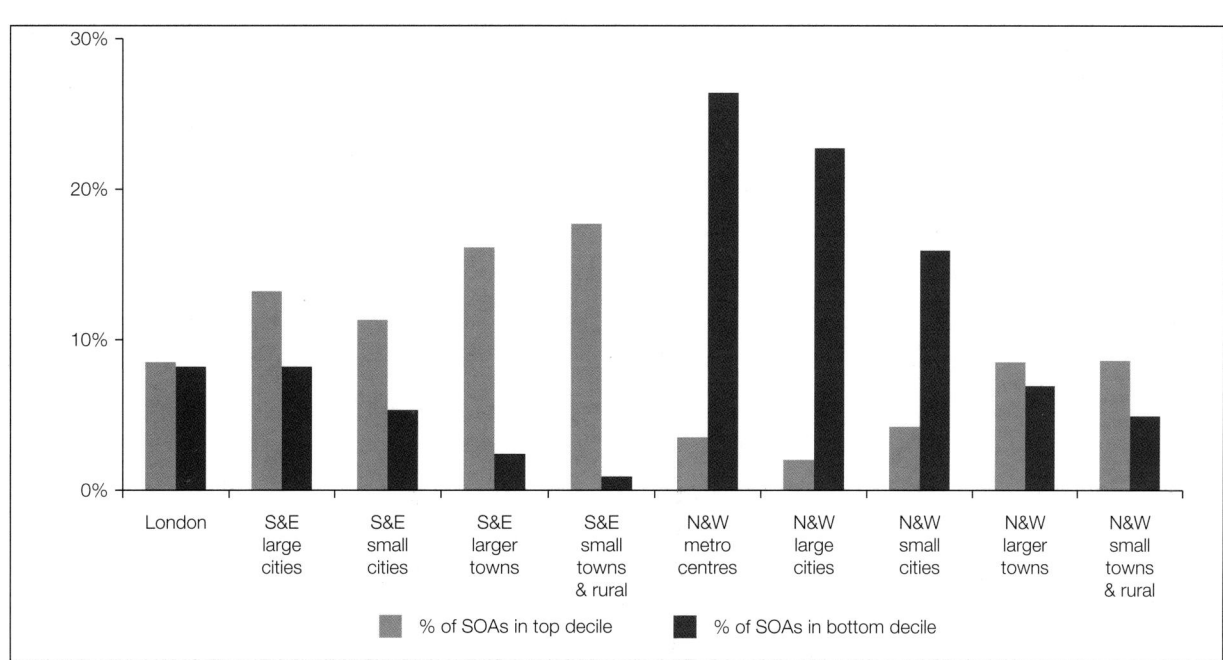

5.3.8   This also holds true when individual cities are considered in Figure 5.5. Almost half of the neighbourhoods in Liverpool are in the poorest 10 per cent in the country. This is double the proportion in Birmingham and Manchester. Liverpool also has none of the least deprived neighbourhoods in England. London is more balanced than any of the other major cities, and apparently less polarised than one might have anticipated, with almost its proportionate share of the most and least deprived neighbourhoods. Bristol is quite unlike the other major regional cities with less than its share of poor neighbourhoods and more than its share of least deprived areas.

Figure 5.5: Incidence of the most and least deprived neighbourhoods by major city, 2004

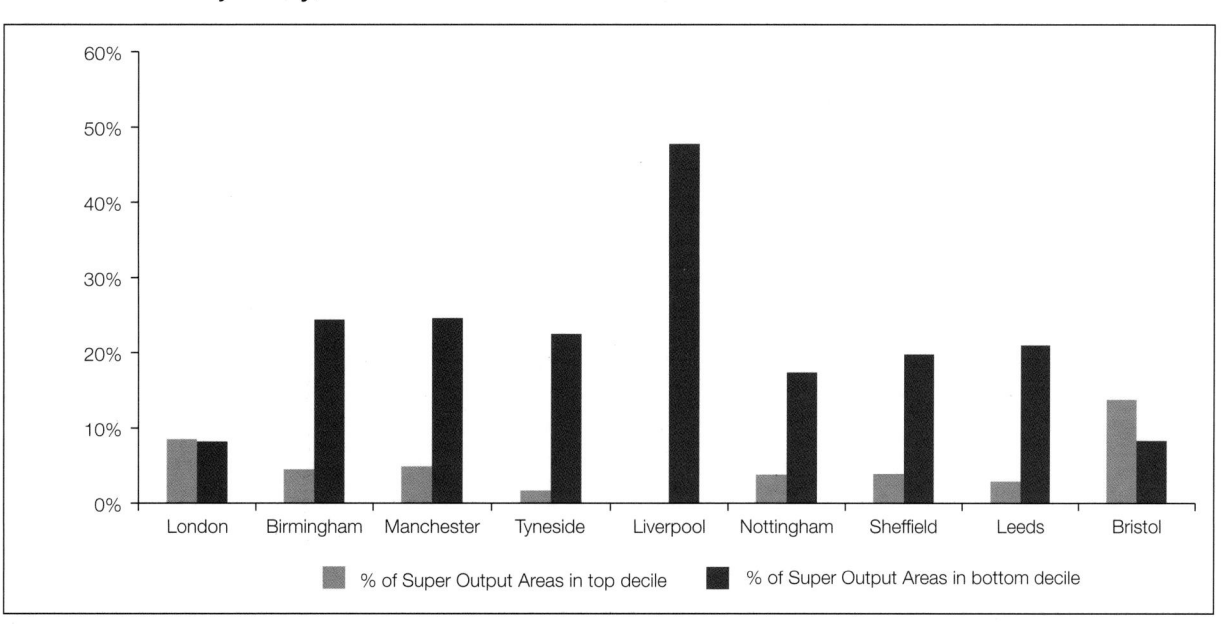

Deprivation amongst ethnic minority groups

5.3.9   In order to explore the relationship between deprivation and ethnic status we linked ethnicity data from the Census with deprivation data from the IMD. The summary findings are shown in Figure 5.6. It reveals that Non-Whites are indeed more likely to live in the poorest neighbourhoods. The percentage living there is roughly twice as high as the percentage living in the rest of the city. In London there are many more Non-Whites living in the poorest areas simply because there are many more Non-Whites in the city as a whole. Looked at more closely, the figure shows that Non-Whites are represented disproportionately in the poorest neighbourhoods in cities in the north and west compared with the south and east.

5.3.10   In London the correspondence between the most deprived neighbourhoods and the Black Caribbean population was much stronger than for the Asian population, suggesting that Asians tend to be better off in the capital. Elsewhere in the south east there was not much difference between the Black Caribbean and Asian populations. The pattern was reversed for cities in the north and west, with a stronger correspondence between the most deprived neighbourhoods and the Asian population.

Figure 5.6: Percentage of Non-Whites in the most deprived neighbourhoods and rest of the city, 2001

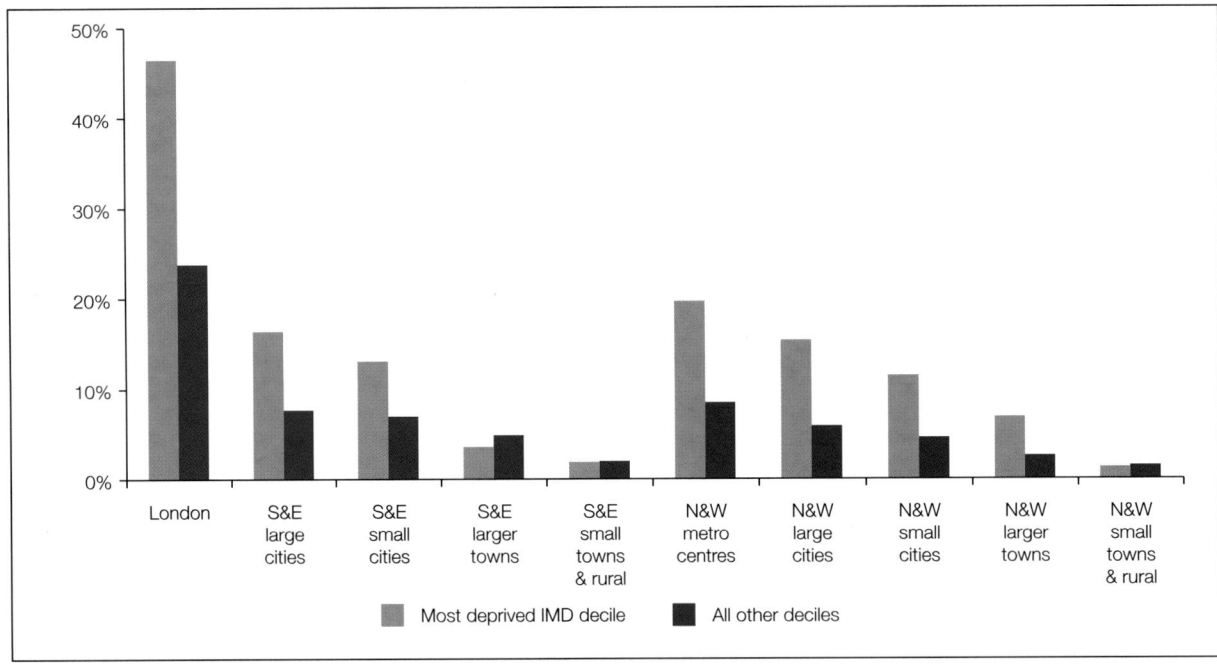

5.3.11   Figure 5.7 shows the data for individual cities in England, limited to those with Non-White populations of over 6 per cent of their total populations. There are three cities where Non-Whites are less likely to live in the most deprived neighbourhoods: Leicester, Milton Keynes and Oxford. In contrast, there are five cities where Non-Whites are more likely to live in the most deprived neighbourhoods: Bradford, Preston, Derby, Peterborough and Burnley. London has a much more balanced representation of Non-Whites in the poorest neighbourhoods.

Figure 5.7: Percentage of Non-Whites in the most deprived neighbourhoods and rest of the city, by individual city, 2001

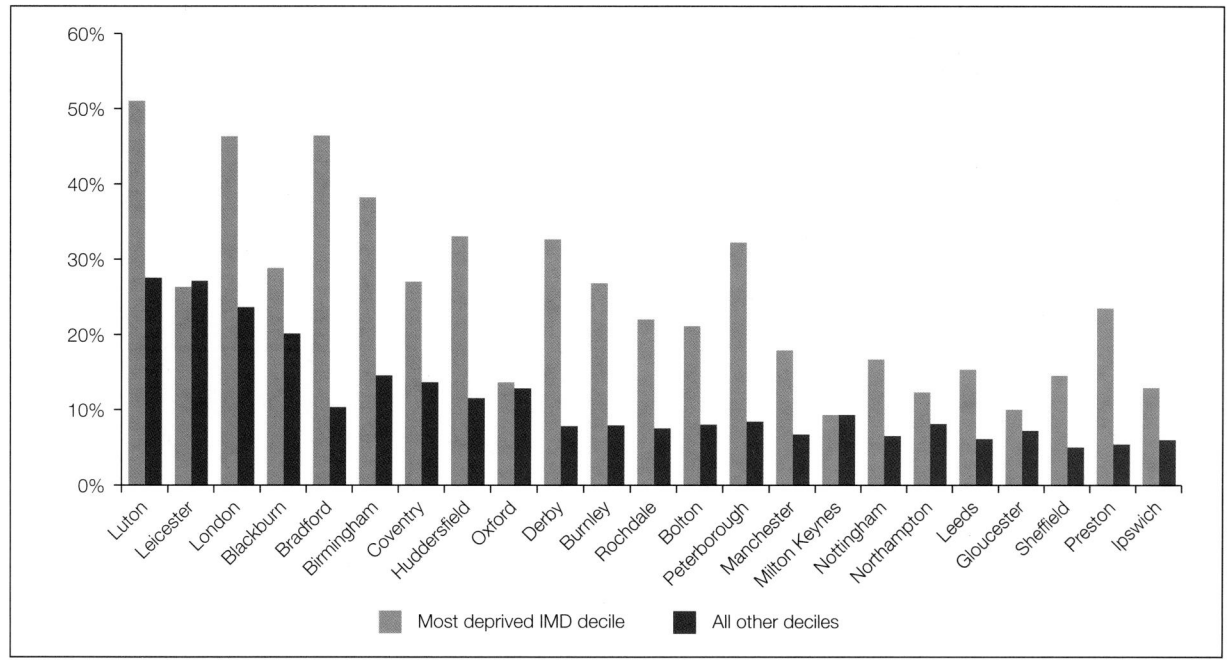

5.3.12 The greater prevalence of the Non-White population in the most deprived neighbourhoods in many cities does not mean that there is a more general relationship between cities with a large Non-White population and cities with a high level of deprivation. Figure 5.8 shows a scatter plot comparing the proportion of the population of the 56 cities that is Non-White with the deprivation level as measured by the IMD. The most deprived cities have small Non-White populations and the cities with the largest Non-White populations have below average IMD scores.

Figure 5.8: Relationship between Non-White population and level of deprivation

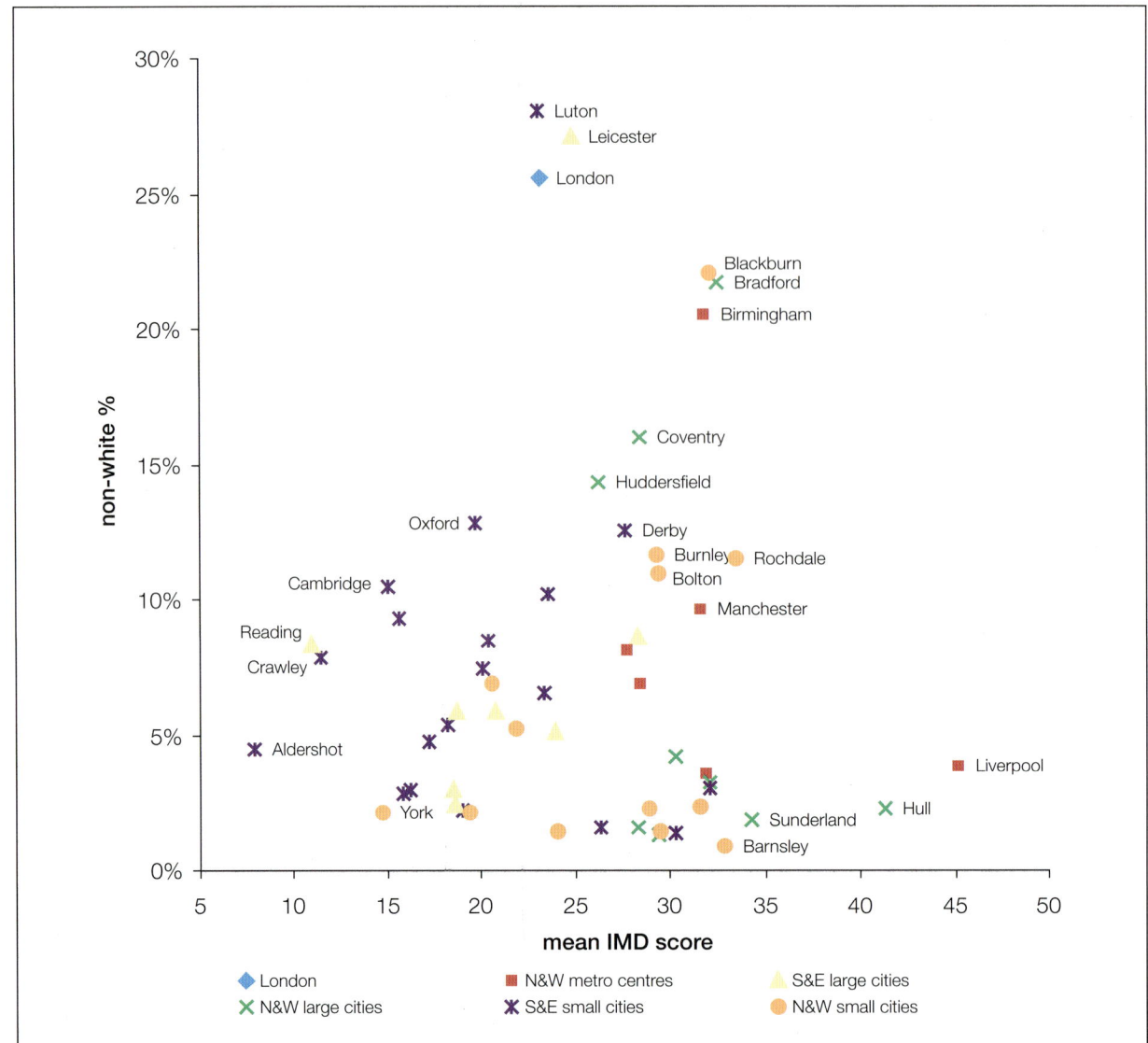

Reliance on welfare benefits

5.3.13   The principal source of income for deprived groups is state benefits. Income Support (IS) is the most important of these. It is paid to people under 60 who are on low incomes, have less than £8,000 in savings, are lone parents, sick or disabled, blind, home carers and are not registered unemployed. Job Seekers Allowance (JSA) is the key benefit for people who are registered unemployed. The combination of these two benefits provides one of the longest reliable time series available for small areas. Map 5.1 shows the proportion of working age adults claiming IS or JSA in August 2003. The highest figure was for Liverpool at 18 per cent, followed by Hull at 17 per cent. The next four cities with claimant rates of 13 per cent were Birmingham, Middlesbrough, Newcastle and Hastings.

5.3.14 There have been substantial falls in recorded unemployment in the last decade. We can obtain an indication of how this has affected the level of income deprivation in the cities by considering changes in the rate of IS and JSA benefit claims. Map 5.2 shows the change in the proportion of working age adults claiming IS or JSA between August 1998 and August 2003. The proportion has fallen almost everywhere, and by most where it was highest. In Liverpool it fell by 3.6 per cent. The other big falls have been along the south coast – Hastings, Brighton and Plymouth – followed by selected cities in the north including Doncaster, Barnsley, Hull, Wakefield, Nottingham and Mansfield. There were two places where claimants rose slightly; Reading and Leicester. Changes in benefit claimants are too complex to describe in terms of either regional location or city size, although there are clear regional clusters on the maps.

Map 5.1: Adults claiming Income Support or JSA in 2003

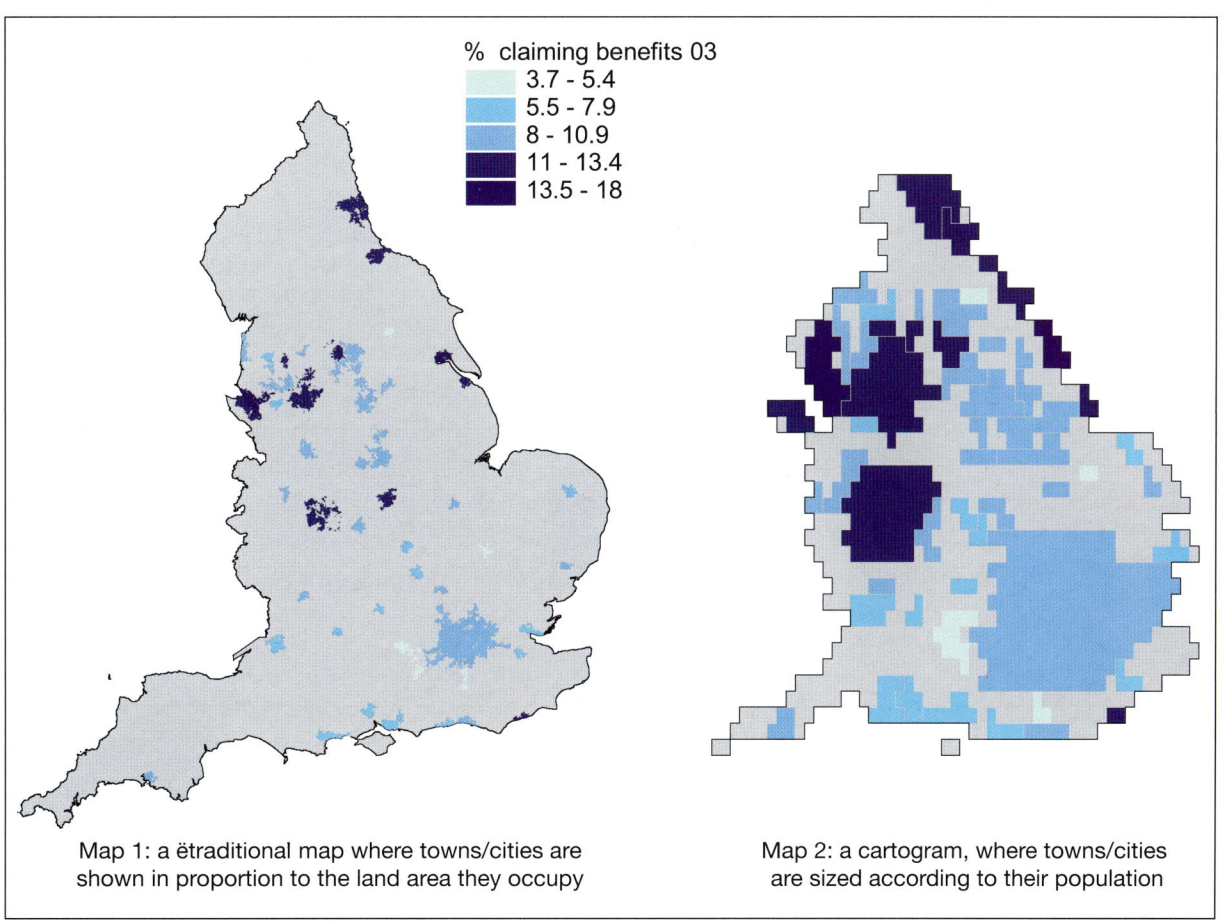

% claiming benefits 03
- 3.7 - 5.4
- 5.5 - 7.9
- 8 - 10.9
- 11 - 13.4
- 13.5 - 18

Map 1: a ëtraditional map where towns/cities are shown in proportion to the land area they occupy

Map 2: a cartogram, where towns/cities are sized according to their population

Map 5.2: Changes in adults claiming IS or JSA, 1998-2003

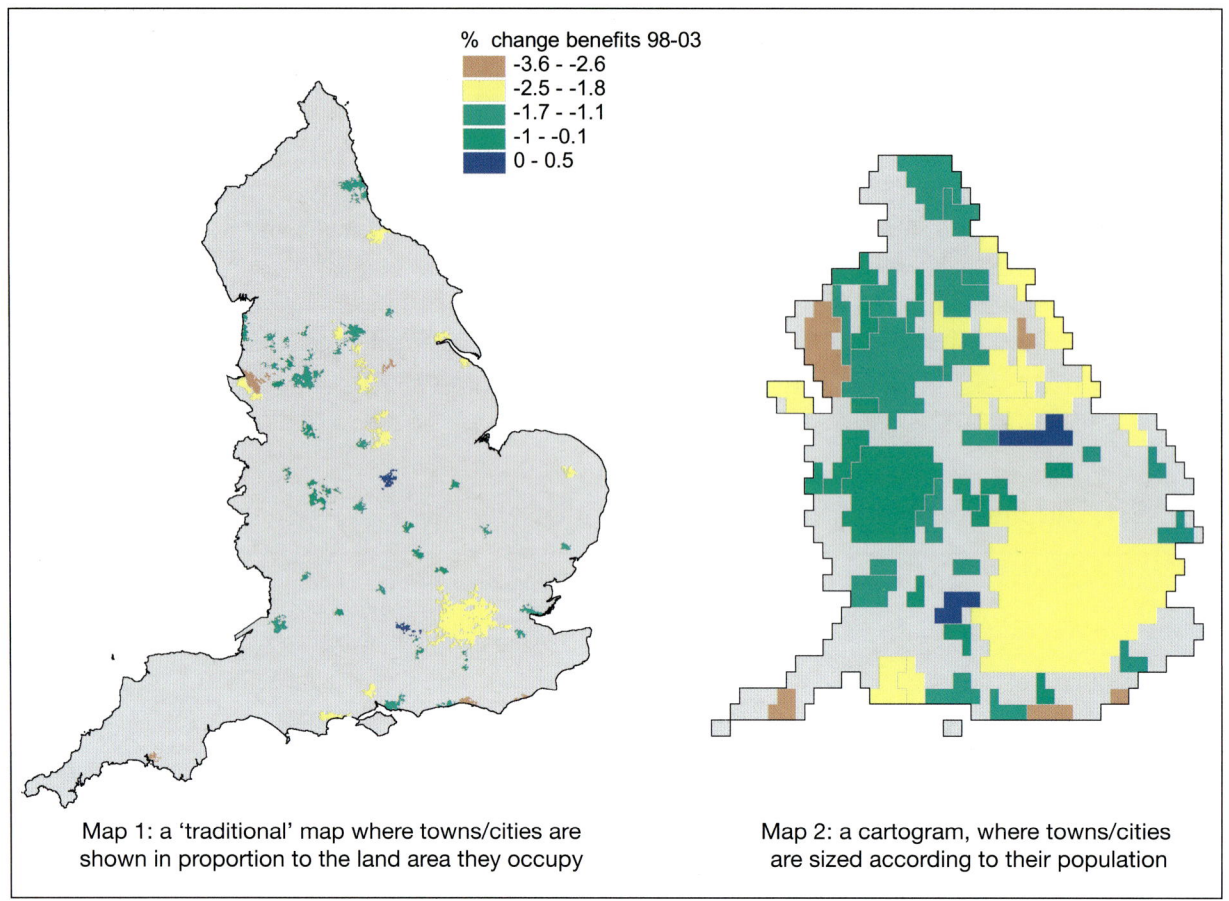

% change benefits 98-03
- -3.6 - -2.6
- -2.5 - -1.8
- -1.7 - -1.1
- -1 - -0.1
- 0 - 0.5

Map 1: a 'traditional' map where towns/cities are shown in proportion to the land area they occupy

Map 2: a cartogram, where towns/cities are sized according to their population

5.3.15   Figure 5.9 shows the distribution of lone parents based on census data rather than benefit claims. It also allows for a comparison of trends over time. The figure confirms that cities have higher rates of lone parenthood than towns and rural areas, and that major cities in the north and west have the highest rates. It also shows a sizeable – and general – increase in lone parenthood between 1991 and 2001.

Figure 5.9: Lone parents as a % of all households, by city type, 1991 & 2001

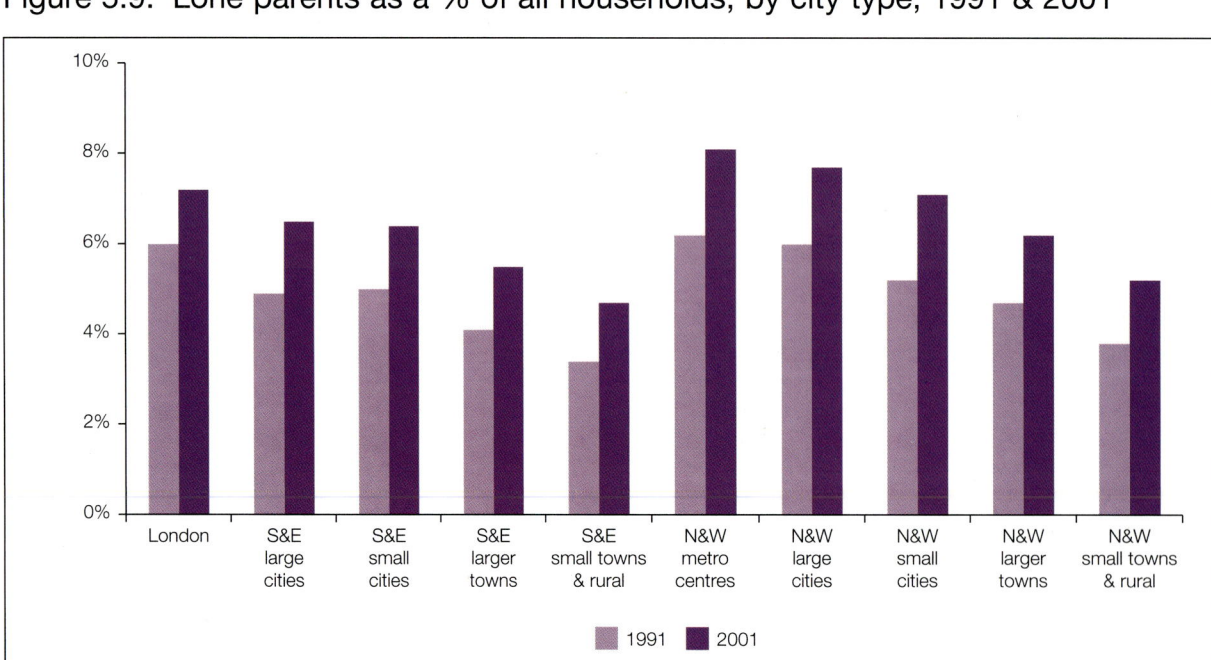

5.3.16 We know that the proportion of adults reliant on benefits is higher in some
cities than elsewhere, but less about the geography of benefit reliance within
cities. The pattern may be highly concentrated in particular neighbourhoods
within the city or widely dispersed across the city, or something in between.
Figure 5.10 shows the breakdown of ward level data on IS claimants by
deciles for the city types. The claimant rate for the ward with the highest rate
is shown, along with the claimant rate for the 9th decile. The figure shows
that cities in the north and west not only have some wards with extremely
high IS claimant rates, but also a more even spread across the city. In contrast,
towns and rural areas, and to a lesser extent, cities in the south and east, have
a more concentrated geography of deprivation. This may have implications for
the relative importance of small area versus city-wide approaches to tackling
deprivation.

Figure 5.10: IS claimants by ward, decile and city type, 2004

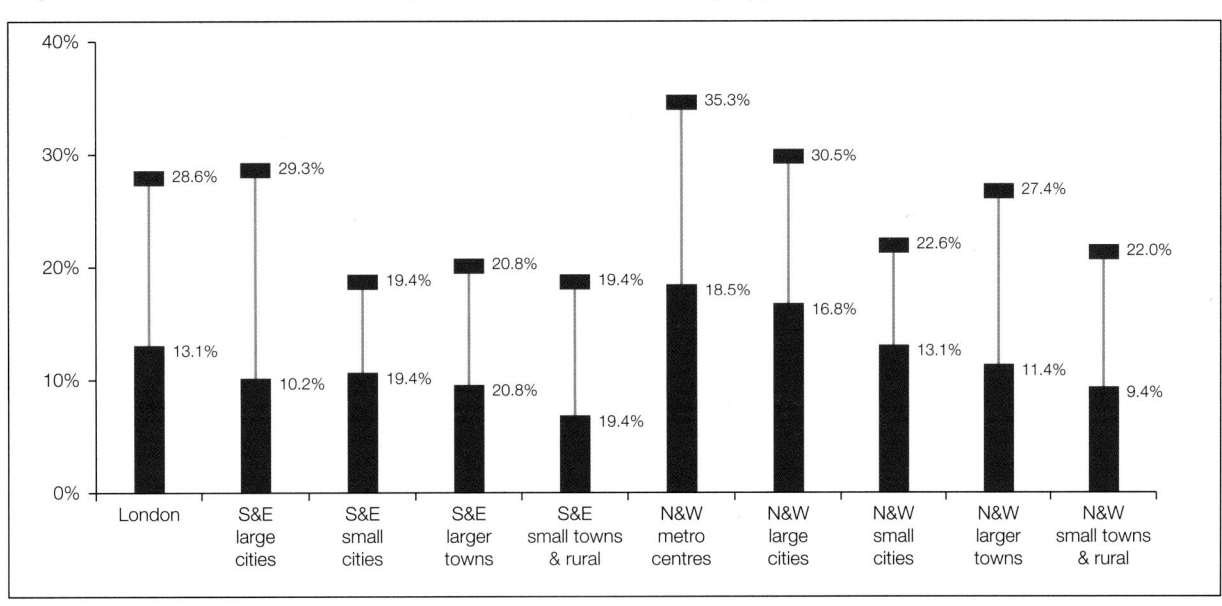

5.3.17 The balance sheet on income and deprivation:

- The level of deprivation is higher and more widespread in cities.

- The gap between the most and least deprived neighbourhoods is bigger
  in cities.

- The poorest neighbourhoods tend to be in the largest cities in the north
  and west.

- Child poverty and lone parenthood are highest in the major cities in the
  north and west.

- A greater proportion of Non-Whites live in the poorest neighbourhoods,
  although cities with a large Non-White population are not more deprived.

- Conditions have been improving in most cities, especially in some of the
  poorest.

5.4   Employment

5.4.1   Employment is fundamental to the general well being of communities and to the level of social cohesion in cities. Involuntary exclusion from employment is probably the principal cause of poverty and disaffection in advanced economies, where paid jobs are the main source of income, social status, personal identity, morale and self-esteem, social interaction outside the family, daily time-structure and meaningful activity. Long-term or recurrent unemployment with low expectations of progress is often synonymous with social exclusion.

5.4.2   The main questions addressed in this section are:

- Is there a strong link between employment and income at the level of the city?

- How does the level of worklessness vary between cities and towns?

- Where are the neighbourhoods with the highest and lowest worklessness?

- How does the employment gap vary between different groups in different cities?

- Have employment conditions been getting better or worse in different cities?

The relationship between employment and income

5.4.3   The relationship between employment and household income can be tested at the level of the city using data from the IMD. Figure 5.11 shows a scatter plot comparing the proportion of the population of the 56 cities that have a low income as measured by the IMD with the proportion that have a high level of employment deprivation. Low income is defined as below 60 per cent of the national median income, excluding housing benefit and before housing costs. The figure shows a very strong, statistically significant relationship, demonstrating that places with a high rate of unemployment and worklessness have many people on low incomes. Liverpool and Middlesbrough feature at one end of the spectrum, and Aldershot, Crawley and Reading at the other.

Figure 5.11: Relationship between income and employment deprivation, by individual city, 2004

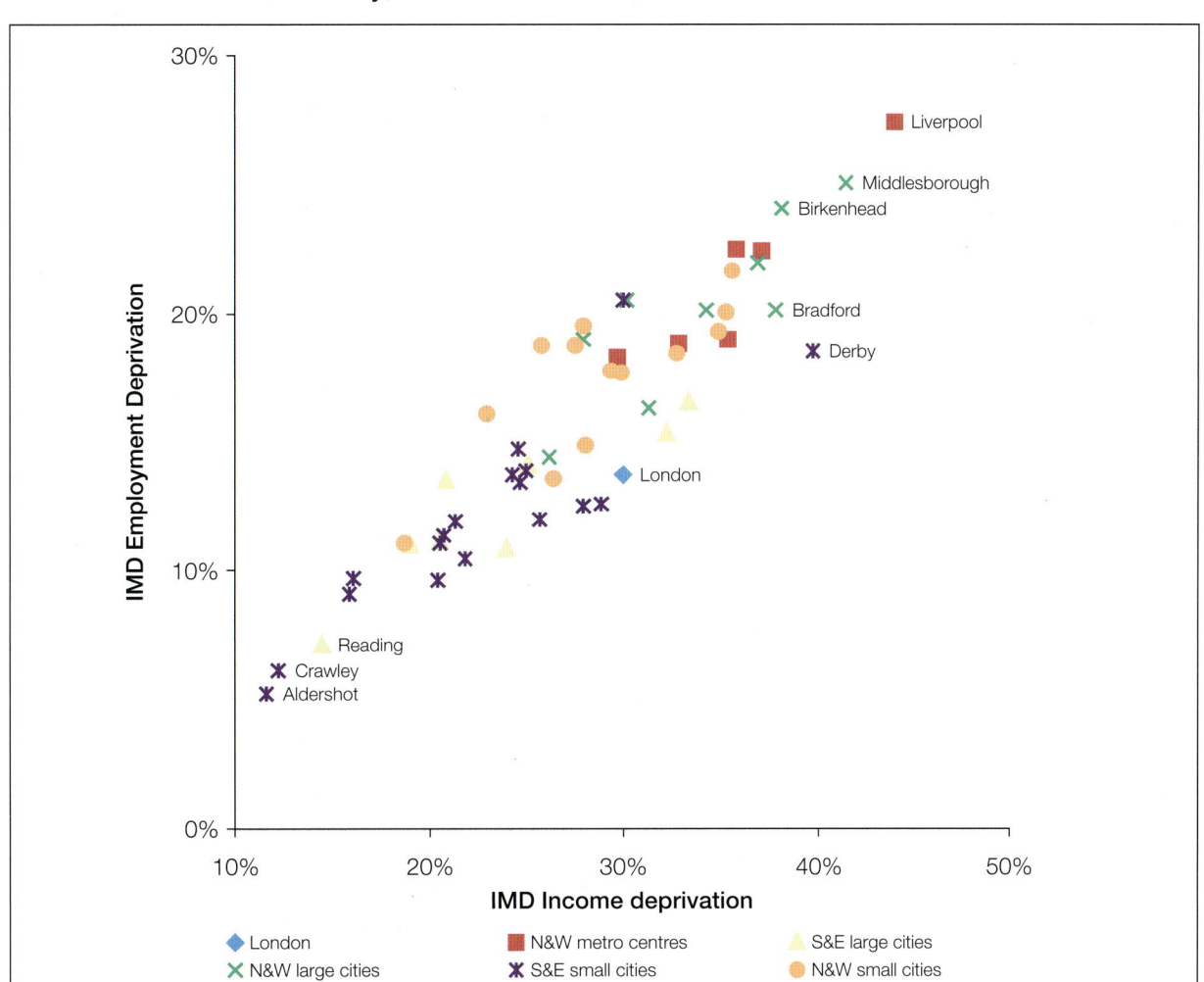

The overall level of worklessness in cities

5.4.4   Registered unemployment is an incomplete measure of labour market conditions because of the big growth in recorded economic inactivity at the expense of the 'claimant count' as people registered for sickness and disability benefits. Consequently it has become common to refer instead to the broader concept of 'worklessness'. This includes people of working age who are out of work but most of whom are not actively looking for work. With the improvement in the UK labour market over the last decade, the Government has acknowledged the broader challenge of reducing worklessness.

5.4.5   Figure 5.12 shows the overall level of involuntary worklessness for the different settlement types. It shows that the problem is much bigger in cities in the north and west than in the south and east. Looked at more closely, both urban size and region seem to matter, although the regional dimension matters more. Every type of settlement in the north and west does worse than every type in the south and east. London's position is consistent with its size and region.

5.4.6   The level of involuntary worklessness varies enormously for individual cities. The disparities are naturally much wider than between different categories of city. Liverpool has by far the highest level of worklessness, followed by Sunderland and Barnsley. Aldershot has the lowest level of worklessness, followed by Reading and Crawley. The metropolitan centres vary quite widely, with Leeds the best performing. Hastings and Mansfield stand apart from the other large and small cities in the south and east for relatively high worklessness. York stands apart from everywhere else in the north and west with low worklessness. London is in the middle of the spectrum – well below worklessness levels in the north and west, but above most places in the south and east.

Figure 5.12: Level of involuntary worklessness, by city type, 2004

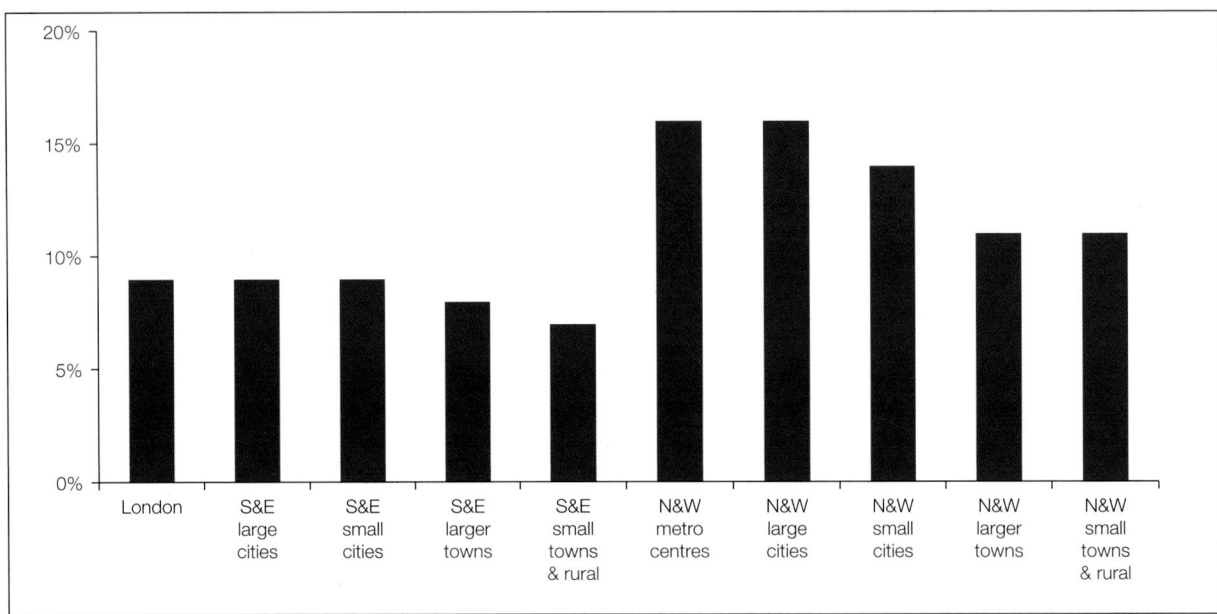

5.4.7   The employment rate measures the proportion of the working age population in paid work. It is effectively the opposite of the worklessness rate, ignoring the impact of full-time students, people with family and caring responsibilities, and early retired. Map 5.3 shows the employment rate for different cities. The importance of the regional dimension is clear. Cities with the lowest employment rates in England are Liverpool, Hull, Middlesbrough and Sunderland. Cities with a relatively high employment rate in the north and west include York, Burnley, Preston and Telford. Cities with the highest employment rate are all west and south of London – Swindon, Reading, Aldershot, Crawley and Worthing.

Map 5.3: Employment rate by individual city, 2003

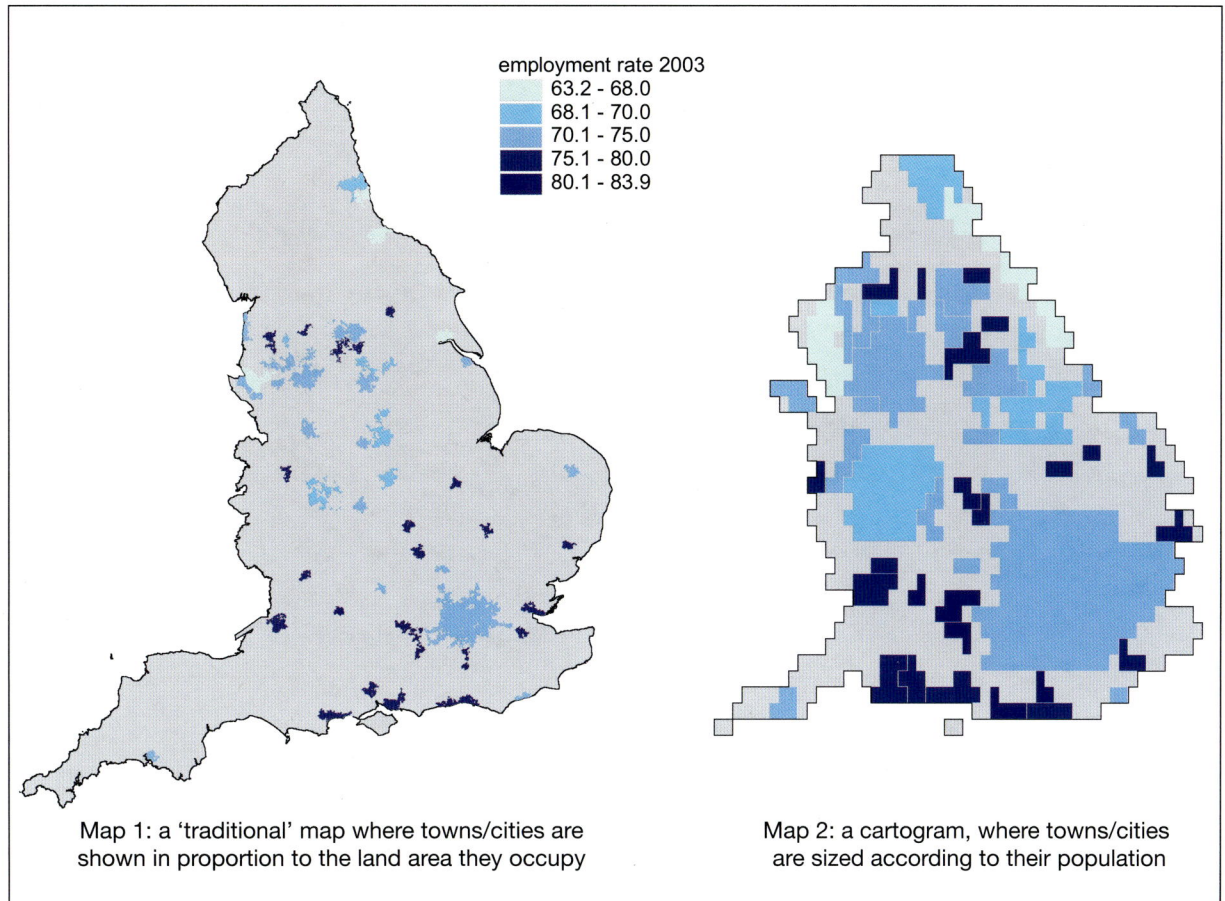

employment rate 2003
- 63.2 - 68.0
- 68.1 - 70.0
- 70.1 - 75.0
- 75.1 - 80.0
- 80.1 - 83.9

Map 1: a 'traditional' map where towns/cities are shown in proportion to the land area they occupy

Map 2: a cartogram, where towns/cities are sized according to their population

The location of workless neighbourhoods

5.4.8   The overall level of worklessness is highest in major cities in the north and west. Where are the neighbourhoods with the highest and lowest levels of worklessness? Figure 5.13 shows the proportion of neighbourhoods in each type of city which fall within the country's top and bottom 10 per cent of neighbourhoods defined by worklessness. Every bar in the graph would be 10 per cent if every settlement type had its proportionate share of these areas. In fact, the major cities in the north and west have more than two and a half times their share of workless neighbourhoods and very few of the well-off areas. Cities, towns and rural areas in the south and east have less than half their share of workless neighbourhoods and more than their share of well-off areas. The regional dimension therefore seems to be crucial. Settlement size also matters, particularly in the north and west. London actually has a slightly smaller share of workless neighbourhoods than other cities in the south and east.

Figure 5.13: Incidence of high and low workless neighbourhoods by city type, 2004

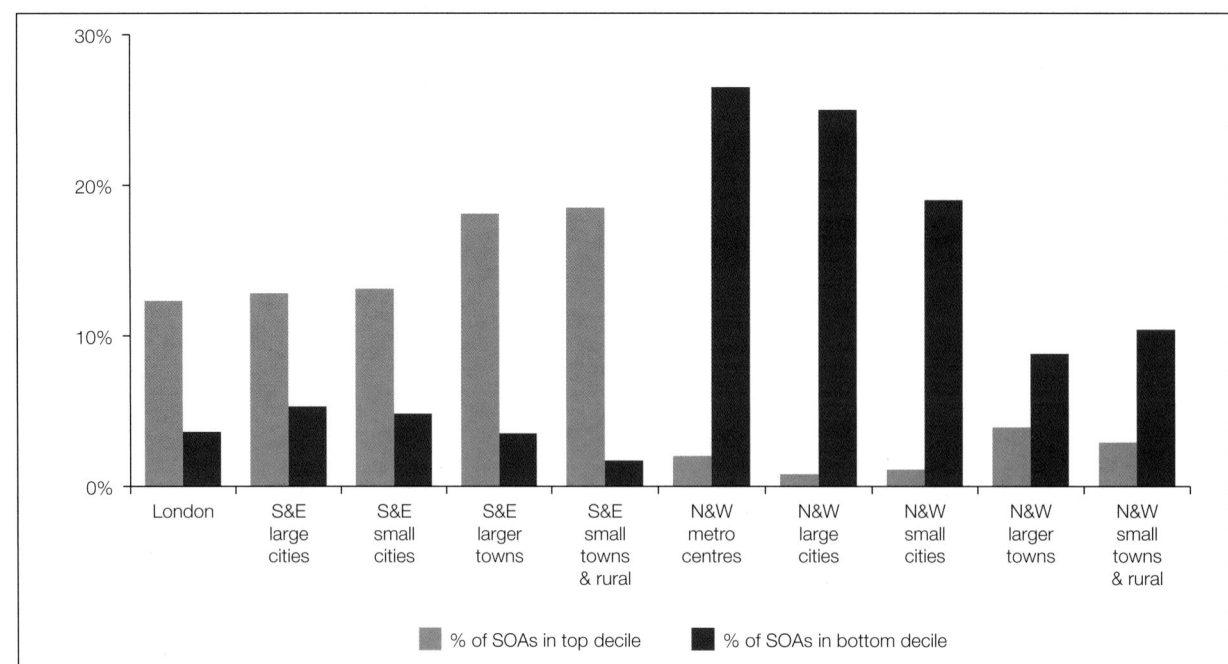

5.4.9   The regional contrast is very striking when individual cities are considered in figure 5.14. London and Bristol are quite unlike the major northern cities in having a larger share of well-off neighbourhoods than workless neighbourhoods. In complete contrast, more than half of the neighbourhoods in Liverpool come into the category of the highest workless neighbourhoods in the country. This is far higher than anywhere else.

Figure 5.14: Incidence of high and low workless neighbourhoods by major city, 2004

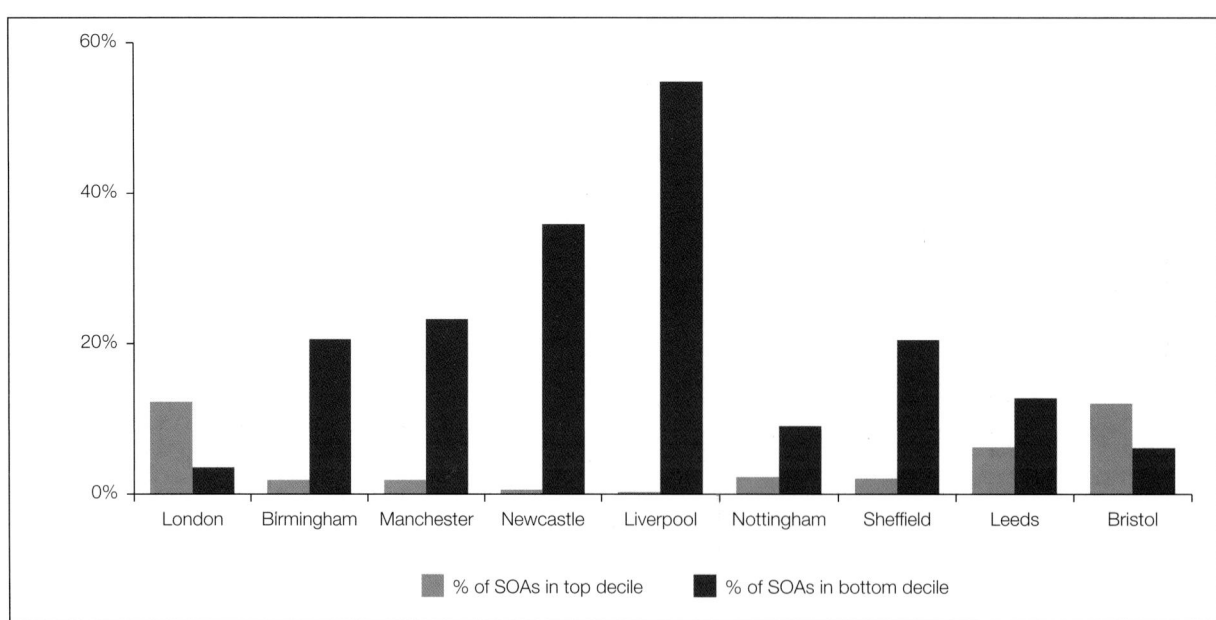

Employment rates for ethnic minority groups

5.4.10　The employment rate for the Non-White population in the UK was 58.4 per cent in 2003/04 compared with 75.6 per cent for Whites. This is obviously a sizeable disparity, attributable to a range of factors including lower skills and qualifications, cultural differences among some groups, for example, attitudes to women working and racial discrimination in the workplace. This employment gap is also reflected in lower average earnings for Non-Whites and is very important for reasons both of social cohesion and economic growth – including making more effective use of a changing labour force and removing barriers to effective economic integration and upward mobility. Ethnic minority groups currently make up about 8 per cent of the UK population but will account for half the growth in the working age population over the next decade.

5.4.11　Data on the employment rate for Non-Whites are unavailable for the PUAs because of the small sample sizes in many areas. Indeed it is only available for a small number of urban local authorities outside London. Table 5.1 compares the employment rate for the whole population of each area with the employment rate for Non-Whites. In general the rates are higher for both groups in the south and east than in the north and west. In London, the biggest problems are in the boroughs of inner and east London. Elsewhere in the south and east, Nottingham and Leicester have low overall employment rates and Nottingham and Luton have very low rates for Non-Whites. In the north and west, every area has employment rates below the national average for both groups. Major cities like Manchester and Birmingham have very low employment rates for Non-Whites. Across England, the gap ranges from no less than 26.4 per cent in Blackburn to – 1 per cent in Sutton, where the employment rate for Non-Whites was higher than for Whites. The size of the gap is likely to be affected by a range of factors, including the proportion of the population that is Non-White, the composition of different minority groups some of whom – Indians and Chinese – are more successful in the labour market than others, the relative skills of the populations and the state of the local labour market.

Table 5.1: Employment rate for Non-Whites and all groups for selected local authorities, 2003

London	Working age employment rate for:		Outside London	Working age employment rate for:	
London boroughs	All (%)	Non-White (%)	Cities in S & E	All (%)	Non-White (%)
Sutton	79.6	80.6	Bristol	77.2	69.8
Merton	79.1	69.6	Peterborough	77.1	67.2
Croydon	75.8	69.5	Reading	77.8	64.8
Barnet	74.9	68.7	Leicester	63.8	57.4
Enfield	69.4	67.5	Luton	70.7	51.8
Hillingdon	77.4	66.3	Nottingham	62.4	48.9
Harrow	70.3	65.5			
Redbridge	70.9	64.7	Cities in N&W		
Greenwich	64.8	61.1	Coventry	71.3	58.3
Hounslow	71.6	60.6	Leeds	73.9	56.8
Ealing	70.2	60.2	Derby	72.0	54.6
Barking & Dagenham	64.5	59.6	Birmingham	64.1	48.5
Lewisham	69.4	59.4	Rochdale	69.1	47.9
Lambeth	68.3	58.9	Bradford	67.8	45.2
Wandsworth	74.6	58.3	Manchester	58.9	43.6
Waltham Forest	68.7	58.3	Blackburn	67.4	41.0
Brent	62.7	56.5			
Southwark	64.1	54.3			
Hammersmith & Fulham	69.4	54.3			
Westminster	64.1	49.9			
Camden	66.4	48.8			
Kensington & Chelsea	64.0	47.3			
Newham	52.7	47.0			
Haringey	63.4	46.9			
Hackney	60.0	44.0			
Islington	62.7	44.0			
Tower Hamlets	52.5	33.4			

Source: Annual Local Area Labour Force Survey, 2002/03

Recent improvement in employment trends

5.4.12 Changes in the employment rate provide an insight into whether conditions have been improving in different cities. Table 5.2 shows the overall employment rate for the six different types of city and the rest of England over the last decade. Although towns and rural areas have consistently had the highest employment rates, the general trend in all categories has been one of improvement, including cities in the north and west. This is an important turnaround from the two previous decades. London and the south and east achieved significant gains between 1994 and 2000, but they have fallen back slightly since then. In contrast, cities in the north and west have continued to make progress. Given the legacy of industrial decline and deconcentration discussed above, it is clearly important that this is sustained.

Table 5.2 Employment rate by city type, 1994-2003 (%)

	1994	1997	2000	2003
London	68.2	71.3	72.7	71.5
South and east large cities	72.0	75.1	77.5	76.6
South and east small cities	73.7	74.8	78.2	77.2
Metropolitan centres	66.1	68.3	69.8	70.6
North and west large cities	67.1	68.7	70.0	71.6
North and west small cities	70.5	70.7	74.4	74.6
Rest of England	75.2	77.3	78.5	78.5

Source: Labour Force Survey, quarterly unweighted data.

5.4.13 Figure 5.15 confirms the slight downturn in employment conditions in all areas of the south and east over the last two years or so, compared with a small upturn in all areas of the north and west. The improvement in the position of cities in the north and west is better than the metropolitan centres. The greatest employment challenges remain there.

Figure 5.15: Employment rate trends by city type, 2000–2004

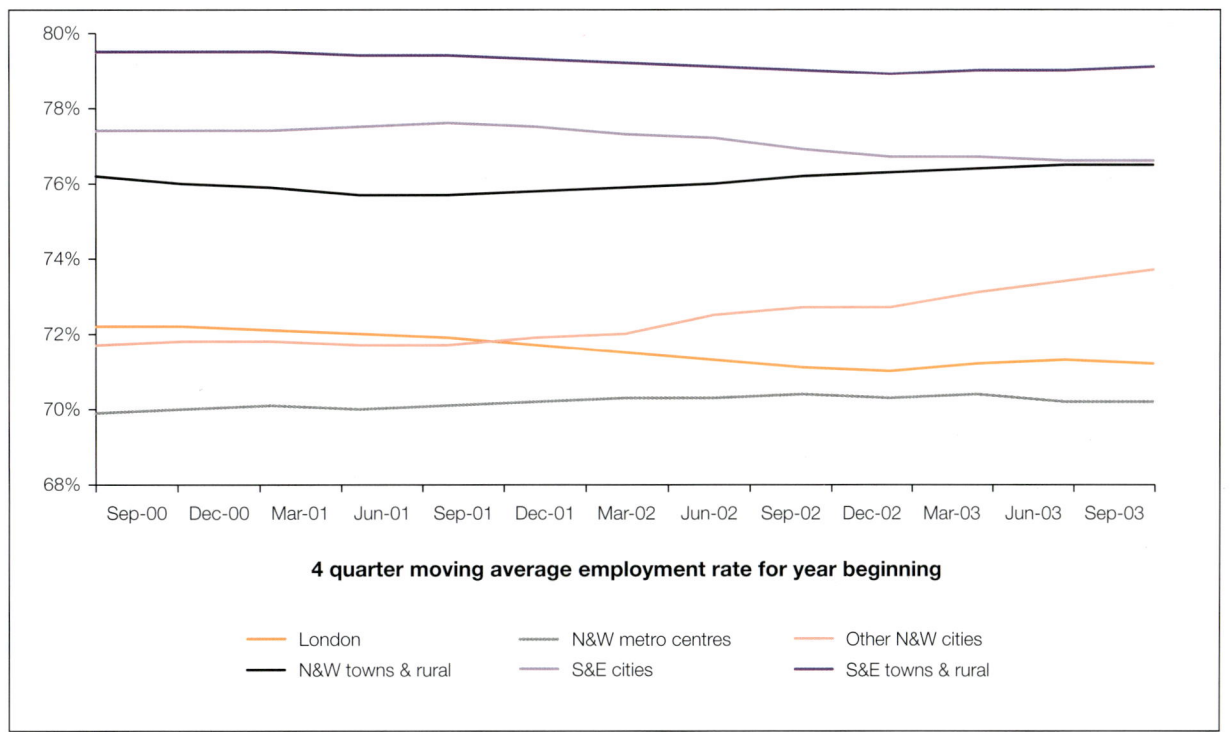

5.4.14 The balance sheet on worklessness:

- Cities with high worklessness have low incomes, so increasing employment is a key to tackling deprivation.

- Involuntary worklessness is higher in cities in the north and west.

- The employment rates for people with disabilities and for the over-50s are lower than average, with cities in the north and west worst off.

- The employment rate for Non-Whites is much lower than for Whites.

- Conditions have improved although there is variation between cities.

5.5 Education and skills

5.5.1 Learning and earning were not always intimately connected in Britain. During the industrial era and until fairly recently, there were many well-paid manual jobs available in manufacturing that required no formal qualifications. However, circumstances have changed a great deal. Education and skills now have a big influence on career prospects and lifetime earnings. Low skills and poor qualifications severely limit people's chances of gaining secure employment and are associated with household poverty and neighbourhood deprivation. They relate directly to two of the three core dimensions of social cohesion: social inequality and social exclusion. Poor schools also influence where people with a choice decide to live. It contributes to selective out-migration from cities and segregation within them, which affects social relationships. In addition, human capital influences the productivity and performance of the economy. This is another reason why improving people's skills and qualifications is a major objective of government policy at local and national levels.

5.5.2 The main questions addressed in this section are:

- How does the skills base vary between regions, cities and towns?

- Is settlement size or regional location a stronger source of differentiation?

- Has the proportion of people with degrees been increasing faster in some places than in others?

- Where are the neighbourhoods with the lowest and highest educational performance?

- How do school results vary across the country and have recent improvements been spread evenly?

The skills base of cities

5.5.3 The level of skills and qualifications varies significantly across the country. Figure 5.16 summarises a complex picture by distinguishing between people of working age with no qualifications, people with degrees or equivalent qualifications, and people in between. The intermediate group includes people with NVQ1, NVQ2, NVQ3 and trade apprenticeships. The qualifications which are equivalent to degrees are mostly medical qualifications.

5.5.4 The first and most important observation is that cities in the north and west have substantially more people with no qualifications than places in the south and east. There is little variation between types of settlement in the south and east in this respect. In contrast, there is an apparent connection between city size and the proportion of the population with no qualifications in the north and west – the larger the city the more unqualified people there are. This is likely to reflect the historical development of former industrial cities – the larger the more successful they were, but the bigger the legacy of low qualifications. Map 5.4 shows the detailed geography of people with no qualifications, confirming the significance of the regional dimension and city size in the north and west.

Map 5.4: Proportion of working age population with no qualifications, 2003

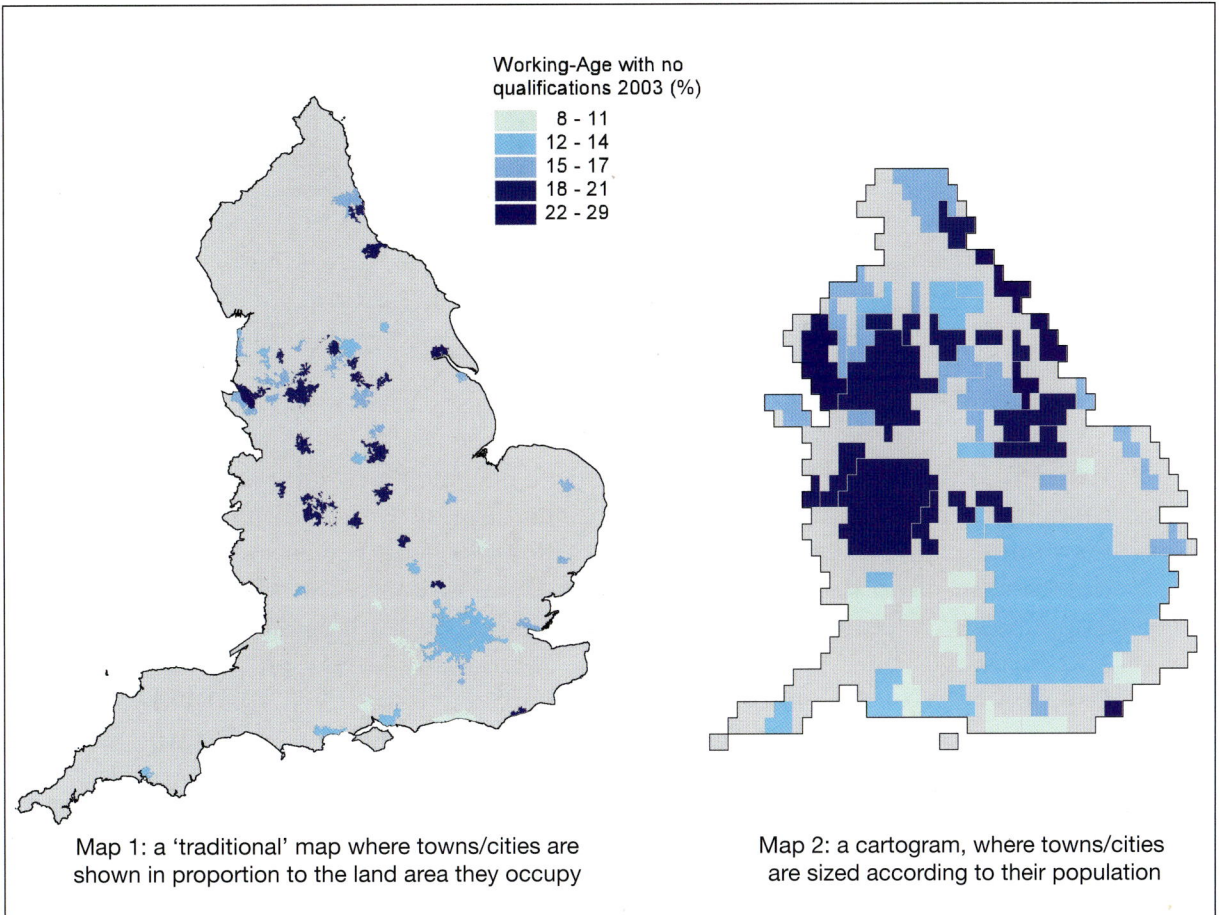

Working-Age with no qualifications 2003 (%)

- 8 - 11
- 12 - 14
- 15 - 17
- 18 - 21
- 22 - 29

Map 1: a 'traditional' map where towns/cities are shown in proportion to the land area they occupy

Map 2: a cartogram, where towns/cities are sized according to their population

5.5.5   Turning to the graduate population, cities in the north and west have fewer people with degrees than elsewhere in the country. London has the highest proportion of graduates, followed by other large cities in the south and east. It appears from this that large cities in the south and east are slightly more attractive to graduates than smaller cities, towns and rural areas, but the opposite seems to be the case in the north and west.

Figure 5.16: Skills of the working age population by city type, 2003

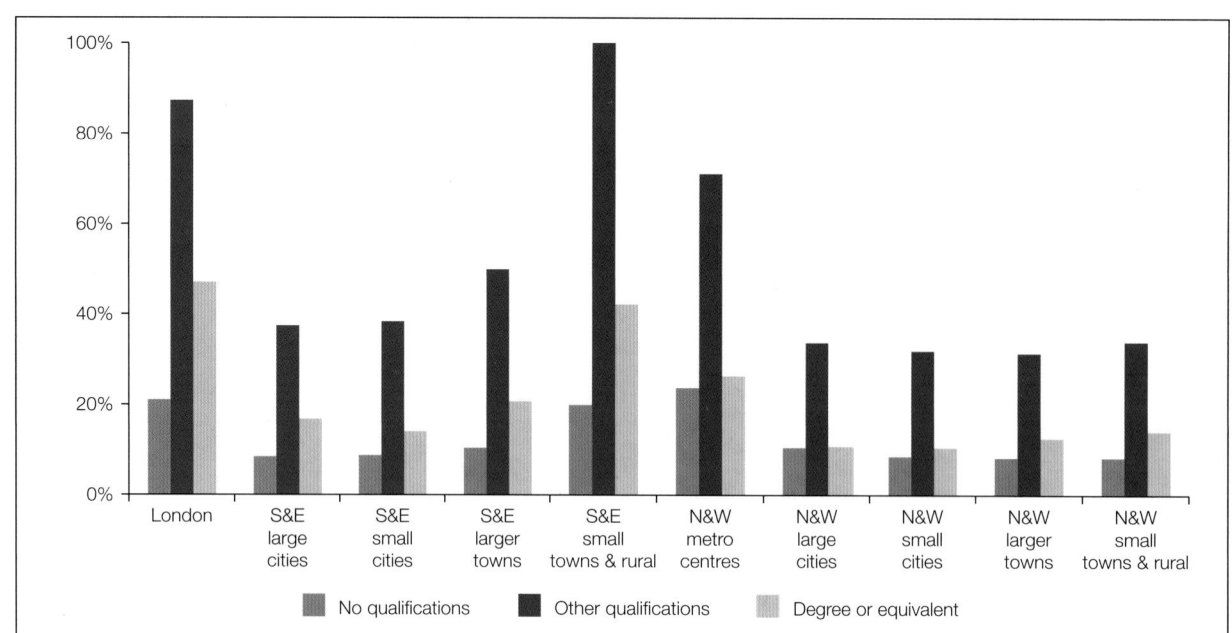

5.5.6   Four of the six cities with the largest proportion of people with no
qualifications are in the north and west – Liverpool, Hull, Stoke and Barnsley.
Ipswich and Leicester are the other two. The cities with fewest people with no
qualifications are Crawley, Cambridge, Reading and Aldershot – all in the
south and east. In terms of graduates, the cities with fewest people with
degrees are all in the north – Hull, Mansfield, Grimsby, Sunderland and Stoke.
The cities with most people with degrees are Cambridge, Oxford, Brighton
and Reading. There is generally a close relationship between places where
few people have no qualifications and many have degrees, and vice versa.
There has been a big increase in the proportion of people in England with
degrees in the last two decades. But the increase has not been distributed
evenly across cities and towns. The first and most important point is that the
disparity has been widening between cities which already had many graduates
in 1981 and those that did not. Cities such as Cambridge, Oxford, London,
Reading, Brighton, York and Bristol – all in the south and east except for York
– have experienced dramatic increases, and from a strong position to begin
with. London's increase between 1991 and 2001 is very striking. At the other
end of the spectrum, cities such as Mansfield, Hull, Grimsby, Barnsley,
Doncaster, Stoke and Sunderland – all in the north and west – have had much
smaller increases, and from a low base. The metropolitan centres performed
quite well between 1991 and 2001, although less well than some of the large
cities in the south and east.

Variations in educational attainment

5.5.7   Schooling is the foundation for high-level skills and qualifications. One of the
key measures of educational performance is the proportion of 15-year-olds
who achieve five or more GCSEs with grades A*-C. Figure 5.17 shows the
results for 2002/03 for different places by gender. It is clear that females
consistently perform better than males. Beyond this there are wide variations
in the results achieved in different settlement types. The biggest variation is

between cities, on the one hand, and towns and rural areas, on the other. In addition, places in the south and east tend to achieve better results than equivalent places in the north. London's position is better than the other city types, but worse than towns and rural areas.

Figure 5.17: GCSE results by gender – 15-year-olds with 5+ grades A*-C, 2003

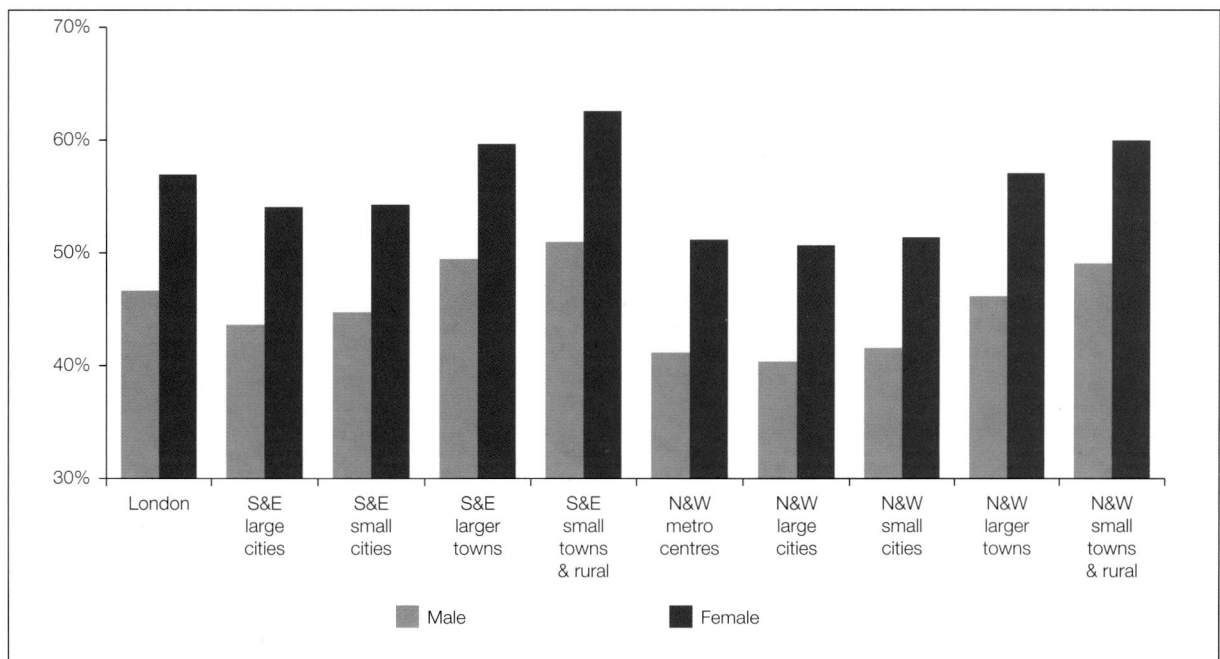

5.5.8   The variations between cities are wide, both within categories and between them. The pass rate in Southend in 2004 was 60 per cent higher than in Mansfield. Other poor results were in Bradford, Hull and Barnsley. Good results were in Bournemouth, Gloucester, York, Preston, Wakefield and generally in towns and rural areas. London's position is better than all the other large cities except Bournemouth and Reading. There has been a big all-round improvement, with some apparent catch-up between many major cities in the north and west and the rest. Nevertheless, the gap remains.

More comprehensive measures of education

5.5.9   The educational attainment of 15-year-olds is only one of many measures of educational performance. The IMD provides a broader basket of measures of educational deprivation, including the average points score of pupils at Key Stages 2, 3 and 4, secondary school absence rates, the proportion of people not staying on in school after 16 and the proportion of those under 21 not entering higher education. Figure 5.18 shows the mean score of this indicator for different settlement types. All city types perform considerably worse than towns and rural areas, with London in between. Major cities in the north and west are the most deprived in educational terms on this measure.

Figure 5.18: Educational deprivation of children (IMD mean score), 2004

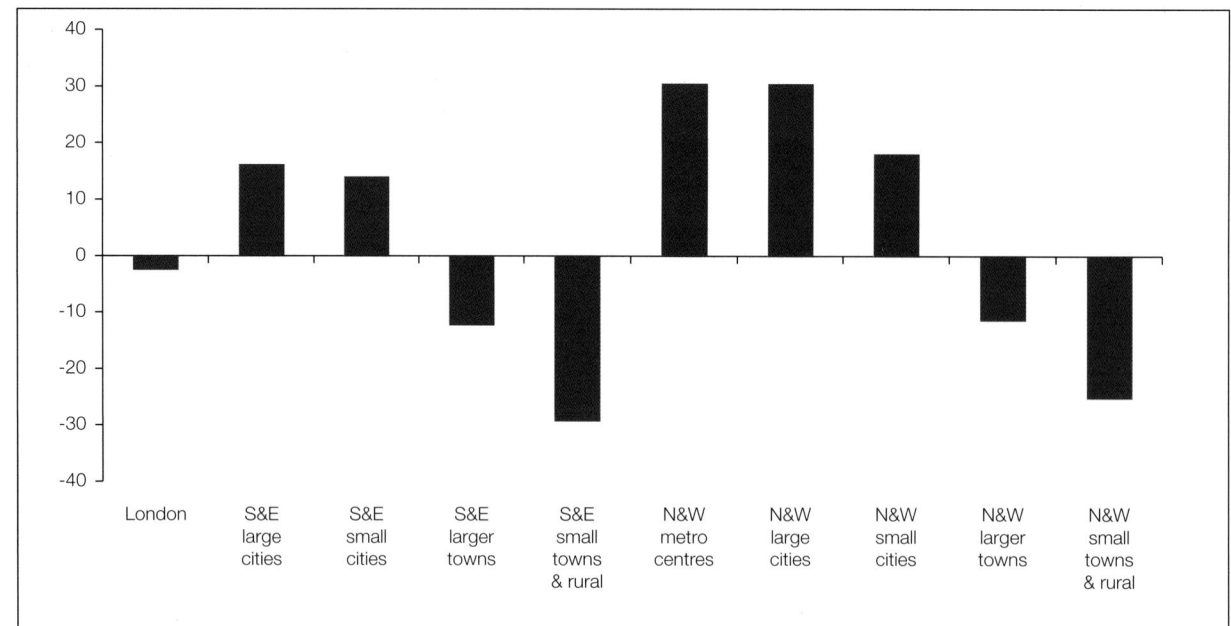

5.5.10 Once again the variations are very wide within and between categories. None of the metropolitan centres perform well. The city with the poorest educational performance for children is Hull, followed by Barnsley, Hastings, Liverpool, Doncaster and Mansfield. Cities with strong performance include Aldershot, Reading, Crawley, York, Warrington and Preston. The last three of these are exceptional among cities in the north and west.

5.5.11 Figure 5.19 shows a strong relationship between the overall level of deprivation in a city and the proportion of its population with no qualifications. Cities in the north and west tend to be concentrated in the top right end of the distribution and cities in the south and east in the bottom left. There are complex two-way causal processes at work suggesting that improved educational performance is unlikely to be a quick fix for other urban problems.

Figure 5.19: Relationship between deprivation and lack of qualifications, 2004

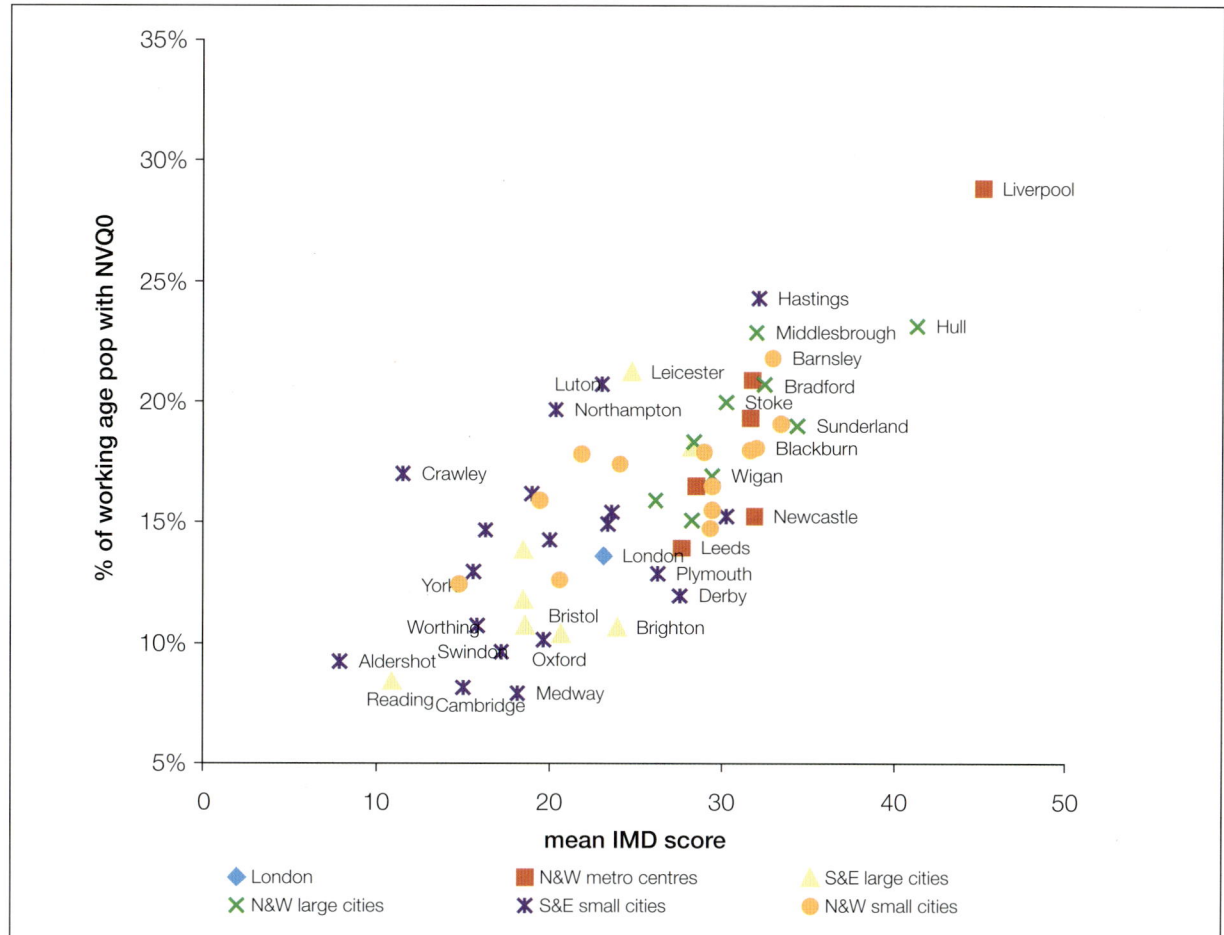

5.5.12 The balance sheet on education:

- Cities in the north and west have more people with no qualifications and fewer people with degrees than elsewhere.

- There is a strong relationship between deprivation and people with no qualifications at city level.

- The proportion of people with degrees has risen everywhere in the last decade, particularly in cities that already had many graduates.

- There is a big variation in the level of educational attainment between cities and the rest of the country. But the gap has narrowed slightly in recent years.

5.6   Crime and community safety

5.6.1   Reducing crime is a major objective of government policy at local and national levels. For example, the national strategy for neighbourhood renewal includes floor targets for reducing the gap between the highest Crime and Disorder Reduction Partnership Areas and the best comparable areas. It aimed to reduce:

- vehicle crime by 30 per cent from 1998/99 to 2004 in all areas;

- domestic burglary by 25 per cent from 1998/99 to 2005 in all areas; and

- robbery by 14 per cent from 1999/00 to 2005 in the ten Street Crime Initiative areas.

5.6.2   The main questions addressed in this section are:

- How do different common crimes vary between regions, cities and towns?

- Do settlement size and regional location affect the rate of crime?

- Have common crimes been increasing or declining in recent years?

- Which cities have had the best and worst experience of crime?

- Are crime patterns related to socio-economic factors?

Overall patterns of crime

5.6.3   The level of crime tends to be higher in larger cities than in smaller cities, and higher in the north and west than in the south and east. However, there are substantial variations between individual cities. Cities in the north and west with low rates of crime include Blackpool, Preston and Warrington. Cities with low crime in the south and east include a variety of places circling London, such as Swindon, Worthing, Aldershot, Crawley, Medway and Southend. Cities with higher rates of recorded crime include Hull, Grimsby, Nottingham and Peterborough (Map 5.5).

Map 5.5: Incidence of crime by individual city, 2003/04

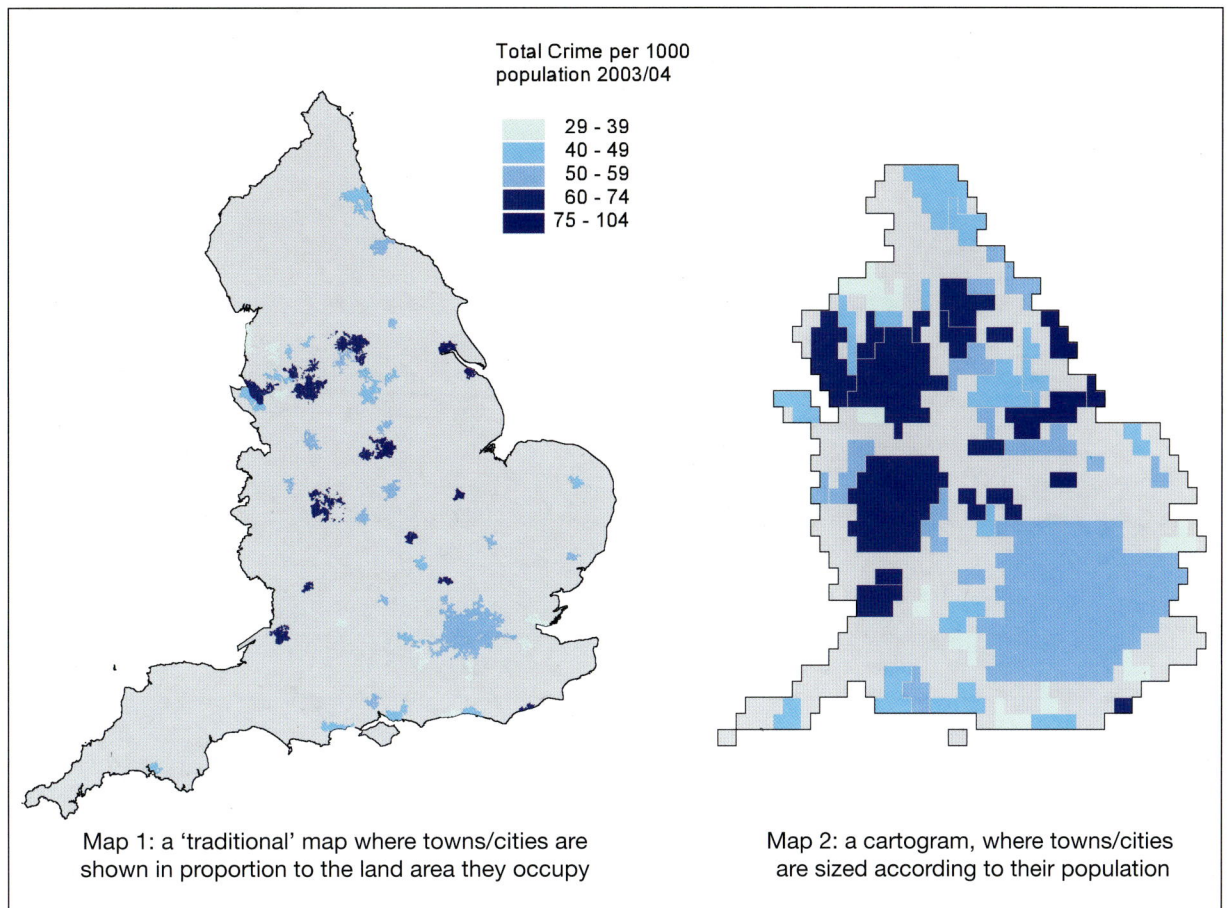

Total Crime per 1000
population 2003/04

29 - 39
40 - 49
50 - 59
60 - 74
75 - 104

Map 1: a 'traditional' map where towns/cities are shown in proportion to the land area they occupy

Map 2: a cartogram, where towns/cities are sized according to their population

Robberies

5.6.4   The rate of robberies per 1,000 population varies a great deal across the country, and broadly in line with city size. London has the highest rate, followed by the metropolitan centres, large cities, smaller cities and other settlements. It is difficult to detect a broad trend over the period 1999-2004 because of the volatile pattern with a peak in 2001/02. But comparing 1999 and 2004 there appears to have been a small increase in every category of city (Figure 5.20).

Figure 5.20: Robberies by city type

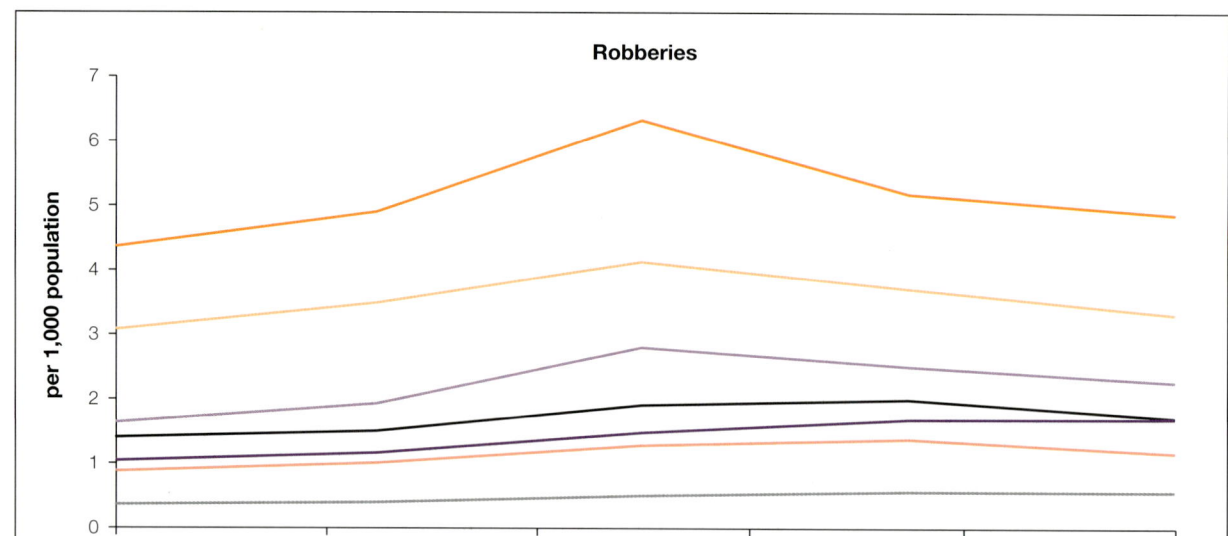

5.6.5   Looked at in more detail, the relationship between size and robbery rate is less straightforward. Among England's major cities, London, Manchester and Birmingham have the highest rates, followed by Bristol, Leeds, Nottingham and Liverpool. Sheffield and Newcastle have the lowest rates. Most cities peaked in 2001/02. Overall, most cities experienced an increase in the robbery rate between 1999 and 2004. Nottingham experienced the largest increase over the period, from having one of the lowest rates to one of the highest (Figure 5.21).

Figure 5.21: Robberies by major city

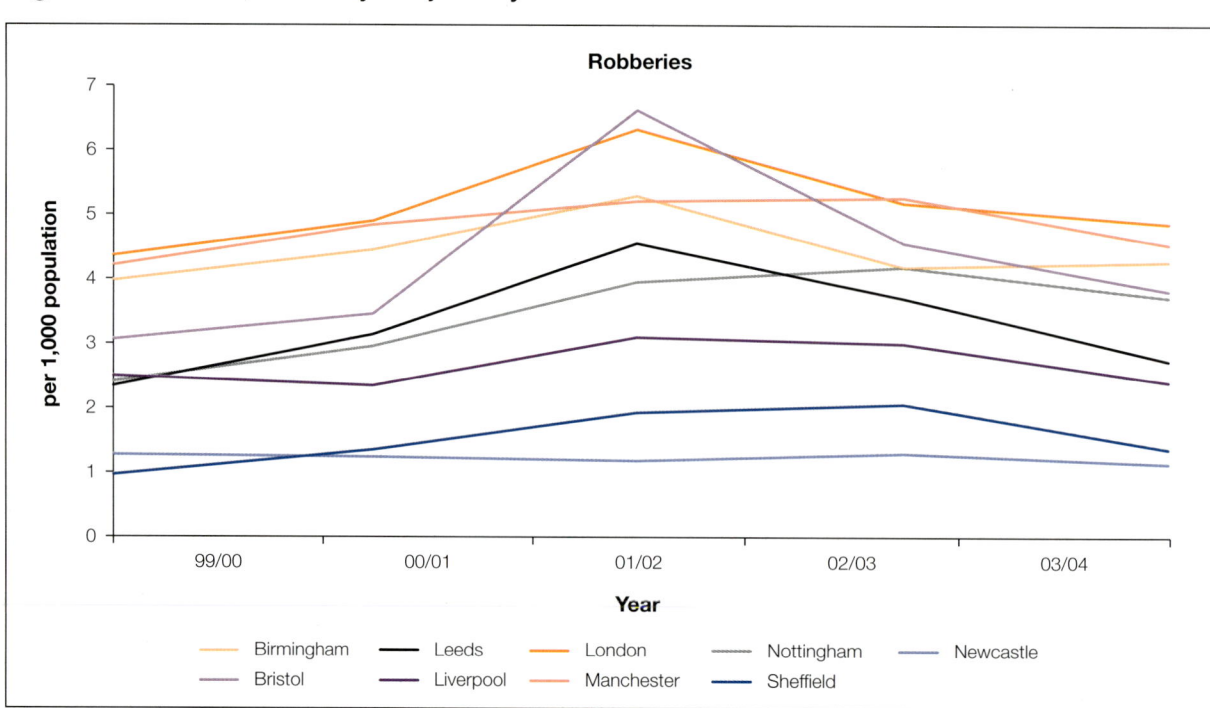

Vehicle crime

5.6.6   Rates of vehicle crime per 1,000 population do not show such a strong relationship with city size, partly because London has fewer of these than the large cities and the differences between city types is much smaller than for robberies. Vehicle crimes are much lower outside the cities. In contrast to robberies, rates of vehicle crime declined slightly over the period 1999/00 to 2003/04, but particularly in the metropolitan centres, where the rate fell to a similar level to the other types of city (Figure 5.22).

Figure 5.22: Vehicle crime by city type

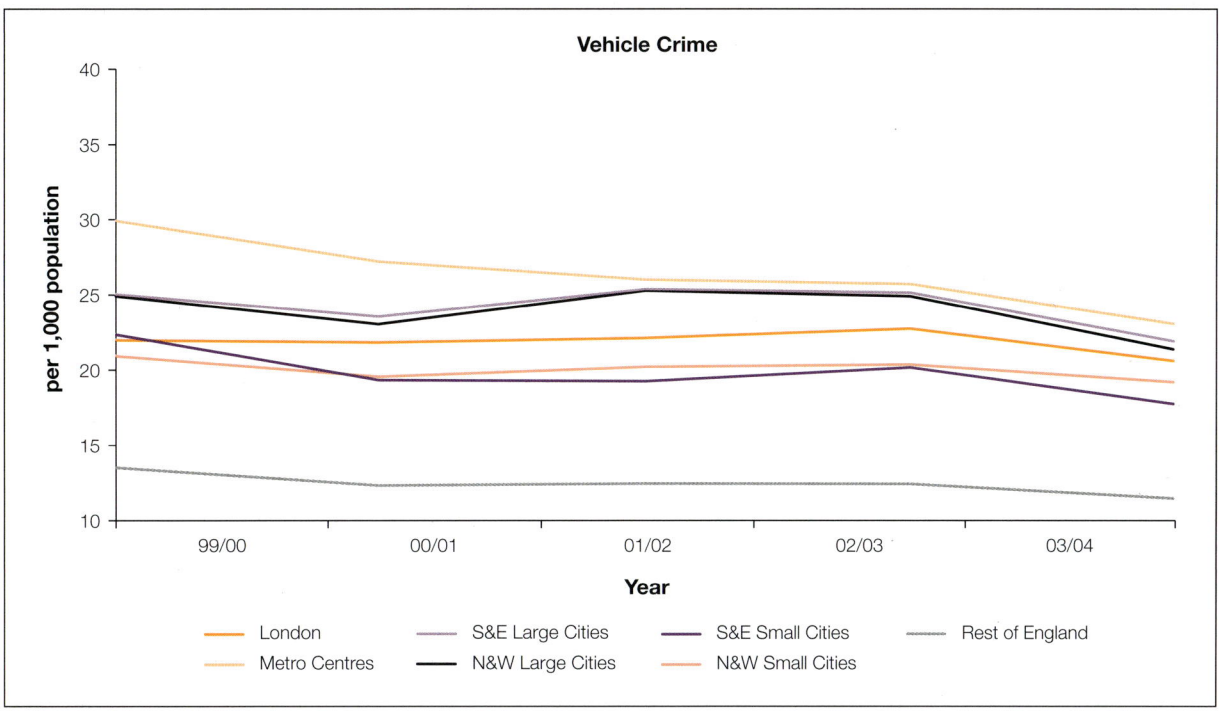

5.6.7   The variation between individual cities is greater than between city types. Most cities experienced a decline over the period 1999-2004 apart from Nottingham, which rose to the highest level among these cities, and Sheffield, which rose slightly. From having the highest rate of vehicle crime in 1999/00, Manchester enjoyed a very significant improvement. Liverpool and Birmingham also experienced consistent improvements. Newcastle enjoyed a decreasing rate of vehicle crime from an already low level (Figure 5.23).

Figure 5.23: Vehicle crime by major city

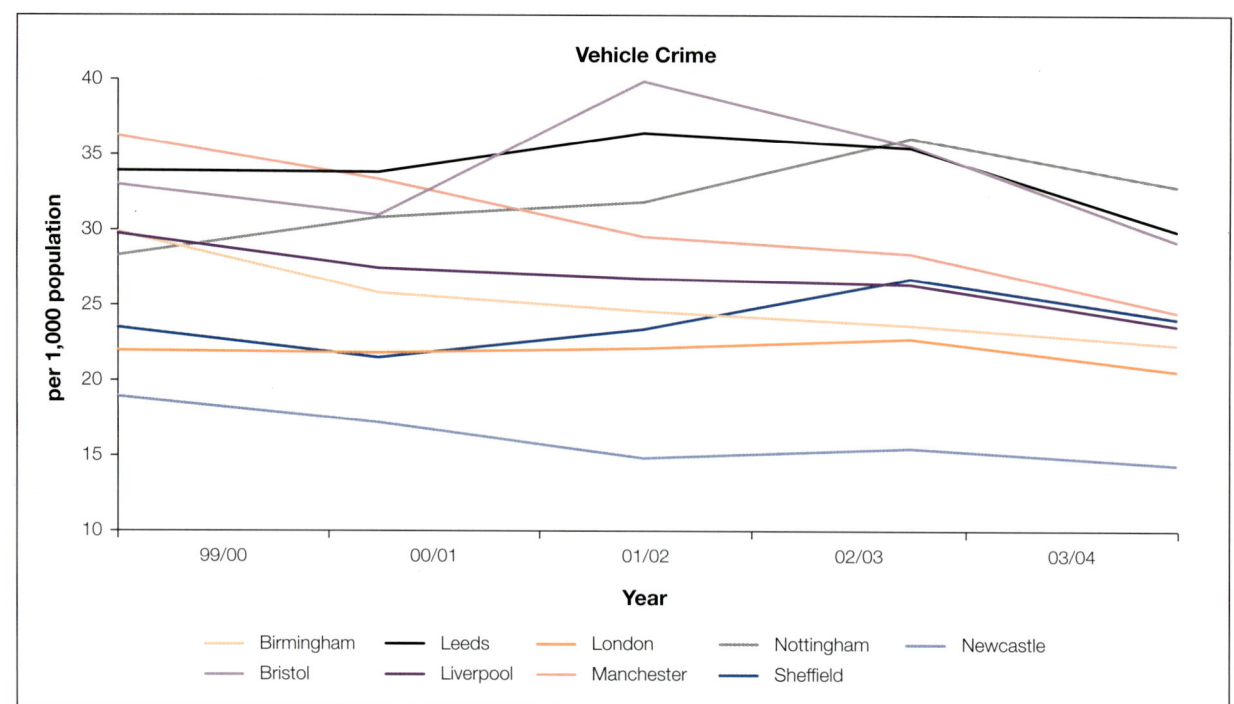

Burglaries

5.6.8   The pattern of burglaries is slightly different from vehicle crimes, being higher in the north and west than in the south and east. City size also seems to matter slightly, with the obvious exception of London, where burglaries are relatively low. Once again, the lowest rates of all are outside the cities. The trend over the period 1999-2004 was broadly stable, with a slight decline in most types of place (Figure 5.24).

Figure 5.24: Burglaries by city type

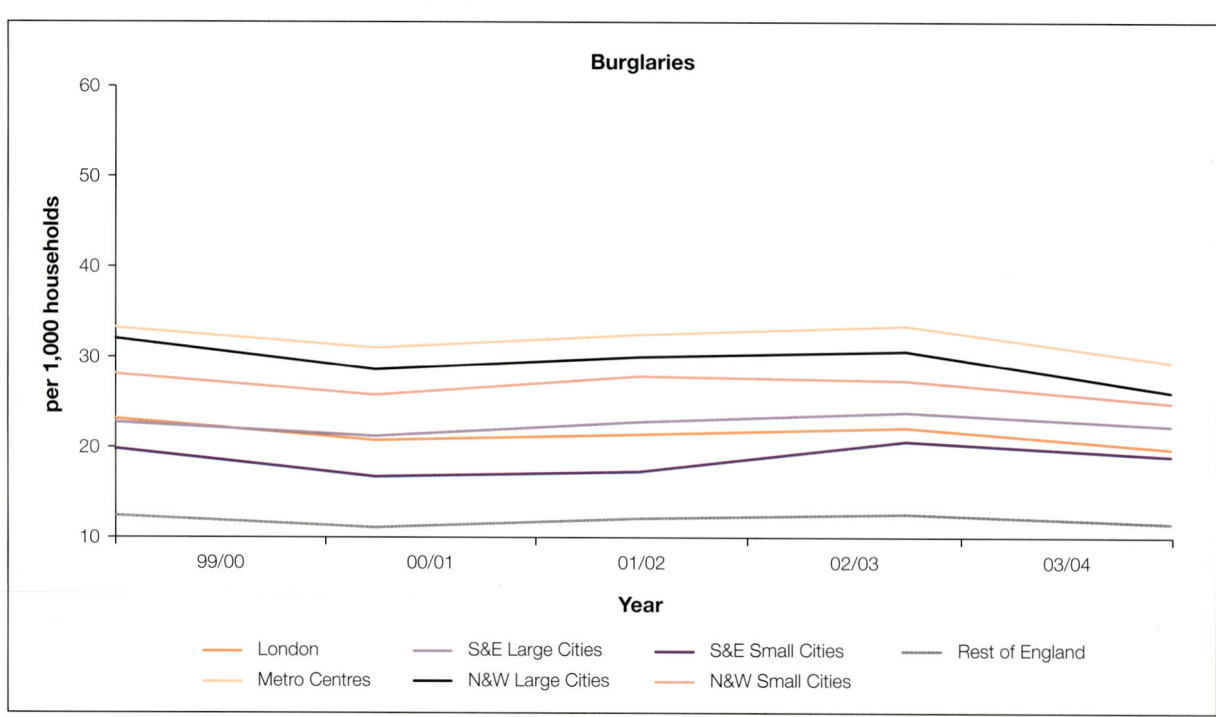

5.6.9   There are wide variations in the rate of burglaries between the major cities (Figure 5.25). Leeds has the highest rate, followed by Nottingham, which has experienced a steady rise. London and Newcastle have the lowest rate of burglaries. Manchester, Bristol, Birmingham, Liverpool and Sheffield enjoyed a decline in burglaries over the period.

Figure 5.25: Burglaries by major city

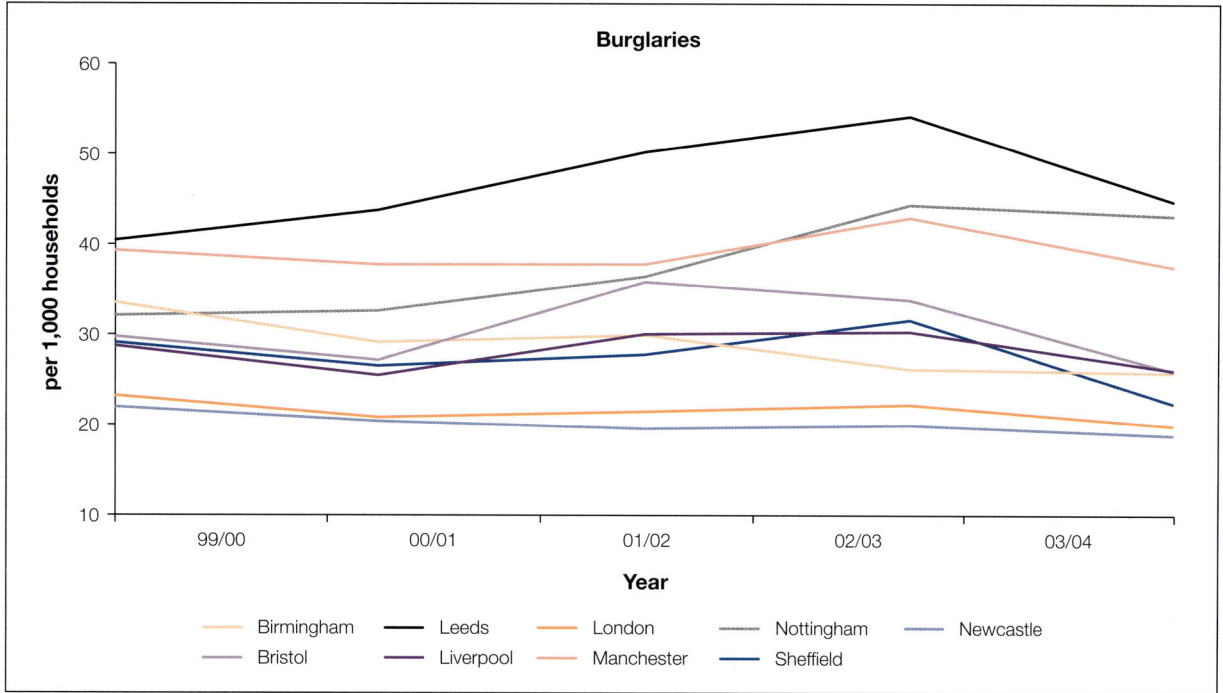

5.6.10   The balance sheet on crime:

- Crime is generally higher in cities than in towns and rural areas.

- Crime tends to be higher in larger cities than in smaller cities, and in the north and west than in the south and east.

- There are big variations between individual cities.

- Robberies generally increased slightly between 1999 and 2004, but peaked in 2001/02.

- Vehicle crime rates declined slightly between 1999 and 2004.

- Burglaries declined very slightly between 1999 and 2004.

5.7   Health

5.7.1   Health is a crucial aspect of the quality of life and a reflection of underlying social and economic conditions. Inequalities in life expectancy – premature mortality – and other health outcomes are among the most striking features of social cohesion or lack of cohesion. The state of health of individuals can be related to a variety of tangible and less tangible neighbourhood and community characteristics, including housing conditions, feelings of safety and security, involvement in physical activity and voluntary work, as well as unemployment, income, education and socio-economic status.

5.7.2   Health can also contribute to the state of cohesion in various ways. People who are unhealthy or have a limiting long-term illness tend to be disadvantaged in the labour market and have lower incomes. They are likely to be less involved in social, community and political activities. Consequently, they may feel more isolated and excluded from the normal day-to-day activities of civic society. Poor health also contributes to absenteeism from work, reduces the size of the effective workforce and can thereby constrain the performance of the economy.

5.7.3   The main questions addressed in this section are:

- How does health vary between regions, cities and towns?

- Is settlement size more significant than regional location?

- What has been the rate of improvement in different aspects of health in recent years?

- Which cities have experienced the greatest and least improvements?

- Are health patterns related to socio-economic conditions at city level?

Life expectancy

5.7.4   Life expectancy varies greatly between different parts of the country. People living in the south and east live longer than those in the north and west. People living in towns and rural areas also live longer than those in cities. Life expectancy has increased steadily over the decade 1992-2002. This increase is faster among men – two to three years – than women – one to two years, although women had a higher starting point. The gap between different parts of the country has not changed significantly over the last decade. Life expectancy also varies greatly between different major cities (Figure 5.26). Men in Bristol and London can expect to live three years longer than men in Liverpool. People everywhere are living longer than they were a decade ago, although the gap between different cities has not changed significantly.

Figure 5.26: Male life expectancy by city type

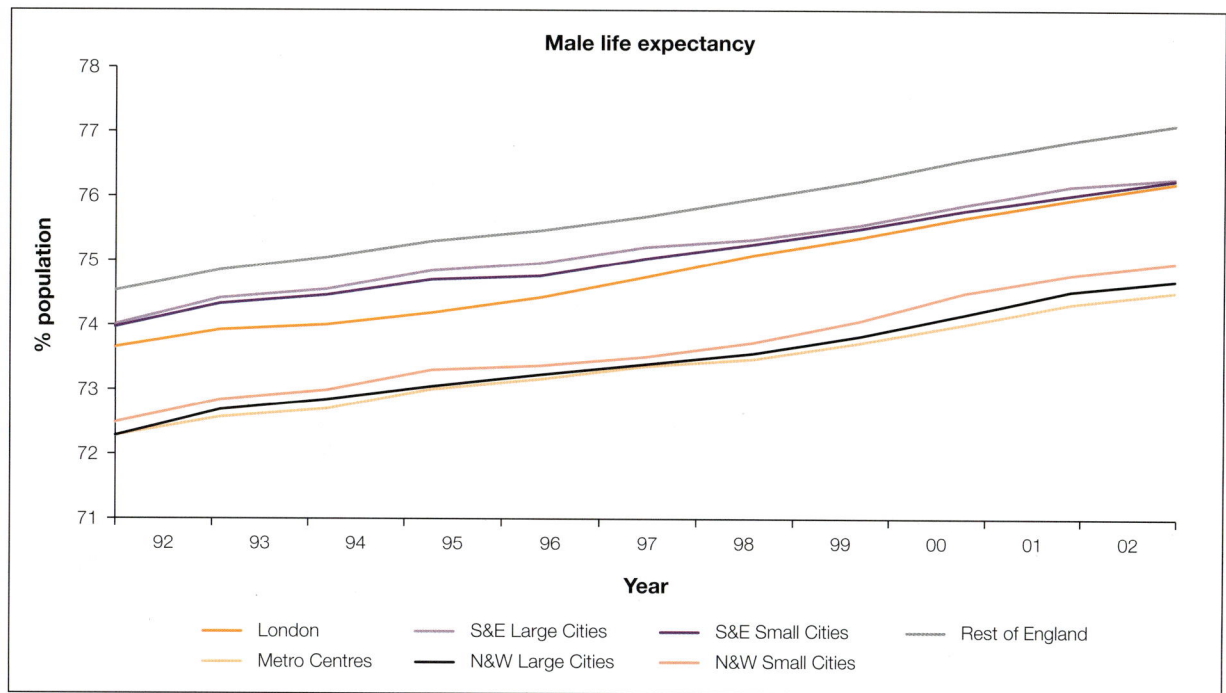

Long-term limiting illness

5.7.5   A much higher proportion of people in the north and west suffer from a long-term limiting illness than in the south and east (Figure 5.27). The size of cities or towns does not seem to affect the incidence of long-term limiting illness. London has the lowest rate. There was an increase in long-term limiting illness across the country between 1991 and 2001.

Figure 5.27: Long-term limiting illness by city type, 1991 and 2001

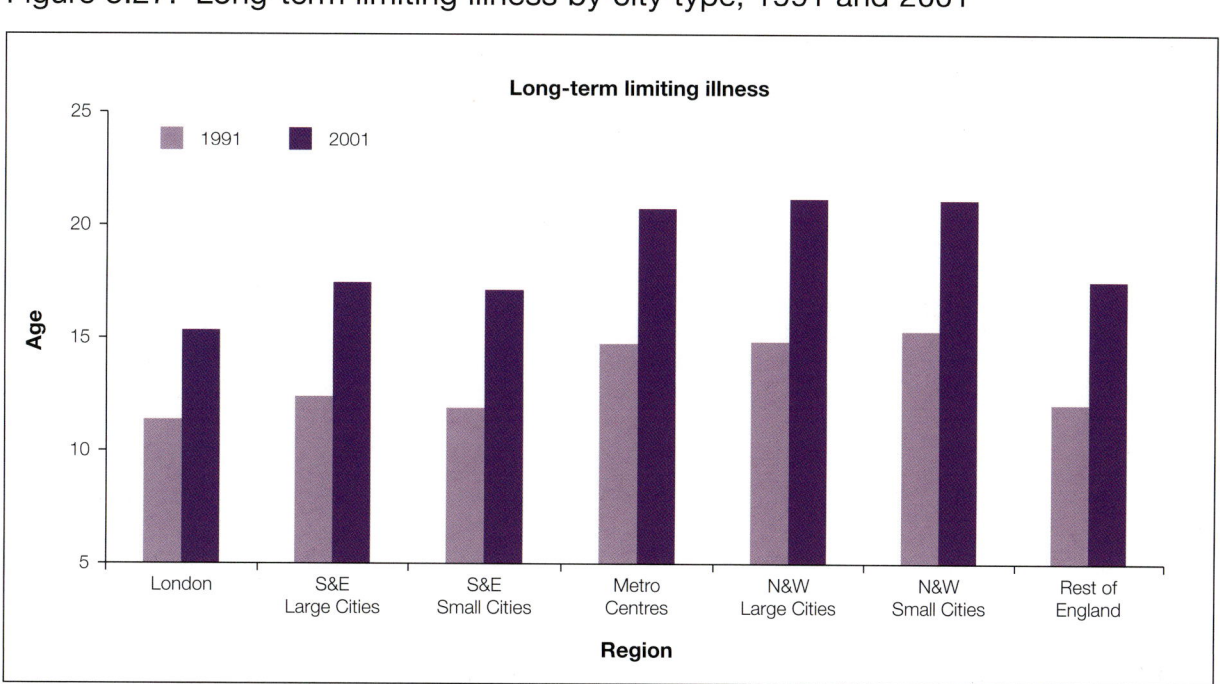

5.7.6   Long-term limiting illness also varies greatly between different major cities (Figure 5.28). Liverpool has the highest level, followed by Newcastle, and London has the lowest. The biggest increase in absolute terms between 1991 and 2001 was in Liverpool and the smallest in London.

Figure 5.28: Long-term limiting illness by major city, 1991 and 2001

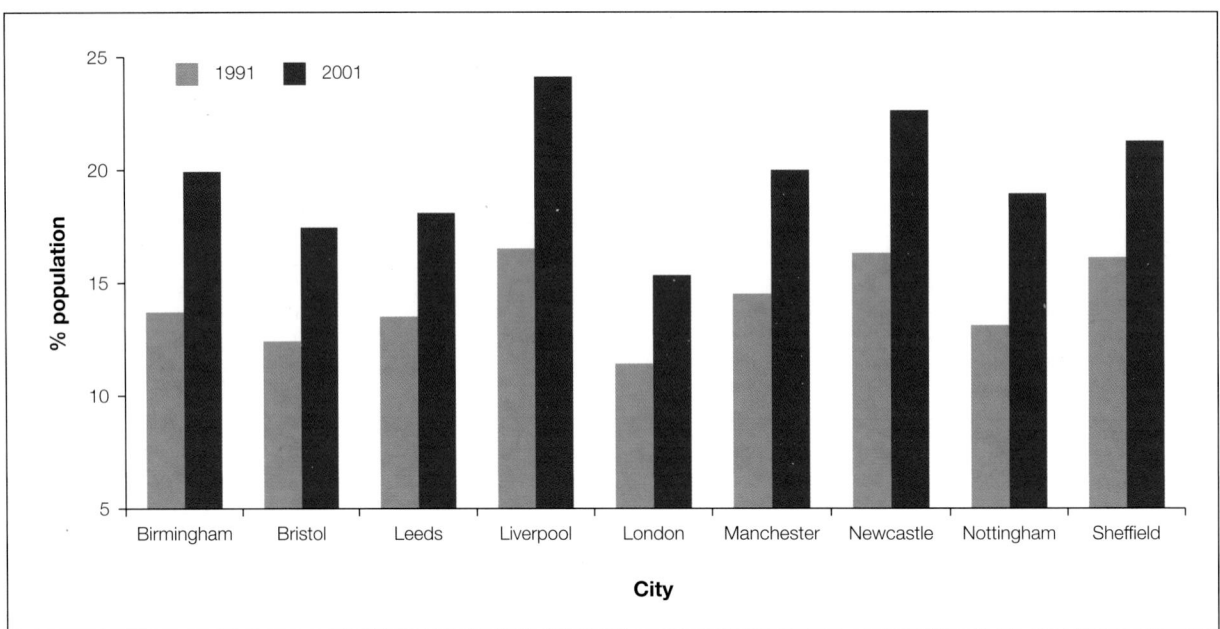

Health variations between cities

5.7.7   Many factors influence the health of individuals and therefore the wider population. Simple statistical analyses of the relationship between health and a range of socio-economic factors provided clues to the underlying processes. The strongest of the various relationships tested turned out to be between health and employment – see Figure 5.29. The correlation coefficient is 0.95, indicating a very strong positive relationship and convincing evidence that cities with high levels of unemployment have poor health.

Figure 5.29: IMD 2004 Health by Employment score over PUA

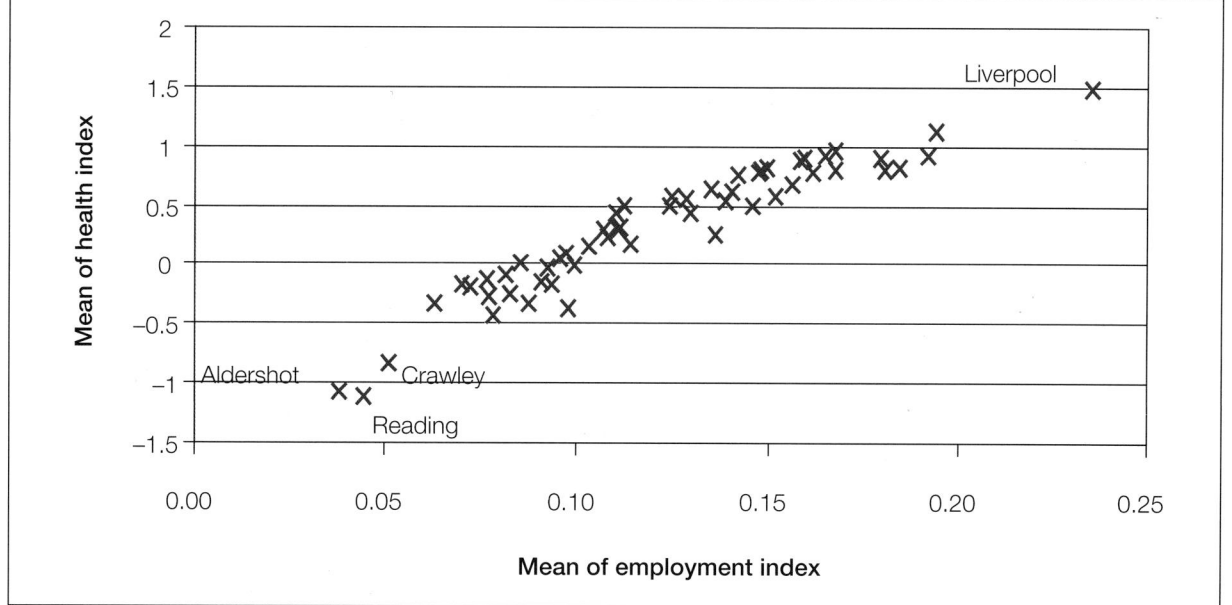

5.7.8   The balance sheet on health:

- Health conditions are generally improving and people everywhere are living longer.

- Employment, income and education are important determinants of health in cities.

- Cities and towns in the south and east have better all-round health profiles than the north and west. There is little sign that this gap has narrowed during the last decade.

- Larger cities tend to have worse health than towns and rural areas.

- London is an exception to this pattern. Its health profile is relatively good, although there are wide inequalities.

5.8   Social cohesion, segregation and integration

5.8.1   The themes of integration and segregation are directly relevant to the issues of social and community cohesion. The independent review team set up by the Home Office to examine the violent disorders in three northern English cities in 2001 concluded that housing, and in particular, residential segregation, were responsible for the disconnection between people of different cultural, religious and racial backgrounds (Home Office, 2001). This section reviews the arguments and evidence around integration and segregation and provides a new analysis of the nature, extent and significance of this phenomenon in England.

5.8.2   This section:

- describes the levels and patterns of segregation between Whites and Non-Whites, but also between White, Black and Asian groups;

- compares this with other forms of residential segregation, for example by social class;

- investigates whether segregation is associated with other social outcomes in cities;

- investigates whether segregation is increasing or decreasing.

Methods and data sources

5.8.3   Three sources of data were used: the Census 2001, the IMD and the SOCD. Ethnicity was defined by the main categories in the Census, i.e. visible minorities or Non-White groups and sub-divided for some analyses into Black (including Black Caribbean, Black African and Black Other), Asian (Indian, Pakistani, Bangladeshi, Other Asian), Chinese, and Other. The Index of Dissimilarity (ID) is used to measure segregation. It measures the unevenness in distribution between two social groups, e.g. a minority and a majority group. The ID score indicates the proportion of one group which would have to move in order for there to be no segregation between the groups, i.e. for the distribution of the two groups across space to be the same. The index varies in value between 0 and 100, with values under 40 generally considered as low segregation, 40 –59 moderately high, 60-69 high, and 70+ very high.

Levels and patterns of segregation

5.8.4   Table 5.3 shows the ID scores for all 56 cities for three types of segregation: White versus Non-White; White versus Asian; and White versus Black residents. In each case, the largest group of cities have moderately high segregation (ID 0.4-0.59) rather than high or very high segregation (ID 0.60+). However, there are more cities with high or very high segregation between Whites and Asians than between Whites and Blacks or Whites and Non-Whites (all Non-White minority groups).

Table 5.3: Segregation between Whites and ethnic minority groups, 2001

White/Non-White		White/Asian		White/Black	
City	ID Score	City	ID Score	City	ID Score
Blackburn	0.72	Blackburn	0.73	Barnsley	0.73
Bradford	0.71	Bradford	0.73	Sunderland	0.65
Burnley	0.68	Rochdale	0.71	Burnley	0.63
Rochdale	0.67	Burnley	0.70	Middlesbrough	0.62
Huddersfield	0.62	Derby	0.68	Leeds	0.60
Bolton	0.62	Huddersfield	0.66	Liverpool	0.59
Sheffield	0.59	Preston	0.66	Blackpool	0.59
Preston	0.59	Bolton	0.65	Manchester	0.59
Derby	0.59	Sheffield	0.64	Wakefield	0.58
Leicester	0.59	Manchester	0.63	Huddersfield	0.57
Birmingham	0.58	Birmingham	0.63	Grimsby	0.56
Middlesbrough	0.57	Middlesbrough	0.62	Sheffield	0.56
Manchester	0.57	Leicester	0.62	Bristol	0.54
Stoke	0.54	Wakefield	0.62	Birkenhead	0.53
Leeds	0.54	Stoke	0.61	Newcastle	0.53
Wakefield	0.52	Gloucester	0.59	Blackburn	0.52
Doncaster	0.49	Leeds	0.57	Birmingham	0.52
Liverpool	0.49	Doncaster	0.56	London	0.51
Newcastle	0.48	Peterborough	0.55	Warrington	0.51
Nottingham	0.48	Nottingham	0.55	Doncaster	0.50
Peterborough	0.47	Newcastle	0.53	Bradford	0.49
Hull	0.45	Liverpool	0.52	Nottingham	0.49
Sunderland	0.44	Hull	0.51	Preston	0.48
London	0.44	Luton	0.51	Plymouth	0.47
Gloucester	0.43	London	0.50	Leicester	0.47
Southampton	0.42	Portsmouth	0.49	Stoke	0.47
Bristol	0.42	Southampton	0.49	Reading	0.47
Luton	0.41	Sunderland	0.48	York	0.47
Portsmouth	0.41	Wigan	0.47	Southend	0.46
Coventry	0.40	Plymouth	0.47	Hull	0.46
Telford	0.39	Barnsley	0.47	Bolton	0.45
Barnsley	0.39	Grimsby	0.47	Portsmouth	0.45
Plymouth	0.38	Ipswich	0.47	Bournemouth	0.45
York	0.37	Telford	0.45	Derby	0.44
Reading	0.36	Coventry	0.45	Norwich	0.44
Norwich	0.35	Mansfield	0.44	Wigan	0.43
Wigan	0.34	Blackpool	0.43	Mansfield	0.42
Grimsby	0.34	Bristol	0.43	Rochdale	0.41
Mansfield	0.33	Birkenhead	0.43	Worthing	0.40
Ipswich	0.33	York	0.42	Southampton	0.40
Southend	0.33	Warrington	0.39	Telford	0.39
Bournemouth	0.32	Crawley	0.39	Gloucester	0.39
Crawley	0.32	Southend	0.39	Aldershot	0.38
Warrington	0.31	Norwich	0.38	Brighton	0.35
Blackpool	0.31	Reading	0.38	Swindon	0.35
Swindon	0.29	Bournemouth	0.36	Coventry	0.33
Chatham	0.28	Northampton	0.36	Crawley	0.33
Northampton	0.28	Swindon	0.34	Ipswich	0.32
Birkenhead	0.28	Chatham	0.32	Chatham	0.32
Milton Keynes	0.25	Oxford	0.28	Hastings	0.31
Brighton	0.24	Milton Keynes	0.28	Northampton	0.30
Worthing	0.21	Brighton	0.26	Peterborough	0.29
Aldershot	0.20	Worthing	0.26	Luton	0.29
Hastings	0.20	Hastings	0.26	Oxford	0.28
Oxford	0.18	Aldershot	0.25	Milton Keynes	0.28
Cambridge	0.17	Cambridge	0.19	Cambridge	0.18

5.8.5   Cities in the north and west dominate the group of places with the highest levels of segregation. The top eight cities on White/Non-White segregation are all from here. All the places with high or very high segregation are Pennine towns crossing from West Yorkshire into Lancashire, north of Greater Manchester. Five of the top 10 most segregated places are small cities in the north and west. Seventeen of the top 20 most segregated cities are in the north and west. In contrast, 17 of the 26 cities with low segregation between Whites and Non-Whites are in the south or east (Map 5.6).

Map 5.6: Levels of ethnic minority segregation 2001

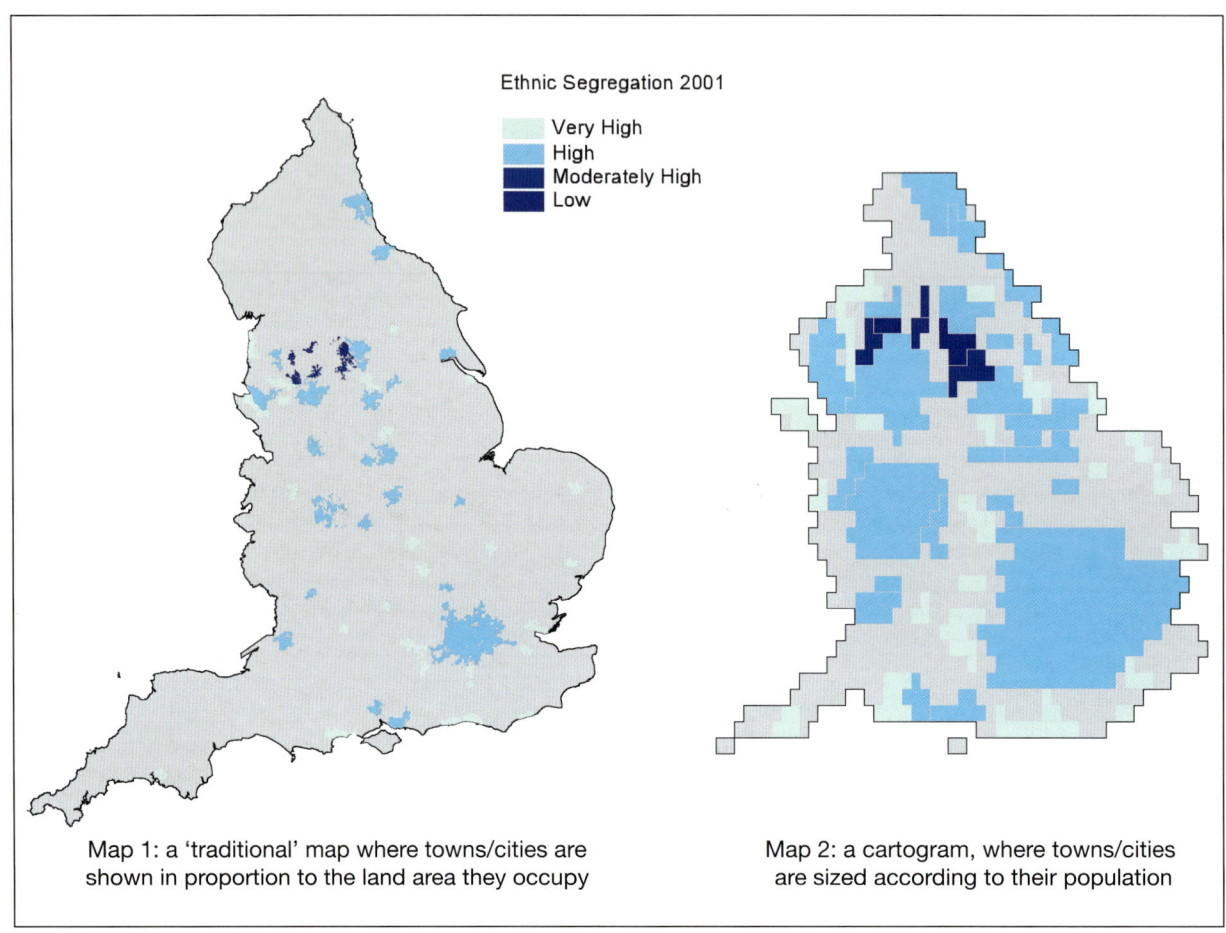

Map 1: a 'traditional' map where towns/cities are shown in proportion to the land area they occupy

Map 2: a cartogram, where towns/cities are sized according to their population

5.8.6   There is a relationship between size of ethnic minority population and level of segregation, as shown in Table 5.4. The mean city ID score rises as the proportionate size of the Non-White population increases.

Table 5.4: Segregation by size of ethnic minority population, 2001

Non-White Population as % of Total City Population	Number of Cities	Mean Segregation (ID) Score (Whites vs. Non-Whites)
Less than 5.0%	31	0.37
5.0 – 9.9%	12	0.42
10.0 – 19.9%	8	0.51
20.0% +	5	0.57

5.8.7   The variations between different forms of segregation are also shown by analysis of segregation at Super Output Area level within regional urban groupings as shown in Table 5.5. In the case of six out of the 10 groupings, segregation between Whites and Asians is higher than that between Whites and Blacks. There are three places where White/Asian segregation is at least 20 points higher than White/Black segregation, all in the north and west: Rochdale (+0.30); Bradford (+0.24); and Bolton (+0.20). In contrast, there are also three north and west cities where White/Black segregation is at least 10 points higher than White/Asian segregation – Sunderland, Blackpool and Warrington – though in each case the Black population is very small. For large and small cities and smaller towns in the south and east, the highest mean levels of segregation are between Indians and Pakistanis. However, the highest levels of segregation anywhere are those recorded between Indians and Pakistanis in north and west large and small towns (with ID scores of 0.80+). North and west larger towns also exhibit markedly higher segregation between Blacks and Asians than between Whites and Blacks.

Table 5.5: Segregation levels by city type, 2001

	White/ non-White	White/ Asian	White/ Black	Black/ Asian	Indian/ Pakistani	Black C/ B African
London	0.44	0.50	0.51	0.49	0.38	0.28
N/W Metros	0.54	0.59	0.56	0.47	0.55	0.47
S/E Large Cities	0.41	0.45	0.45	0.39	0.51	0.46
N/W Large Cities	0.48	0.55	0.50	0.51	0.59	0.63
S/E Small Cities	0.32	0.39	0.35	0.38	0.54	0.49
N/W Small Cities	0.49	0.56	0.53	0.54	0.57	0.69
S/E Larger Towns	0.51	0.61	0.54	0.41	0.58	0.50
N/W Larger Towns	0.51	0.62	0.52	0.62	0.83	0.74
S/E Smaller Towns & Rural	0.41	0.50	0.52	0.52	0.70	0.68
N/W Smaller Towns & Rural	0.45	0.57	0.64	0.62	0.81	0.80

Ethnicity and deprivation

5.8.8   We compared the ethnicity of the most deprived decile of neighbourhoods (SOAs) with the ethnicity for all other neighbourhoods. The results are shown in Table 5.6. In many cases, the Non-White population is more than twice as prevalent in the most deprived as in other neighbourhoods, most notably the case for large cities and larger towns in the north and west – the latter including places such as Carlisle, Darlington, Lancaster and Stafford. However, this is not the case in smaller towns and rural areas; nor in larger towns in the south and east such as Basildon, Guildford, Lincoln, Stevenage where the ethnic minority presence is in fact lower in the most deprived neighbourhoods.

Table 5.6: Ethnicity and deprivation by city type, 2001

	Ethnicity in most deprived areas (IMD bottom decile) (% Non-White) – (A)	Ethnicity in all other areas (% Non-White) (B)	Ratio of ethnic presence (A/B)
London	46.4	23.7	1.96
Metros	19.6	8.4	2.33
South/Eastern Large Cities	16.3	7.6	2.14
North/Western Large Cities	15.3	5.8	2.69
South/Eastern Small Cities	13.0	6.9	1.88
North/Western Small Cities	11.4	4.5	2.53
South/Eastern Larger Towns	3.5	4.8	0.73
North/Western Larger Towns	6.8	2.5	2.72
S/E Smaller Towns & Rural	1.8	1.9	0.95
N/W Smaller Towns & Rural	1.2	1.4	0.86

5.8.9   Taking this analysis further, we can look at the position of specific ethnic groups in individual cities, which we have done for all cities with a Non-White population of at least six per cent. Table 5.7 shows the position for Asians, and Table 5.8 that for Blacks. Comparing the two tables we can see that concentration in deprived areas reaches higher levels for Asians than for Blacks, with four cities where five times as many Asians live in the most deprived neighbourhoods as live in all other neighbourhoods. However, at the other end of the spectrum, there are also four cities where fewer Asians live in the most deprived neighbourhoods as live in other areas, which is not the case for Blacks in any city.

5.8.10   Concentrations in deprived areas for both groups are more marked in north and western cities than in south and eastern cities: eight of the top ten cities for concentrations of Asians in deprived areas are in the north and west as are eight of the top ten cities for concentrations of Blacks in deprived areas. Some cities exhibit marked differences in their treatment of Asians and Blacks. The top three cities for degree of concentration of Blacks in deprived areas – Manchester, Leeds and Nottingham – all have a concentration index for Blacks which is approximately twice that for Asians in the same places. Similarly, Leicester markedly concentrates Blacks in deprived areas whilst deconcentrating Asians from deprived areas. Other south and east small cities exhibit lower levels of concentrations of Asians in deprived areas. Six of the bottom ten cities on the Asian concentration index come from this grouping.

Table 5.7: Asian concentration in deprived areas, 2001

City	Grouping	Asian presence in most deprived areas (%) – (A)	Asian presence in all other areas (%) – (B)	Concentration Index: ration of Asian presence (A/B)
Derby	S/E: Small Cities	24.8	4.6	5.4
Peterborough	S/E: Small Cities	27.9	5.2	5.4
Bradford	N/W: Large Cities	42.1	8.3	5.1
Preston	N/W: Small Cities	19.4	3.8	5.1
Burnley	N/W: Small Cities	25.4	7.1	3.6
Rochdale	N/W: Small Cities	20.0	6.1	3.3
Sheffield	N/W: Metros	8.4	2.7	3.1
Huddersfield	N/W: Large Cities	25.8	9.3	2.8
Bolton	N/W: Small Cities	18.2	6.5	2.8
Birmingham	N/W: Metros	25.8	9.6	2.7
Manchester	N/W: Metors	10.3	3.9	2.6
Ipswich	S/E: Small Cities	4.1	1.6	2.6
Leeds	N/W: Metros	8.3	3.5	2.4
Coventry	N/W: Large Cities	19.3	9.6	2.0
Nottingham	S/E: Large Cities	6.1	3.1	2.0
Luton	S/E: Small Cities	34.6	17.9	1.9
Blackburn	N/W: Small Cities	27.3	18.8	1.5
London	London	15.6	10.4	1.5
Gloucester	S/E: Small Cities	3.7	2.7	1.4
Milton Keynes	S/E: Small Cities	3.1	3.7	0.8
Northampton	S/E: Small Cities	2.7	3.3	0.8
Leicester	S/E: Large Cities	17.2	23.1	0.7
Oxford	S/E: Small Cities	2.9	4.8	0.6

Table 5.8: Black concentration in deprived areas, 2001

City	Grouping	Black presence in most deprived areas (%) – (A)	Black presence in all other areas (%) – (B)	Concentration Index: ration of Black presence (A/B)
Manchester	N/W: Metros	3.7	0.8	4.6
Leeds	N/W: Metros	3.7	0.8	4.6
Nottingham	S/E: Large Cities	5.7	1.4	4.1
Preston	N/W: Small Cities	1.6	0.4	4.0
Huddersfield	N/W: Large Cities	3.9	1.0	3.9
Sheffield	N/W: Metros	2.9	0.9	3.2
Leicester	S/E: Large Cities	5.2	1.7	3.0
Bolton	N/W: Small Cities	1.2	0.4	3.0
Birmingham	N/W: Metros	7.9	2.7	2.9
London	London	23.2	8.2	2.8
Derby	S/E: Small Cities	3.7	1.3	2.8
Bradford	N/W: Large Cities	1.6	0.6	2.7
Northampton	S/E: Small Cities	5.6	2.3	2.4
Ipswich	S/E: Small Cities	3.9	1.7	2.3
Coventry	N/W: Large Cities	3.5	1.5	2.3
Burnley	N/W: Small Cities	0.2	0.1	2.0
Oxford	S/E: Small Cities	4.7	2.5	1.9
Luton	S/E: Small Cities	11.3	6.2	1.8
Rochdale	N/W: Small Cities	0.5	0.3	1.7
Peterborough	S/E: Small Cities	1.9	1.2	1.6
Gloucester	S/E: Small Cities	3.3	2.2	1.5
Blackburn	N/W: Small Cities	0.3	0.2	1.5
Milton Keynes	S/E: Small Cities	3.4	2.4	1.4

Racial segregation and other urban outcomes

Segregation and social outcomes

5.8.11 To assess the relations between segregation by ethnicity and other social outcomes we examined those 26 cities with a Non-White population of six per cent or more – approximately the UK rate of Non-White population excluding mixed races. The ID score for the city was correlated against the city values for a range of other variables as well as against the standard deviation for those variables that were also available at the SOA level. The variables in question covered issues of resources, household type, crime, housing and education. The strongest and most consistent relationships between level of segregation and other variables relate to poverty and further education. For both north and west and south and east cities, higher segregation is associated with lower average earnings, higher deprivation, fewer people in the professional and managerial classes, and more housing in the lowest council tax band. Higher segregation is also associated with fewer young people in further or higher education. The poverty related associations are slightly stronger in the south and east than in the north and west, but the relationship with further education is stronger in the north and west, though it also exists in south and east cities.

How important is segregation for urban performance?

5.8.12   Segregation by ethnicity is important in a number of ways. Higher segregation is associated with lower earnings, higher unemployment, and fewer managerial and professional class employees at the city level, though these relationships are stronger in the south and east than in the north and west. Right across the country, a strong relationship exists between the level of segregation and the rate of participation in further and higher education.

Segregation by income, wealth and employment is greater than segregation by ethnicity

5.8.13   Segregation by ethnicity is much higher than segregation by social class, yet lower than segregation based on income, wealth and employment status. The bigger division is between the rich and poor, especially in south and east cities. Significant spatial divisions along these lines may equally undermine community cohesion due to the gap in quality of life, lack of shared experiences and absence of contact between social groups that may result.

Segregation is decreasing in most cities

5.8.14   Segregation between Whites and Non-Whites, measured at ward level, has fallen in the vast majority of cities between 1991 and 2001, usually by five points (0.05) or less. There are only eight cities – four each in the north and west and south and east) – where segregation has increased over the past decade. In only two cases was it by a significant amount, Blackburn +0.08 and Norwich +0.06. In the other six cases – Hull, Sunderland, Portsmouth, York, Southend and Plymouth – it was by very small amounts.

5.8.15   The balance sheet on cohesion and segregation:

   • Segregation by ethnicity has fallen. It declined between 1991 and 2001 in 48 out of 56 cities. It increased very slightly in six and significantly in only two.

   • Segregation by income, wealth and employment is greater than segregation by ethnicity.

   • Higher segregation is associated with lower employment, lower earnings, lower education participation and higher levels of deprivation.

   • Segregation is significantly higher in cities in the north and west of England.

   • The connection between segregated minorities and deprived areas is critical.

5.9 The balance sheet on social cohesion in cities

5.9.1. There has been improvement in social cohesion in most cities in recent years. This reflects better national performance in spheres such as employment, health and education. Employment conditions have improved in most cities over the last decade, by more than average in some of the poorest cities. Income levels have risen and deprivation levels fallen in most cities, again especially in some of the poorest. People are living longer everywhere although regional or urban-rural gaps have not narrowed. Recorded vehicle crime and burglaries have declined slightly although robberies have increased slightly. The gap in school educational attainment has narrowed a little between cities and the rest of England. The proportion of people with degrees has risen everywhere in the last decade, especially in the prosperous cities which already had many graduates. Segregation by ethnicity, contrary to some assumptions, declined in most cities.

5.9.2 However, despite this progress, cities still face challenges of social exclusion and inequality. The level of deprivation is higher and more widespread in cities than in other parts of the country. There are higher levels of unemployment and worklessness. The health of the population is generally less good. The gap between poor and better-off neighbourhoods is bigger than elsewhere. Residential segregation is quite high, based on income, wealth, employment status and ethnicity. Educational attainment in schools is lower than elsewhere. The rate of recorded crime is generally higher. There is a marked regional difference. Cities in the north and west face bigger challenges than those in the south and east. So there have been improvements in levels of social cohesion in English cities in recent years but there is more to do.

Chapter 6: Liveability in English cities

6.1   Introduction

6.1.6   This chapter assesses the liveability of English cities at the outset of the 21st century. It reviews existing literature and data organised around four overarching themes: environmental quality, physical place quality, functional place quality, safer places. It explores the following kinds of questions:

- Are English cities becoming more or less liveable?

- In what ways? Which parts of them? For whom?

- What is the evidence base?

- What process lessons can be learnt?

- What are the methodological issues and difficulties?

- What work is needed to better define and understand these issues?

6.1.7   In addition to the existing literature it also explores the state of liveability in two case studies, Leicester and Manchester. Both cities have invested significant energy, in terms of organisational process and resources, in a range of liveability programmes. Manchester in particular has seen a series of initiatives aimed at improving local environmental quality. Our analysis suggests that this focus and investment has yielded significant results, both in terms of performance and residents' perceptions.

6.1.8   Our initial look at the different kinds of data suggests the following conclusions to our initial questions:

- Getting better and more liveable? A cautious yes, on most indicators, though not on all counts but set against a consensus of previous decline. And the evidence base is often very thin.

- How, where, for whom? The picture is particularly positive in terms of urban management and cleanliness. It is less so in terms of broader environmental pollution. It is better in both central and inner urban areas. It is difficult to say if any particular groups are greater or lesser beneficiaries.

- Process is important. Process innovations in our two case study cities point to promising areas of potential in the field of liveability and urban management. However, further research is required into good practice in order to establish what works well and under what conditions.

6.1.9   A number of lessons can be drawn in attempting to measure liveability:

- Liveability is a relatively new topic. The current range of desired indicators are not sufficiently robust, and few time series data are available. A clear baseline needs to be established against which future progress can be assessed.

- Liveability is local. Many elements of liveability are locally-specific and not readily comparable on the basis of local-authority-level data. A full picture of liveability is only likely to emerge as a result of case-by-case analysis.

- The importance of perception. Liveability is a softer area of government policy, and one where perceptions are crucial.

6.2   What is liveability?

6.2.1   Liveability is at the forefront of government policy. It has become increasingly important for citizens, as surveys by local authorities, government and market researchers attest. It is a complex and diverse area, where responsibility spans several government departments. In the absence of a generally-agreed definition, we follow the line set by the ODPM, seeing liveability as concentrating on the public realm and the built environment, in terms of both observed outcomes and citizens' perceptions of their local urban environment. Liveability is concerned with the quality of space and the built environment. It is about how easy a place is to use and how safe it feels. It is about creating a sense of place by creating an environment that is both inviting and enjoyable. The government's emphasis on 'Cleaner, Safer, Greener' focuses on identifying with citizens' desires and aspirations for their neighbourhoods and cities. Crucially, liveability is also one of five key interdependent themes within the Sustainable Communities agenda, which is driving major public investment in housing and communities across England.

6.2.2   Liveability has risen in importance recently, with the government seeking to coordinate the activities of several departments through its 'Cleaner, Safer, Greener' programme. It emphasises the role of two departments in particular – the ODPM through the PSA8 target, and the Home Office through its PSA2. But it also stresses links to other departments such as DCMS, DfT, DEFRA, DoH, DfES, DTI and Treasury.

6.2.3   The liveability agenda is essentially about creating places where people choose to live and work. In this sense liveability can be understood as a key competitive element between cities in terms of attracting both people and businesses to a city. This is a point noted in the 2004 report on Competitive European Cities; where do the core cities stand? *"Evidence from the Core Cities in the UK highlighted that the mixture of ingredients that improve quality of life and make a sustainable community 'with the assets of good environment, distinctive architecture and cultural facilities, diverse housing stock and access to natural amenities' are an essential mix to attract the right kind of labour force to make a city economically competitive."*

6.2.4   For clarity a brief separation of definitions is useful here. 'Quality of life' is often confused with liveability, when in fact it covers a much broader range of topics. Liveability can be regarded as a subset of 'quality of life' – with 'quality of life' covering a broader range of factors such as education, poverty, economic deprivation, health, the environment, congestion and so on. 'Quality of life' is monitored by DEFRA as the main set of indicators of its Sustainable Development programme.

6.2.5   The basic principles of sustainable development are covered by the following widely accepted and quoted definition 'development which meets the needs of the present without compromising the ability of future generations to meet their own needs'. Sustainability and quality of life are both key drivers of the government's Sustainable Communities programme, whose overarching aim is to deliver places where people want to live and work now and in the future. This recognises the implicit connection between liveability and places that are economically and socially successful.

6.3   What does the literature tell us?

6.3.1   Since 1997, government has adopted a six-fold approach to improving the liveability of urban residential environments. It has:

- analysed residents' concerns and aspirations about their neighbourhood and assessed environmental quality in that light;

- improved the quality of development by setting up the Commission for Architecture and the Built Environment in 1999 and later CABE Space in 2003 to improve the quality of public spaces, initially focussed on parks and green spaces;

- provided a strategic framework for government departments, local authorities, public agencies, local communities and others with responsibility for, or a stake in, local environmental assets;

- boosted implementation capacity through granting additional funding to local partners, including community led regeneration;

- introduced special initiatives to improve neighbourhoods, especially the most disadvantaged, including the Living Spaces Programme, the Liveability Fund, and supporting the introduction of community wardens and community support officers;

- monitored environmental standards more closely and systematically.

6.3.2   Evidence of the impact of government policy in this wider sense is extremely limited both because of the lack of comprehensive urban quality of life data and also the fact that evaluators have never been handed such an all-encompassing brief. Although some components of liveability are familiar, it is a comparatively recent concept and policy has not yet been analysed in such terms. In this section, we restrict attention to the quality of space and the built environment in residential areas though recognise that many policies explored elsewhere affect urban quality of life.

6.3.3   The current government has assembled an extensive body of evidence on what makes urban areas good places to live (DETR, 2000; DTLR, 2002; ODPM, 2002, 2004a). Residents have repeatedly emphasised the importance to their quality of life of safer and cleaner streets and public spaces, less rubbish and dog fouling, improved parks and street infrastructure and more activities for children and young people (ODPM, 2005). Mounting public concern about the steady deterioration in the quality of streets, parks and open spaces triggered a series of government reports and initiatives from the late 1990s onwards analysing the problem in depth and proposing a range of solutions (for example, Urban Parks Forum, 2001; DTLR, 2002). The thrust of resulting government initiatives such as 'Cleaner, Safer, Greener Communities' (CSGC) and related 'Together' campaign has been to address such concerns, desires and aspirations (ODPM, 2002). Policies have also sought to address traditional weaknesses in environmental management such as lack of resources, co-ordination, poor design and management and lack of community involvement. Cross-departmental working on liveability issues has increased as a result of the CSGC programme.

6.3.4   CABE Space's brief closely addresses the most salient issues in public space management identified in commissioned research. It has sought to help local authorities develop a more strategic approach, provided benchmarks and exemplars to inspire good practice, raise awareness across professional disciplines of the economic, environmental and social importance of well designed and managed urban spaces and improve professional skills. Assessments of CABE, generally, have repeatedly shown that it is very highly regarded by national, regional and local organisations for the quality of its advice to developers, local authorities and government departments regarding development proposals and also its research into best practice and training activities (OPM, 2004; ODPM Committee, 2005). There is also extensive evidence to suggest that CABE has helped to compensate for the shortage of design skills within local authorities and put pressure on developers to raise the standard of master plans and new homes (e.g. CABE, 2004). Research therefore suggests that CABE has effectively championed the cause of good design.

6.3.5   Trend information regarding liveability has significantly improved as a result of government policy. New liveability targets have recently been introduced (ODPM's PSA8), including a floor target for closing the gap between deprived areas and the rest of the country on cleanliness (NRU). There is now better longitudinal data about urban environmental quality (for example, Local Environmental Quality Survey of England 2002-4; ENCAMS, 2004) and the level of public satisfaction with local authority environmental and waste services (Best Value User Satisfaction Surveys, 2000/1-2003/4 – ODPM, 2004b) and concern about neighbourhood issues through the British Crime Survey (BCS), EHCS, SEH etc. However, the state of the urban environment has only been systematically analysed on one occasion (Environment Agency, 2002). Nor are there any evaluation reports which assessed the overall effectiveness of policymaking using available trend information and other intelligence. Evidence is scattered and uneven, partly because responsibility for the public realm is shared amongst so many parties.

6.3.6   Some broad inferences about policy can be drawn from the available evidence, however. Table 6.1 shows that resident satisfaction with local parks has risen sharply in both Neighbourhood Renewal Fund (NRF) areas and the rest of England in the period 1999/2000- 2003/4. Government Best Value Performance Indicators show that satisfaction levels with local authority parks and open space services have moved from a mid-ranking position to being one of the most popular types of local authority service. The recent increase in the number of local authorities receiving Green Flag awards confirms this.

Research suggests that this improvement is due to a combination of better central and local government policies and funding since 1998/9, generous Lottery funding, for example, Millennium Greens; Public Parks Initiative, Heritage Lottery Fund (HLF); New Opportunities Fund Green Space and Sustainable Communities Programme and better advice and promulgation of best practice by CABE Space and other organisations (Worpole, 2003; ODPM, 2004a).

6.3.7   The combination of the joint Government/NOF (£170m) Fair Share programme in NRF areas and the latter's commitment to prioritising deprived urban areas probably accounts for increasing satisfaction in deprived areas, although the rate of increase there has been slightly less than nationally. Early results from the evaluation of HLF's £125m Green Spaces and Sustainable Communities Programme suggest that it is improving recreational provision, increasing community pride and self-esteem, achieving environmental and social benefits and improving the popularity of previously hard-to-let properties (Baker & Millward Associates, 2004). No evaluation results are yet available, however, for recently begun government programmes such as the £30m Living Spaces Scheme which provides support to community groups wishing to improve local spaces and the £89m Liveability Fund which is being piloted in 27 local authorities. The latter is geared to supporting service reforms to ensure sustainable capital works on issues including fly-tipping, litter, graffiti, abandoned vehicles, anti-social behaviour and public space improvement.

6.3.8   Longitudinal data relating to other aspects of the urban residential environment suggest a more uneven picture. The Best Value Performance Indicator relating to household waste collection shows that public satisfaction with services has recently been high. On the other hand, the performance of urban authorities in terms of the cleanliness of public land has remained much the same over the period 2000/1-2003/04 and the proportion satisfied is relatively low at around 60 per cent. MORI data tends to corroborate this and shows that satisfaction with street cleaning fell steadily during the period 1995-2001. Table 6.1 shows that abandoned vehicles were an increasing problem until 2003/4 although government moves to grant local authorities the power to remove such vehicles at much shorter notice has helped and additional legislation is coming forward through the Clean Neighbourhoods and Environment Act. Research suggests that such environmental degradation has occurred for variety of reasons including inadequate resources, the relatively low priority attached to public space management compared with other local services, the multitude of different stakeholders involved, the way in which different local authority departments operate in a compartmentalised fashion and societal behaviour (ODPM, 2004a).

6.3.9   There have recently been signs of improvement, however. Although resident satisfaction with their local environment generally has steadily declined both in NRF areas and nationally over the period 1999/2000-2002/3, the 2003/4 figures suggest a slight upturn in fortunes. This is corroborated by results from the Local Environmental Quality Survey, produced by ENCAMS. From 2002/3-2003/4, the proportion of sites rated by ENCAMS as good or satisfactory has climbed 4 per cent points to 40, the percentage judged poor has fallen 2 per cent points to 4 per cent and the balance were rated unsatisfactory. Treatment of fly-posting, graffiti and fly-tipping has markedly improved but this has been offset by a rapid increase in certain types of litter – sweet wrappers, snack packaging, drink cans – partly because of the increasing tendency for people to eat on the move. More densely populated urban areas tended to score less well. Low density private housing, rural roads, public open spaces, waterside areas and public transport stations were rated relatively clean, while low density social housing and roads registered average scores and industrial, retail – especially secondary – areas and high density housing areas were judged relatively dirty.

6.3.10   Evaluation of the government's own liveability initiatives suggests that they have had a favourable impact since 2000 especially when set against a backdrop of a long term decline in public expenditure on public open spaces over the preceding 20 years. However, the benefits have arisen from targeted measures and limited real increases in government expenditure on the environmental services and cultural services block since 2000. For example, local authority spending on parks was an estimated £1.3bn lower in 2001 than in 1980, however, it has risen since. Lottery funding has been critical in compensating for significant public under-investment in either new or refurbished public spaces. Residents' surveys have shown that the Neighbourhood Wardens programme has improved residents' perceived quality of life, for example, 6 per cent increase in residents thinking the areas were getting better in 2003 than in 2001, due to the mixture of crime reduction measures and environmental improvements such as removal of graffiti, fly-tipping, litter and dog fouling (ODPM, 2004c). Similar results have been achieved in some Neighbourhood Management Pathfinder areas (ODPM, 2004d).

6.3.11   While sustainable funding remains a fundamental problem, many local authorities have displayed considerable ingenuity in spreading the responsibility and financial burden for managing parks – with support from government, Groundwork and other environmental organisations. They have achieved this by more closely engaging communities, sharing management responsibility to local people, generating income through establishing local charitable trusts and related revenue generating activities. Many recently upgraded public parks are consequently better designed, maintained and well-used by all sections of the community. The same can be said of key public spaces within major city centres such as Manchester, Birmingham and Sheffield. The outstanding challenge is to extend these achievements throughout urban areas. 3.3m households, 16 per cent of all households live in poor quality environments and almost a third of those in deprived areas (English House Condition Survey, 2003). Also, visual street clutter arising from various signage and street furniture is still a significant problem in many commercial and neighbouring residential areas (ODPM, 2004a).

6.3.12   BVPI user satisfaction surveys show that liveability measures only tackle some of the things that make somewhere a good place to live (ODPM, 2004b). These include quality of health, educational, retail and recreational facilities and transport provision. While many of these are being tackled by other initiatives, research suggests that certain aspects of urban quality of life have received less attention by successive governments such as transport and accessibility and environmental sustainability issues. The SEU has shown that transport policy does not connect very well with wider social agendas and that many government departments and agencies have not paid proper regard to the transport implications of service delivery (SEU, 2003). Many poorer people are unable to access key services because they cannot be reached by public transport, which critically affects liveability. Research has shown that there are many local examples of good practice in accessibility planning which integrates land use, regeneration and transport considerations, joint planning of service delivery across public services and development of community transport (Lucas, 2004). However, a variety of funding, legislative and institutional barriers will have to be overcome if such approaches are to become the norm.

6.3.13 Increased traffic congestion and related problem of noise and pollution are also having a major detrimental effect on urban quality of life (Environment Agency, 2002). Increased investment in various modes of public transport such as buses and light rail transit has encouraged modal shift and reduced city centre traffic in cities such as Oxford, York and Manchester. Cycling in London has doubled following significant investment. However, the overall picture has been one of rising car ownership and long term decline in public transport patronage. The latter trend is only just beginning to bottom out. Public satisfaction with bus services and local transport information is starting to improve but is still comparatively low – 54 per cent and 50 per cent respectively, 2003/4. Despite increases in vehicular movements, the government and local transport authorities have secured slightly greater reductions in traffic accidents in deprived urban areas than the rest of England by a combination of lower speed limits, traffic calming, other traffic management measures and the Safer Routes to School initiative (Table 6.2).

6.3.14 Environmental indicators reveal an upward trend in transport congestion, waste generation and energy consumption. They underline the conclusions of a recent research report which recommended that the definition of liveability needs to be broadened to ensure that liveability policies are environmentally sustainable (ODPM, 2004e). This would ensure that greater emphasis is placed upon questions of energy efficiency, public health and sustainable lifestyles.

Table 6.1: Liveability Trends in Neighbourhood Renewal Areas compared with English average.

	% residents satisfied with local parks		% residents satisfied with local environment		Rate of abandoned vehicles/'000 households	
	NRF	England	NRF	England	NRF	England
1999/2000	62	63	61.9	66.9	N/a	N/a
2000/1	N/a	N/a	61.5	66.1	N/a	10.7
2001/2	N/a	N/a	60.9	64.8	N/a	13.8
2002/3	N/a	N/a	60.4	63.7	N/a	14.8
2003/4	69	72	61.1	64.3	N/a	N/a

Sources: Local parks – Best Value User Satisfaction Survey, ODPM; local environment (average of 6 household attitude factors officially recorded as 18 month rolling average but re-estimated here on annual basis); abandoned vehicles – DEFRA

Table 6.2: Road accident casualties, 1999-2003

	Disadvantaged districts	England
% change in road accident casualties, 1999-2003	−10.6	−9.0

Note: Target to reduce road accident casualty numbers in deprived areas by more than the percentage decline across the country

Source: DoT STATS 19 personal injury accident database

The balance sheet

6.3.15 Our review of the limited available literature and trawl of potential data and indicator sources suggests the following complex kaleidoscope:

- Liveability in terms of urban management within local government is becoming increasingly important.

- Environmental quality in particular is under increasing pressure from more intense use and continued development pressures: noise pollution and congestion are symptomatic of this.

- Some areas are generally improving, such as air quality, street cleanliness and parks and green spaces.

- Many components, such as street cleanliness, are improving in quantitative terms. But perceptions of quality may not yet be following suit, suggesting that liveability is a growing area of concern for the public at large.

- Place quality has developed substantially as a theme since the Urban Task Force Report, with the need for high quality, sustainable buildings and places achieving widespread policy acceptance. However, despite many positive examples, there is no clear evidence to suggest that standards are systematically improving.

- Providing attractive alternatives to the car in terms of more sustainable modes of travel remains a challenge, but London and Oxford offer positive examples.

- The Urban Renaissance is arguably being felt in cities across the UK, however, substantive evidence remains thin.

- Crime is falling. However, anti-social behaviour has been rising in prominence and is arguably more connected with specific places and hence impacts on the liveability of specific localities.

Methodological points

- A great deal of the data required to assess many of the categories is not currently being systematically collected. This is particularly true of design-related, and many place-specific, elements such as public realm quality and walkability.

- Where they are being collected, they often use proxies which cannot answer the key question of how the 'place/space' is changing.

- The effort to ground PSA8 in measurable data and changes is starting to produce some potentially useful data. But this is a recent initiative and so there is no time series on which to base conclusions.

- Measuring liveability in English cities is virtually impossible from pure desk-based research.

- Even if existing data sets and times series data were available, there are considerable areas of place quality in particular, where highly locally specific and detailed studies would be the only way to judge conditions and progress.

- Certain topics such as anti-social behaviour require a new set of indicators to capture the impact on local communities and relationship with other agendas.

6.4   What does it look like on the ground?

6.4.1   In this section we examine two cities, Leicester and Manchester, to explore liveability on the ground. Leicester is a medium-sized middle England city, characterised by its status as the 'Environment City'. Manchester, on the other hand, is not only one of the great Core Cities of the north, but also well known for its recent investment in new public realm initiatives, such as Cathedral Square or the URBIS project. The case studies contain two major components. The first concentrates on the PSA8 indicators which form part of the government's 'Cleaner, Safer, Greener' agenda. Table 6.4 provides an overview of how well the PSA8 indicators 'fit' with the list of desirable indicators (Table 6.3). The PSA8 targets also have the advantage of being nationally comparable allowing cities and city regions to benchmark their overall performance against their peers. This analysis of PSA8 targets provides us with a citywide overview of how the case study cities are performing in general liveability terms. We look at citywide liveability under two broad methodological headings, namely 'Observed Change' and 'Perceived Change'.

Table 6.3: Desirable Liveability Indicators

13 Desirable Indicator Areas
A.   Environmental Quality
1.   Noisier-Quieter?   2.   Dirtier-Cleaner?   3.   More or less congested?   4.   Building quality, Better or Worse?
B.   Place Quality (Physical)
5.   Quality of the built environment 'product'   6.   Levels of derelict land   7.   Quality of parks and green spaces   8.   Public realm quality
C.   Place Quality (Functional)
9.   Pedestrian journeys: easier-or harder?   10. Public transport quality   11. Vitality and viability of services
D.   Safer Places
12. Crime levels   13. Anti-social behaviour

Table 6.4: PSA8 Targets and Desirable Liveability Indicators

Key Targets	Corresponding Desirable Indicators	Indicators	Availability (Baseline)	Spatial Level
1. Reduce the percentage of local authority districts nationally judged to have unacceptable levels of litter and detritus.	A2	BV199 Also ENCAMS Local Environmental Quality Surveys	Available Autumn 2004	Local Authority
2. Reduce the number of abandoned vehicles.	A2	Municipal Waste Management	2002-03 – however this measure is to be changed in 2004-05 to the Wastedataflow Survey	Local Authority
3. Increase the proportion of local authorities with at least one park or green space that meets Green Flag Award standard.	B7	Civic Trust Data	2003-04	Local Authority
4. Reduce the number of Local Authorities achieving a Comprehensive Performance Assessment (CPA) score of 'one' for the Environment Services Block.	B6/7/8; A2	Audit Commission CPA	None – also CPA's being revised with a view to implementation in 2005 – results 2008	Local Authority
5. Reduce the percentage of households living in poor quality environments.	B5	English House Condition Survey (EHCS)	Baseline: 2003-04 – now available on an annual basis	Sub-regional/ regional (sample now only 8,000 per annum)
6. Increase the percentage of residents satisfied with local parks and open spaces.	B7 (Perceived)	Bv119e	2003-04	Local Authority
7. Increase the percentage of households satisfied with the quality of the places in which they live above the baseline year of 2003-04.	A4; B5/7/8; C10; D12/13 (Perceived)	Survey of English Housing	2003-04 – Trends available from 1999	Mostly Regional – some aggregated sub-regional data

The question of 'fit'

It has been impossible to identify a sufficient range of robust data to cover the thirteen identified areas. The table above illustrates how the seven ODPM PSA8 targets relate to our thirteen desirable areas. As previously acknowledged, this is an imperfect solution, but nonetheless, the seven ODPM PSA8 targets do cover elements of nine of the thirteen areas – on balance a reasonable proportion. The strength of the PSA8 data is that it allows for national comparison. The weakness is that is does not capture those elements that are more localised and connected with function, form and design, such as the ease of pedestrian journeys, or the quality of place. These areas are never likely to be covered by easily comparable national data and rather are likely to be measured on a much more localised level. We suggest later that this might take the form of a local liveability audit tool – although this is unlikely to take the place of the PSA8 targets in the short term.

6.4.2   The second component focuses on more local level information and also includes two sub-divisions. The first of these follows on from the interviews with people who are key players in delivering liveability related services and projects in the two case study cities. It seeks to identify lessons from the successes and failures of these two cities in their efforts to deliver on the liveability agenda. The second adds available local level data, such as local level Best Value Residents' Surveys or Citizen's Panels, to offer a more localised version of the city-wide level data that are presented from the PSA8 data above. We also explore some early attempts to monitor and develop local level neighbourhood indicators, which may provide some useful lessons in developing a framework for monitoring local level liveability in the future.

Manchester

6.4.3   Manchester has invested significant corporate energy and focus in the wider liveability agenda. The plethora of initiatives and programmes outlined above represent a consistent focus on the core place-specific elements in particular. The PSA8 results and local level information indicate firstly that liveability is important. Two of the top three areas in which citizens expect improvements in Manchester have a 'place dimension'. They are the issues of crime and vandalism, which can have a direct impact on the appearance of a place and the quality of local amenities, parks and leisure facilities.

6.4.4   The key issues are common to the region and the country, but the levels of concern are greater in the Manchester areas. So whilst liveability is important across the country, this case study illustrates that cities in particular need to continue to invest in the quality of place and services and lifestyle offer if they are to retain and attract residents and crucially investment. In terms of the role of government and local authorities one thing is clear in relation to delivering qualitative improvements to liveability. The key to enhancing liveability in cities is through careful and consistent urban management and to be effective it requires a coordinated approach from a variety of public sector organisations.

6.4.5   Manchester is responding to these aspirations. There is clearly an improvement in the quality of parks as shown by the growing number of green flag awards. This is matched by a clear increase in the levels of user satisfaction with parks from 62 per cent in 2000 to 71 per cent in 2003, a rating consistent with the national average. Efforts have also been made to remove abandoned vehicles, an important mechanism to discourage anti-social behaviour which might undermine place quality. The data, both local and national, indicate that this attention and focus has resulted in a significant improvement in the quality of urban management in Manchester and the satisfaction levels of it citizens.

6.4.6   Many of the officers involved were convinced that, although important, liveability is only part of the picture. Manchester is clear that economic development to provide opportunity for all is crucial. A high quality environment on its own is insufficient to address structural neighbourhood issues like major social or housing quality problems, although intensive management can help stabilise them in the short term. The changing patterns in citizens' priorities over the last decade from largely socio-economic concerns such as employment to broader quality of life concerns suggests an intuitive hierarchy of priorities for citizens. The current favourable economic climate, combined with a greater public awareness of local environmental quality, has made liveability far more important in terms of citizen's priorities than before. The balance of results for Manchester point to significant observed improvements in a number of the core liveability topics, which are slowly starting to be reflected in residents' perceptions of their environment.

Leicester

6.4.7   The overall thrust of the findings for Leicester show that liveability is clearly the single greatest priority for Leicester's residents and is an increasingly important priority for the city council. Data show significant improvements in the observed quality of the local environment – parks and local amenities – and also evidence that it remains one of the greatest priorities for improvement among residents. This suggests that while the council is allocating additional resources to better urban management and maintenance, the bar itself has been raised by citizens' rising expectations for their environment. This highlights how liveability issues have risen up the local agenda in Leicester. Indeed the top three areas of resident concern focus on elements which have a significant 'place dimension'. They are:

● the quality of the shopping facilities;

● the issue of crime and vandalism, which have a direct impact on the appearance of a place;

● local amenities, parks and leisure facilities.

6.4.8   The results are not universally positive for Leicester and there are clearly areas where the council is failing to meet its own targets. Park quality is one example, which features highly in people's areas for improvement. It is clear that in order to meet its own targets the council will have to invest significant resources to achieve its goal of eight Green Flag awards by 2006. The CPA figures for 2004 also point to some areas of concern – with the elements which most closely fit the 'Cleaner, Safer, Greener' agenda slipping somewhat in 2004.

6.4.9   However, the percentage of citizens who identify this area as particularly needing improvement is broadly similar to the England average and up to 20 per cent lower than in the Manchester case study. In terms of 'quality of life', Leicester performs better than the national average. A similar trend is apparent in the user satisfaction ratings on litter and cleanliness. At 59 per cent satisfaction, Leicester is significantly ahead of Manchester and the Core Cities and near to the national average. So whilst there is room for improvement, this suggests that Leicester's efforts to be an 'environmental city' have had a positive impact on liveability in the city.

6.4.10   The satisfaction of citizens has yet to be fully recognised within some national quality assurance measures. The case study also shows that the perception of quality of life does not necessarily equate to relatively strong performance in all of the PSA8 domains: the number of abandoned vehicles is higher than in Manchester, and the number of Green Flag awards lower. In fact, despite only one Green Flag award, Leicester still achieves satisfaction ratings for its parks and green spaces which are significantly above the national average.

6.4.11   It is clear that a more nuanced and locally specific analysis is required to supplement a review of the PSA8 targets. The local level data, although patchy, along with the results of the Best Value Residents' Survey suggest that there remains room for improvement. But the increasing focus on liveability is being reflected in the measured outcomes. The current emphasis on liveability in Leicester, along with the current benchmarking process, should yield better results in the future and allow a more in depth picture of Leicester's performance.

6.4.12   Table 6.5 below provides a summary of the main findings from the two case studies. Manchester has performed very strongly across the majority of areas. This positive change is starting to alter residents' perceptions of their neighbourhood and their city. Leicester started from a very different base which partly explains its relatively neutral performance. Of the PSA8 indicators, abandoned vehicles and park quality as measured by the Green Flag Awards stand out as areas for improvement. There are signs of a refocus in corporate terms on liveability initiatives, especially to parks. There are a couple of useful trends in both authorities. Liveability concerns have risen substantially in both areas in terms of what residents would like to see improved. In terms of positive messages, particular progress has been made in street cleanliness and park quality. Engaging the public and effective communication are key components in improving the impact of liveability investment.

Table 6.5: Summary of Case Study Findings

Category	Indicator	Manchester	Leicester
Observed Change	(a) Cleanliness and Litter	✪	✪
	(b) Abandoned Vehicles	✪	☒
	(c) Park Quality	✪	◇?
	(d) Overall Environmental Services Performance	◇?	◇?
	(e) Quality of Living Environment	◇?	◇?
Perceived Change	(a) Satisfaction with Parks and Open Spaces	✪	✪
	(b) Perception of Local Area	☒	✪
Local Indicators	Best Value Surveys	✪	✪
	Manchester PSA 10	✪	NA

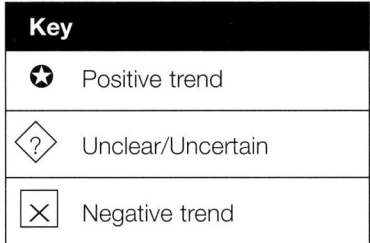

Key	
✪	Positive trend
◇?	Unclear/Uncertain
☒	Negative trend

6.5   Is liveability in our cities improving?

6.5.1   The analysis in the case studies concentrates on the PSA8 indicator set, supplemented by additional local level data and the results from the structured interviews. Although this represents a promising start, the main government liveability indicators fall short of the range of desirable indicators, which would adequately measure the performance of cities on liveability. In the absence of such data we supplement the analysis with the findings from the literature and data review and identify national trends to give as rounded as possible a view of the current state of urban liveability in England today. For those topics where neither section has been able to provide an indication of how English cities are performing, we make a suggestion of what could be used as an indicator, and why it is important. The four liveability themes are detailed below, along with a summary of the current situation, where possible.

Table 6.6: Key Liveability Themes and Desirable Indicators

A.	**Environmental Quality**		
1.	Noisier-Quieter?	↘	
2.	Dirtier-Cleaner?	↗	
3.	More or less congested?	↘	
4.	Building quality, Better or Worse?	↗	(?)
B.	**Place Quality (Physical)**		
5.	Quality of the built environment 'product'	↔	(?)
6.	Levels of derelict land	↗	
7.	Quality of parks and green spaces	↗	
8.	Public realm quality	–	(?)
C.	**Place Quality (Functional)**		
9.	Pedestrian journeys: easier-or harder?	–	(?)
10.	Public transport quality	↔	(?)
11.	Vitality and viability of services	↗	(?)
D.	**Safer Places**		
12.	Crime levels	↗	
13.	Anti-social behaviour	–	(?)

Key	
↘	Poor or worsening trend
↗	Good or improving trend
↔	Unclear/ambiguous – no clear trend
(?)	Insufficient data/research to support judgement – trend based on anecdotal evidence and/or professional judgement

Local environmental quality

6.5.2 This category concentrates on the environmental quality of places as opposed to design considerations. The four elements cover noise pollution, street cleanliness, congestion and building quality.

6.5.3 Noise pollution is a significant element of concern, especially within urban areas and this problem has worsened. While aspects of attitudes to noise are contained within the Survey of English Housing, noise is not included in local Best Value Residents' Surveys or in any of the local level data that we identified. There is clearly progress at a national level, with for example a national ambient noise mapping exercise underway under the auspices of DEFRA and the corresponding development of a national ambient noise strategy. The absence of significant and comparable levels of monitoring at local level is of concern. Noise is a substantial liveability issue, with almost 30 per cent of homes in England and Wales reporting that noise had adversely impacted upon their quality of life. Effective and consistent local level indicators and targets are urgently required.

6.5.4   Significant progress has been made in relation to street cleanliness in recent years. Both observed and attitudinal data are available and the current indicators provide a robust and nuanced picture of the quality of urban management and residents' perceptions of litter and street cleaning in their local environment. Both of our case study cities report similar patterns of results. In Manchester and Leicester, the quality of urban management has been consistently improving, whereas people's expectations continue to rise. Cleanliness is among the most often cited elements identified by citizens in terms of liveability. The current indicator set is comprehensive and should allow local authorities to target and allocate resources effectively, in line with residents' priorities. Manchester provides a useful example of very localised and effective micro-management in relation to its ward level Street Environment Management teams. The PSA8 indicators provide robust data on both the observed and perceived quality of street cleanliness. Our cities are becoming cleaner and resources better managed, however citizens' expectations are not yet being realised. The BVPI 199 suite of indicators represents a major step forward in providing the necessary levels of information on local environmental quality.

6.5.5   Road congestion is a growing problem in the majority of urban areas in the UK. Despite certain initiatives to measure and identify levels of congestion in cities, no widely available and comparable local level indicators are available and being monitored by local authorities as part of the wider liveability agenda. Road congestion needs to be monitored more effectively, and less simplistically, at a local level. Local authorities should consider how congestion impacts upon liveability, and how liveability investment could potentially aid in the reduction of congestion, for example, through improved public realm leading to greater use of walking, cycling and public transport. Congestion is increasingly impacting upon the ability to deliver the wider liveability agenda in many urban areas. More effort is needed to effectively monitor levels of congestion in local areas and to integrate congestion data into the other liveability indicators. While congestion is a local issue, with locally experienced impacts, solutions to congestion can often require non-local action.

6.5.6   In terms of the quality of the living environment, this report has not been able to establish a clear picture. At a national data level the levels of "decent" housing are reported in the English House Condition Survey (EHCS). In addition, liveability problems are recorded as part of the survey based on the professional surveyors' assessments of problems in the immediate environment of the home. This assessment of the quality of the local environment forms part of the ODPM's PSA8 targets, but is not producing information at Local Authority level. It is likely that the most reliable source of this data at a local level will come from local authorities' own data/research rather than national level surveys.

Place quality (physical)

6.5.7   This category covers four primary areas, of which PSA8 and the local level indicators only adequately cover performance and residents' perceptions for one – the 'quality of parks and open spaces'. CABE have pointed to the second rate nature of urban design in many new housing areas and also to the value of investing in high quality design of buildings. Place quality in terms of design is not, however, included within PSA8. But the case studies did provide an opportunity to discuss with the cities whether they felt that the design quality of their city was improving. Both cities underlined that the quality of the built environment is less susceptible to change than the public realm, given the lifespan of buildings and the low level of renewal of the urban fabric on an annual basis. Both cities can demonstrate that a determined effort to improve the urban design quality can reap rewards.

6.5.8   Place quality in terms of design of new development remains largely mediocre across England, although there are significant signs of an increasing focus on the quality of new buildings. This is resulting in excellent examples across the country, but the pace of improvement is very slow and is not widespread. Emphasising high quality design in both the planning and development process can lead to a step change in the quality of new developments. Measuring this liveability topic is only likely to be achieved on a case-by-case basis. This could in turn form part of any future liveability audit. Inevitably, inter-district comparison will be difficult, but crucially longitudinal monitoring will be possible allowing performance to be assessed against agreed objectives.

6.5.9   Levels of derelict land are recorded in the National Land Use Database with the change in the level of derelict land nationally pointing to a marginally positive trend. However, Previously Developed Land (PDL) is not being included as part of the systematic liveability analysis of local neighbourhoods. More and more PDL is coming back into use. The rate of reuse is faster in the twelve SOC Case Study Cities than nationally, although progress remains slow. Derelict land does represent a good potential indicator for liveability. It should become one of the targets for any neighbourhood liveability programme. It also reflects on the quality of local level urban management.

6.5.10   Public realm quality is not being systematically monitored, with the majority of councils lacking a strategy to monitor the topic. This has implications for the effective allocation and prioritisation of liveability and environmental resources. It is especially important given the emphasis on public realm within the government's liveability agenda. Given the absence of data, it has not been possible to establish a clear trend in relation to the quality of the public realm. This absence of comparable data needs to be tackled. Tools such as Placecheck should be integrated into the monitoring process in order to assess the quality of current and planned public realm environments.

Place quality (functional)

6.5.11   This category covers three areas, namely pedestrian journeys, public transport quality and the vitality and viability of key services. These topics are not covered under the PSA8 Indicator suite and also not being actively monitored by either of our case study cities in the context of liveability. But they represent good indicators on how cities and spaces are being used, with implications for the liveability agenda. The first two are arguably liveability indicators in their own right, whereas the third represents a reflection of the success of liveability in attracting and retaining people and businesses to and in an area.

6.5.12   The relative ease of pedestrian journeys is not currently being measured systematically at either national or local level to reflect how pedestrian-friendly the public realm is. Some research does exist which points to the importance of high quality walking environments both for the economy and in terms of quality of life. As yet, it is not possible to monitor whether investment in liveability measures is leading to an observable increase in the quality of walking environments. We cannot judge whether such measures are helping to promote increased use of more sustainable modes of travel and more intensive use of urban environments, with resultant improvements in the perception of public realm quality and also safety.

6.5.13   The inclusion of a walkability audit as part of the development of local liveability initiatives would enhance the profile of pedestrians as a crucial component of functional place quality. A wider urban walkability audit should form part of a comprehensive walking strategy, as in the recently launched Draft Walking Plan for London (GLA: Feb 2004). Such strategies may help to arrest the secular decline in walking. It is not possible to draw any conclusions about the changing quality of pedestrian journeys, either generally or in the cities. However it is clear that, nationally, the proportion of people walking to work and school has been in decline for decades. Walkability and its role as a reflection of the success of liveability investment need to be more effectively monitored. Community Street Audits and Walkability Audits represent potentially effective methods of evaluating the functionality of local environments.

6.5.14   Public transport links into liveability in terms of how space is used and allocated. The quality of public transport has a direct impact on the proportion of people likely to leave their cars at home. Combined with road pricing and other measures to make town centres less car friendly, an opportunity is presented to reallocate space and to enhance the quality and amount of open spaces within our cities. As an acknowledgement of its potential to contribute towards liveability, accessible public transport has been included as one of the acceptable categories for funding as part of the ODPM's Liveability Fund. There is evidence from London and Oxford that investment in public transport can lead to enhanced local environmental quality, especially in town centres. Both cities are taking opportunities to reallocate space from private vehicles to pedestrians and public transport. This has to be contrasted against a decline in the proportion travelling to work by public transport over the last fifty years. These two cities, and perhaps also Manchester's best value residents' satisfaction survey results, suggest that a renaissance in public transport use could be starting to slow or even reverse the trends of the recent past. Investment in public transport is having a positive impact upon liveability in our cities. Public transport accessibility could be included in a liveability audit. Tools such as the DfT's Accession modelling would allow for a much greater depth to be achieved in looking at this aspect of liveability, both locally and citywide.

6.5.15   Vitality and viability of services provides an opportunity to assess the impact of liveability investment on improving the quality of urban environments in two key ways. Firstly, the data provide an indication of how people are using the town and neighbourhood centres. Second, they give us an indication of the performance of the local retail business environment. This can illustrate how people and businesses are voting with their feet in terms of where they perceive to be attractive places to spend time and ultimately money. Urban centres have stopped the inexorable decline and outward movement of activity. But there is little comparable evidence on how individual and smaller centres are performing, so it is difficult to judge the full impact on or contribution to liveability. Monitoring the vitality and viability of services in towns and neighbourhoods has the potential to provide a barometer of the success of liveability initiatives to attract both businesses and people into specific target areas.

6.6   Next steps

6.6.1   This report highlights a number of issues on the state of liveability in English cities, in the context of a significantly enhanced public policy concentration on this relatively new area. We bring together some key strands for future analysis and action.

Liveability is relatively new

6.6.2   The focus on liveability, as an important characteristic of successful neighbourhoods, is relatively new. It does however chime with a neighbourhood focus for the delivery of services within the two case studies, and quality baselines which map expenditure are in the process of being assembled. However, the data sets do not yet have the robustness of the indicators used in the SOCR Database.

6.6.3   Once a clear set of topics has been agreed upon – we suggest the thirteen areas proposed in this report a clear baseline needs to be established. This will distinguish between those elements that can be monitored at a citywide level, such as street cleanliness, noise or air pollution; and those that will need to be assessed at a more local level, such as building quality, place quality and so on. Central government guidance will be key. But the majority of indicators are likely to be monitored locally.

Liveability is local – place matters

6.6.4   The majority of liveability initiatives are likely to be highly localised in nature, limiting the extent or precision of national or inter-area comparison. A number of the liveability topics, such as cleanliness, noise pollution and park quality can be effectively monitored in qualitative and quantitative terms and comparisons drawn between different local authorities. However, these indicators only provide part of the liveability picture. Topics, such as "functional place quality" in particular, are highly localised in terms of their impacts, making intra-authority comparison difficult. They are also more likely to be beyond the direct influence of the local authority, they depend on a broader range of factors and interactions. Nonetheless, the development of a comprehensive localised liveability audit tool for liveability initiatives, could allow for comparison to be made between different areas and schemes across the country. This could support the development of best practice and help ensure value for money.

Process is important

6.6.5 Both Manchester and Leicester have introduced holistic street management teams which have yielded very encouraging results. Both are in the process of developing more robust indicator sets to allow for future performance to be monitored. The qualitative monitoring reports by Manchester's SEM terms in particular are low on resource requirements but provide an effective monthly monitoring tool.

The importance of perception

6.6.6 As the constitution of PSA8 shows, perception of the quality of the environment is a key component of what makes for a 'liveable' neighbourhood. It is not enough to invest, however heavily, in management and maintenance – unless efforts are made to communicate achievements. Neither case study has formally constituted liveability strategies which captured the range of their initiatives and the successes to date. Where there has been an investment in communication, for example around the "100 Days" campaign, there have been significant benefits in terms of improved perception.

Getting the message across

6.6.7 Local liveability initiatives should educate and inform the public about liveability and the quality of their local environment. The example set by Manchester shows that engaging the community offers the potential to engage and activate people in taking ownership and responsibility for their neighbourhood and public spaces. Establishing and disseminating best practice in this regard is crucial.

What works?

6.6.8 Further research is needed in order to identify liveability best practice. Many different models are currently being experimented with across the country. It would be useful at this stage to identify and disseminate best practice across local authorities. This includes not only the operational elements, but also the monitoring of performance and local targets and standards to improve the comparability of projects and interventions.

Develop a local liveability audit tool

6.6.9 We recommend the development of a local liveability audit tool, which could be rolled out to local authorities and would allow them to assess the impact of liveability initiatives. They could also compare liveability in specific areas with similar areas in the authority area or nationwide. This tool could be based on existing methods such as Placecheck, but expanded to include the full range of desirable liveability indicators, including quantitative, qualitative/judgemental and attitudinal inputs. Central government, either directly, or through non-departmental bodies, such as CABE, IDeA or the Academy for Sustainable Communities, will have to take a lead in the development of the audit tool.

6.7   Conclusions

6.7.1   Liveability is important and its importance has been rising, with the public placing a greater emphasis on local environmental quality. This is reflected in the range of attitude surveys which place street cleanliness, the quality of parks and open spaces consistently among those factors that residents would like to see improved in their local area. It suggests that, as long as the economy continues to perform well, people will continue to focus on liveability. Government policy is likely to evolve further.

6.7.2   Corporate focus matters. Where the public agencies, local and central government have concentrated on cleanliness and park quality, there have been noticeable improvements in terms of observed results. Corporate focus is yielding results. However, despite these observed improvements, the public are becoming more demanding in terms of their expectations of the quality of their local environment. These expectations are not yet being consistently realised. In terms of corporate focus, it is essential that there is a clear division of responsibility on liveability. It needs to be clear who is responsible for setting priorities and targets, delivery and implementation and monitoring and dissemination of best practice. Resolving the relationships and responsibilities between partners at a local, regional and national level is critical here.

6.7.3   The local dimension matters. Although some of the organisational and governance issues are of national reach, the majority of liveability strands are most likely to be best assessed and delivered at a localised level. Public realm quality, quality of parks, street cleanliness, walkability, noise and air pollution, for example, all impact upon residents' local lived experience of their environment. They are more suited to local appraisal and implementation. The Street Environment Managers and their teams at Manchester City Council offer a good example of the delivery of targeted local resources which is effective with minimal resources in terms of monitoring. Other topics need to be monitored and delivered at a citywide level, but still have localised liveability impacts – public transport quality is an example.

6.7.4   The public sector matters. The majority of liveability themes rely on significant public sector input. But this does not always mean implementation. So while the public sector is likely to lead on the delivery of public transport, street cleanliness, park quality and the quality of the public realm, it is more likely to have a supporting and mentoring role in the quality of the built environment 'product' or the vitality and viability of key services. This does not mean that the private sector has no place in this agenda – as is evidenced by high-quality public realms in new private-sector development, such as Birmingham's Brindleyplace, or Duke of York's Square in Chelsea. But the great bulk of the effort will continue to be made by local and central government.

6.7.5   A national lead is required. Overall, the government's liveability agenda is starting to have an impact. The PSA8 targets has helped to focus investment and attention on liveability, especially where there is a clear and direct connection between the indicator and the local authorities' responsibilities. BV199 on Local Environment Quality is an excellent example where there is a clear relationship between the targets and the responsibilities of the local authorities and their ability to effect change. It is important that the government continues to set a clear agenda and takes responsibility for allocating responsibilities and standards in this area.

6.7.6   Invest in liveability. It is clear that the government is taking liveability seriously and investing significant sums of grant funding in response to the 'Cleaner, Safer, Greener' agenda. It is less clear that this national focus is being universally applied at a local level. Some local authorities such as Manchester City Council have developed a range of innovative schemes and delivery mechanisms which are responding to the government's ambitions. But others are not and it is difficult to establish a pattern among local authorities. Research examining best practice might point to a number of models that could be usefully applied in different local authorities in different contexts around the country. The Academy for Sustainable Communities, IDeA and ODPM could play a key role here.

Chapter 7: Public attitudes in English cities

7.1   Introduction

7.1.1   This chapter explores the extent to which people's attitudes and experiences vary dependent on whether they live in urban or non-urban areas, in the south and east or the north and west of England. The analysis is based on data from the *British Social Attitudes* survey series which measures changes in public attitudes towards social, political and moral issues. The numbers in the BSA are not large enough to allow us to use the ten fold typology used elsewhere in this report. We use a typology consisting of five categories, to which people are assigned according to the postcode district in which they live. The categories are:

- Urban: London; cities in south and east England; cities in north and west England.

- Non-urban: towns and rural areas in south and east England; towns and rural areas in north and west England.

7.1.2   The chapter begins by summarising the extent to which these five different areas differ in their basic socio-demographic profile. To what extent, for instance, do those living in urban areas differ in their experiences to those in non-urban parts of England? Do these experiences vary according to geography? Are people living in urban parts of the south and east of England significantly different to those living in urban parts of the north and west? The chapter focuses on four particular areas of interest to the *State of the Cities Report*. We begin by considering different measures of social cohesion. We then focus upon two key indicators of connectivity – transport and the Internet. Our third topic is politics and governance. Finally, we examine a range of measures of quality of life.

7.1.3   For each topic, we begin by examining our most up to date findings usually taken from the 2003 *British Social Attitudes* survey. In some cases we find clear differences between people living in different parts of England, in others a remarkable continuity from one area to the next. For some key issues, we then use multivariate analysis to explore whether the differences we find are best explained by the socio-demographic or socio-economic profile of the area. Does, for instance, the fact that London has a notably 'young' population help explain the distinctiveness of its inhabitants' views on some issues? Where possible, we then examine whether the picture has changed over the last decade. The broadest time period used for this time series analysis is the decade 1993 to 2003.

7.2.   The socio-economic profile of urban and non-urban areas

7.2.1   Earlier chapters in this report contained socio-economic profiles of a range of areas. Here we complement this by providing data specifically about the categories we are using in this section. There are a number of notable demographic and socio-economic differences between the populations living in the five areas. Many of these play an important part in explaining some of the different attitudes and experiences we identify, so we outline some of the most important differences. Later we assess the extent to which these characteristics help to explain any differences found.

Age

7.2.2   A particularly important variation relates to age with London and, to a lesser extent, other south and east urban areas being particularly distinctive in their relatively youthful age profile. Only 15 per cent of Londoners are aged 65 or older, compared with 22 per cent of people in non-urban areas. As a result, a relatively small proportion of people in London and in urban areas of the south and east, are retired. This is 14 per cent in London and 18 per cent in urban areas of the south and east compared with 22 per cent in urban areas in the north and west.

Occupation, education and income

7.2.3   Respondents from the five different areas differ in their occupational backgrounds. However, the most striking differences are between the south and east and the north and west, rather than between urban and non-urban areas. In particular, it is notable that a higher proportion of people in the south and east than in the north and west are in non-manual occupations. For instance, 51 per cent of those in London and 46 per cent of people in urban parts of the south and east are in managerial or professional occupations, or in intermediate non-manual ones. This compares with 36 per cent of people in urban parts of the north and west. Conversely, people in the north and west are the most likely to have manual occupations: 47 per cent of those in urban parts of the north and west, compared with 36 per cent of those in urban parts of the south and east and 28 per cent in London.

7.2.4   Given these occupational differences, it is not surprising to find that another important distinction between different areas relates to education. When it comes to having a degree London has a distinctive profile – over a quarter of Londoners are graduates, compared with 18 per cent of those in urban areas of the south and east and 13 per cent of those in urban areas in the north and west. Having no qualifications is particularly common in the north and west urban and non-urban areas where around three in ten are in this position, compared to around two in ten in the south and east including London.

7.2.5   The highest proportion of people living on an annual household income of less than £12,000 is found in urban areas in the north and west, where this applies to just under a third. The lowest proportion is found in non-urban parts of the south and east, where one in five have a household income in this bracket. Urban/non-urban differences are most marked in the south and east, where a higher proportion of people in non-urban as opposed to urban areas have incomes in the highest bracket. There, for instance, a third of the non-urban population have annual household incomes of £38,000 or more, compared with a quarter of those in the urban south and east.

Table 7.1: Household income, 2003

	London	Urban south and east	Urban north and west	Non-urban south and east	Non-urban north and west	All
	%	%	%	%	%	%
Below £12,000	24	26	32	20	28	26
£12,000 to £22,999	18	21	25	23	25	23
£23,000 to £37,999	22	28	25	23	28	25
£38,000 plus	36	25	17	33	19	26
Base (all who answered question)	492	530	776	938	473	3209

Ethnicity and religion

7.2.6 The ethnic make-up of the different areas differs markedly. In London, 72 per cent of respondents describe themselves as White, 10 per cent as Black and nine per cent as Indian or Pakistani. By contrast, in urban areas in the north and west and south and east, nine in ten respondents describe themselves as White. In non-urban areas, the proportion of White respondents is higher still, at 98 per cent in the north and west and 94 per cent in the south and east.

7.2.7 There are marked religious belief differences between urban and non-urban areas but little geographical variation beyond this. Most notably, there are fewer Anglicans and more who follow non-Christian religions in urban areas than there are in towns and rural areas. For instance, in urban parts of the north and west, 27 per cent are Anglican and seven per cent are non-Christian. The equivalent figures for non-urban areas in the north and west are 33 and one per cent respectively. The highest proportion of people who follow non-Christian religions is found in London, which, at 18 per cent, contains more than double the proportion found in other cities.

Housing tenure

7.2.8 Housing tenure is a characteristic which distinguishes between urban and non urban areas, with owner-occupation being more common in the latter although differences between the different areas in the north and west are not significant. The lowest proportion of owner-occupiers is found in London, and the highest in non-urban areas of the south and east. Renting from a private landlord is most common in London and urban areas of the south and east.

7.3 Social Cohesion

7.3.1 We turn now to a range of different experiences and attitudes which collectively help us paint a picture of the level of 'social cohesion' in different areas. We focus here on topics such as social networks and support, trust, racial prejudice and participation in community life. This evidence complements but expands on some material presented in Chapter 5.

Local social networks

7.3.2   For many, the length of time they have lived in a particular neighbourhood will be an important determinant of their social networks. Urban dwellers, particularly those in the south and east including London are the most likely to have moved into their neighbourhood comparatively recently. That is, within the last five years. This applies to 31 per cent of people living in urban areas in the south and east and 30 per cent of Londoners, compared to 26 per cent of non-urban areas in the south and east. There is also a clear regional pattern with those in the north and west being more likely than those elsewhere to have lived in an area for a long time. Thus, while nearly a third of people living in non-urban parts of the north and west have lived in their neighbourhood for 28 years or more, the same is true of only 23 per cent of people living in non-urban areas in the south and east.

7.3.3   To what extent are these differences a reflection of socio-demographic differences between the five areas in question? For example, does the relative youthfulness of London's population when compared with, the non-urban north and west explain the differences we have found? To some extent this does appear to be the case. Multivariate analysis shows that the differences do indeed reflect the distinctive characteristics of each of our five areas in relation to age, education, occupation, economic activity and income. Once these variations are taken into account, there is no significant difference between the likelihood of a person in any of the five areas having lived in their neighbourhood for five years or less.

7.3.4   To some extent, this is also true when we focus on those who have lived in their neighbourhood for 28 years or more. Once we take account of variations in the age and educational profiles of the five areas, some of the differences reduce. However, even when such variations are taken into account, those in non-urban parts of the north and west are significantly more likely to have lived in their neighbourhood for 28 years or more, while those in non-urban parts of the south and east are significantly less likely to have done so.

7.3.5   Over the last decade, there has been an increase in the proportion of people who have lived in their neighbourhood for a relatively short period of time; that is, under five years. In 1994, this characterised one in five people, compared with over one in four now. This change has occurred in both urban and non-urban areas, and has taken place in the north and west as well as the south and east although, as we have seen, notable differences still exist between these areas.

7.3.6   As we might expect, there has also been a reduction in the proportion of people who have lived in their neighbourhood for a very long period of time, defined here as 28 years or more. However, this decline is only evident in the south and east, where it has occurred in both urban and non-urban areas. In 1994, for instance, 31 per cent of those in urban parts of the south and east had lived in their neighbourhoods for 28 years or more; this now applies to 22 per cent. A similar pattern is found for non-urban areas in the south and east, but no such change is yet evident among the north and west.

7.3.7   When it comes to the location of close friends and family, there are clear differences between those in the north and west and south and east. In comparison, any urban/non-urban differences are small. In general, those in the north and west are more likely to have close friends or family living nearby than are those in the south and east. For example, 30 per cent of people in urban areas in the north and west say that most of their relatives and family members live in the local neighbourhood, compared with only 23 per cent of south and east city dwellers. Similar differences are apparent between inhabitants of non-urban areas in the north and west and south and east, with the former being more likely to have friends and family living nearby.

7.3.8   The most likely group of all to report that most of their close friends or family live "further away" are those in London. This is particularly true of family members; over a half of Londoners say most of their family live further away (53 per cent), compared with only 30 per cent of those in urban areas in the north and west. This provides a good illustration of the likely differences between these two areas in terms of the prior geographical mobility of their residents.

7.3.9   There has been considerable debate over the last decade about what is termed 'social trust', and the extent to which it has declined within a range of western societies (Putnam, 2000). Although it is clearly impossible to measure as subtle and multi-faceted a concept as social trust though a single survey question, it is useful to examine responses to what has become the 'classic' measure of social trust, last asked on the *British Social Attitudes* survey in 2002. This asks respondents whether, "generally speaking", they would say that "most people can be trusted, or you can't be too careful in dealing with people" (Johnston and Jowell, 2001).

7.3.10   The results are shown in Table 7.2 and demonstrate that, by this measure, Londoners display a significantly *higher* level of social trust than those in urban parts of the north and west. Due to small sample sizes, no other statistically significant differences exist. This difference is likely to reflect the distinctive socio-demographic and economic profile of Londoners compared with those in urban parts of the north and west. We know, for instance, that levels of social trust are highest among graduates, those in professional and managerial occupations, and the affluent; all groups which are more common in London than elsewhere. This is confirmed by multivariate analysis, which shows that the differences in Table 7.2 reflect the unique age, educational, occupational and income profiles of each of the five areas.

Table 7.2: Social trust, 2002

| | | Urban | | Non-urban | | |
	London	south and east	north and west	south and east	north and west	All
Generally speaking would you say that ...	%	%	%	%	%	%
...most people can be trusted ...	43	36	35	40	40	39
or						
...that you can't be too careful in dealing with people	55	61	63	58	59	59
Base	*279*	*310*	*531*	*532*	*272*	*1924*

7.3.11 Between 1998 and 2002 overall levels of social trust have seen a small but significant decline from 43 to 39 per cent. This figure conceals considerable geographical variation, as in London trust has actually *increased* – from 35 in 1998 to 44 per cent in 2000. In all other areas levels of trust have fallen, though the small sample sizes in some of these areas means that the only area to experience a statistically significant decrease is the non-urban south and east. There four in ten people thought that "most people can be trusted", 10 points lower than the figure in 1998.

Table 7.3: Social trust: 1998, 2000, 2002

| | | Urban | | Non-urban | | |
	London	south and east	north and west	south and east	north and west	All
say most people can be trusted	%	%	%	%	%	%
1998	35	43	40	50	47	43
2000	44	46	41	46	37	43
2002	43	36	35	40	40	39
Base (1998)	*278*	*277*	*491*	*519*	*202*	*1,767*
Base (2000)	*317*	*271*	*537*	*557*	*246*	*1,928*
Base (2002)	*279*	*310*	*531*	*532*	*272*	*2,287*

Local and regional attachment

7.3.12 To what extent do people living in types of locality, or different geographical areas of England feel attached to the region in which they live? Those in the north and west irrespective of whether they lived in an urban or non-urban areas, are more likely than those in the south and east to feel a sense of regional attachment. This applies to eight in ten of those living in urban areas of the north and west, but only seven in ten of those in urban areas in the south and east.

7.3.13 People living in towns and rural areas are more likely than those in cities to feel closely attached to their local area. The lowest levels of attachment to the local area are found in London. This pattern holds true even when we take account of the distinctive socio-demographic profiles of our different areas; residents of non-urban areas are more likely than those elsewhere to feel attached to their locality.

7.3.14 There is little clear pattern in the degree to which people feel close either to England as a whole, or to Britain. But it is notable that Londoners are the most likely to say that they feel closely attached to Europe.

Table 7.4: Attachment to different areas, 2003

| | | Urban | | Non-urban | | |
	London	south and east	north and west	south and east	north and west	All
feel closely attached to	%	%	%	%	%	%
... local area	77	83	84	89	89	85
... region (defined as government office region)	77	71	80	70	78	75
... England as a whole	79	86	82	86	87	84
... Britain as a whole	80	83	80	81	83	81
... Europe as a whole	45	36	30	32	38	35
Base (local area/GOR/ England)	576	581	893	1,115	544	3,709
Base (Britain/Europe)	297	308	453	581	278	1,917

Racial prejudice

7.3.15 One of the clearest measures of social cohesion is the extent to which people within particular communities feel that racial prejudice is on the increase or decrease. In fact, the most commonly held view is that such prejudice has increased over the last five years and that it will continue to increase in the future. The most striking finding relates to the distinctiveness of urban areas in the north and west. Over half of those living there think that racial prejudice has increased over the last five years, considerably more than take this view elsewhere. This group is also more likely to think that prejudice will increase over the next five years, 57 per cent doing so. This is likely, at least in part, to reflect the civil disorder that occurred in Bradford, Oldham and Burnley in 2001, and the racial tension associated with this.

7.3.16 Residents of urban areas in the south and east, including London, are significantly less likely than their counterparts in the north and west to think that prejudice has increased, or that it will do so in the future. They are also less likely than residents of non-urban areas in the south and east to take this view.

7.3.17   There has been a significant increase over time in the proportion of people who think that racial prejudice has increased, or will do so in the near future. As Table 7.6 shows, in 1994, 39 per cent of people thought that racial prejudice would increase over the next five years. Over the next four years this proportion fell; by 1998 it was just 23 per cent. However, it then rose again and by 2003 just over half of people (51 per cent) thought that prejudice would increase over the next five years. These changes have affected all areas, but have been most notable in urban areas of the north and west and non-urban areas of the south and east. The changes of view since 1998 in the urban north and west confirm our earlier impression that its distinctive profile on this measure can at least partly be explained by the civil disorder and racial tension evident in 2001 in towns such as Oldham and Burnley. The changes that have occurred in non-urban parts of the south and east are less straightforward to explain. One possibility is that they reflect increasing concern about immigration. Perceptions of levels of racial prejudice correlate closely with attitudes towards immigration, with those who think that prejudice has increased, or will do so in the future, being more likely to think that levels of immigration should be reduced [McLaren and Johnson, 2004].

Table 7.5: Perceptions about levels of racial prejudice, 2003

| | London | Urban | | Non-urban | | All |
		south and east	north and west	south and east	north and west	
Now compared with five years ago	%	%	%	%	%	%
More now	35	41	53	44	44	44
Less now	23	20	18	21	21	21
About the same	39	36	26	31	32	32
Next five years compared with now	%	%	%	%	%	%
More in five years	44	47	57	53	51	51
Less in five years	24	21	14	17	18	18
About the same as now	28	28	25	25	27	26
Base	*576*	*581*	*893*	*1,115*	*544*	*3,709*

Table 7.6: Perceptions as to whether racial prejudice will increase over the next five years: 1994, 1996, 1998, 2003

| | | Urban | | Non-urban | | |
	London	south and east	north and west	south and east	north and west	All
more prejudice in five years	%	%	%	%	%	%
1994	38	38	41	36	41	39
1996	32	29	34	27	39	31
1998	22	20	27	23	15	23
2003	44	47	57	53	51	51
Base (1994)	285	348	543	526	260	1,962
Base (1996)	344	207	562	616	289	2,018
Base (1998)	141	126	257	266	96	886
Base (2003)	576	581	893	1,115	544	3,709

7.3.18 Attempting to measure an individual's own racial prejudice through survey questioning is, of course, far from easy, and doubts have been expressed about the possibility of assessing attitudes towards such a sensitive topic in this way (see Rothon and Heath, 2003, for a discussion). We focus below on one extremely direct method, used consistently on the *British Social Attitudes* survey since it began. This takes the form of a question about the respondent's own racial prejudice, asked after a number of questions about levels of prejudice within Britain as a whole. Despite the likely influence of political correctness on some responses to this question, it is a very useful measure of prejudice and correlates strongly with people's views on related issues such as immigration, equal opportunities and relationships with different ethnic minority groups [McLaren and Johnson, 2004; Evans, 2002].

7.3.19 Although we found earlier that perceptions of racial prejudice vary notably according to geography and urban-rural boundaries, the same is not true of self-expressed racial prejudice which varies far less by these measures. However, urban areas in the north and west contain a slightly higher proportion than elsewhere of people who describe themselves as being "very" or "a little" prejudiced against people of other races, this applying to just over a third. By contrast, those in non-urban areas in the north and west are the *least* likely to describe themselves as prejudiced in this way. Multivariate analysis confirms that these geographical differences reflect the distinctive age, educational, occupational and ethnic profiles of each area. Once these differences are taken into account, there are no significant geographical variations in expressed racial prejudice.

7.3.20 Earlier we saw that there has been an increase since 1998 in the proportion of people who think that racial prejudice is becoming more common across England. However, when we ask people themselves how prejudiced they are, we find that levels of such self-expressed prejudice have dropped. As Table 7.7 shows, the proportion of people who describe themselves as "very" or "a little" prejudiced has fallen since 1994, by an average of six points across England. However it is notable that the proportion has risen since 1998, when only 27 per cent admitted to being prejudiced. In 1994, as in 2003, those in urban parts of the north and west were the most likely to say that they were prejudiced, reflecting the area's distinctive socio-demographic and economic profile.

Table 7.7: Self-reported racial prejudice: 1994, 1998, 2003

| | | Urban | | Non-urban | | |
	London	south and east	north and west	south and east	north and west	All
Very or a little prejudiced	%	%	%	%	%	%
1994	35	33	41	39	33	37
1998	36	30	24	28	12	27
2003	29	31	34	32	27	31
Base (1994)	285	348	543	526	260	1,962
Base (1998)	141	126	257	266	96	886
Base (2003)	576	581	893	1,115	544	3,709

Participation in community life

7.3.21 Levels of social involvement are claimed to be inexorably entwined with phenomena such as social trust and social capital. British research has demonstrated that links between organisational membership and social trust do exist. For instance, previous analysis of British Social Attitudes data has found that those with stronger links to voluntary organisations tended to be more likely to help their fellow citizens, and more trusting of others [Johnston and Jowell, 1999, 2001].

7.3.22 Organisational belonging and participation varies considerably across England, being lowest in the north and west and highest in the south and east. The highest rates of all are found among residents of non-urban areas in the south and east, 62 per cent of whom regularly join in the activities of at least one of the organisations described in Table 7.8. Participation rates are lowest in urban areas in the north and west; just over a half of their populations do so.

7.3.23 There are marked geographical differences in the *types* of organisation with which people are involved. Table 7.8 shows those organisations mentioned by five per cent or more of respondents. It shows, for instance, that sports or recreation clubs are less commonly cited by people living in north and west urban areas, only 15 per cent doing so. But working men's clubs and social clubs are more common there than in any other area (14 per cent). Another notable difference relates to participation in education, arts, drama, reading or music groups. Thirteen per cent of Londoners do so, as do 12 per cent of people in non-urban areas in the south and east, compared with only 7 and 8 per cent respectively of people in urban areas in the north and west and south and east.

7.3.24 A variety of factors underpin these urban/non-urban and regional differences in organisation membership. In particular, it is clear that a number of key socio-demographic groups, for example graduates, are significantly more likely than others to belong to these sorts of organisations. As we have seen, these groups are not evenly spread throughout England. Once multivariate analysis is used to take the unique age, educational, occupational and income profiles of each of the five areas into account, no significant geographical differences in participation remain.

Table7.8: Organisational membership, or regular participation in activities, 2003

| | London | Urban | | Non-urban | | All |
		south and east	north and west	south and east	north and west	
	%	%	%	%	%	%
belongs to an organisation or takes part in activities	56	60	52	62	54	57
% belongs to:						
Sports or recreation club	18	22	15	22	21	20
Religious group, church organisation	13	13	11	13	11	12
Political party or trade union	9	11	9	10	12	10
Education, arts, reading, drama group	13	8	7	12	8	10
Social club, working men's club	4	11	14	8	9	9
Parent-teachers organisation	9	5	6	7	7	7
Tenants/residents association, neighbourhood watch	8	6	5	7	5	6
Environmental or conservation group	5	5	3	6	6	5
Local group who raise money for charity	5	6	4	6	5	5
Base	436	435	666	809	421	2,767

7.3.25 In the past, attending religious services has been one of the most common forms of organisational 'belonging'. To assess the extent to which this is still the case, the BSA survey asks its respondents who saw themselves as belonging to a particular religion, or who were brought up within a religion, how often they attended religious services. As Table 7.9 shows, Londoners are the most likely group to attend religious services regularly. One in five do so at least once a fortnight, a considerably greater proportion than elsewhere in England. This reflects London's unique ethnic and religious profile.

Table 7.9: Attendance at religious services, 2003

	London	Urban south and east	Urban north and west	Non-urban south and east	Non-urban north and west	All
	%	%	%	%	%	%
Weekly or fortnightly	21	13	14	12	10	14
Less often than fortnightly, but at least once a year	26	17	16	21	18	20
Less often than once a year, or never	38	55	56	52	58	52
Question not asked: not religious, and no religious upbringing	13	15	14	14	11	13
Base	576	581	893	1,115	544	3,709

7.3.26   There has been a marked decline in weekly or fortnightly attendance at religious services, with just under one in five doing so in 1993, compared to one in seven in 2003 (Table 7.10). However, this decline has been less apparent in London where there has been a marked increase both in Non-White ethnic groups, and in those following non-Christian religions. This lack of change in London partly explains the very distinctive profile that London now has in this respect. In all other areas, bar urban parts of the south and east where regular attendance was comparatively low in 1993, there has been a decline of at least six percentage points in the proportion attending services regularly.

Table 7.10: Religious attendance: 1993, 1998, 2003

	London	Urban south and east	Urban north and west	Non-urban south and east	Non-urban north and west	All
attend weekly or fortnightly	%	%	%	%	%	%
1993	23	15	20	18	17	19
1998	18	13	13	11	9	13
2003	21	13	14	12	10	14
Base (1993)	282	186	469	409	225	1,571
Base (1998)	402	428	751	812	302	2,695
Base (2003)	576	581	893	1,115	544	3,709

7.4   Connectivity

7.4.1   Urban areas tend, almost by definition, to be characterised as having better levels of connection and communication than non-urban areas, both in terms of their relation to the outside world and the opportunities they offer for connection with others living in the locality. To take perhaps the most obvious example, people living in urban centres usually have at their disposal considerably more choice when it comes to using public transport to get from one place to another.

7.4.2   Here we focus on two different forms of communication, both of which can be seen as contributing to the 'connectivity' of different places. The first is one of the most traditional issues that we consider when thinking of communication and connection; transport. To what extent, for instance, do areas differ in their transport behaviour, links and opportunities? Do these differences translate into different attitudes towards transport, both public and private? The second area we consider is a more recent phenomenon; the Internet. Here we are particularly interested in exploring the 'virtual' opportunities for connection that the internet potentially offers to those who might otherwise be relatively cut off by, for instance, poor mobility or transport links.

Transport use

7.4.3   Car ownership and use varies both by urban/non-urban location and geography. In line with findings from the National Travel Survey, non-urban areas generally report higher levels of car use than urban ones (The Stationary Office, 2005; Department for Transport, 2005). Those living in the south and east report higher levels of car use than those in the north and west. This means that car use is highest of all in non-urban areas of the south and east where 90 per cent of households have access to a car, and lowest in urban areas in the north and west where only 72 per cent do so. Among other things, this is likely to reflect the income profile in these areas as non-urban areas of the south and east have the highest average household incomes, while urban areas of the north and west have the lowest. The exception to the south and east's reliance on the car is London, where both access to, and the use of, cars is relatively low.

7.4.4   Multivariate analysis confirms that these stark differences in car ownership partly reflect income differences across different parts of England, as well as differences in age, education, occupation, and current activity. However, even when these are taken into account, significant urban/non-urban and regional differences remain. In particular, the above average reliance of the non-urban south and east and the below average reliance of urban parts of the north and west and London remains evident [Exley and Christie, 2002].

7.4.5   In line with other surveys, we found an overall increase since 1993 in the proportion of people who live in households that own a car (The Stationary Office, 2005). This is most notable in non-urban areas. In non-urban parts of the north and west, for instance, 75 per cent of households had regular use of a car in 1993; this now applies to 81 per cent. By contrast, urban areas have seen very little, or no, change in this respect (Table 7.11).

7.4.6   A slightly different pattern emerges in relation to the proportion of drivers in different areas. Here there has been a ten percentage point increase across England since 1993, from 60 to 70 per cent. The most dramatic increase is found again in non-urban areas of the north and west where two-thirds of respondents now drive, compared with 53 per cent in 1993. However, there has also been an approximate ten point increase in the proportion of drivers in both urban and non-urban parts of the south and east. This is true even in London.

Table 7.11: Car ownership and use: 1993, 1998, 2003

	London	Urban south and east	Urban north and west	Non-urban south and east	Non-urban north and west	All
% household owns/ has regular use of car	%	%	%	%	%	%
1993	69	78	71	84	75	76
2003	73	81	72	90	81	80
Base (1993)	*409*	*331*	*732*	*705*	*327*	*2,504*
Base (2003)	*576*	*581*	*893*	*1,115*	*544*	*3,709*
% respondent currently drives a car	%	%	%	%	%	%
1993	52	59	59	70	53	60
1998	62	74	60	76	64	68
2003	62	71	64	80	67	70
Base (1993)	*196*	*157*	*369*	*354*	*167*	*1,243*
Base (1998)	*124*	*151*	*260*	*293*	*100*	*928*
Base (2003)	*157*	*162*	*226*	*275*	*155*	*975*

7.4.7   In all areas, the car is the most common form of transport used on a daily basis. Perhaps the most distinctive finding in Table 7.12 relates to the high proportion of people in non-urban areas of the south and east who drive a car each day, or nearly every day. This applies to six in ten people, compared with under five in ten people in every other area of interest. In fact, once we take account of the fact that not all respondents are *able* to drive, this means that three-quarters of drivers in non-urban areas in the south and east do so more or less every day. Far smaller proportions travel daily as a car passenger, although it is notable that this applies to nearly one in five of those living in non-urban areas of the north and west.

7.4.8   The most distinctive pattern to emerge regarding other modes of transport relates to London – a finding also apparent in the National Travel Survey. Londoners are significantly more likely than any other group to walk for at least 15 minutes, four in ten doing so every day, or nearly every day. They are also markedly more likely to travel by bus on a daily basis, or by train. Of course, this is likely largely to reflect the availability of such forms of transport. For example, 51 per cent of Londoners report having a train station within half a mile of their home, compared with 23 per cent in north and west urban areas and 17 per cent in south and east non-urban areas.

7.4.9   Few people in any area cycle each day. Although no significant differences exist in this respect between the different areas considered in this report, people in urban areas of the north and west are significantly less likely than those in urban areas of the south and east to report ever riding a bike – 17 and 29 per cent respectively. Bar car use, cycling is the one mode of transport that Londoners are less likely than other groups in the south and east to use. Only 18 per cent of Londoners report ever riding a bike.

Table 7.12: Daily use of different modes of transport, 2003

	London	Urban south and east	Urban north and west	Non-urban south and east	Non-urban north and west	All
% reporting travel every day or nearly every day	%	%	%	%	%	%
By car, as driver	36	44	42	60	45	47
By foot, 15 minutes walk	40	31	34	28	23	31
By car, as passenger	8	11	11	13	18	12
By bus	19	5	9	2	4	7
By train	11	4	1	1	1	3
By bicycle	4	7	5	5	3	5
Base (all)	*157*	*162*	*226*	*275*	*155*	*975*

7.4.10 Londoners were the most likely to have travelled by air in the previous year, nearly two-thirds having done so. This compares with 54 per cent of people in north and west urban areas and 57 per cent of those in urban areas in the south and east.

7.4.11 The distinctive nature of attitudes in London is also clear when we consider attitudes towards different ways of raising money for public transport. Londoners tended to be the most supportive, and those in the north and west the least. For example, 44 per cent of Londoners would support a £5 levy on those entering city centres at peak times, three times the proportion found among those in urban areas in the north and west (15 per cent). Fieldwork for the 2003 survey took place after the introduction of the congestion charge in London. People living in the north and west were also notably less enthusiastic than those in the south and east, including London, about the introduction of charges for driving on motorways. The distinctiveness of Londoners on this issue is in line with other research carried out during the same period (Department for Transport, 2004). In many areas of England, the only realistic alternative to the car is the bus. However, outside London, clear majorities would only travel by bus if they had no other alternative. It is also notable that over one in five in urban parts of the north and west see bus travel as predominantly being the domain of the poor.

Internet use

7.4.12 The last decade has seen an immense increase in the proportion of people able to make personal use of the Internet, from 33 per cent in 2000 to 51 per cent in 2003 (Bromley, 2004). Considerable interest exists in the extent to which this new technology can help liberalise access to hitherto inaccessible resources and services, as well as providing new opportunities for communication and knowledge transfer. However, concern also exists over the extent to which the Internet has resulted in a new 'digital divide' between those able to make use of the undisputed opportunities which the Internet offers, and those who are not.

7.4.13 Just over a half of respondents in the 2003 survey report making personal use of the Internet, whether at home, at work or elsewhere. There are marked geographical and urban/non-urban variations, with people in urban areas, particularly in the south and east, being the most likely to use the technology. For instance, six in ten in urban areas of the south and east, including London, make personal use of the Internet, compared with only just over four in ten in urban areas of the north and west. These differences partly reflect differences in home internet access, which is more common in the south and east than in the north and west. They also reflect the different educational profiles of the areas, as internet use is significantly higher than average among graduates [Bromley, 2004; Gardner and Oswald, 2001].

7.4.14 There are also regional and urban/non-urban variations in the extent to which people use the Internet at work. The most likely groups of workers to do this are in London – 57 per cent, followed by those in cities in the south and east – 46 per cent. The least likely are workers in urban areas of the north and west – 39 per cent.

Table 7.13: Internet access, 2003

| | | Urban | | Non-urban | | |
	London	south and east	north and west	south and east	north and west	All
% make personal use of internet	60	60	42	51	46	51
% with internet access in household	57	55	44	57	47	52
% ever uses internet for work*	57	46	39	44	40	45
Base	576	581	893	1,115	544	3,709
*Base (all in work)	237	264	315	438	219	1,473

7.4.15 Table 7.14 shows the huge increase between 2000 and 2003 in the proportion of people who have home internet access or who use the Internet. This increase has taken place throughout England, but is most notable in urban parts of the south and east. There home Internet access has increased by 20 points since 2000, to 55 per cent, while the proportion using the Internet has doubled, to 60 per cent. Although there has been an increase in Internet access and use throughout the country, a significant digital divide still exists between the more well-connected south and east and the less connected north and west.

Table 7.14: Internet access, 2000, 2003

| | London | Urban | | Non-urban | | All |
		south and east	north and west	south and east	north and west	
% with internet access in household	%	%	%	%	%	%
2000	41	35	32	39	34	36
2003	57	55	44	57	47	52
% ever uses internet						
2000	43	30	29	37	27	33
2003	60	60	42	51	46	51
Base (2000)	317	271	537	557	246	1,928
Base(2003)	576	581	893	1,115	544	3,709

7.5   Politics and Governance

7.5.1   We now turn to examine the extent to which there are geographical differences in people's views about politics, their engagement with the political process, and their views about the way in which Britain is governed.

7.5.2   Despite the lack of any regional or urban/non-urban differences in party attachment, there is a clear difference between the level of political interest shown in the south and east and that shown in the north and west. While 38 per cent of Londoners, and 33 per cent of those in urban areas of the south and west have a great deal or quite a lot of interest in politics, this applies to only around a quarter of people in the north and west, irrespective of whether they live in urban or non-urban areas.

Views about politics and politicians

7.5.3   The last two decades have been marked by a quite dramatic decline in levels of political trust, suggesting that the electorate has become increasingly cynical. There are no significant regional or urban/non-urban differences in the extent to which people trust the British government. 18 per cent say that they do so "just about always" or "most of the time", 49 per cent say "only some of the time", and 30 per cent say "almost never". However, mistrust in politicians seems to be higher in the north and west than elsewhere, with 57 per cent in urban areas saying they would almost never trust politicians to tell the truth when in a tight corner. Multivariate analysis shows that these differences reflect the socio-demographic characteristics of these areas and, in particular, their educational and income profile.

7.5.4   Public confidence in the electoral system does not depend simply upon political trust. It also relates to the extent to which people feel that the system can take account of their needs and desires, a perception known as 'system efficacy'. Londoners display the highest levels of system efficacy. They are the least likely to agree about the limited responsiveness of Britain's political system. This is likely to reflect the educational profile of Londoners, as graduates tend to display particularly high levels of political efficacy and a higher than average proportion of Londoners are graduates. There also seems to be a regional difference between north and west and south and east, with those in the former having slightly lower levels of faith that the system is responsive than those in the south and east. The fact that Londoners feel more able to influence government hints at an interesting regional divide, whereby those in the north and west have particularly low levels of faith in their own ability to understand and influence politics and government. For instance, 63 per cent in urban areas of the north and west think that politics can be too complicated to understand, compared with 55 per cent in London and 57 per cent in south and east urban areas. There has been an overall decrease in the proportion of people who do not feel confident in their ability to understand politics and government.

7.5.5   There is a widespread belief that the government favours some parts of England over others (Table 7.15). This view is particularly widespread in the north and west, where it is held by 81 per cent of people in urban and non-urban areas. However, even in London, where this view is least common, over two-thirds believe it to be true. There is also fairly unanimous agreement as to which areas are favoured. Over nine in ten think that either the south of England in general, or London in particular, gets preferential treatment.

Table 7.15: Perceptions of government bias in its treatment of the English regions, 2003

| | | Urban | | Non-urban | | |
	London	south and east	north and west	south and east	north and west	All
	%	%	%	%	%	%
% think government favours some areas of England over others	68	76	81	74	81	76
Base	*157*	*162*	*226*	*275*	*155*	*975*
think government favours:	%	%	%	%	%	%
London	39	42	38	38	39	39
South of England	43	37	56	40	52	46
Rest of England	9	6	1	9	1	5
Base (all who think government favours some areas over others)	*112*	*130*	*184*	*218*	*130*	*774*

7.6   Quality of Life

7.6.1   While politics and constitutional matters are topics which clearly have an impact on people's lives in the long run, they can seem somewhat removed from day-to-day existence for many. So we turn now to examine issues which arguably have a more noticeable impact on people's quality of life: their assessments of the local area, schools and traffic problems.

The local area

7.6.2   We first explore in Table 7.16 whether people believe that their area had got better, worse or remained about the same as a place to live during the last two years. Unfortunately this question was last asked in 1999 so the evidence is a little dated. At that time the most common view, held by over a half, was that there had been no change to the area over the previous two years. People in London were the most likely to think that things had got better, and those in urban areas of the north and west were the least likely – 19 and 9 per cent respectively. The most negative view was held in these same urban parts of the north and west, where over a third thought that their local area had got worse as a place to live over the previous two years. Similar findings emerge when considering people's views about the sorts of change they expect over the next two years, with people in urban areas of the north and west being the most likely to think that their area will get worse – 32 per cent – compared with 22 per cent of people in urban parts of the south and east.

7.6.3   Multivariate analysis confirms the importance of geographical area when it comes to views about the local area. Even when other characteristics between the areas are taken into account, most notably age and education, those in urban areas of the north and west are significantly more likely to think that their local area has got worse over the last two years.

Table 7.16: Has local area changed over last two years? 1999

| | | Urban | | Non-urban | | |
	London	south and east	north and west	south and east	north and west	All
	%	%	%	%	%	%
Got better	19	15	9	13	14	13
Got worse	26	27	36	27	28	29
No change	51	56	53	55	55	54
Base	356	425	765	855	317	2,718

7.6.4   The comparatively high levels of disenchantment found among people living in urban parts of the north and west are reflected in their views about the extent to which local people can actually make an impact upon their area. For example, nearly a half of people in urban parts of the north and west think that it is "too difficult" to do much about improving the local area, compared with 37 per cent in urban parts of the south and east, and 40 per cent in London.

Assessments of local schools

7.6.5   People in urban areas are more likely than elsewhere to take a pessimistic view of their local primary and secondary schools, irrespective of geography. As Table 7.17 shows, 44 per cent of Londoners think that local secondary schools have got worse over the last few years, as do a third of people in other urban areas. This does not, of course, indicate that schools have actually got worse, but does indicate that people's perceptions, and perhaps expectations, of schools vary considerably across England. In London, a quarter think that secondary schools have improved, as do a third of those in other cities. By contrast, only a quarter of people in non-urban areas feel that their local secondary schools have got worse over the last few years. The same pattern is evident in relation to primary schools, although far fewer overall (16 per cent) feel that they have got worse than was the case with regard to secondary schools, rising to 26 per cent in London.

Table 7.17: Views about local secondary schools, 2003

| | London | Urban | | Non-urban | | All |
		south and east	north and west	south and east	north and west	
	%	%	%	%	%	%
Got better	24	34	33	38	38	34
Got worse	44	34	34	26	26	32
Stayed about the same	31	33	33	36	35	34
Base (all with opinion)	*305*	*291*	*506*	*586*	*324*	*2,012*

7.6.6   It is noteworthy that for each of the three areas of state secondary school performance we asked about, the proportion of people who think they are doing a good job increased significantly between 1993 and 2003 (Table 7.18). When it comes to whether schools do well in preparing young people for work, London and urban parts of the north and west showed significant increases, from 36 to 52 per cent in the case of London. When asked about teaching young people basic skills, the proportion of people in the urban north and west and the non-urban south and east thinking they do "very" or "quite well" increased by 11 and 12 points respectively. Finally, in urban parts of the north and west there was a significant increase in the proportion of people who thought that schools did well in bringing out young people's natural abilities, up from 44 per cent to 54 per cent.

Table 7.18: How well state secondary schools perform: 1993, 1998, 2003

	London	Urban south and east	Urban north and west	Non-urban south and east	Non-urban north and west	All
very or quite well	%	%	%	%	%	%
Prepare young people for work						
1993	36	43	40	47	41	42
1998	41	45	42	44	50	44
2003	52	49	51	49	50	50
Teach basic skills						
1993	64	69	64	64	71	66
1998	58	67	70	62	59	64
2003	71	73	75	76	74	74
Bring out natural abilities						
1993	41	44	44	48	50	46
1998	41	49	49	51	50	49
2003	47	50	54	53	57	52
Base (1993)	*177*	*154*	*319*	*312*	*151*	*1,113*
Base (1998)	*103*	*114*	*209*	*221*	*74*	*721*
Base (2003)	*348*	*357*	*550*	*691*	*359*	*2,305*

Traffic

7.6.7   Earlier, in the connectivity section, we found considerable variation between urban and non-urban residents' transport choices and their views about transport issues, such as congestion charging. Here we focus upon the extent to which people in these areas feel that they suffer from some of the negative consequences of traffic, particularly car traffic. We asked about four issues, as listed in Table 7.19.

7.6.8   People in London or other urban parts of the south and east are the most likely to feel that each of these traffic consequences is a serious problem for them. In particular, with the exception of motorway congestion, Londoners are significantly more likely than those in urban parts of the north and west to feel that traffic issues pose a serious problem. Two-thirds, for instance, think this of traffic congestion, compared with a half in urban parts of the north and west. The distinctiveness of London in this respect is in line with other research (Department for Transport, 2005).

7.6.9   In particular, Londoners are more likely than average to feel that they suffer from exhaust fumes and traffic noise, and people in urban parts of the south and east are also significantly more likely than average to feel that they suffer from traffic noise.

Table 7.19: Traffic problems, 2002

	London	Urban south and east	Urban north and west	Non-urban south and east	Non-urban north and west	All
% very serious or serious problem:	%	%	%	%	%	%
Congestion on motorways	36	36	29	34	31	33
Traffic congestion in towns and cities	66	64	51	61	53	59
Traffic exhaust fumes in towns and cities	73	69	58	58	52	61
Traffic noise in towns and cities	47	48	33	37	35	39
Base	*138*	*160*	*259*	*272*	*144*	*973*

The rural idyll

7.6.10 Chapter 3 identified the significance of the rural idyll for much of English society. Table 7.20 throws light on this. It shows that the most popular 'ideal' place to live is a country village. This was chosen by 37 per cent of people in England. The second most popular choice was a small city or town, chosen by 28 per cent. Only 5 per cent said that they would choose to live in a big city.

7.6.11 There were clear variations in preference between urban and non-urban areas. In particular, nearly a half of Londoners – 46 per cent said that they would choose to live in a big city or on its outskirts, over double the proportion in any of our other categories. It is also notable that more than a half of all urban dwellers including Londoners would not choose to live in a big city or its outskirts. After Londoners, those already living in urban areas, whether in the south and east or north and west, were the most likely to opt for life in a big city or its outskirts. People currently living in non-urban areas were the least likely to find this prospect attractive.

Table 7.20: Where people choose to live, if have free choice, 1999

	London	Urban south and east	Urban north and west	Non-urban south and east	Non-urban north and west	All
	%	%	%	%	%	%
Big city	15	3	6	3	2	5
Suburbs/outskirts of a big city	31	17	21	7	5	15
Small city or town	18	34	22	33	33	28
Country village	25	32	38	42	37	37
Farm or house in the country	9	12	11	13	23	13
Base	*248*	*280*	*521*	*555*	*212*	*1,816*

7.7   Conclusion – what is the balance sheet on public attitudes?

7.7.1   What does this chapter tell us about people's attitudes to social cohesion, connectivity, politics and governance and the quality of life in cities?

Social cohesion

7.7.2   Some of our measures show urban areas being less 'cohesive' than others. This is particularly true of cities in the south and east, including London. People were less likely than those elsewhere in England to have lived in their neighbourhood for long periods of time. Inhabitants of urban areas, irrespective of region, had a lower sense of attachment to their local area than those in non-urban areas. There was a lower sense of 'neighbourliness' in urban areas than elsewhere in England. However, many of our measures of cohesion varied more by region than they did by any urban/non-urban divide. For instance, those in the north and west of England tend to live nearer to and maintain higher levels of regular contact with family and friends. They are also notably more likely than people in the south and east to feel a high level of attachment to, and pride in, their region. According to these measures, the inhabitants of urban centres in the north and west have more in common with non-urban areas in the same region than with cities in the south and east of the country. Overall, urban areas in the north and west of England emerge as more 'cohesive' than those elsewhere.

7.7.3   On some measures of social cohesion, particular parts of England, most notably London and urban areas in the north and west, stand out. London is unique in having relatively high levels of regular church attendance, no doubt a reflection of its very particular ethnic composition. London also had particularly high levels of social trust, a reflection of its socio-demographic profile. It was the only area which saw increased levels of trust between 1998 and 2002. Meanwhile, people in urban areas of the north and west have very distinctive views about racism. They are substantially more likely to feel that racism has increased over the last five years and would continue to do so. Self-expressed racial prejudice is also slightly higher in these areas; the result of their distinctive socio-economic profile. Based on these measures there are also marked differences in attitudes between urban and non-urban parts of the north and west.

Connectivity

7.7.4   There are notable differences between urban areas in the south and east and north and west of the country. In relation to transport, attitudes and behaviour varied markedly between urban and non-urban areas, as well as by region. The highest proportion of households with cars and regular car drivers is found in non-urban parts of the south and east. The lowest is in London and urban parts of the north and west. Travel behaviour has changed notably over the last decade, particularly in non-urban areas.

7.7.5 To some extent, these differences are reflected in attitudes towards transport and different transport policies. Londoners, with their relatively low levels of car dependence have particularly distinctive views. They support the idea that drivers should pay higher taxes and are the least likely to think that driving is just too convenient to give up. People in urban parts of the north and west, despite their comparatively low dependence on the car, are less supportive of drivers paying higher taxes than those in urban parts of the south and east who are more likely to drive.

7.7.6 There are notable regional differences in attitudes towards policies aimed at curbing transport use. Londoners again emerge as being the most supportive of policies such as charging motorists to enter town centres or introducing motorway tolls, followed by other areas of the south and east. Those in the north and west are by far the least in favour of such policies.

7.7.7 Overall, there are marked differences between the three urban areas. London stands out as having relatively low levels of dependence on the car, as well as notably tolerant views about policies aimed at reducing car dependence. People in cities in the north and west, despite their relatively low levels of car use, are very unenthusiastic about such policies.

7.7.8 In terms of Internet access and use, there are significant differences between urban and non-urban areas, and between regions. The highest levels of use are in urban parts of the south and east including London. The lowest are in urban parts of the north and west. This difference reflects the differing socio-economic profiles of these areas, particularly in terms of age, occupation and education. There has been a marked increase in the proportion using, or with access to, the Internet between 2000 and 2003. The most notable increase is in the urban south and east.

Politics and governance

7.7.9 Only one political issue, proportional representation, attracted a significantly different reaction in urban and non-urban areas, with the latter being more in favour. On most other issues, the main division was between the south and east and north and west of England, rather than between cities and their less urban counterparts. In nearly all cases, these differences point towards the north and west being less politically engaged than the south and east. For instance, people in the south and east were more likely than those in the north and west to express an interest in politics. They have slightly higher levels of trust in politicians. There is some evidence that people in the south and east are more likely than those in the north and west to believe that the political system is responsive to public demands and to be confident in their ability to understand politics and government. Once again, Londoners stand out. They have particularly high levels of belief in the system's responsiveness and confidence in their own political abilities. This is likely to reflect the unique socio-demographic profile of London, particularly in levels of education.

7.7.10 There were differences in the extent to which people reported ever having engaged in political protest. People in urban parts of the north and west were markedly less likely than those elsewhere to have done so, a reflection of this area's socio-demographic profile.

Quality of life

7.7.11 There are clear differences between urban and non-urban areas on a number of measures of quality of life. People in cities were the most likely to report living near to a range of services and facilities. They were also more likely than those in non-urban areas to think it important that such services were nearby. However, they tended to express lower levels of satisfaction with current services. People in cities were, for instance, less likely to be satisfied with the quality of schools in their local area. Meanwhile, urban areas particularly in the south and east were the most likely to experience congestion, air pollution and traffic noise.

7.7.12 It is also clear that urban areas particularly in the south and east are the most likely to experience problems caused by traffic and congestion. Around two-thirds of those in cities in the south and east, including Londoners, report that traffic congestion is a serious problem for them, compared with a half of those in cities in the north and west. Problems caused by exhaust fumes also vary considerably by location, with nearly three-quarters of Londoners seeing these as problematic, compared with under six in ten in cities in the north and west.

Does living in cities shape people's views?

7.7.13 Sometimes city dwellers appear markedly different to their non-urban counterparts. However, in many cases, there is a clear regional aspect to this. Those in cities in the south and east often differ from those in urban parts of the north and west. At times, London corresponds to other cities in the south and east. On other occasions, it appears to be unique.

7.7.14 There are two possible explanations for these differences. On the one hand, these differences, though 'real' in the sense that they describe our findings for a particular area, might be purely a reflection of the demographic and economic make-up of cities across England. It is simply that more people of a certain type, for instance graduates, live in cities, and they happen to have distinctive views. On the other hand, the experience of living in a city might affect a person's views about particular topics.

7.7.15 Multivariate analysis allows us to explore these issues. It shows that, in relation to social cohesion, Internet use, politics and governance, most of the findings reported reflect differences in the socio-economic make-up of the different areas in question. For instance, the fact that the residents of urban areas in the north and west are more likely than those in other urban areas to express concern about racism, or to admit to being prejudiced themselves, is best explained by their educational, class and age profile. Similarly, the marked differences we found between access to the Internet in different parts of England largely reflect the varying socio-economic profiles of these areas.

7.7.16 However, our findings on transport and quality of life suggest that the experience of living in a city does indeed influence residents attitudes and experiences. For instance, even when we take account of socio-economic differences, Londoners and those in cities in the north and west are notably less likely than average to make regular use of a car. Location does clearly make a difference both to a person's behaviour and to their views. The same appears to be true in relation to quality of life. The lower levels of satisfaction reported by people in cities and higher problems with traffic and air pollution clearly relate to city life itself, rather than reflecting the unique composition of urban areas. Cities do matter and do shape people's views.

Chapter 8: English cities in an international context

8.1 Introduction

8.1.1 This chapter looks at trends in cities and urban policy in the US and Europe. It identifies key changes taking place in policy and process in both continents to see what lessons can be learned in the United Kingdom. It reviews quantitative data sets including the US Census and the EU Urban Audit to identify the ways in which English cities lead or lag behind counterparts elsewhere. It draws upon a wider range of literature to identify some key policy implications for government. Given the scale and diversity of experience of both continents, this chapter does not enter into great detail about policy instruments. Rather it identifies some key policy principles and messages. It examines the American experience first and the European second.

8.2 Lessons from America?

8.2.1 This section addresses four major questions:

- What are the current trends and drivers of change in US cities?

- What factors measure and explain city success in the US?

- What policies have promoted the success of US cities?

- What can English cities learn from this?

While the US and England are marked by significant cultural and political differences in their views of cities, the two are undergoing similar economic and demographic changes which allow valuable comparative policy dialogue about policies and prospects for urban areas.

8.2.2 Americans concerned about the future of cities look upon their English counterparts with envy. Most people in England live in cities and their immediate surroundings, while the US is, by any measure, a suburban nation. Federal and state governments in the US give only occasional attention to the important issues confronted by the nation's major cities, even as the UK government holds biennial summits dedicated to fostering an urban renaissance. As England develops more and more of its new housing in and around existing communities, the US population heads further into the ex-urban hinterland to escape not just cities, but increasingly older suburbs as well.

8.2.3 Although American cities do not occupy the same place in the national agenda as their English counterparts, there are signs that the US – like Britain – may be entering a new urban age. Beneath the dominant story of sprawl and metropolitan decentralisation in the US lies an emerging narrative about the power and potential of cities and urban places. Broad demographic and market forces are fuelling a visible, though uneven and incomplete, renaissance of American cities. These forces are not confined to cities alone, and are reshaping suburbs in ways that force Americans to rethink what is urban.

8.2.4   The policy context in which city renaissance is occurring in the US differs greatly from that in the UK, however. Thriving American cities have benefited from strong leadership by local elected officials who have taken bold steps to transform their cities' physical, economic, and social landscapes. They have succeeded despite federal and state government policies that neglect, and in some cases impede, the progress of cities. For cities that continue to fall behind, the consequences are severe. In a decentralised fiscal system, declining population and employment at the city level lead to a shrinking tax base, and a growing inability to fund the services needed to attract or retain households in a mobile society. In the UK, by contrast, central government devotes considerable effort to reviving city centres and creating sustainable urban communities. Britain's local councillors, however, historically have had far fewer powers to pursue those goals than their American counterparts. Yet UK policymakers are giving new attention to the role of elected city mayors and strategies for promoting fiscal devolution. In this way, the US and UK have much to learn from the recent experiences of one another's cities, and common implications exist for a wide range of policy areas in both countries.

8.3   Cities matter to a suburban nation

8.3.1   Even in a suburban nation such as the US, cities and city-regions remain important to the national economy and identity. Roughly one-fifth of the US population lives in its 100 largest cities, and two-thirds live in the urban areas surrounding large cities. Whilst the US is not as urban a nation as the UK, its inhabitants are at least as likely to live in and around big cities as their former colonial counterparts in Canada and Australia.

8.3.2   The nation's largest central cities employed 31 million workers in 2001, accounting for roughly 27 per cent of all US jobs. In this sense, employment remains more concentrated in cities than population. US metropolitan economies, anchored by large cities, account for the bulk of the nation's economic output. In 2003, the 318 US metropolitan areas generated aggregate output valued at $9.4 trillion, more than 85 per cent of total US output, slightly exceeding their share of US population.

8.3.3   High-value growth industries in the US are largely located in big cities. Urban areas have led the nation's transition to a service-dominated economy (Figure 8.1). Finance, business services, and engineering/management employment have all grown faster, pay higher wages, and are more concentrated in cities than employment generally.

Figure 8.1: Urban Areas have Led the Transition to a Services-Dominated Economy

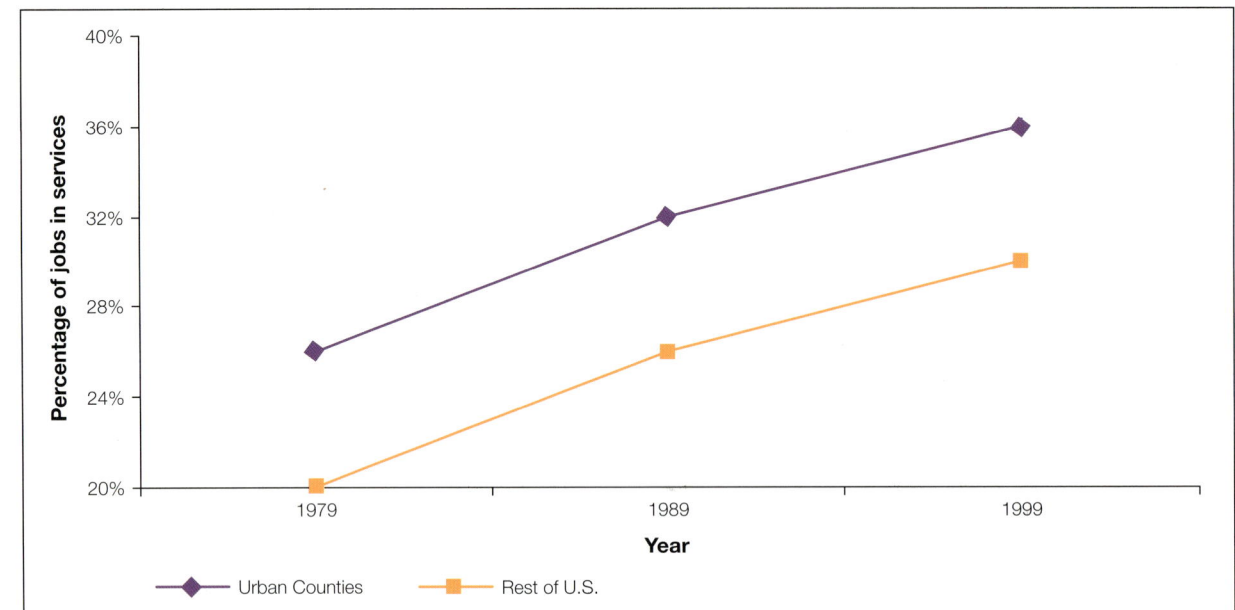

8.3.4 Metropolitan areas, particularly the cities at their core, remain an important lens through which Americans identify their communities. Newspapers, sports teams, and cultural institutions reinforce residents' connections with their broader city-regions. Of course, these strengths are found in varying degrees in individual cities. They are more characteristic of America's global and national cities – New York, Los Angeles, Chicago, Atlanta, Washington, DC – than its regional cities, especially those dealing with a legacy of heavy industrial employment like Cleveland, St. Louis, and Baltimore. Yet cities remain crucial to the success of their metropolitan areas. Indeed, in a country as large as the US, the metropolitan context is far more relevant than the national one for defining and measuring the performance of cities. Population and economic growth in suburbs remain highly correlated with what occurs in their central cities.

8.4 Drivers of Change

8.4.1 Changes in US cities reflect larger structural changes occurring in the population and economy which affect cities, suburbs, and rural areas to varying degrees. Four macro-level trends are most important.

8.4.2 *Population growth.* The US is growing nearly as fast today as it did in the late 1960s, at the end of the country's postwar baby boom. It ranked fourth among the 30 OECD countries on population growth from 1991 to 2003 (Figure 8.2). Demographers expect this rapid population expansion to persist over the next few decades, fuelling the continued expansion of US metropolitan areas. As a result, by 2030, about half of the buildings in which Americans live, work, and shop will have been built after 2000.

Figure 8.2. The United States is the fourth fastest-growing OECD country

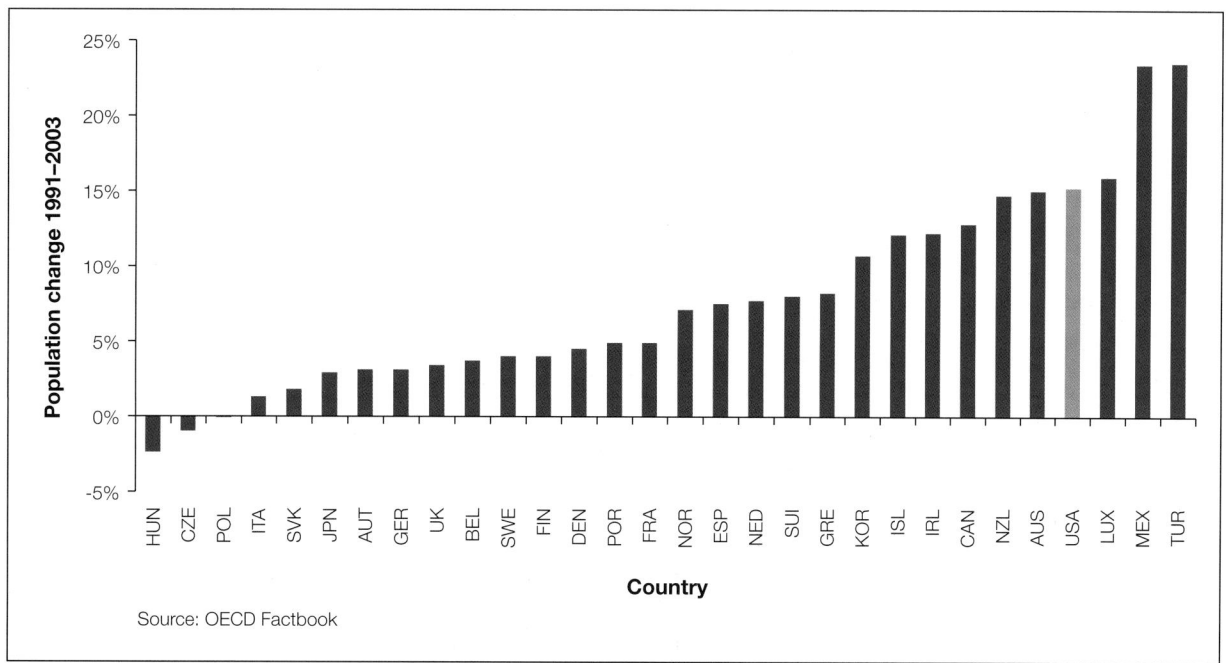

Source: OECD Factbook

8.4.3   *Growing racial/ethnic diversity.* As in western Europe, fertility and mortality have fallen to relatively low levels among the native-born US population. The nation's continued growth owes in large part to immigration, as foreign-born individuals and their children today make up more than one-fifth of US residents. Because most migrants to the US come from Latin American and Asian nations, the country has become more racially and ethnically diverse as well. Thirty-two per cent of the population is Non-White or Hispanic.

8.4.4   *An aging society.* America's 76 million strong 'Baby Boom' cohort is nearing retirement, posing new demographic and fiscal challenges. The greying of America, and delayed childbearing among younger adults, has contributed to the nation's household diversity, increasing the number of single person and childless married couple households in the US In 2000, the average US household contained 2.6 people, down significantly from 3.4 people in 1950.

8.4.5   *Widening inequality within broader growth.* During America's economic expansion in the 1990s, a tight labour market produced broad-based economic gains for American workers and families. Labour force participation and incomes rose for Blacks and Hispanics, and the nation's poverty rate declined. Since 2000, some of these gains have been erased due to economic recession and a jobless recovery. These cyclical changes, however, did not suspend longer-term secular changes, including the continued decline of manufacturing employment and the rise of service employment. The resulting increase in the economic return to skills and education, amid demographic transitions such as immigration, have further widened the gap between the highest and lowest income families in the US.

8.5   Trends in American Cities

Cities are growing overall in response to large trends

8.5.1   With economics, demographics, and shifting consumer tastes putting new wind in their sails, major American cities in the 1990s registered their largest population gains in several decades. City observers hailed the 'urban turnaround' and the 'downtown rebound.' In contrast to earlier censuses, the results from Census 2000 gave cities much to celebrate.

City populations increased in the 1990s

8.5.2   The post-war years were, in general, unkind to American cities. The 1970s, in particular, saw most big cities lose population. Boston, Chicago, New York, Philadelphia, and Washington, along with dozens of other older cities, saw their populations decline by at least 10 per cent. A poor economy, high crime rates, municipal mismanagement, and rapid suburban development combined to drain cities of their upwardly mobile residents. The 50 largest cities together lost two per cent of their population in that decade. The 1980s were somewhat kinder to cities, as they showed a combined six per cent population increase. However, several big cities continued to lose residents. In the 1990s, however, population gains were larger and spread more widely (Figure 8.3). The overwhelming majority of big US cities – 74 out of the top 100 – showed increases. Their combined population grew by nine per cent. Some cities which had lost residents during the 1980s, including Atlanta, Chicago, and Denver, actually reversed their slides during the 1990s. The difference between the decades was most noticeable in very large cities of at least one million people. They grew by seven per cent in the 1990s, in contrast to one per cent in the 1980s. And only 20 of the 100 largest cities lost significant population over the decade, a considerable improvement on the 37 which suffered that fate during the 1980s.

Figure 8.3. Large US cities grew more rapidly in the 1990s

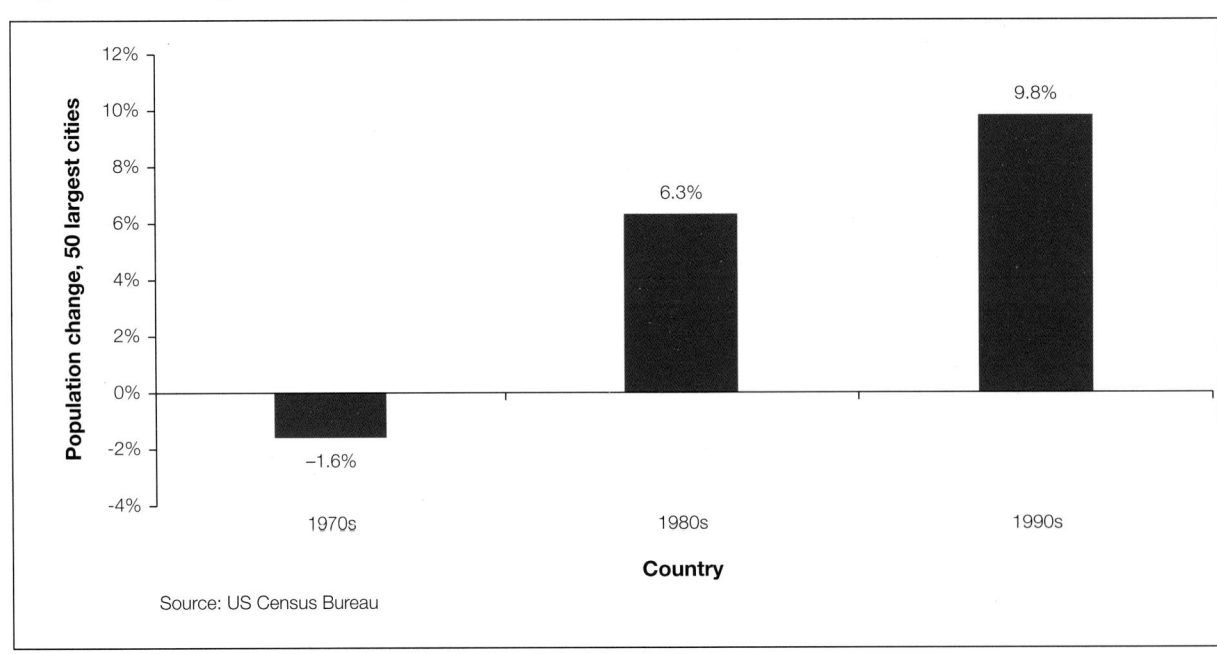

Source: US Census Bureau

Most city centres grew

8.5.3   One notable pattern in the resurgence of city populations was the widespread upturn in city centre living. Little more than two decades ago, many US downtowns were devoid of residents, home almost exclusively to office and retail space. But in the 1990s, city centre living gained in popularity. Analysis of 36 major American downtowns found that three-quarters gained inhabitants over the decade. Even some cities which lost population overall gained downtown residents, including the older industrial cities of Cleveland, Baltimore, Philadelphia, and Milwaukee. The experience has encouraged most city governments to continue developing city centres attractive to wealthier residents, especially young workers and empty-nest Baby Boomers desiring shorter commutes and nearby amenities. One analysis found that 45 per cent of city centre residents in 2000 had college degrees, nearly twice the national proportion.

But city growth was uneven

8.5.4   While the dominant population trend was positive, a booming economy did not produce gains for all places. Several older cities continued their long post-war population slide. Baltimore, Buffalo, and St. Louis all registered double-digit decreases and Detroit's population dipped below 1 million for the first time since 1920. Medium-sized cities had an uneven experience as well. Among the 100 cities with 1990 populations from 100,000 to 170,000, 25 lost population over the decade or did not grow at all. Cities in this size category with a heavy industrial heritage were hit especially hard.

8.5.5   Moreover, among those cities which did increase in population, significant disparities separated the high fliers from the modest gainers. As broader regional patterns indicate, Sunbelt cities – especially those in the West – grew very rapidly over the decade, while their Northeastern and Midwestern counterparts declined or barely expanded. Las Vegas, the nation's fastest-growing city in the 1990s, nearly doubled in population in just 10 years. Of the nearly 200 cities with populations of at least 100,000 in 1990, the top ten growers were all located in the Western US or Texas. Eight of the top 10 decliners, meanwhile, were found in the Northeast or Midwest.

City job gains were widespread

8.5.6   Job growth in cities during the 1990s actually outpaced population growth. Of 114 large cities tracked by the Department of Housing and Urban Development, 102 experienced at least modest job growth between 1992 and 2001. The 114 cities combined gained 4.5 million jobs during that time, a 17 per cent increase. For the most part, the job growth pattern mirrored that for population growth. Sunbelt cities such as Las Vegas, Austin, and Orlando topped the list and rust belt cities such as Buffalo, Detroit, and Dayton appearing near the bottom. One promising trend was that several cities which lost residents in the 1990s – including St. Louis, Cleveland, Baltimore, and Philadelphia – had modest job gains during that time.

Population and employment decentralisation remains the rule

8.5.7   Although welcome after decades of decline or sluggish growth, the upward population and job trends for cities did not diminish the broader story of nearly every American metropolis – continued decentralisation of people and jobs. The economic and population centre of metropolitan America continued to move further into the suburbs.

Suburbs grew faster than cities

8.5.8   In general, city and suburban populations travelled in tandem during the 1990s. The fastest growing cities were located in fast-growing metropolitan areas, and declining cities were found in slow-growing regions. Phoenix, and Cleveland were model examples of this tendency. Phoenix grew at a torrid 34 per cent rate, as its metropolitan area expanded by 45 per cent. Meanwhile Cleveland, which lost five per cent of its population, occupied a metropolitan area that grew by only two per cent over the decade. The economic and demographic forces affecting cities and their suburbs, while not uniform, did reflect broader regional trends in the 1990s.

Employment continued to suburbanise

8.5.9   As people went, so went the jobs. Despite consistent job growth in cities over the past decade, more Americans work in suburbs today than ever before. Across the largest 100 metropolitan areas, only 22 per cent of people work within a three-mile radius of the city centre, and more than 35 per cent work at least ten miles from the urban core. Around cities like Chicago, Atlanta and Detroit, more than 60 per cent of regional employment is now located 10 or more miles from the downtown. None of this evidence contradicts the fact that cities performed better in the 1990s than in previous decades. For most cities, their worst days seem to be behind them. However, the 1990s hardly stifled the decentralising forces in metropolitan areas that have made the United States the suburban nation it remains today.

Lines between cities and suburbs have blurred

8.5.10   The decentralisation of jobs and population in metropolitan America has reached the point where many suburbs themselves are coming to resemble central cities in their demographic and economic makeup. In previous generations, planning systems and exclusionary housing development kept suburbs as the exclusive province of middle and upper class White families. Today more suburbs are diversifying along racial and ethnic, income, and household lines, especially in rapidly-growing parts of the nation.

Immigrants made cities 'majority minority'

8.5.11   Cities lead the nation's growing racial and ethnic diversity. Between 1990 and 2000, the 100 largest cities in the United States moved from being majority non-Hispanic White to majority minority. Whites went from representing more than half to less than half of the overall population of these cities. The transformation was not marginal, as their combined White share of population dropped dramatically from 52 per cent in 1990 to 44 per cent in 2000 (Figure 8.4).

8.5.12 Immigration fuelled this transition. The arrival of residents from abroad helped boost population growth in US cities in the 1990s, and in several cases prevented them from losing residents overall. Older cities including New York, Chicago, Minneapolis, and Boston, all typical of the urban renaissance in the 1990s, would each have lost population if not for increases in foreign-born residents. Even Dallas, which grew by 18 per cent over the decade, would have experienced only two per cent growth without the addition of immigrants.

Figure 8.4. Cities and suburbs are home to diversifying populations

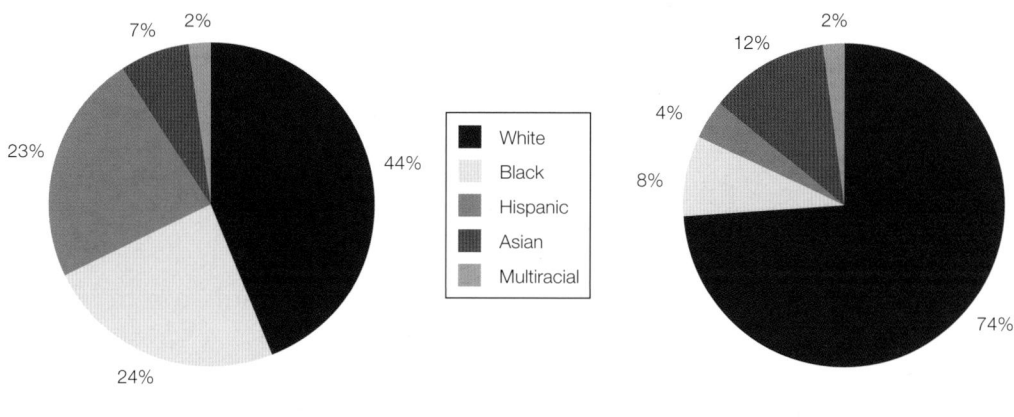

Source: Brookings (2001); Frey (2001)

Minority groups are also moving to suburbs

8.5.13 Diversifying populations were not confined to big cities, however. The decade saw a dramatic increase in minority suburbanisation, especially in what have been called Melting Pot Metros. These large, multi-ethnic metropolitan areas, like Los Angeles, Chicago, San Francisco, and Houston are major ports of entry for immigrants and are where the impact of rising Hispanic and Asian populations is most obvious. Non-Whites and Hispanics accounted for the bulk of suburban population gains in most large metropolitan areas. In 2000, they represented 27 per cent of suburban populations, up from 19 per cent one decade earlier. Today, the majority of Hispanics and Asians in large US metropolitan areas live in suburbs rather than cities.

Poverty is suburbanising

8.5.14 The shifting geography of poverty demonstrates this growing economic similarity between many cities and suburbs. Historically, cities and rural areas have been home to the nation's poor. As recently as 1967, these areas contained 81 per cent of all Americans living below the poverty line. A little over one generation later, suburbs today contain more than 40 per cent of the nation's poor. In major metropolitan areas, half of the poor reside in suburbs. And while the poverty rate in cities (18.4 per cent) remains more than twice as high as that in suburbs (8.3 per cent), the city-suburb poverty rate gap narrowed slightly in the 1990s. Fewer than half of the nation's big cities saw their poverty rates increase in the 1990s, compared to three-fourths in the 1980s. Perhaps the best news for cities, was that the pockets of extreme poverty that have long characterised many inner cities dissipated significantly during the 1990s. Even though many cities experienced only moderate declines in their overall poverty rates, the strong economy and other policy tools seem to have broken up many of the worst concentrations of economic distress plaguing inner cities during the late 20th century.

Population and economic dynamics are widening gaps across cities and metro areas

8.5.15 As cities and suburbs converged in some important respects in the 1990s, cities and regions themselves however, diverged on major indicators of economic and social health. A widening gap among US cities and metropolitan areas in the 1990s and beyond appeared along a range of outcomes: population growth, migration, human capital, income, and wealth. The resurgence and continued growth of some cities and regions occurred alongside social and economic decline in other areas.

8.5.16 Although the 1990s saw population increase in most cities, not every city grew by the same degree, or even grew at all. The following three factors help explain the remainder of the wide disparity in city population trajectories:

- high human capital cities – those with larger shares of college-educated residents, higher median incomes, and lower poverty rates – tended to grow faster;

- industrial mix mattered. Cities with high percentages of workers employed in manufacturing tended to grow much more slowly. By contrast, cities specialising in trade and services grew rapidly;

- newer cities grew faster than older cities. Population increased more in cities where people tend to drive to work, and in cities with newer housing.

8.5.17 Migration patterns, especially among younger workers, helped to widen the gap between highly educated cities and suburbs and less dynamic labour markets. What attracted these workers to certain cities and not others? Job growth, especially in the high technology sector, and a healthy supply of cosmopolitan amenities were associated with increases in young, educated workers in the 1990s. Many have highlighted the role that labour market density plays in attracting these young and restless workers. With today's typical US worker remaining at their job for under five years, these cities may be attractive because of the wide range of employment options they offer within easy reach.

Income and wealth

8.5.18 These dividing lines on population, migration, and human capital had obvious consequences for the economic health of cities. Because higher-income, higher-educated households are generally more mobile, and can exercise greater choice in their metropolitan location, struggling cities lost these households over the past two decades. Meanwhile, other cities and regions enjoyed income growth at the high end of the spectrum, though that presented its own set of challenges.

8.5.19 Most cities still lack a representative number of middle and higher income households to contribute to their tax base and support local market vitality. This is particularly the case in the distressed cities of the Northeast and Midwest. Widening income gaps across cities highlight the challenge for most urban areas: to attract, retain, and grow from within a larger base of middle income workers and families. The story for US cities and metropolitan areas is positive overall. But deep divisions and further divergence in the 1990s on several indicators suggest a more complicated, uneven picture of urban health.

8.6 What's driving the urban recovery?

8.6.1 What helps to explain the resurgence of some cities amid the continued long-term decline of others? As we saw with English cities in Chapter 3, American cities are benefiting from demographic, economic, and cultural forces that suggest a possible return to urban living.

8.6.2 Declining household size and increasing racial and ethnic diversity could benefit cities. They offer a more diverse housing stock attractive to more young singles and couples and older childless couples. Though more immigrants live in suburbs today than in previous generations, they still live disproportionately in cities and will continue to regenerate urban neighbourhoods which need population and economic activity.

8.6.3 Perceptions of cities have improved dramatically during the past 20 years, assisted by television and film depictions of life in the big city, as well as dramatic declines in violent crime rates in cities after 1990 (Figure 8.5).

Figure 8.5 Decline in violent crime

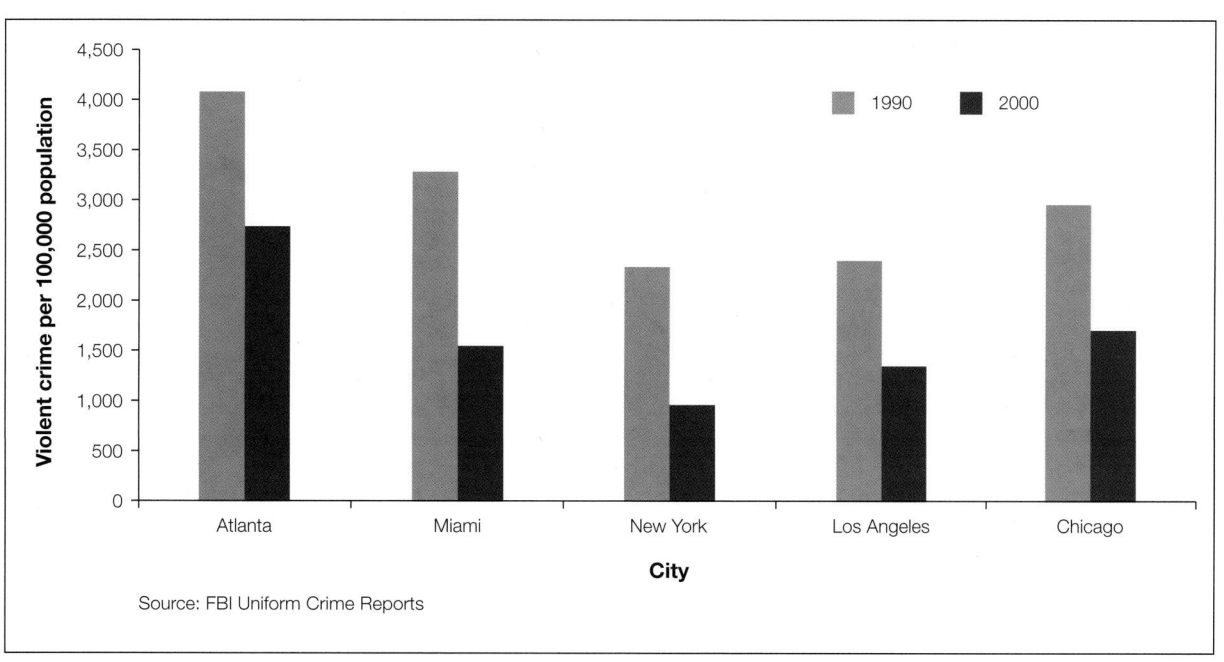

Source: FBI Uniform Crime Reports

8.6.4   As the economy continues to shift from manufacturing to services, ideas and innovation are driving economic growth and changing the value of density itself. Firms in large metropolitan areas value their workers more highly, because workers there are more productive. They grow more productive over time because of the variety of jobs and information spillovers within and between industries. Cities today are not merely centres of production, but are increasingly centres of consumption, with distinctive amenities valued by wealthier households. Furthermore, an aging society and the pressures of globalisation should drive the nation towards more cost-efficient land use in coming decades.

8.7   Policy responses

8.7.1   The demographic and economic forces shaping US cities have spurred a wave of local innovation in the United States. This innovation, a product of strong local governments and entrepreneurial leaders, has helped fuel the partial resurgence of American cities and enabled them to respond more effectively to competitive pressures.

8.7.2   American cities have greater powers and responsibilities than English cities. They raise revenue for and deliver a wide range of basic local services. They implement large numbers of programmes financed by federal and state governments. They have significant land use and planning powers. This devolved system has advantages and disadvantages. It has bred a new generation of entrepreneurial local politicians who have brought about significant transformation of their cities. At the same time, it has resulted in a degree of inequality among cities and their residents which would create serious concern in the UK.

8.7.3   Successful cities in the US have enjoyed far-sighted leadership that pursues bold strategies. In particular, these leaders – typically elected city mayors – have acted on five fronts. These include:

8.7.4   *Fixing basic services.* More than any one urban policy – good schools, safe streets, efficient basic services, and efficient planning systems – dictate residential choices and business investments in the US Mayors of successful US cities have used innovative policing strategies, assumed responsibility for schools, overhauled fiscal management, tackled decline, and upgraded basic infrastructure such as roads and sewers. This dramatic break from past practices reinforces the basics as a focus for city governance.

8.7.5   *Building on core assets of cities.* Rather than pursue the hot new industry, or copy other cities' economic development strategies, a growing number of American cities have tried to build on their unique existing assets. These include ports and airports, historic neighbourhoods, waterfronts, universities and medical institutions and a dense collection of people with drive, talent, and ideas. By investing in these economic and physical assets, cities have improved their competitive position for jobs and residents.

8.7.6   *Creating neighbourhoods of regional choice.* The strongest cities have demonstrated that they can build and sustain neighbourhoods of every variety. They are trying to invigorate the local businesses and commercial corridors around which diverse neighbourhoods grow. They understand that neighbourhoods need to be integrated economically with the rest of the region, especially in terms of access to regional labour markets. Some have conducted complex neighbourhood analyses to target scarce resources and achieve market and social impact. Some have actively marketed neighbourhoods to outsiders, including middle class households looking for affordable housing, or immigrants who have helped to revitalise inner-city communities. Still others have used the redevelopment of failed public housing as the catalyst for large-scale public and private sector investment in housing, business, and schools.

8.7.7   *Growing a strong, urban middle class.* While many US cities have set off in search of the creative class, most remain home to disproportionate numbers of low and moderate income working households. Though the condition of the national economy greatly influences their economic and social mobility, these workers and families rely on local governments in several ways. They need them to connect to education and training which link them to growth sectors of the economy; to reduce the costs of basic goods and services which are often more expensive in low-income neighbourhoods; and to generate opportunities for wealth-building and financial security through homeownership in stable communities. These strategies recognize that the economic and social futures of cities rely far more on the progress made by current residents than the migration decisions of a small group of elite younger workers.

8.7.8   *Driving balanced city-regional growth.* In the end, cities are not islands unto themselves. They exist as part of broader metropolitan communities and economies. They operate as labour markets, since their residents invariably work throughout the broader region, often in key sectors. For that reason, urban policies must relate to the city-regional geography – the real geography of housing markets, labour markets and educational opportunity. Policy-makers must treat the borders of cities as porous boundaries rather than fixed barriers. And cities need to understand their own position in the city-region.

8.7.9   In recent years, urban leaders have begun to position their cities within the city-regional landscape and link residents to the broader geography of opportunity. The more far-sighted urban leaders are looking for ways to collaborate with their suburbs on everything from improving transportation and infrastructure to promoting trade to developing regional workforce training systems. Business leaders have known for years that local economies and the challenges they face are regional in scope. Political leaders have begun to catch on.

8.7.10   These are all crucial developments, a signal that institutional expertise is crucial to successful local governance. In particular, they indicate that cities recognise that they are in a new context, and that the economy in which they operate, the people who live in and around them, the politics of funding and running them have created a new urban dynamic. The competitive strategies described above share some unifying themes. What unites these efforts is their focus on transformation of the physical, economic and social landscape. These are big, entrepreneurial efforts at a time when both national parties rarely offer solutions to the daily challenges – housing, congestion, jobs, sprawl – that bedevil working families living in metropolitan areas.

8.7.11   What also unites these efforts is their intense focus on competitiveness. Urban leaders in the US embrace the proposition that a strong economy is a necessary precondition for a wide range of social and environmental objectives – growing a middle class, reducing racial and ethnic disparities, promoting balanced growth. They also accept the reality that cities must compete with each other, their suburbs and places abroad for talented workers, quality firms, and the enhanced tax base that accompanies them.

8.7.12   A related theme is the reliance on local innovation. City leaders understand that they – not the federal government or state governments – are primarily responsible for their own economic destiny. This understanding – and the substantial powers that have been devolved to cities – lays the foundation of the entrepreneurial attitude that permeates urban leaders in the United States. This reliance on local innovation, of course, has its limits. City strategies, no matter how strategic or well executed, cannot undo structural changes in the economy.

8.7.13   Yet the design and implementation of the new competitive agenda does not rest with local government or directly elected mayors alone. Even with economic restructuring, many American cities still have a rich network of non-government leaders in the private and voluntary sectors – business improvement districts, community development corporations, philanthropists, business alliances. They play an active role in the development and implementation of initiatives and are a major reason that US cities have performed relatively well.

8.7.14   These strategies confirm the significant role played by government, corporate, civic and community leaders. Many of these actions have helped cement an image of the new mayor – pragmatic, entrepreneurial, no nonsense, above politics. This highly favourable image stands in sharp contrast to the public's perception of politicians at higher levels of government. Yet it would be inaccurate to paint the US federal and state governments as uniformly hostile to the urban agenda. Although historic and some contemporary ones have exacted a toll on the health of cities, many of the positive changes that have occurred in cities more recently are at least partly attributable to policy shifts at the national level. The liberalising of national immigration policy in the 1960s, the devolution of transportation planning to metropolitan entities, the transformation of public housing in the 1990s to promote residential mobility, and the subsidising of low wages through the federal tax code all contributed to improved city performance. States, too, have experimented with efforts to stimulate the redevelopment of older areas, seeking to level the playing field between cities and suburbs. Without this more supportive policy environment, cities would not have enjoyed the degree of success they have in recent years.

8.8   Lessons for English cities

8.8.1   What does the experience of American cities mean for English cities? The primary lessons are about local governance. The powers of US cities run broad and deep, and have fostered an entrepreneurial culture and attracted strong city leadership. The fortunes of English cities depend to a much greater degree on the involvement of central government, which may be less well-equipped to keep pace with the dynamic changes shaping urban areas today. There are five areas in which English cities might benefit from the experiences of their American counterparts.

8.8.2   The direct election of mayors in England could help realise the potential of cities and City-Regions. Strong city leadership could help urban places adapt in the changing economy, especially where serious governance reforms are needed. Accountable local leaders could greatly assist Whitehall in delivering on national priorities. They would be in a unique position to reach across programmes in a particular place to achieve results, taking a wider view that is often beyond the reach of more targeted efforts like Local Strategic Partnerships (LSPs). England could go one step further and consider the direct election of mayors for larger City-Regions. Even if the direct election of mayors is not widely adopted in England, other American experiments in local government structure – combined mayor/city council systems, metropolitan mayors' caucuses – could be considered.

8.8.3   Local government reform, especially with greater financial powers given to cities, would provide the foundation for responsive city leadership. In fact, considerations of elected mayors must be accompanied by greater understanding of what powers such new arrangements might bring. In the US, cities reap the benefits of investments through increased tax revenues, which they are able to reinvest in other priorities. In England, cities must return the bulk of their tax increases to central government. That creates little incentive to innovate and a significant lag between when problems are identified and local resources available to address them. England could award additional fiscal and economic development powers to cities while guarding against the emergence of the significant disparities between cities found in the US.

8.8.4   English cities should also seek to engage non-governmental leaders in the private and voluntary sectors, who form such a critical component of the civic leadership class in the US Encouraging them to play an active role in agenda setting and policy implementation is crucial. Elected city mayors who serve as a sort of CEO for local governments can find helpful partners in the leaders of these other large organizations.

8.8.5   US cities have succeeded partly by embracing economic and demographic diversity. England is in general a more economically integrated country than America. The broader embrace of racial and ethnic diversity, particularly concerning immigrants, is less evident at national or local level in Britain. The nature of immigration to the US remains quite distinct from that in the UK However, the fact that England is aging even more rapidly than America makes the attraction and integration of new immigrant populations a potentially more relevant issue for English cities than American ones. Many local officials in the US have taken the lead in promoting the geographic and cultural integration of immigrant populations, recognising their importance to the long-term economic health of cities.

8.8.6   Finally, the American experience issues a stark warning about the relationship between national policy and local innovation. In the end, the United States devolves too much power and responsibility to local levels of government. England should guard against the emergence of extreme inequities which characterise American cities today. The challenges of modern life and a global economy demand the right mix of investment by higher levels of government and the strategic leaders who are closer to the ground. Devolution of power is not a licence for withdrawal of central government investment and interest.

8.9   Messages from Europe

8.9.1   Given the very different histories, social structures, institutional and constitutional arrangements and urban experiences across the continent, this section cannot review in detail the experience of cities and urban policy across Europe. Rather it focuses upon a set of key trends and policy messages which emerge from the European experience and which have significance for cities and city policy in the UK. It addresses the following questions:

- What trends are there in cities and why do they matter to Europe?

- How do English cities compare with European cities?

- What policies have European governments adopted and what key principles have emerged?

8.10   What trends in cities and why do they matter to Europe?

8.10.1   In the last decade there has been a transformation in the perceptions of the role cities play within Europe. They are now high on the European agenda for a variety of reasons. Traditionally cities have been seen in their respective national economic hierarchies. Increasingly they are seen in a wider European economic context at least. There has been a rapid growth in the development of networks between cities at a European level designed to promote trading links, exchange good practice and promote the interests of cities at a European level. There has been growing awareness of the contribution and potential of cities to Europe's economic competitiveness. Cities are increasingly seen as economic assets, not liabilities, which need to be exploited not only at a national but also at a European level. This is a crucial part of the European Council's Lisbon Agenda[4]. But there has also been growing recognition of the double-edged character of much economic change in cities during this period. The search for economic growth has not always led to social equity; indeed it has often been associated with social exclusion. This juxtaposition of success and failure, growth and decline, innovation and stagnation, wealth and poverty, great architecture and environmental

4 At its meeting in Lisbon in March 2000, the European Council launched its new mid-term strategic goal: to make the European Union by 2010 "the most competitive and dynamic knowledge-based economy in the world, capable of sustainable growth with more and better jobs and greater social cohesion". EU leaders also agreed a detailed strategy for achieving this goal – the Lisbon Strategy – aimed at:
- Preparing the transition to the knowledge-based economy;
- Promoting economic reforms for competitiveness and innovation;
- Renewing the European social model by investing in people and combating social exclusion; and
- Keeping up with a macro-economic policy mix for sustainable growth.

deterioration poses a major challenge to the social cohesion of Europe. Linking increasing economic competitiveness to increasing social inclusion is a crucial challenge for policy-makers at all levels of government and all social partners in all European countries.

8.10.2 Of course, urban Europe remains enormously diverse. There is not a single model of a European city and the challenges are not the same in every city. Important differences in their economic structure and functions, social composition, size and geographical location shape the challenges cities face. Equally, national differences in traditions and cultures, economic performance, institutional arrangements and government policy have an important impact upon cities. The problems of global cities like London or Paris are not those of medium-sized cities. Declining large industrial cities with exhausted manufacturing economies, less skilled work forces and substantial immigrant communities face different dilemmas from fast growing cities based upon high tech industries. Cities in the periphery face different economic, social and environmental challenges than those at the centre of Europe. The challenges of cities in the new member states of the EU are different from those in the west.

8.10.3 Despite this diversity some general urban trends are clear from the EU Urban Audit, which showed that:

- City population levels are stabilising but populations at wider conurbation levels are growing.

- Cities are becoming more international and more cosmopolitan. 10 per cent of the population of the cities were non-nationals, around one third from the EU and two-thirds from outside.

- Cities have relatively small households and are getting smaller.

- Cities bear the brunt of unemployment and long-term unemployment.

- Income disparities and poverty are growing. About 25 per cent of households had income which was less than 50 per cent of national household income.

- Home ownership is increasing. Ninety-five per cent of cities had experienced an increase in levels of ownership.

- Cities are improving on some health indicators.

- Crime rates are higher in cities especially northern and capital cities.

- Service sector employment is increasing. Over three-quarters of employment is now in services and less than a quarter in industrial employment.

- Voter participation in city elections is relatively low and declining. Average voting in local elections varied enormously from 20 per cent to 60 per cent. But the percentage had fallen in two-thirds of all cities between most recent elections.

- Educational levels are rising. Cities lag behind at lower educational levels but most have more graduates than the national average.

- Travel is increasing, car ownership is increasing and public transport is declining.

Tertiary Education in European countries and cities

8.10.4 Cities differ in some important respects. For example, Figure 8.6 from the European Urban Audit shows that three out of four cities attract a higher share of tertiary-educated residents than their country as whole. Some cities, such as Paris and Edinburgh, have managed to attract even twice the national share. Amongst large and medium sized cities, there are still too many who lag far behind, with less than two-thirds of the national share of tertiary-educated residents. The UK and its cities perform better than some but still lag behind several northern European countries.

Figure 8.6: Proportion of the population with tertiary education, 2001.

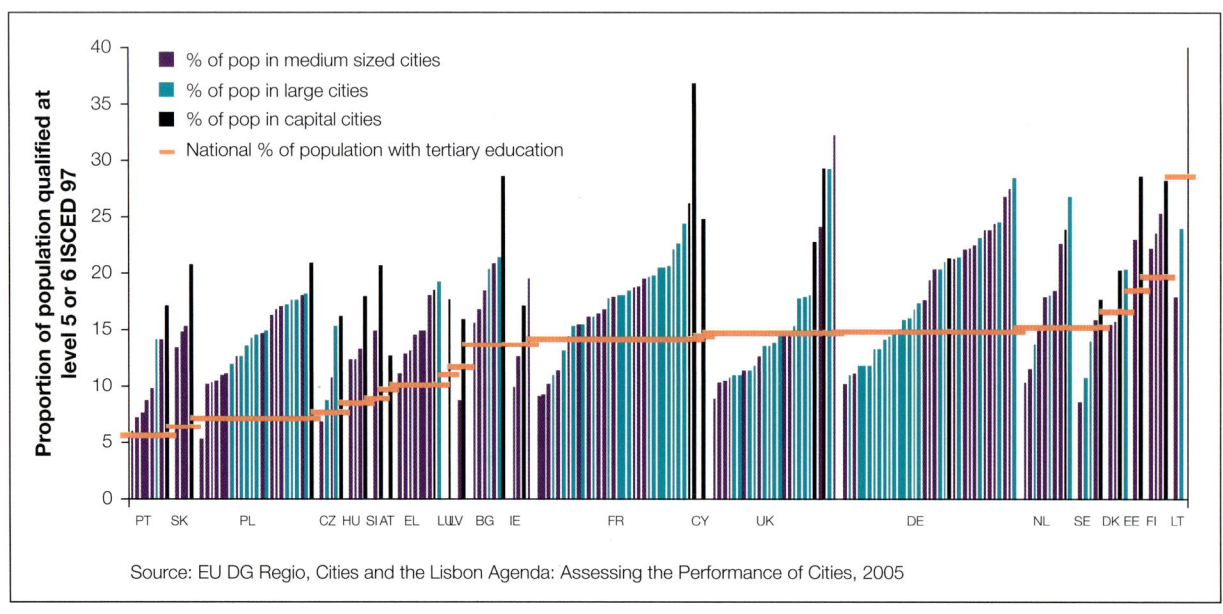

Source: EU DG Regio, Cities and the Lisbon Agenda: Assessing the Performance of Cities, 2005

Figure 8.7: Urban employment rate and employment in private services, 2001.

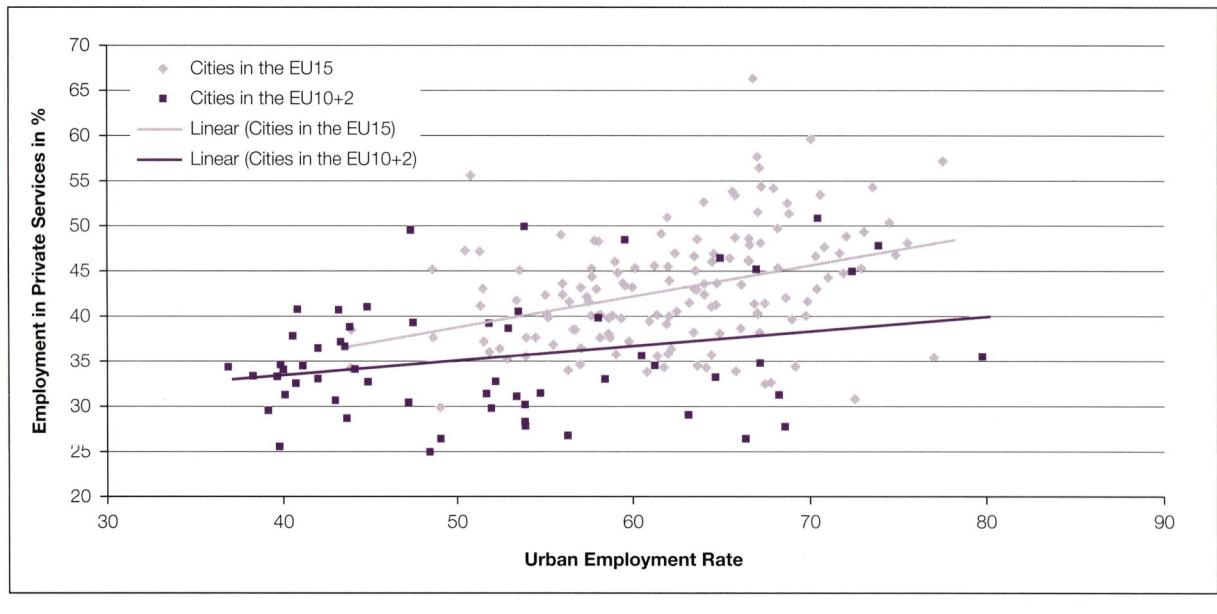

Where are the jobs? Employment in the service sector

8.10.5 Many cities in the EU15 have experienced dramatic economic restructuring, with a steep decline in employment within the heavy manufacturing sector and slow job growth in the service economy. Cities in the new member states still rely to a higher degree on manufacturing. For example, 25 per cent of jobs in cities in the old member states are in manufacturing industries. However, cities have a higher employment rate when they have a higher share of jobs in the private service sector (Figure 8.7).

Urban employment rates tend to be lower

8.10.6 The Lisbon Agenda set the goal of increasing the European employment rate to 70 per cent, by 2010. In 2001, only 10 per cent of the cities in the Urban Audit had reached this level, with cities lagging behind the national averages. Figure 8.8 shows that urban residents are much less likely to be working than residents of their country. In many countries, none of the cities or only one or two of the cities have an employment rate higher than the national rate. Overall, three out of four cities have a lower employment rate than their country as a whole. The UK is not the worst, but still lags behind some north European countries.

Figure 8.8: National and city employment rates, 2001.

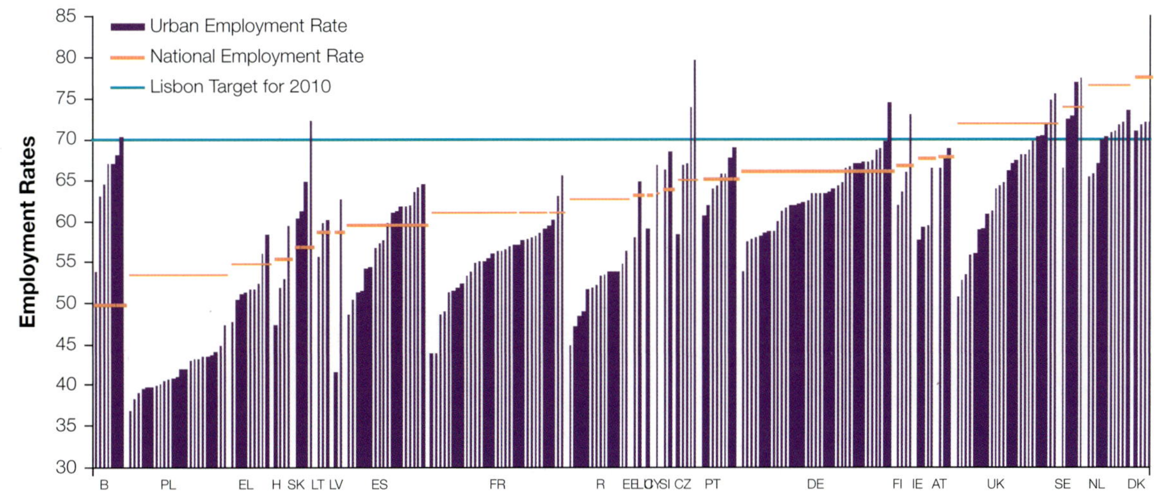

Source: EU DG Regio, Cities and the Lisbon Agenda: Assessing the Performance of Cities, 2005

Urban unemployment rates tend to be higher

8.10.7 Unemployment also tends to be concentrated in cities. Figure 8.9 shows that in 67 per cent of UA cities, the unemployment rate is higher than the national rate. In certain cities, the unemployment rate is far higher. For example, in Naples, an unemployment rate of 32 per cent was more than three times higher than the national average of nine per cent in 2001. The UK and its cities perform relatively well on this indicator.

Figure 8.9: City and national unemployment rates 2001

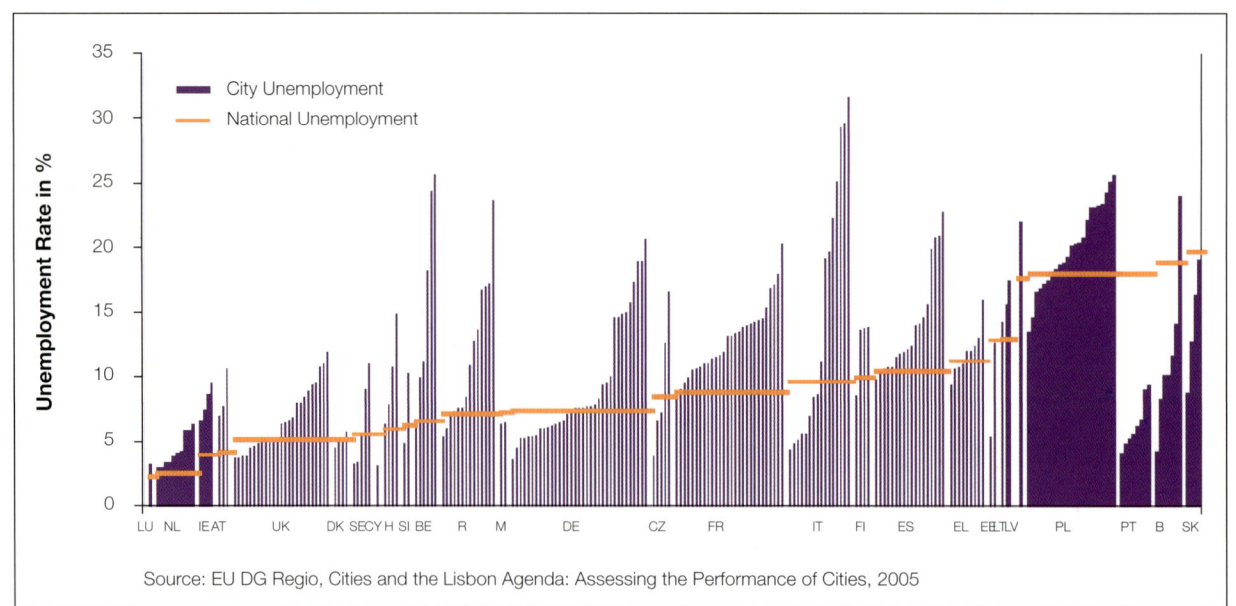

Source: EU DG Regio, Cities and the Lisbon Agenda: Assessing the Performance of Cities, 2005

Crime

8.10.8   Crime is concentrated in cities. Almost all cities have higher crime rates than the national rate. In almost half, crime rates are even 50 per cent higher than the national rate. Not all cities face the same crime issues, however. For example, the Urban Audit Perception Survey showed than in 22 cities out of 31, the majority did not always feel safe. Yet in some cities, four out of five residents always felt safe. This limited data shows that the UK does not perform well (Figure 8.10).

Figure 8.10: Perception of safety, 2004.

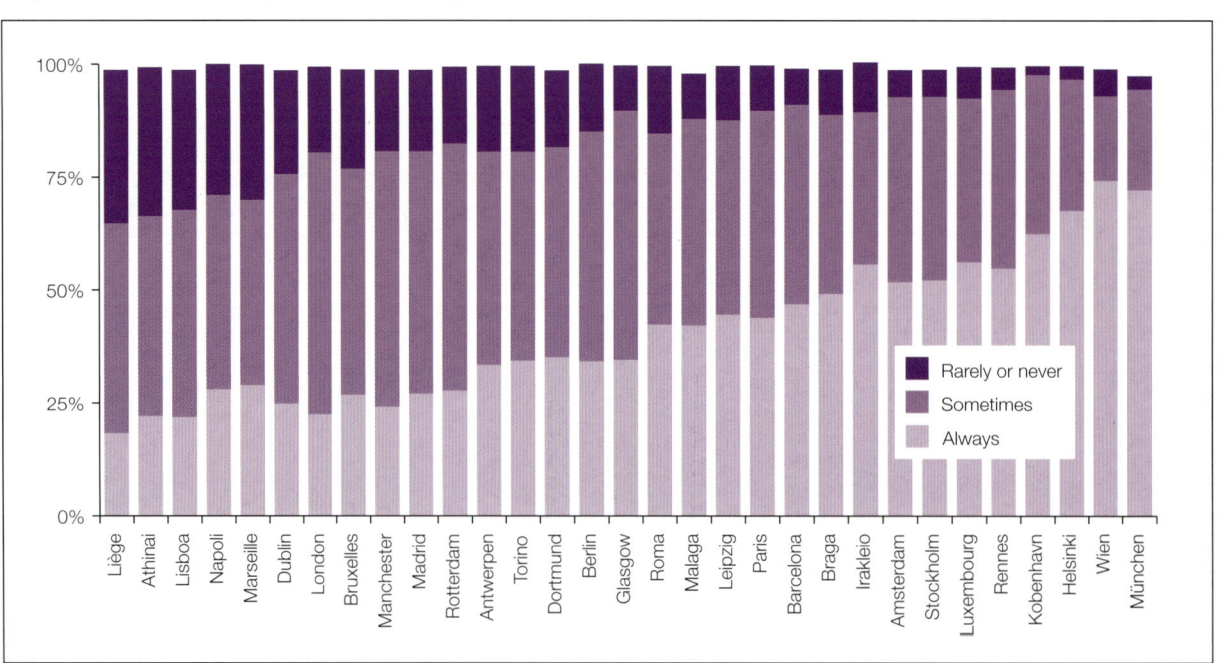

How much do cities matter economically?

8.10.9   Given the diversity of circumstances there is much discussion about the economic significance of cities in Europe. However, the essential argument of most analyses is that they are important to national and regional economic growth and their importance is increasing. For example, much European evidence on the performance of regions indicates that the urbanised regions are the most successful. The ODPM study of successful continental large cities and regions found that there was no example of a successful region, which did not have a successful city at its core. (ODPM 2004) Herschel and Newman's comprehensive review of the evidence concluded that the degree of urbanization was directly related to economic performance, emphasising the importance of City-Regions as economic core areas. For example in the EU, regions characterised as 'urban' have a GDP of almost a quarter (22 per cent) above the EU average, jointly generating some 60 per cent of the EU's total GDP. Each of the ten regions with the highest level of wealth creation in the EU includes at least one major conurbation. In particular, capital cities emerged consistently as the main centres for investment and innovation and thus prosperity. (Herschel and Newman 2002)

8.10.10 This review is underlined by the most authoritative empirical analysis of urban and regional performance in Europe by Rodriguez-Pose. (Rodriguez Pose 1998). His review of economic performance over almost two decades concluded that the economic winners in Europe were dynamic systems of cities and metropolitan City-Regions. Capital and urban regions achieved growth rates above the European average during the 1980s and 1990s. Almost all of the ten leading regional economies in Europe were centred on metropolitan cities. His separate analysis of corporate behaviour in Germany during the past decade demonstrated how a small number of leading cities were becoming increasingly significant as national economic drivers. What explained cities' economic success? A number of factors did. Although capital and information were increasingly mobile with technological change and deregulation, both had become increasingly concentrated in large metropolitan areas. The concentration of highly skilled people in the main metropolis offered companies advantages over other areas. Metropolitan regions were characterized by a high level of qualifications, positive rates of population growth, low demographic dependency, low unemployment, and a fuller integration of women in the labour market. They also enjoyed greatest social dynamism and their stock of qualified labour, top-level universities and relative absence of social conflict had eased the assimilation of technological advances, encouraged innovation and fostered economic growth.

If cities matter, where are their boundaries?

8.10.11 If cities matter – where do they start and end? The appropriate relationship between cities and their economic hinterlands is an increasingly important issue in the UK. The growth in significance of City-Regions underlines the fact that the current relationships are sub-optimal. However, the UK is not alone in these concerns. There is great awareness in continental Europe of the importance of the economic relationships between cities and regions.

Despite the assumption that things work better on the continent, this is not the case. In fact there are a series of regional-urban difficulties which are also experienced in the UK. These include: local government fragmentation, economic competition between adjacent local authorities, worries about the environmental impact of residential and job decentralisation, fiscal exploitation of the central city by suburban service users, the segregation of excluded communities as municipalities contest to attract richer and repel poorer people and housing, failures to market the sub-region effectively, and concerns that the central city is too small to punch its weight in European and global markets.

8.10.12 Many in Europe recognise that city administrative boundaries do not correspond with current economic realities and that the wider sub-region is critical for long-term policymaking. However, few urban areas have yet devised a satisfactory set of arrangements that capture the wider economic territory. There are a series of territorial tensions. Smaller municipalities are reluctant to be overwhelmed by the larger city. National governments are often reluctant to strengthen the position of already powerful central cities.

8.10.13 There is a mixed picture across Europe, but some general patterns are clear. Firstly, there are increased efforts to devise sub-regional institutional relationships so that cities and their surrounding regions can work together more efficiently. This is partly to manage internal issues – economic development, physical infrastructure, human capital, environment, transport issues – and partly to market their regions externally. Secondly, the nature of the relationships ranges from formal to informal. Both approaches have costs and benefits. Thirdly, these urban-regional relationships are never simple with a range of economic and political tensions making it difficult to get easy solutions. Fourthly, drawing boundaries and deciding who is in who is out – formally or informally – is not simple. Different cities have worked with different boundaries. Political realities and relationships are a key consideration. In many urban areas there are efforts to build relationship between neighbouring local authorities, or occasionally between more distant towns and cities, which all emphasise the economic advantages derived from critical mass and increased collaboration.

8.10.14 One message for English cities is that their counterparts in Europe are convinced that to be competitive in the global marketplace in future they have to organise and act at a wider metropolitan or sub-regional level. Another message is that most of them have decided that it is not worth attempting to create formal institutions to achieve this, since they are unlikely to be implemented. The most common view is that informal strategic alliances between willing partners which can be mobilised around agreed territories and powers and resources are better than the alternatives of acting only on a local basis or spending a great deal of time and energy fighting unwinnable battles for formal change.

8.10.15 There is substantial evidence regarding the problems of using formal institutional or constitutional changes to achieve sub-regional collaboration. Many attempts in the Netherlands and Germany have been unsuccessful. The one genuinely formal approach in Stuttgart still relies upon internal collaboration and partnership, which is not always achieved. The majority of places are attempting to collaborate informally on policy issues across boundaries and with partners where they can. This emphasises the need for informal sub-regional collaboration. A number of European national governments are attempting to incentivise that collaboration. There is a policy message for the UK here.

8.11 How do English cities compare with the best European cities?

8.11.1 The previous section looked at the performance of a wide range of cities. English cities did not always perform well but they were not the worst. This next section focuses upon the performance of a much smaller number of more successful continental cities to see how English cities compare. It tries to throw some light on the economic performance of European cities drawing upon on recent research work on Competitive European Cities for the ODPM in over 20 European cities (ODPM 2004). It analyses the comparative performance of English cities in three critical areas of competitiveness identified in Chapter 4 – innovation, connectivity and human capital. This is a complex area. There is disagreement about the relative merits of indicators. There is never perfect data with which to illustrate such indicators. Boundaries are always problematic. But this section uses the best available evidence from the most robust sources. As a measure of competitiveness, it uses GDP per capita. As indicators of innovativeness it uses the EU innovation score for regions, which is a composite of public and private investment in research and development (R&D), percentage of the workforce in high tech activities and patents registered. For a measure of the skilled workforce, it uses the percentage of the workforce with qualifications to ISCED level 3. For connectivity it uses accessibility to air, rail and Internet connections.

8.11.2 Table 8.1 shows the GDP per capita of the top 61 cities in Europe. A number of features are obvious. Capital cities tend to be at the top of the league table. Large cities tend to do well. German cities, despite the country's economic difficulties, perform very well, with 15 in the top 20. UK cities outside London do not perform well. Bristol and Leeds, at 34 and 43 respectively, perform best. Several are at the bottom of the list with GDPs per capita less than one-third of the richest cities in Europe.

Table 8.1: GDP of 61 Cities in Europe

Rank	City	Euros per capita	Rank	City	Euros per capita
1	Frankfurt am Main	74,465	32	The Hague	30,110
2	Karlsruhe (Germany)	70,097	33	Essen (Germany)	29,760
3	Paris	67,200	34	Bristol	29,437
4	Munich	61,360	35	Lyon (France)	28,960
5	Düsseldorf	54,053	36	Bologna (Italy)	28,282
6	Stuttgart	53,570	37	Bochum (Germany)	27,900
7	Brussels	51,106	38	Parma (Italy)	27,491
8	Copenhagen	50,775	39	Dortmund (Germany)	26,548
9	Hanover	47,223	40	Rotterdam	26,227
10	Hamburg	43,098	41	Strasbourg (France)	26,015
11	Mannheim	41,674	42	Florence (Italy)	25,693
12	Nuremburg	41,456	43	Leeds	25,619
14	Augsburg (Germany)	39,360	44	Duisburg (Germany)	25,259
14	Cologne	39,108	45	Eindhoven (Netherlands)	25,226
15	Amsterdam	38,203	46	Turin	25,042
16	Münster (Germany)	38,149	47	Toulouse	24,852
17	Wiesbaden (Germany)	37,454	48	Rome	24,766
18	Dublin	36,591	49	Bordeaux	24,252
19	Vienna	36,572	50	Malmo (Sweden)	24,233
20	Stockholm	35,733	51	Gothenberg (Sweden)	24,065
21	Gelsenkirchen (Germany)	35,688	52	Grenoble (France)	24,026
22	Helsinki	35,322	53	Verona	23,954
23	London	35,072	54	Berlin	23,428
24	Bremen (Germany)	35,022	55	Marseilles	22,809
25	Edinburgh	35,018	56	Birmingham	22,069
26	Bonn	34,112	57	Manchester	22,099
27	Antwerp (Belgium)	33,090	58	Newcastle-upon-Tyne	20,499
28	Milan	32,122	59	Lille	20,191
29	Glasgow	31,893	60	Barcelona	18,449
30	Utrecht	31,712	61	Liverpool	16,466
31	Saarbrücken (Germany)	30,368			

Source: Barclays Bank 2002

How innovative are European cities?

8.11.3   Table 8.2 shows the performance of the top 50 European regions – rather than cities – on innovation.

Table 8.2: European Innovation Index – Top 50 scoring regions

Region	City	Country	Rank	Score
Stockholm	Stockholm	Sweden	1	225
Uusimaa	Helsinki	Finland	2	208
Noord-Brabant		Netherlands	3	191
Pohjois-Suomi		Finland	4	161
Eastern		UK	4	161
Île de France		France	6	160
Bayern	Munich	Germany	7	151
South East		UK	8	150
Comunidad de Madrid		Spain	9	149
Baden-Württemberg	Stuttgart	Germany	10	146
Sydsverige		Sweden	11	143
Berlin		Germany	12	140
Östra Mellansverige		Sweden	12	140
South West	Bristol	UK	14	147
Västsverige		Sweden	15	146
Midi-Pyrénées	Toulouse	France	16	141
Wien		Austria	17	126
Etelä-Suomi		Finland	18	124
Utrecht		Netherlands	19	123
Flevoland		Netherlands	20	114
Vlaams Gewest		Belgium	22	112
Lombardia	Milan	Italy	22	112
Kärnten		Austria	23	111
Région Bruxelles		Belgium	23	111
Rhône-Alpes	Lyon	France	23	111
Lazio		Italy	26	110
Piemonte	Turin	Italy	27	109
Zuid-Holland	Rotterdam	Netherlands	27	109
Hessen		Germany	29	108
Southern and Eastern		Ireland	29	108
West Midlands	Birmingham	UK	29	108
Groningen		Netherlands	32	107
Comunidad Foral de Navarra		Spain	33	105
Noord-Holland		Netherlands	33	105
Limburg (NL)		Netherlands	33	105
North West	Manchester Liverpool	UK	36	104
Hamburg		Germany	37	103
Scotland		UK	38	102
Cataluña	Barcelona	Spain	39	101
Gelderland		Netherlands	39	101
Väli-Suomi		Finland	41	100
London		UK	41	100
Mellersta Norrland		Sweden	43	99
East Midlands	Nottingham	UK	44	98
Övre Norrland		Sweden	45	97
Ceuta y Melilla		Spain	46	95
Franche-Comté		France	46	95
Sachsen		Germany	48	94
Lisboa e Vale do Tejo		Portugal	48	94
Attiki		Greece	50	93

Source: European Trend Chart on Innovation Technical Paper No3 EU Regions 2002

8.11.4   Even though the precise ranking varies, a familiar pattern emerges. Northern European cities and countries – Sweden, Finland, Netherlands and Germany perform well. Few southern European cities perform well, except for Madrid. German cities as a group perform well. From the UK, only London and the south east make the top ten. Of the UK cities, Bristol leads. But the remainder fall in the bottom 25, with innovation scores about half that of the high performing regions.

How well educated is our workforce?

8.11.5   Figure 8.11 shows the qualifications of the workforce of 23 cities in their regional context. A familiar pattern emerges. Northern European cities especially German ones perform well. Bristol and Leeds perform best of the UK provincial cities. However, again the majority congregate at the bottom end of the league table.

Figure 8.11: Percentage of population (25–34 years) with 3rd level education – 2000

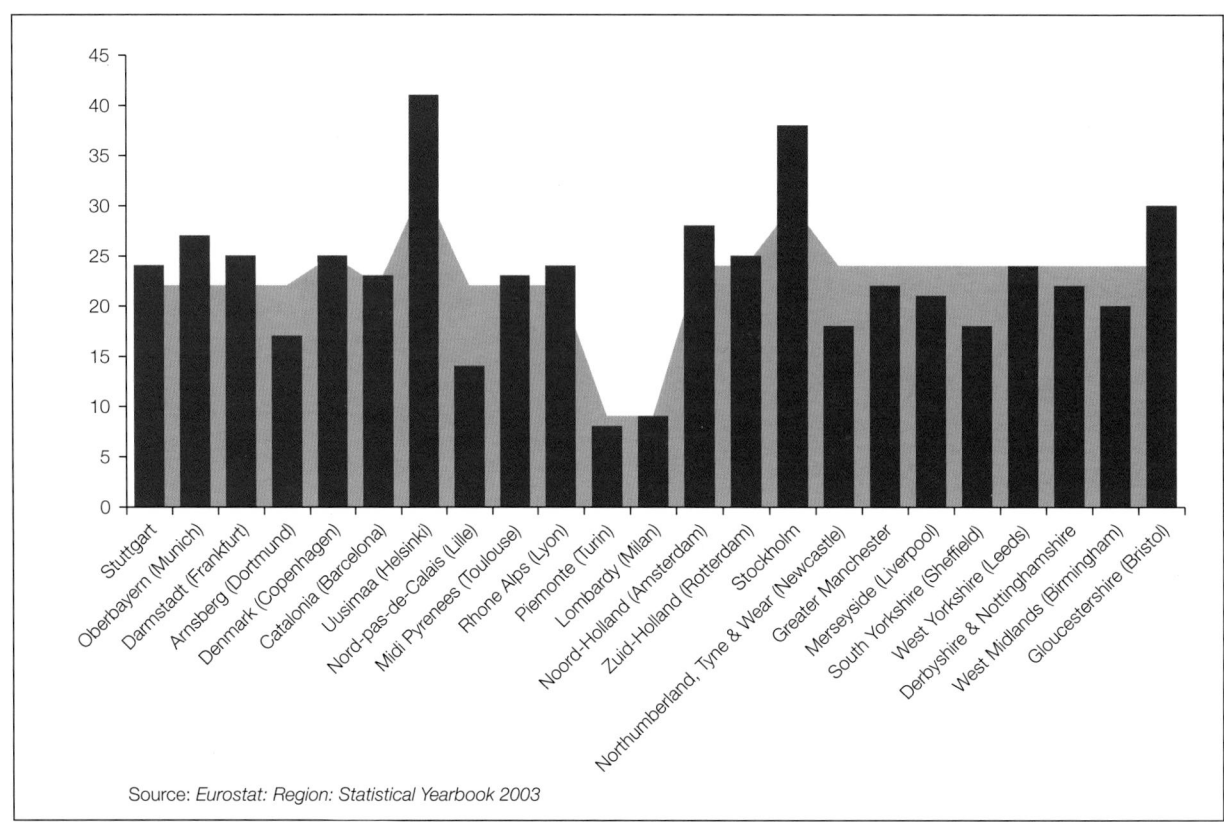

Source: *Eurostat: Region: Statistical Yearbook 2003*

8.11.6   Further evidence about innovation and the quality of the labour force can be found in Figures 8.12, 8.13 and 8.14. These again demonstrate the higher percentages of the workforce in high tech manufacturing, services and knowledge intensive services in many continental cities than in UK cities.

Figure 8.12: % Employees working in high tech manufacturing sectors

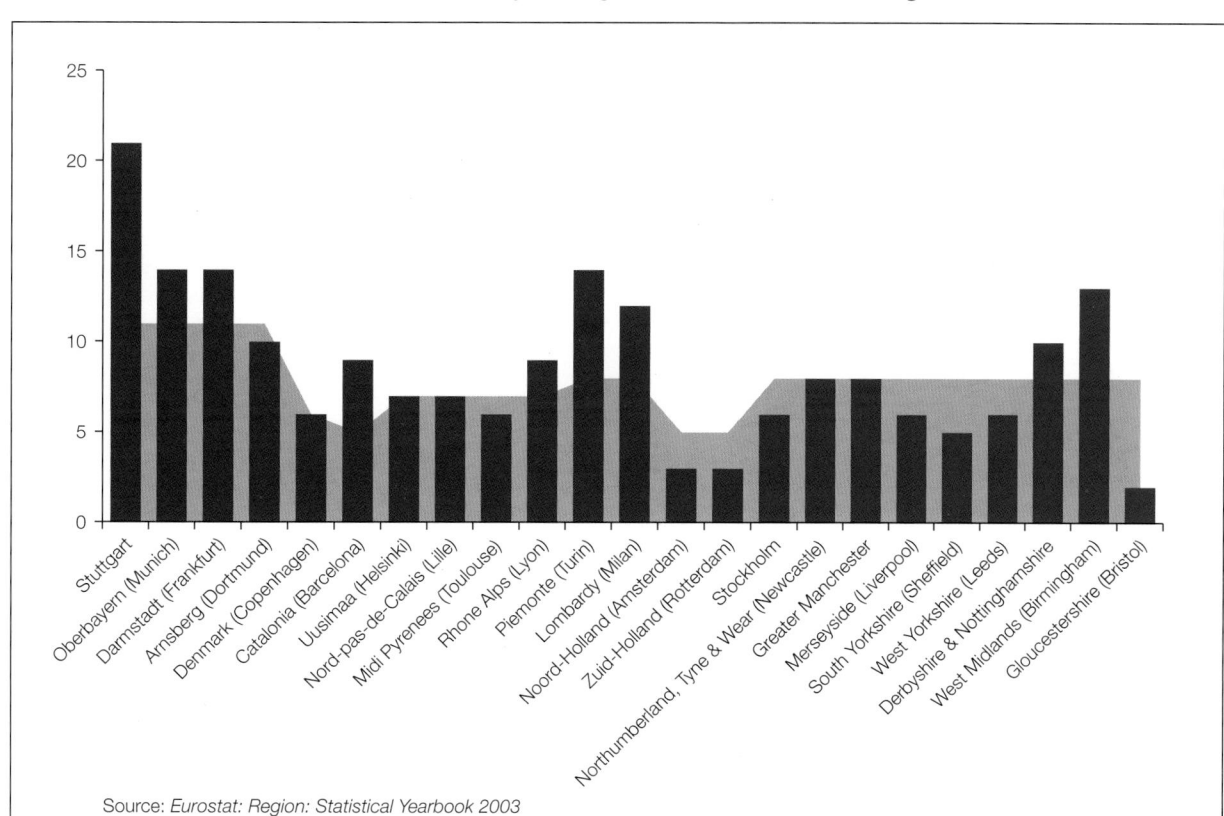

Source: *Eurostat: Region: Statistical Yearbook 2003*

Figure 8.13: % Employees working in high tech service sectors

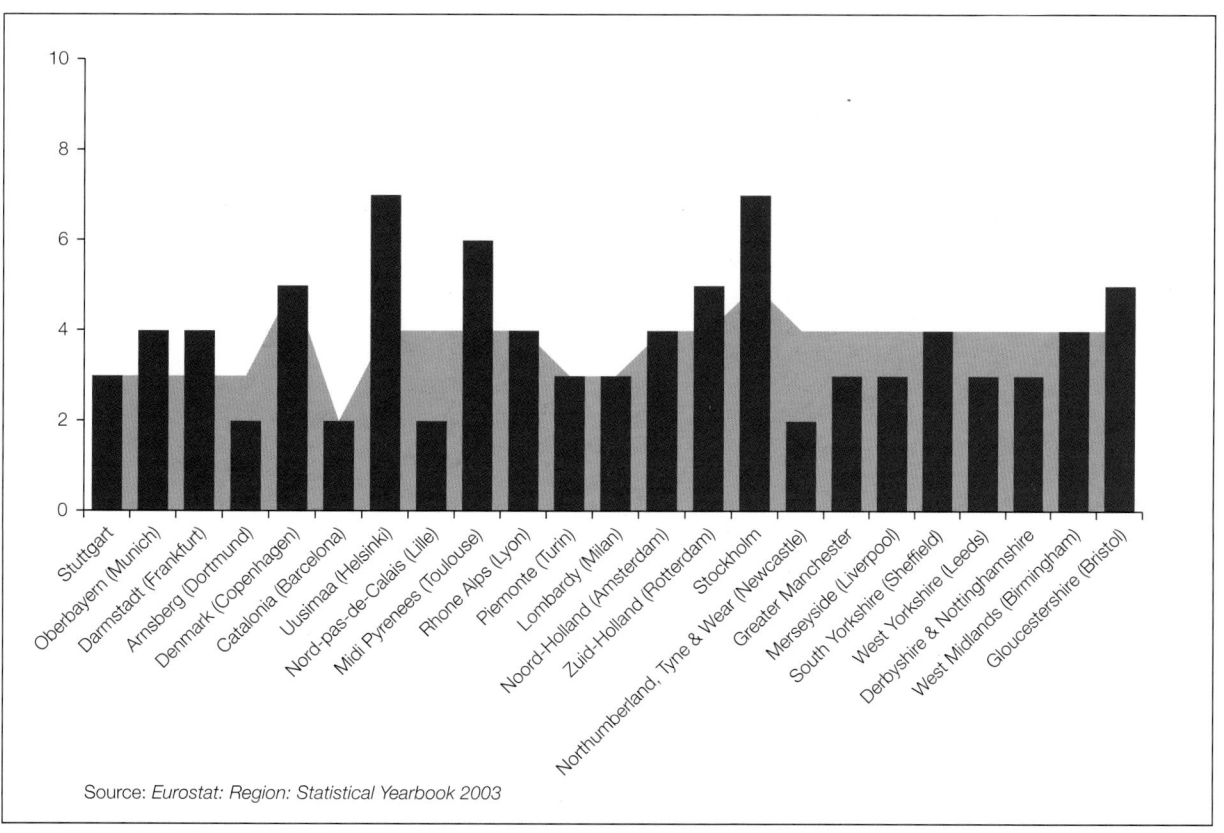

Source: *Eurostat: Region: Statistical Yearbook 2003*

Figure 8.14: % Employees working in knowledge intensive sectors

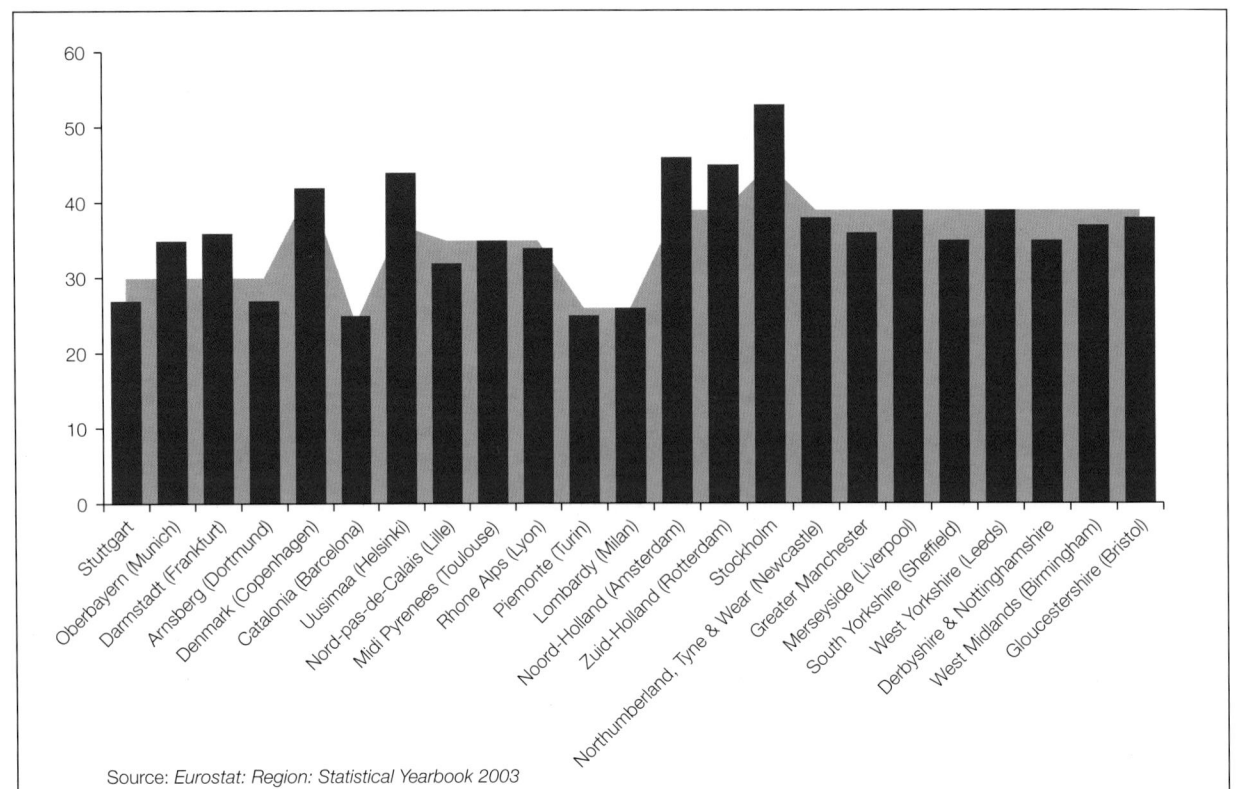

Source: *Eurostat: Region: Statistical Yearbook 2003*

How active is our labour force?

8.11.7 Drawing upon the recent EU Urban Audit Table 8.3 shows economic activity rates in a range of European cities. A familiar pattern again emerges showing the same leading cities and with English cities lagging behind the best continental cities.

Table 8.3: Economic activity rates in European cities

2001			Activity rates	2001			Activity rates
1	Helsinki	Finland	77.6	25	Inner London	UK	69.3
2	Munich	Germany	77.3	26	Sheffield	UK	69.3
3	Vienna	Austria	76.0	27	Cardiff	UK	67.8
4	Aarhus	Denmark	76.0	28	Lyon	France	67.3
5	Utrecht	Netherlands	75.8	29	Valencia	Spain	67.2
6	Copenhagen	Denmark	75.4	30	Dublin	Ireland	66.5
7	Edinburgh	UK	74.5	31	Toulouse	France	66.2
8	Paris	France	74.3	32	Leicester	UK	66.2
9	Eindhoven	Netherlands	74.1	33	Birmingham	UK	65.3
10	Amsterdam	Netherlands	73.1	34	Grenoble	France	65.2
11	Paris et petit couronne	France	73.0	35	Saint-Etienne	France	65.1
12	Madrid	Spain	72.6	36	Dortmund	Germany	64.5
13	Hamburg	Germany	72.5	37	Athens	Greece	64.4
14	Barcelona	Spain	72.4	38	Marseille	France	64.4
15	Bristol	UK	72.0	39	Lille	France	64.3
16	Leeds	UK	71.8	40	Newcastle	UK	64.1
17	London	UK	71.8	41	Rennes	France	63.8
18	Dusseldorf	Germany	71.6	42	Cambridge	UK	63.6
19	Gothenburg	Sweden	71.6	43	Glasgow	UK	62.7
20	Stockholm	Sweden	71.4	44	Antwerp	Belgium	62.1
21	Frankfurt	Germany	70.5	45	Brussels	Belgium	60.3
22	Berlin	Germany	70.1	46	Liverpool	UK	60.2
23	Rotterdam	Netherlands	69.9	47	Thessalonica	Greece	58.2
24	Leipzig	Germany	69.9	48	Manchester	UK	55.8

Source: Urban Audit

How well connected are European cities?

8.11.8 Again drawing upon the Urban Audit, Tables 8.4 and 8.5 assess the connectivity of English cities in comparison with the best continental cities. A familiar pattern emerges. Although there is some obvious diversity, cities which have high GDPs, high innovation levels, high educational qualifications, high activity rates and high percentages in high tech occupations are often better connected by air and rail than many UK cities.

Table 8.4: European cities rated according to 'accessibility by air' 2001

2001			Accessibility by air (EU27=100)	2001			Accessibility by air (EU27=100)
1	Frankfurt	Germany	187	27	Turin	Italy	119
2	Dusseldorf	Germany	184	28	Dublin	Ireland	119
3	Brussels	Belgium	177	29	Leicester	UK	117
4	Paris	France	175	30	Leeds	UK	114
5	Amsterdam	Netherlands	175	31	Sheffield	UK	112
6	Milan	Italy	166	32	Liverpool	UK	112
7	Berlin	Germany	165	33	Athens	Greece	111
8	London	UK	164	34	Bristol	UK	110
9	Copenhagen	Denmark	156	35	Toulouse	France	110
10	Hamburg	Germany	155	36	Gothenburg	Sweden	110
11	Antwerp	Belgium	153	37	Newcastle	UK	109
12	Utrecht	Netherlands	153	38	Marseille	France	108
13	Vienna	Austria	153	39	Thessalonica	Greece	105
14	Birmingham	UK	144	40	Helsinki	Finland	105
15	Dortmund	Germany	143	41	Lille	France	103
16	Manchester	UK	143	42	Cambridge	UK	103
17	Rotterdam	Netherlands	140	43	Glasgow	UK	103
18	Munich	Germany	140	44	Valencia	Spain	101
19	Barcelona	Spain	135	45	Edinburgh	UK	97
20	Rome	Italy	128	46	Stockholm	Sweden	97
21	Bologna	Italy	126	47	Cardiff	UK	94
22	Lyon	France	124	48	Grenoble	France	93
23	Eindhoven	Netherlands	123	49	Saint-Etienne	France	86
24	Genoa	Italy	123	50	Aarhus	Denmark	86
25	Madrid	Spain	122	51	Rennes	France	74
26	Leipzig	Germany	120				

Source: Urban Audit

Table 8.5: 51 European cities rated according to 'accessibility by rail' 2001

2001			Accessibility by rail (EU27=100)	2001			Accessibility by rail (EU27=100)
1	Dusseldorf	Germany	233	27	Sheffield	UK	116
2	Frankfurt	Germany	230	28	Bristol	UK	113
3	Paris	France	225	29	Marseille	France	113
4	Brussels	Belgium	217	30	Genoa	Italy	109
5	Dortmund	Germany	213	31	Liverpool	UK	108
6	Lille	France	206	32	Leeds	UK	104
7	Eindhoven	Netherlands	202	33	Vienna	Austria	103
8	Antwerp	Belgium	201	34	Cardiff	UK	102
9	Utrecht	Netherlands	197	35	Rennes	France	100
10	Rotterdam	Netherlands	191	36	Roma	Italy	85
11	Amsterdam	Netherlands	180	37	Newcastle	UK	79
12	Lyon	France	162	38	Toulouse	France	75
13	Munich	Germany	161	39	Glasgow	UK	63
14	Leipzig	Germany	161	40	Copenhagen	Denmark	60
15	Hamburg	Germany	156	41	Edinburgh	UK	60
16	London	UK	153	42	Barcelona	Spain	57
17	Milan	Italy	152	43	Aarhus	Denmark	56
18	Berlin	Germany	150	44	Madrid	Spain	52
19	Turin	Italy	142	45	Valencia	Spain	38
20	Grenoble	France	142	46	Dublin	Ireland	35
21	Saint-Etienne	France	128	47	Gothenburg	Sweden	30
22	Birmingham	UK	127	48	Thessalonica	Greece	28
23	Leicester	UK	123	49	Stockholm	Sweden	24
24	Cambridge	UK	121	50	Athens	Greece	23
25	Bologna	Italy	119	51	Helsinki	Finland	22
26	Manchester	UK	117				

Source: Urban Audit

8.11.9 By contrast some limited data from the Urban Audit in Table 8.6 indicates that in terms of Internet connections, many English cities compare quite favourably with continental cities.

Table 8.6: Percentage of households with Internet access at home, 2001

1	Helsinki	Finland	44.6
2	Utrecht	Netherlands	44.0
3	London	UK	42.9
4	Amsterdam	Netherlands	41.0
5	Edinburgh	UK	39.6
6	Bristol	UK	35.3
7	Leeds	UK	35.3
8	Rotterdam	Netherlands	34.0
9	Manchester	UK	32.7
10	Newcastle	UK	32.0
11	Dublin	Ireland	31.0
12	Sheffield	UK	31.0
13	Birmingham	UK	29.9
14	Cambridge	UK	28.6
15	Antwerp	Belgium	27.5
16	Brussels	Belgium	27.1
17	Glasgow	UK	23.7
18	Leipzig	Germany	23.0
19	Vienna	Austria	23.0
20	Leicester	UK	22.4
21	Cardiff	UK	15.4

Source: Urban Audit

8.11.10 Accessibility has important economic implications. For example, analysis of Urban Audit data in Figure 8.15 shows that GDP and multimodal and air accessibility of cities are extremely closely linked, underlining the growing importance of air connections for European cities.

Figure 8.15: GDP per capita and multimodal accessibility, 2001

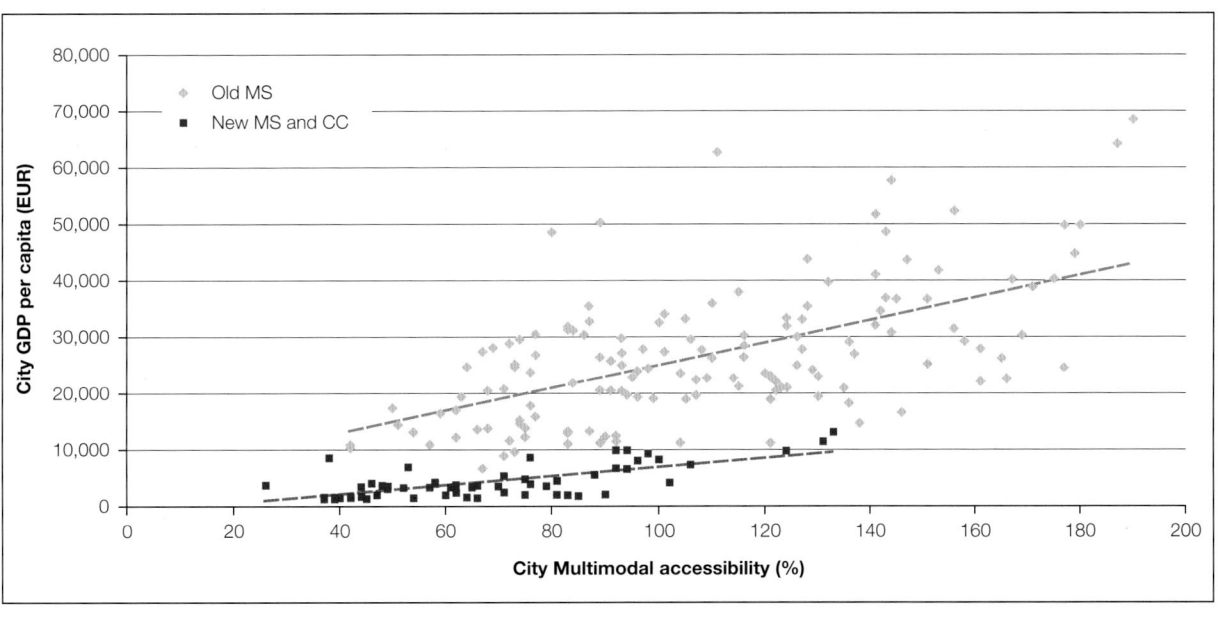

Is the problem national or urban?

8.11.11 One question which arises from these data, is whether the UK cities perform relatively poorly because the UK national performance is poor or whether the cities themselves are under-performing. Figure 8.16 provides evidence on this. The picture is very clear. The competitive cities in our sample considerably outperform their national GDPs. Recent improved performers like Helsinki or Barcelona match or beat their national performance. The cities included in the study as comparable to the Core Cities – Dortmund, Rotterdam, and Lille – perform less well, as we would expect. With the exception of Bristol, UK cities lag significantly behind the UK average. Just as the continental cities are arguably leading their nation's performance, arguably the Core Cities are constraining the UK performance. The implication must be that if the Core Cities could improve their performance to match that of their continental counterparts, the gains to the UK national economy would be enormous.

Figure 8.16: National and urban economic competitiveness: a comparison

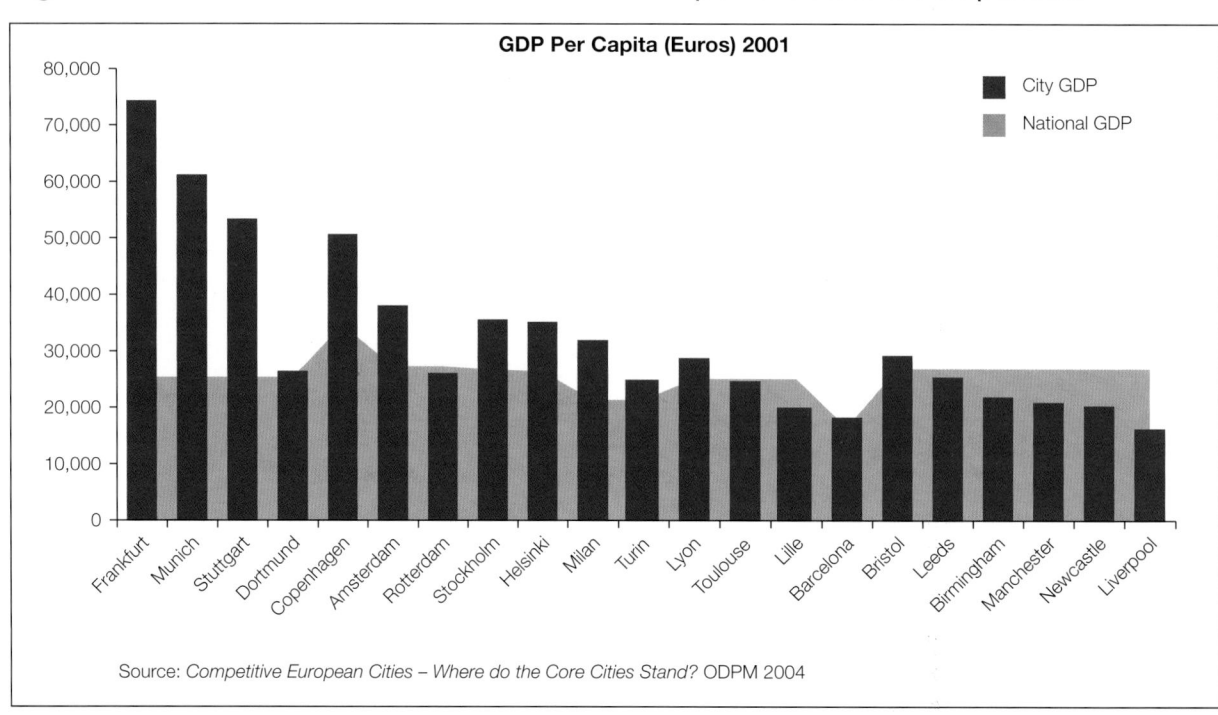

Source: *Competitive European Cities – Where do the Core Cities Stand?* ODPM 2004

8.11.12 This section has shown that in many important ways, English cities outside London lag behind many of the highest performing continental cities in measures of economic competitiveness. Figure 8.17 puts the European experience in a global perspective. A number of health warnings have to be entered. The figure does include some small states and some regions as well as cities. It is not therefore always comparing like with like. Nevertheless, it shows that Europe itself lags behind international competitors in terms of regional competitiveness. With some notable examples, the best performing regions in terms of competitiveness lie outside Europe. Only two UK regions appear in the leading set. In other words, the bigger picture about the scale of the gap between UK and leading world city and regions is confirmed.

Figure 8.17: Regional competitiveness: labour productivity

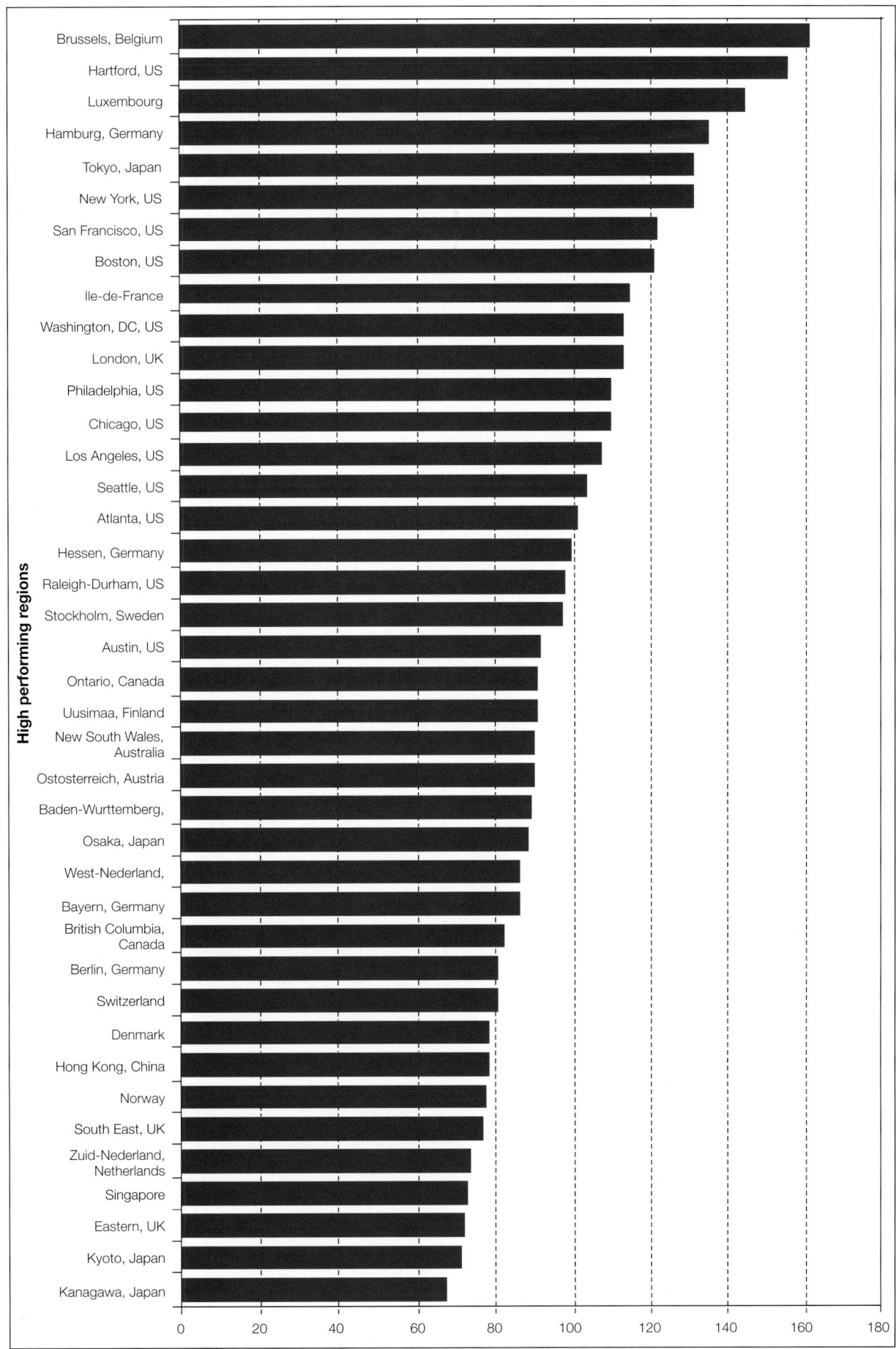

Source: Huggins, R. Associates *Global Index of regional Knowledge Economies: Benchmarking South East England*, Guildford, SEEDA.

8.12   What messages about urban performance?

The urban hierarchy is stable – but cities can improve quickly

8.12.1   The evidence underlines the structural characteristics of competitiveness, which are acquired over a long period of time and not lost quickly. The cities, which performed well a decade ago and were well regarded by the private sector as places to do business then, still head the league table. Nevertheless, there is evidence that cities can change their performance. The quantitative evidence showed how in Spain, Barcelona and Madrid had improved their position as had Helsinki in Finland. In the longer term it is also instructive to recall the experience of the three most successful non-capital cities in Europe – Frankfurt, Stuttgart and Munich. Fifty years ago all had been virtually destroyed. Indeed, there is a strong view in those cities that this destruction of older industrial structures and attitudes encouraged the view that change, innovation, reinvention were both desirable and possible.

National and regional government matters

8.12.2   Cities have to maximise their opportunities if they are to succeed economically. And the framework set by national government matters a great deal. Although there are differences, the trend in continental Europe is to decentralise and regionalise decision-making, placing powers at the lowest level. Continental cities typically have more diverse forms of local revenue and more buoyant tax bases, which make them less fiscally dependent upon the national state and more proactive in their development strategies. Continental cities have responsibility for a wider range of functions which affect their economic competitiveness than do their UK counterparts. Although it is not a straightforward relationship, the evidence does suggest that where cities are given more freedom and autonomy they have responded by being more proactive, entrepreneurial and successful. Decentralisation in France has invigorated provincial cities during the past 20 years. The most successful cities in Europe have been German, which is the most decentralised European country. The renaissance of Barcelona, in part, stems from the move towards regionalisation and the lessening of the grip of the capital city, Madrid. A second point can be underlined about the relationship between national and local governments. Both France and the Netherlands have been moving towards more long-term contractual relationships between national and local government to deliver economic performance.

Cities can help themselves

8.12.3   Cities operate within a set of powerful structural economic social, physical and institutional constraints but are not powerless to shape their economic trajectories. The evidence from our successful – and currently less successful – continental cities indicates that cities need to:

- develop their long-term strategic view of their economic role and trajectory;

- build upon and deepen existing strengths in clusters and sectors to modernise and upgrade the functions they undertake in those economic sectors;

- build strategic alliances with private partners;

- develop sub-regional territorial alliances and initiatives;

- maximise their internal and external connections;

- develop a local innovation strategy;

- encourage the skilled labour force to come, stay and contribute;

- encourage university and city links in which universities see the importance of their economic contribution to the local economy;

- develop their cultural infrastructure and improve their quality of life.

8.13 European policies for cities – what messages for the UK?

8.13.1 This final section asks what have other governments been doing about cities in recent years and what policy messages are there for UK government? It draws heavily upon recent research undertaken for the Dutch government in 2004 when it held the Presidency of the European Union. (Van den Berg, 2006). The policies have varied from country to country since they face different challenges and opportunities and have different histories, cultures, constitutional arrangements and decision-making systems. There is no single policy response but there have been some common policy challenges and trends.

Trends

8.13.2 There have been three broad trends. Firstly there has been a redrawing of the balance between national, regional and local actions with many countries reducing the role of the national government and providing greater responsibilities – if not always resources – to cities. Secondly, there has been growing recognition by many European countries and governments of the potential contribution that cities can make to national economies and a more coherent attempt to boost their economic performance. Thirdly there has been a growing recognition of the need for more explicit national urban polices which specifically address the challenges and opportunities facing cities, their communities and residents.

8.13.3 Four countries have formulated extensive explicit national urban policies – the United Kingdom, France, The Netherlands and Belgium. Six countries – Germany, Finland, Sweden, Denmark, Italy, Portugal – have put urban issues on their national agendas, although the policy responses do not have the same critical mass as in the first four.

8.13.4 There is evidence that giving greater powers to cities has become more common during the past decade. There is more scope for manoeuvre for the cities in the national policy frameworks, at least for the four countries with explicit urban policies. The empowerment of cities has been associated with more national support for bottom-up initiatives. Traditional top-down approaches have become less popular. There have been several examples of cities – independently or through organisations – generating important policy initiatives which have influenced the national urban policy agenda.

8.13.5 Increased attention for local partnerships and the importance of civic involvement are common themes in urban policies. Most national governments regard partnerships – among cities and public and private partners – almost as a precondition for the effective delivery of national urban policies. Another major trend is the attempt to achieve a more integrated approach in the delivery of national urban policies. Equally, the growth in area-based initiatives indicated that the national governments had confidence in these policies. However, the selection criteria, the spatial scope and mismatch with mainstream policies remain barriers to successful area-based policies.

8.13.6 Social exclusion has been the most difficult problem to solve in most large cities across Europe. The policy responses to combat it differ considerably and include: urban renewal; more affordable housing; promoting compact cities; supporting social mix in neighbourhoods; providing cheap public transport; integration policies of ethnic minorities. In most countries the integration of ethnic minorities and immigrants is a major challenge to cities. Integration problems were increasingly linked to social exclusion and feelings of insecurity. In a number of the relatively prosperous Western European countries explicit integration policies are becoming an part of national urban policy-making.

8.13.7 Despite this concern to promote social cohesion, governments in several countries have shifted their policy emphasis from social, problem-led policies to economic, opportunity-led policies. In several countries, large-scale flagship projects have been important catalysts for urban revitalisation and economic competitiveness. Some countries still regard spatial planning policies as a way of trying to maintain a balanced urban system. However, others are increasingly concerned to improve the international competitive position of their major urban areas.

Policy messages

8.13.8 This section has demonstrated the growing contribution that cities are making and can make to the development of Europe. It has also shown how a wide range of organisations – national, European and international – have developed increasingly sophisticated understandings of the challenges and opportunities facing cities and a range of policies to address them. What has been learned from the experiences of those policies so far that we can build upon for a more coherent approach to cities and urban policy in future? The review undertaken by the Dutch government suggests that the key principles for successful urban policies at European level would include:

Priorities for urban policy

- *Policy should focus upon economic competitiveness, social cohesion and environmental sustainability to achieve balanced development.* Policies have frequently focused upon one or the other goal. The experience is that this does not work. Policy needs to focus upon opportunity and need at the same time.

- *Policies should recognise that liveability as well as economic success is crucial to people's choice of places in which they want to live.* This leads to a concern about the public as well as the private realm and the quality of services offered, as opposed to simply the economic opportunities that are offered.

- *Cities and neighbourhoods must become places of choice and connection rather than compulsion and exclusion.* Many cities have become places where people without real choices are required to live. Successful cities attract an economic and social mix of people and communities.

- *Cities are important as sources of identity, culture recognition and connection between communities and cultures.* Cities are more than economic market places. They can encourage social integration, community engagement, and cultural recognition. This points to a wider set of policy goals than simply economic ones.

Mechanisms for successful urban policy

- *Policies for economic, social and environmental development in urban areas should be integrated not treated separately.*

- *Policies that support people and places are not mutually exclusive.* It is possible and desirable to have strategies that focus upon individual needs and also upon the social and physical infrastructure which make cities attractive in the long term.

- *Urban policy should recognise the linkages between housing, education, transportation, security, health and welfare policies and not treat them separately.* Urban problems are not separated into functional specialisms. It is important that policies are not segregated into such specialisms. National, regional and local governments need to be more flexible and integrated in this regard.

- *Mainstream government departments programmes and resources – in addition to special urban initiatives – are crucial to cities.* All the services which affect cities- housing, education, transport, social security, security – make the difference to urban success or failure. Those policies and the departments which deliver them, need to be committed to urban areas if they are to succeed.

- *Cities and urban policy must have long-term support rather than short-term interventions.* Urban policy experiments are often limited in their time span. However, urban problems are long-term. Meeting urban challenges is a marathon not a sprint. There are no quick fixes.

- *Policy should balance leadership from the top by national government with leadership and engagement from below by community and local partners.* Government must give strategic leadership, vision and long term commitment to sustainable development. However, the full engagement of citizens and communities is crucial to the successful ownership and implementation of sustainable urban development.

- *Government should build long-term contracts between different partners and levels of government, which focus upon the outcomes of policies rather than upon short-term policy inputs.* Contractual arrangements where responsibilities for results and sanctions and incentives are clear and agreed – but where local partners have freedom to determine the best way of delivering them – are better than national governments attempting to micro-control local partners.

Engaging stakeholders

- *Partnership, which engages the public, private, and community sectors on an equal footing, should be encouraged.* Government must actively encourage and facilitate the engagement of the community and private sectors.

- *Partnership mechanisms must be balanced with democratic political accountability.* Partnerships are typically appointed not elected. However, elected governments, local and regional, have democratic accountability. Policy-making needs to ensure that the inclusiveness of partnerships does not dilute the democratic element of decision-making.

Achieving the right spatial balance

- *Area-based approaches where particular areas of opportunity or need in cities receive concentrated attention should be encouraged.* The sustained concentration of resources upon carefully defined areas can make a difference to their economic and social prospects.

- *Policy should adopt a wide territorial focus which links the social challenges faced at neighbourhood level to the larger metropolitan or sub-regional economy where the problems are often created.* The economic problems of deprived areas cannot be solved in terms of the opportunities within those areas. Neighbourhood-based policies need to be linked to wider regional economic processes.

- *Economic and institutional collaboration between urban and regional areas should be encouraged.* The interests of cities and regions are inter-connected. However, policy-making systems and institutions often do not recognise this. Relationships should be developed which at least encourage collaboration, not conflict, between cities and regions.

Encouraging good practice, policy learning and capacity

- *Governments need to learn from experience and good practice – nationally and internationally.* There is much good practice. It is foolish to reinvent the wheel.

- *Governments need to evaluate policy with robust audits of policies and places, reliable socio-economic baselines, systematic collection of intelligence and independent reviews of impact.* Increasingly good urban policy builds assessment and evaluation of policy initiatives into the process from the beginning. This makes it possible to know what has worked and what has not, and what should and should not be done in future.

- *Governments need to improve the skills and capacity of professionals, politicians, community partners and the private sector involved in running cities.* This will require new relationships between partners in the urban scene and possibly new institutional arrangements.

8.13.9 Finally, this review of policies made clear that although some governments had recognised that cities were potential national economic assets, not all had done so. Also, while national ministries with responsibility for cities have increasingly accepted their significance, this was not true of all government departments. The conclusion of the research was that if cities were to contribute more to the national and European economies, their significance and potential should be recognised more systematically in more countries and by more departments of national government. As in the UK, the research underlined that the sectoral policies of different government departments should be better integrated if cities were to become more socially coherent and contribute more to increased national competitiveness. Many of these themes and issues from both continents are taken up in the later chapters of this report.

References
Glossary

State of the English Cities: A Research Study

References

Volume 1 State of the English cities report

Chapter 1: Towards a new urban agenda

Amin, A. & Tomaney, J. (eds.) *Behind the Myth of the European Union: Prospects for Cohesion,* London, Routledge.

Begg, I. (1999), *Cities and competitiveness", Urban Studies,* Vol.36, Nos. 5-6, 795-809.

Boddy, M. & Parkinson, M. (eds.), (2004), City Matters: Competitiveness, Cohesion and Urban Governance, Policy Press.

Buck, N., Gordon, I., Harding, A., and Turok, I. (eds) (2005) *Changing Cities: Rethinking Urban Competitiveness, Cohesion and Governance,* London: Palgrave.

CCWG (2004) Parkinson, M., *Cities and Regions: Institutions, Relationships and Economic Consequences, A Review of the Evidence,* Core Cities Working Group.

Commission of the European Communities (2005), *Cohesion Policy and Cities: The Urban Contribution to Growth and Jobs in the Regions,* Brussels.

ODPM (2004) Parkinson, M. et al, *Competitive European Cities: Where do the Core Cities Stand?* London: ODPM

ODPM (2005), *Conclusions of Bristol Ministerial Informal Meeting on Sustainable Communities in Europe,* UK Presidency, Bristol.

Pyke, F. & Sengeberger, ", (1992), *Industrial Districts and Local Economic Regeneration,* Geneva, International Institute for Labour Studies.

Van den Berg, Leo et al (2006), *National Policy Responses to Urban Challenges in Europe,* Ashgate.

Chapter 2: Evaluating policy for English cities

DETR (1999) *Towards an urban renaissance: final report of the Urban Task Force* London

DETR (200) *Our Towns and Cities: The Future – Delivering an Urban Renaissance* (The Urban White Paper) London

ODPM (2004) Parkinson, M. et al, *Competitive European Cities: Where do the Core Cities Stand?* London: ODPM

ODPM (2003) *Sustainable Communities: Building for the Future* London

Social Exclusion Unit (1998) Bringing Britain Together. A National Strategy for Neighbourhood Renewal. London: TSO.

Social Exclusion Unit (2001) A New Commitment to Neighbourhood Renewal. National Strategy Action Plan. London: TSO

Chapter 4: The competitive economic performance of English cities

Amin, A. and Tomaney, J. (eds.) *Behind the Myth of the European Union: Prospects for Cohesion,* London, Routledge.

Amin, A. and Thrift, N. (1992) "Neo-Marshallian nodes in global networks", *International Journal of Urban and Regional Research*, Vol. 16, No. 4, pp. 571 587.

Atkinson, R. D. (2002) *The 2002 State New Economy Index,* Washington: Progressive Policy Institute.

Atkinson, R. D. and Gottlieb, P. D. (2001) *The Metropolitan New Economy Index,* Washington: Progressive Policy Institute.

Baldwin, R., Forslid, R., Martin, P. Ottaviano, G. and Robert-Nicoud, F. (2003) *Economic Geography and Public Policy*, Princeton: Princeton University Press.

Begg, I. (1999) Cities and Competitiveness, *Urban Studies* 36, 5/6, pp. 795-810.

…….. (2002) *Urban Competitiveness: Policies for Dynamic Cities*, Bristol: Policy Press.

Bennett, R. J., Daniel, J. G. and Bratton, W. (1999) "The location and concentration of businesses in Britain: business clusters, business services, market coverage and local economic development", *Transactions of the Institute of British Geographers*, NS 24, pp. 393-420.

Boschma, R. (2004) Competitiveness of regions from an evolutionary perspective, *Regional Studies*, 38, pp. 1001-1014.

Boscham, R. and Lambooy, J.G. (1999) Evolutionary economics and economic geography, *Journal of Evolutionary Economics*, 9, pp. 411-429.

Bowling, A. (1995) "What things are important in people's lives?", *Social Science and Medicine*, Vol. 41, pp. 1447-1462.

Bristow, G. (2005) Everyone's a winner: problematising the discourse of regional competitiveness, *Journal of Economic Geography*, 5, pp. 285-304.

Brown, G. (2001) The conditions for high and stable growth and employment, *Economic Journal*, 111, pp. 30-44.

Bryson, J. R. and Daniels, P. W. (1998) "Business link, strong ties, and the walls of silence: small and medium sized enterprises and external business advice", *Environment and Planning C: Government and Policy*, Vol. 16, pp. 265-80.

Camagni, R, (2002) On the concept of territorial competitiveness: sound or misleading? *Urban Studies*, 39, 13, pp. 2395-2411.

Caves, R.E. (2000) Creative Industries: Contact between Art and Commerce, Cambridge, Mass: Harvard University Press.

Cellini, R. and Soci, A. (2002) Pop Competitiveness, Banca Nazionale del Lavoro, *Quarterly Review*, LV, 220, pp. 71-101.

Chatterji, M. and Dewhurst, J. H. L. (1996) "Convergence clubs and relative economic performance in Grate Britain: 1977-1991", *Regional Studies*, Vol. 30, pp. 31-40.

Cheshire, P. and Gordon, I.R. (Eds) (1995) *Territorial Competition in an Integrating Europe*, Aldershot: Avebury.

City Corporation of London (2003) Financial Services Clustering and its Significance in London, Report prepared by Manchester Business School and Loughborough, Department of Geography, London, City Corporation.

Coase, R.H. (1937): "The nature of the firm". *Economica* NS 4, 386-405.

…….. (1988): "The nature of the firm: origin". *Journal of Law, Economics and Organisation* 4,1, 3-47.

Cooke, P. and Morgan, K. (1993) "The network paradigm: new departures in corporate and regional development", *Environment and Planning D*, 11, pp.543-564.

Core Cities (2004) *Core Cities Working Group: Innovation Group: Final Report*

Council on Competitiveness (2001) *US Competitiveness, 2001: Strengths, Vulnerabilities and Long-term Priorities*, Washington: Council on Competitiveness:

Department of Environment, Transport and the Regions (1999) *Quality of life Counts*, London, DETR.

Department for Environment, Food and Rural Affairs (2002) *Survey of Public Attitudes to Quality of Life and to the Environment*, London, DEFRA.

Department of Trade and Industry (1998) *Our Competitive Future: Building the Knowledge-Driven Economy*, London: DTI.

…….. 2003) *Prosperity for All*, London: DTI.

…….. (2003a) *Regional Competitiveness & State of the Regions*, London, DTI.

…….. (2003b) *UK productivity and Competitiveness Indicators 2003*, DTI Economics paper No. 6, London, DTI.

…….. (2004) *Creating Wealth from Knowledge*, The DTI five year programme, London, DTI

Dosi, G; Freeman, C; Nelson, R; Silverberg, G; Soete, L (1988) *Technical Change and Economic Theory*. Pinter, London.

Duffy, H. (1995) *Competitive Cities: Succeeding in the Global Economy*, London: Spon.

Dunford, M. (1993) Regional disparities in the European Community: Evidence from the REGIO databank, *Regional Studies*, 27, pp. 263-275.

…….. (1997) "Divergence, instability and exclusion: regional dynamics in Great Britain" in Lee, R. and Wills, J. (eds.) *Geographies of Economies*, London, Arnold.

Dunford, M. and Smith, A. (2002) Catching up or falling behind? Economic performance and the trajectories of economic development in an enlarged Europe, *Economic Geography*, 76, 2, pp. 169-195.

European Commission (1997) *Report on the competitiveness of the EU*, DG III (mimeograph).

…….. (1999) *Sixth Periodic Report on the Social and Economic Situation of Regions in the EU*, Brussels: European Commission.

…….. (2003) *European Competitiveness Report*, 2003, Brussels: European Commission.

…….. (2004) *A New Partnership for Cohesion: Convergence, Competitiveness and Cooperation*, Brussels: European Commission.

Eurostat (2004) *Urban Audit perception Survey: Local perception of Quality of Life in 31 European Cities*, www.urbanaudit.org

Evans, P. (2000) Income dynamics in countries and regions, in Hess, G.D. and van Wincoop, E. (Eds) *Intra-national Macro-economics*, Cambridge: Cambridge University Press, pp. 131-155.

Findlay, A., Morris, A. and Rogerson, R. (1988) "Where to live in Britain in 1988", *Cities*, Vol. 5, pp. 268-273.

Florida, R. (2002) *The Rise of the Creative Class: and how it is transforming work, leisure, community and everyday life*, New York, Basic Books.

Freeman,C. (1986)"The role of technical change in national economic development", in A. Amin and J. Goddard eds. *Technological Change, Industrial Restructuring and Regional Development*, pp. 100-114, London, Allen and Unwin.

Fujita, M., Krugman, P. and Venables, A. (1999) *The Spatial Economy: Cities, Regions and International Trade*, Cambridge, Mass: MIT Press.

Fujita, M. and Thisse, J-F. (2002) *Economics of Agglomeration: Cities, Industrial Location and Regional Growth*, Cambridge: Cambridge University Press.

Grabher,G. (1991)*The Embedded Firm: the Socio-Economics of Industrial Networks*, London, Routledge.

…….. (1993) "The weakness of strong ties. The lock-in of regional development in the Ruhr area." In *The Embedded Firm: on the socio-economics of industrial networks*, G. Grabher (ed.), pp. 255-277, London, Routledge.

…….. (2001) "Ecologies of creativity: the village, the group and the heterarchic organisation of the British advertising industry", *Environment and Planning A*, Vol. 33, pp. 351-74.

Gripais, P. & Bishop, P. (2005) *Government Output and Expenditure in UK Regions and Sub-Regions: An Analysis of the New Experimental Accounts Data, Regional Studies*, 39(6), 805-813

Group of Lisbon (1995) *Limits to Competition*, Cambridge, Mass: MIT Press.

H.M. Treasury (2001) *Productivity in the UK: 3-The Regional Dimension*, London: H.M. Treasury.

…….. (2003) *Productivity in the UK: 4-The Local Dimension*, London: H.M. Treasury.

…….. (2004) *Devolving Decision Making: Meeting the Regional Economic Challenge – Increasing Regional and Local Flexibility*, London: H.M. Treasury

Huggins, R. (2005) *UK Competitiveness Index 2005*, Cardiff, Robert Huggins Associates.

Jacobs. J. (1984) *Cities and the Wealth of Nations*, New York: Random House.

Jensen-Butler, C. (1997) "Competition between cities, urban performance and the role of urban policy: a theoretical framework", in C. Jensen-Butler, A. Schachar and J. van Weesep (eds.) *European Cities in Competition*, pp. 3-42, Aldershot, Avebury.

Jensen-Butler, C, Schacher, A. and Weesep, J. van (Eds) (1997) *European Cities in Competition*, Aldershot: Avebury.

Kaldor, N. (1981) The role of increasing returns, technical progress and cumulative causation in the theory of international trade and economic growth, *Économie Appliquée*, 34, pp. 593-617.

Kitson, M., Martin, R. L. and Tyler, P. (2004) Regional competitiveness: An elusive yet key concept? *Regional Studies*, 38, pp. 991-999.

Krugman, P. (1990) *The Age of Diminished Expectations*, Cambridge, Mass: MIT Press.

.... (1991) Increasing returns and economic geography, *Journal of Political Economy*, 99, pp. 483-499.

.... (1994) Competitiveness: A Dangerous Obsession, *Foreign Affairs*, 73, 2, pp. 28-44.

.... (1996a) *Pop Internationalism*, Cambridge, Mass: MIT Press.

.... (1996b) Making sense of the competitiveness debate, *Oxford Review of Economic Policy*, 12, pp. 17-35.

.... (2003) Growth on the Periphery: Second Wind for Industrial Regions? *The Allander Series*, Fraser Allander Institute, Scotland.

Lambert (2003) *Review of Business-University Collaboration*, Norwich, HMSO.

Lever, W. (1993) "Competition within the European urban system", *Urban Studies*, Vol. 30, pp. 935-948.

MacPherson, A. (1997) "The role of producer service outsourcing in the innovation performance of New York State manufacturing firms", *Annals, Association of American Geographers*, Vol. 87, 52-71.

Markusen, A. (1996) "interaction between regional and industrial policies: evidence from four countries", *International Regional Science Review*, Vol. 19, pp. 49-78.

Martin, R.L. (1989) The Growth and Geographical Anatomy of Venture Capitalism in the United Kingdom, *Regional Studies*, 23, pp. 389-403.

.... (1992) Financing Regional Enterprise: The Role of the Venture Capital Market, in Townroe, P. and Martin, R.L. (Eds) *Regional Development in the 1990s: The British Isles in Transition*, London: Jessica Kingsley.

Martin, R.L. Berndt, C., Klagge, B., Sunley, P. and Herten, S. (2003) *Regional Venture Capital Policy: UK and Germany Compared*, London and Berlin: Anglo German Foundation.

Martin. R.L. and Sunley. P.J. (1998) Slow convergence? The new endogenous growth theory and regional development, *Economic Geography*, 74, 3, pp. 201-227.

.... (2003) Deconstructing clusters: chaotic concept or policy panacea? *Journal of Economic Geography*, 3, pp. 5-35

Mason, C. M. and Harrison, R. T. (2003) "Closing the regional equity gap? A critique of the Department of Trade and Industry's regional venture capital funds initiative", *Regional Studies*, Vol. 37.8, pp. 855-868.

Mott Report (1969), Cambridge Futures 2.

Muller, E. and Zenker, A. (2001) "Business services as actors of knowledge transformation: the role of KIBS in regional and national innovation systems" *Research Policy*, Vol. 30, pp. 1501-1516.

McCombie, J. and Thirlwall, A. (1994) *Economic Theory and the Balance of Payment Constraint*, London: Macmillan.

Oakley, K. (2004) Not so Cool Britannia: The Role of the Creative Industries in Economic Development, *International Journal of Cultural Studies*, 7, pp. 67-77.

Office of the Deputy Prime Minister (2004a) *Competitive European cities: where do the Core Cities Stand?*, Urban Research Paper 13, London, ODPM.

.... (2003) *Cities, regions and competitiveness*, London: ODPM

.... (2004b) *Our Cities Are Back: Competitive Cities Make Prosperous Regions and Sustainable Communities*, London, ODPM.

.... (2005) "What does regional and urban policy tell us about city regions and what are the key questions we still need to answer?", Working Draft Position paper for Cross Departmental City-regions Policy, Residential Workshop, Selsdon Park Hotel, 5-6 January.

OECD (2003) *OECD Science, Technology and Industry Scoreboard*, Paris, OECD.

O'Mahony, M. and Van Ark, B. (Eds) (2003) *EU Productivity and Competitiveness: An Industry Perspective – Can Europe Resume the Catching-up Process?* Luxembourg, European Commission.

Perroux, F. (1955) "Note sur la notion de 'pole de croissance', *Economie Appliquee*, Jan-June, pp. 307-320.

Piore, M. J. and Sabel, C. F. (1984) *The Second Industrial Divide: Possibilities for Prosperity*, Basic Books.

Porter, M.E. (1992) *Competitive Advantage: Creating and sustaining Superior Performance*, Issue 10, London: PA Consulting Group,

.... (1998a) *On Competition,* Boston, Mass: Harvard Business School Press.

.... (1998b) Location, clusters and the new economics of competition, *Business Economics*, 33, 1, pp. 7-17.

.... (2000) Location, competition and economic development: local clusters in the global economy, *Economic Development Quarterly*, 14, 1, pp. 15-31.

.... (2001) Regions and the new economics of competition, in Scott, A.J. (Ed) *Global City Regions*, Oxford: Blackwell, pp. 139-152.

.... (2002) "Regional foundations of competitiveness and implications for government policy", DTI workshop, London 16.4 2002.

.... (2003) The economic performance of regions, *Regional Studies*, 37, 6/7, pp. 549-578.

Porter, M. E. and Ketels, C. H.M. (2003) *UK Competitiveness: Moving to the Next Stage*, DTI Economics Paper 3, London: Department of Trade and Industry.

Power, D. and Scott, A.J. (Eds) (2004) *Cultural Industries and the Production of Culture*, London: Routledge.

Pyke, F. and Sengeberger, W. (1992) *Industrial Districts and Local Economic Regeneration,* Geneva, International Institute for Labour Studies.

Reich, R. (1990) But now we're global, *The Times Literary Supplement,* Aug 31-Sep 6.

Robert Huggins Associates (2003) *World Knowledge Competitiveness Index,* Robert Huggins Associates, Pontypridd.

…….. (2005) *UK Competitiveness Index: The Changing State of the Nation, 1997-2005,* Robert Huggins Associates, Pontypridd.

Roberts, M. (2004) "The growth performance of the GB counties: some new empirical evidence for 1077-1993", *Regional Studies,* Vol. 38.2, pp. 149-163.

Rodriguez-Pose, A. & Gill, N. (2005) *On the 'Economic Dividend' of Devolution, Regional Studies,* 39(4), 405-420.

Rogerson, R. J. (1999) "Quality of life and city competitiveness", *Urban Studies,* Vol. 36, Nos 5-6, pp. 969-985.

Rogerson, R. J., Findlay, A., Morris, A. and Paddison, R. (1989) "Variations in quality of life in urban Britain", *Cities,* Vol. 6, pp. 227-233.

…….. (1990) *Quality of Life in Britain's District Councils,* Glasgow, University of Strathclyde.

Rowthorn, R. (1999) "The political economy of full employment in modern Britain", *Kalecki Memorial Lecture,* Department of Economics, University of Oxford, October 19.

Schumpeter, J.A. (1939) *Business Cycles: a theoretical, historical and statistical analysis of the capitalist process.* McGraw-Hill, New York.

Scott, A.J. (2000) *The Cultural Economy of Cities: Essays on the Geography of Image-Producing Industries,* London: Sage.

Scott, A.J. and Storper, M. (1987) "High Technology industry and regional development: a theoretical critique and reconstruction". *International Social Science Journal* 112, 215- 232. Press, Cambridge.

Setterfield, M. (1997) *Rapid Growth and Relative Decline: Modelling Macroeconomic Dynamics with Hysteresis,* London: Macmillan.

Simmie, J. M. (ed.) (2001) *Innovative Cities,* London, Spon.

Simmie, J. M. (2002) "Trading places in the global economy", *European Planning Studies,* Vol. 10, 2, pp.201-214.

Simmie, J. M. (2003) "Innovation and urban regions as national and international trading nodes for the transfer and sharing of knowledge", *Regional Studies,* Vol. 37, 6&7, August/ October pp. 607-620

Smith Institute (2005) *Working Cities,* Seminar Briefing, 8 June, London.

Steinle, W.J. (1992) Regional competitiveness and the single market, *Regional Studies,* 26, 4, pp. 307-318.

Storper, M. (1995) Competitiveness policy options; the technology-regions connection, *Growth and Change*, Spring, pp. 285-308.

.... (1997) *The Regional World: Territorial Development in a Global Economy*, New York: Guilford Press.

Storper, M.J. and Harrison, (1991) "Flexibility, hierarchy and regional development: the changing structure of industrial production systems and their forms of governance in the 1990s", *Research Policy*, 20, pp. 407-422.

Strambach, S. (2001) "Innovation processes and the role of knowledge-intensive business services" in Koschatzky, K., Kulicke, M. and Zeniker, A. (eds.) *Innovation Networks – Concepts and Challenges in the European Perspective*, Heidleberg, Physica, pp. 53-68.

Thirlwall, A. (1983) A plain man's guide to Kaldor's growth laws, *Journal of Post-Keynesian Economics,* 5, pp. 345-3548.

Tyson, L. (1992) *Who's Bashing Whom? Trade Conflicts in High-Technology Industries*, Washington, DC: Institute for International Economics.

Urban Studies (1999) Special Issue on Competitive Cities, *Urban Studies*, 36, 5/6.

Witt, U. (2003) *The Evolving Economy*, Cheltenham: Edward Elgar.

Yeung, H. (1994) "Critical reviews of geographical perspectives on business organisations and the organisation of production: towards a network approach", *Progress in Human Geography*, 18, pp. 460-490.

Chapter 6: Liveability in English cities

Armitage, R. forthcoming, '*Secured by design refined: environmental risk factors, offenders' modus operandi and costs and incentives*'.

ATCM (Undated) *"Key Performance Indicators"*.

Atkinson, R. Flint, F. Blandy S., Lister, D. (2003) *"Gated Communities in England"* Final report of the Gated Communities in England 'New Horizons' Project.

Audit Commission (2002) '*Street Scene*', London: Audit Commission.

.... (2003) *"Quality of Life Indicators A good practice guide"* http://www.auditcommission.gov.uk/reports/NATIONAL-REPORT.asp?CategoryID=&ProdID=ACDE5F73-1CEB-4936-9675-6FD06664CC7F

Baker Associates/Alison Millward Associates (2004) Green Spaces and sustainable communities. Programme evaluation on behalf of the New Opportunities Fund. Second Annual Report. Baker Associates: Bristol.

British Crime Survey: http://www.crimestatistics.org.uk/

Budd, T. (1999) '*Burglary of domestic dwellings: findings from the British Crime Survey*', Home Office Statistical Bulletin 4/99.

BVPI *Data on Local Government Performance:* http://www.bvpi.gov.uk/pages/Index.asp

CABE (2002a) *"The Value of Good Design"*, London.

…….. (2002b) *'Streets of Shame' – Summary of findings from 'Public Attitudes to Architecture and the Built Environment'*, London.

…….. (2004) *"Housing Audit: Assessing the Design Quality of New Homes"* http://www.thehomebuyersguide.org/downloads/housing_audit_2004.pdf

…….. (2005) *'Does Money Grow on Trees?'* , London: CABE http://www.cabe.org.uk/data/pdfs/DoesMoneyGrowonTrees.pdf

CBRE (2005) *'Market View: UK Retail Briefing'*, Issue 1 2005; London.

Champion, A. & Green, A. (1987) *"Changing places: Britain's Demographic, economic and social complexion"* Edward Arnold.

Civic Trust Green Flag Awards: http://www.greenflagaward.org.uk/

Clarke R. (1997) *'Situational Crime Prevention: Successful Case Studies'* 2nd Edn. Albany, N.Y.: Harrow and Heston.

DEFRA *Quality of Life Counts indicators:*

http://www.sustainable-development.gov.uk/index.htm

DETR & CABE (2000) *"By Design, Urban Design in the Planning System: Towards better practice"*, London.

DETR (2000a) *'Living in Urban England: Attitudes and Aspirations'*, London.

…….. (2000b) *'Our Towns and Cities: the Future. Delivering an urban renaissance'*, London.

DETR (2001) Literature Review of Public Space and Local Environments for the Cross Cutting Review. Final Report. K.Williams, S. Green et al Oxford Centre for Sustainable Development, Oxford Brookes University. DETR: London.

DFT Road Travel Speeds in English Urban Areas: http://www.dft.gov.uk/stellent/groups/dft_control/documents/contentservertemplate/dft_index.hcst?n=8171&l=4

DfT Bus passenger satisfaction ratings: http://www.dft.gov.uk/stellent/groups/dft_transstats/documents/page/dft_transstats_031294.hcsp

DTLR (2002) Green Spaces, Better Places Final report of the Urban Green Spaces Taskforce. DTLR: London.

Ekblom, P. (2002a*) 'From the Source to the Mainstream is Uphill: The Challenge of Transferring Knowledge of Crime Prevention Through Replication, Innovation and Anticipation.'* in: N. Tilley (ed.) Analysis for Crime Prevention, Crime Prevention Studies 13: 131-203. Monsey, N.Y.: Criminal Justice Press/ Devon, UK: Willan Publishing.

…….. (2002b) *'Future Imperfect: Preparing for the Crimes to Come.'* Criminal Justice Matters 46 Winter 2001/02:38-40. London: Centre for Crime and Justice Studies, Kings College.

EnCams (2003) 'Local Environmental Quality Survey of England', London: EnCams *English House Condition Survey:*

http://www.odpm.gov.uk/stellent/groups/odpm_housing/documents/page/odpm_house_603834.hcsp

…….. (2004) Local Environmental Quality Survey in England, 2002-4. EnCams: London.

Environment Agency (2002) *"The urban environment in England and Wales"*, London: Environment Agency.

Frontier Economics (2004) *"Quality of place and regional economic performance"*, unpublished.

Grayson, L. & Young K. (1994) *'Quality of Life in Cities – An Overview and Guide to Available Literature'* London: The British Library.

GLA (2004) *'The London Plan: Spatial Development Strategy for Greater London'*, London: GLA.

Hillier, B. & Shu, S. 1999, *'Do burglars understand defensible space?: New evidence on the relation between crime and space'*, Planning in London, April 1999.

Home Office/RDS (2004) *'Defining and measuring anti-social behaviour'* London.

Institute for Criminal Policy Research (2005) *'Anti-social behaviour strategies: Finding a balance,'* Bristol: The Policy Press for the Joseph Rowntree Foundation.

Jacobs, J. (1961) *'The Death and Life of Great American Cities'.* New York: Random House.

LGA (2004) *'What drives public satisfaction with local government?'*, London.

Llewelyn Davies in association with DTLR & The National Retail Planning Forum (2002) 'Going to Town: Improving Town Centre Access – a Companion Guide to PPG6'.

…….. (2003) "Quality Streets: The Economic Benefits of Good Walking Environments" http://www.c-london.co.uk/files/pdf/Quality%20Streets%20-%20main%20report.pdf

…….. (2004) *"Safer Places: The Planning System and Crime Prevention"* London: ODPM.

Lucas, K., (ed.) (2004) Running on Empty: Transport, social exclusion and environmental justice. The Policy Press: Bristol.

Lynch, K (1960) *"A theory of good city form"* Cambridge: MIT Press.

McLeod, G. (2003) *"Privatising the City? The tentative push towards edge urban developments and gated communities in the United Kingdom"* Unpublished report for the ODPM.

Manchester City Centre Management Company and Manchester City Council (2003) *'Manchester City Centre Strategic Plan 2004-2007'.*

Manchester City Council (2004) Environment and Operations Directorate Environmental Service Department, Street Management Group *Business Plan 2004/5.*

Markosky, C (2004) *"The Good Village Guide"* Article in The Sunday Telegraph, November 14th 2004.

MORI (2005) 'MORI — Physical Capital: Liveability in 2005'. London.

National Land Use Database: http://www.nlud.org.uk

Nelson, S. Gibson, P. Ginham D. (2004) "*From Zero to Hero* & *Is Britain the Dirty Man of Europe*", London: Encams.

ONS *(2004) Survey of English Housing 2000/1-2002/3 aggregated results:* http://www.odpm.gov.uk/stellent/groups/odpm_housing/documents/page/odpm_house_6

ONS/DEFRA (2004) '*Quality of Life Counts: 2004 Update'* http://www.sustainable-development.gov.uk/documents/publications/qolc2004.pdf

ODPM (2002) Living Places Cleaner, Safer, Greener. ODPM: London.

…….. (2003) English House Condition Survey. Key Findings for 2003. Decent Homes and Decent Places. ODPM: London.

…….. (2004a) Living Places: Caring for Quality. Bartlett School of Planning, UCL. ODPM: London.

……..   (2004b) Best Value User Satisfaction Survey 2003/4. ODPM: London.

……..   (2004c) Neighbourhood Wardens Scheme Evaluation Research Report 8. Neighbourhood Renewal Unit. ODPM: London.

……..   (2004d) Neighbourhood Management Pathfinder Programme National Evaluation Annual Review 2003/04. SQW report for ODPM, London.

…….. (2004e) Liveability and Sustainable Development: Synergies and Conflicts. Brooklyndhurst for ODPM: London.

……..   (2004f) *"Government Blitz on Nuisance Vehicles"* http://www.odpm.gov.uk/pns/displaypn.cgi?pn_id=2004_0280

……..   (2005) Sustainable Communities: People, Places and Prosperity – A Five Year Plan. Office of the Deputy Prime Minister. ODPM: London.

……..   (2005) The Role and Effectiveness of CABE. ODPM Housing, Planning and Local Government and the Regions Committee Report. Cm6509. HMSO.

……..   (2005) '*How To Manage Town Centres'*, London

Office of Public Management (2004) CABE Stakeholder Review OPM: London.

Parkinson, M., Hutchins, M. Simmie, J. Clark, G. Verdonk, H. (2004) *"Competitive European Cities: Where do the Core Cities Stand?"*, London: ODPM.

Power, A., (2004) Neighbourhood Management and the Future of Urban Areas CASEpaper 77. London School of Economics: London.

Poyner, B. & Webb, B. (1992) '*Crime free housing'*, Oxford: Butterworth Architecture.

Retail Property Research (1993) '*Central London Shopping Study: All Centre Report'*, London.

Social Exclusion Unit (2003) Making the Connections: Final Report on Transport and Social Exclusion. Report by SEU. ODPM: London.

SRA *National train performance:* http://www.sra.gov.uk/pubs2/statistics

Tilley, N. (1993) *'After Kirkholt: Theory, Methods and Results of Replication Evaluations.'* Crime Prevention Unit Paper 47. London: Home Office.

Todorovic J. & Wellington, S. (2000) *"Living in Urban England: Attitudes and Aspirations"* London: DETR.

Town S. (2002) *'Permeability, Access Opportunities and Crime'.* Unpublished paper, West Yorkshire Police.

Urban Parks Forum (2001) Public Park Assessment. A survey of local authority owned parks focusing on parks of historic interest. UPF: Caversham.

Urban Task Force (1999) *'Towards an urban renaissance: report of the Urban Task Force'*

URBED (1994) *'Vital and Viable Town Centres: Meeting the Challenge'*, London: URBED.

Wilson, J & Kelling, G. 1982, *"Broken windows"*, The Atlantic Monthly, March 1982, 29-38.

Woolley, H., Rose, S. Carmona, M. Freedman, J. (2004) *"The Value of Public Space"*, London: CABE.

Worpole, K., (2003) A space – or a place – for everyone? Town and Country Planning. Vol 72 no 8.

Chapter 7: Public attitudes in English cities

Bromley, C. (2004), 'Can Britain close the digital divide', in Park, A., Curtice, J., Thomson, K., Bromley, C. and Phillips, M. (eds.), *British Social Attitudes: the 21st Report*, London: Sage.

Bromley, C. and Curtice, J. (2002), 'Where have all the voters gone?', in Park, A., Curtice, J., Thomson, K., Jarvis, L. and Bromley, C. (eds.), *British Social Attitudes: the 19th Report*, London: Sage.

Butler, D. and Stokes, D. (1969), *Political Change in Britain*, London: Macmillan.

Clarke, H., Sanders, D., Stewart, M. and Whiteley, P. (2004), *Political Choice in Britain*, Oxford: Oxford University Press.

Curtice, J. and Jowell, R. (1997), 'Trust in the political system', in Jowell, R., Curtice, J., Park, A., Brook, L., Thomson, K. and Bryson, C. (eds.), *British Social Attitudes: the 14th Report*, Aldershot: Ashgate.

Curtice, J. and Sandford, M. (2004), 'Does England want devolution too?', in Park, A., Curtice, J., Thomson, K., Bromley, C. and Phillips, M. (eds.), *British Social Attitudes: the 21st Report*, London: Sage.

Curtice, J. and Seyd, B. (2003), 'Is there a crisis of political participation?', in Park, A., Curtice, J., Thomson, K., Bromley, C. and Phillips, M. (eds.), *British Social Attitudes: the 21st Report*, London: Sage.

Dalton, R. (1999), 'Political support in advanced industrial democracies', in Norris, P., *Critical Citizens: Global Support for Democratic Governance*, Oxford: Oxford University Press.

Department of the Environment, Transport and the Regions (DETR) (2000), *1998 British Social Attitudes Survey: Secondary Data Analysis of the Local Government Module*, www.local.dtlr.gov.uk/research/surv1998.

Department of Transport (2004), *Attitudes to Roads, Congestion and Congestion Charging*, www.dft.gov.uk/stellent/groups/dft_transstats/documents/page/dft_transstats_029806.hcsp

.... (2005), *Results from the ONS Omnibus Survey*, www.dft.gov.uk/stellent/groups/dft_transstats/documents/page/dft_transstats_039667.hcsp

Electoral Commission and the Hansard Society (2004), *An Audit of Political Engagement*, London: The Electoral Commission.

.... (2005), *An Audit of Political Engagement: Research Report, March 2005*, London: The Electoral Commission.

Evans, G. (2002), 'In search of tolerance', in Park, A., Curtice, J., Thomson, K., Jarvis, L. and Bromley, C. (eds.), *British Social Attitudes: the 19th Report*, London: Sage.

Exley, S. and Christie, I. (2002), 'Off the buses?', in Park, A., Curtice, J., Thomson, K., Jarvis, L. and Bromley, C. (eds.), *British Social Attitudes: the 19th Report*, London: Sage.

Gardner, J. and Oswald, A. (2001), 'Internet use: the digital divide', in Park, A., Curtice, J., Thomson, K., Jarvis, L. and Bromley, C. (eds.), *British Social Attitudes: the 18th Report*, London: Sage.

Home Office (2004), *2003 Home Office Citizenship Survey: People, Families and Communities*, Home Office Research Study 289, Home Office: London.

Jeffery, C., Harding, A. and Humphrey, L. (2005), *Before the Referendum: Public Views on Elected Regional Assemblies in the North of England*, Devolution Briefing No. 17, Swindon: ESRC.

Johnston, M. and Jowell, R. (1999), 'Social capital and the social fabric', in Jowell, R., Curtice, J., Park, A., and Thomson, K. (eds.), *British Social Attitudes: the 16th Report*, London: Sage.

.... (2001), 'How robust is British civil society', in Park, A., Curtice, J., Thomson, K., Jarvis, L. and Bromley, C. (eds.), *British Social Attitudes: the 18th Report*, London: Sage.

McLaren, L. and Johnson, M. (2004), 'Understanding the rising tide of anti-immigrant sentiment', in Park, A., Curtice, J., Thomson, K., Bromley, C. and Phillips, M. (eds.), *British Social Attitudes: the 21st Report*, London: Sage.

Office of the Deputy Prime Minister (ODPM) (2003), *Public knowledge and attitudes to the balance of funding survey*, www.local.odpm.gov.uk/finance/balance/public.ppt.

Park, A., Curtice, J., Thomson, K., Bromley, C. and Phillips, M. (eds.) (2004), *British Social Attitudes: the 21st Report*, London: Sage.

Putnam, R. (2000), *Bowling Alone – the collapse and revival of American community*, New York: Simon and Schuster.

Rao, N. and Young, K. (1999), 'Revitalising local democracy', in Jowell, R., Curtice, J., Park, A. and Thomson, K. (eds), *British Social Attitudes: the 16th Report: Who Shares New Labour Values?*, Aldershot: Ashgate.

Rothon, C. and Heath, A. (2003), 'Trends in racial prejudice', in Park, A., Curtice, J., Thomson, K., Jarvis, L. and Bromley, C. (eds.), *British Social Attitudes: the 20th Report: Continuity and change over two decades*, London: Sage.

Stratford, N. and Christie, I. (2000), 'Town and country life', in Jowell, R., Curtice, J., Park, A., Thomson, K., Jarvis, L, Bromley, C. and Stratford, N. (eds.), *British Social Attitudes: the 17th Report*, Aldershot: Ashgate.

The Stationary Office (2005), *Focus on Personal Travel: England*, London: The Stationary Office.

Chapter 8: English cities in an international context

Alba, Richard D. et al, "Immigrant Groups in the Suburbs: A Reexamination of Suburbanization and Spatial Assimilation." *American Sociological Review* 64 (1999): 446–460.

Apgar, Mahlon, "Deconcentration: A Strategic Imperative in Corporate Real Estate." *Journal of Real Estate Portfolio Management* 8 (4) (2002): 50–60.

Berman, Eli, Bound, John and Griliches, Zvi , "Changes in the Demand for Skilled Labor within U.S. Manufacturing: Evidence from the Annual Survey of Manufacturers." *The Quarterly Journal of Economics* 109 (2) (1994): 367–397.

Bernstein, Jared, "The Changing Nature of the Economy: The Critical Roles of Education and Innovation in Creating Jobs and Opportunity in a Knowledge Economy." Testimony before the Committee on Education and the Workforce of the U.S. House of Representatives, March 11, 2004.

Berube, Alan , "Gaining but Losing Ground: Population Change in Large Cities and Their Suburbs." In Bruce Katz and Robert E. Lang, eds. *Redefining Urban and Suburban America: Evidence from Census 2000, Volume I* (Washington: Brookings Institution, 2003).

.... "Racial and Ethnic Change in the Nation's Largest Cities." In B. Katz and R. Lang, eds., *Redefining Urban and Suburban America: Evidence from Census 2000, Volume I* (Washington: Brookings Institution, 2003).

Berube, Alan and Forman, Benjamin , "Living on the Edge: Decentralization Within Cities in the 1990s" (Washington: Brookings Institution, 2002).

Berube, Alan and Frey, William "A Decade of Mixed Blessings: Urban and Suburban Poverty in Census 2000." In A. Berube, B. Katz, and R. Lang, *Redefining Urban and Suburban America: Evidence from Census 2000, Volume II* (Washington: Brookings Institution, 2005).

Birch, Eugenie, "Who Lives Downtown?" (Washington: Brookings Institution, 2005).

Bollinger, Christopher, Berger, Mark and Thompson, Eric, "Smart Growth and the Costs of Sprawl in Kentucky: Phase I and II" (University of Kentucky Center for Business and Economic Research, 2001).

Borjas, George J., Richard B. Freeman, and Lawrence F. Katz, "How Much Do Immigration and Trade Affect Labor Market Outcomes?" *Brookings Papers on Economic Activity*: 1–67.

Carlino, Gerald, "Knowledge Spillovers: Cities' Role in the New Economy." *Business Review* Q4 (2001): 17–24.

Ciccone, A. and Hall, R. E. "Productivity and the Density of Economic Activity." *American Economic Review* 86 (1) (1996): 54–70.

Cortright, Joseph and Mayer, Heike, "Signs of Life: The Growth of Biotechnology Centers in the U.S." (Washington: Brookings Institution, 2002).

Economist , The "Minding about the gap", *The Economist,* June 11–17, 2005, p. 32.

Farley, Reynolds "The Unexpectedly Large Census Count in 2000 and Its Implications," Research Report 01-467 (University of Michigan Population Studies Centre, 2001).

Fasenfest, David, Booza, Jason and Metzger, Kurt, "Living Together: A New Look at Racial and Ethnic Integration in Metropolitan Neighbourhoods, 1990–2000" (Washington: Brookings Institution, 2004).

Federal Reserve Bank of Chicago, *1996 Annual Report.*

Fellowes, Matthew and Katz, Bruce, "The Price is Wrong: Getting the Market Right for Working Families in Philadelphia" (Washington: Brookings Institution, 2005).

Florida, Richard, *The Rise of the Creative Class* (New York: Basic Books, 2002); Joseph Cortright and Carol Coletta, "The Young and the Restless: How Portland Competes for Talent" (2004).

Franklin, Rachel S., "Migration of the Young, Single, and College Educated: 1995 to 2000." Census 2000 Special Report 13 (U.S. Census Bureau, 2003).

Frey, William H., "Three Americas: The Rising Significance of Regions." *Journal of the American Planning Association* 68 (4) (2002): 349–255.

.... "Metropolitan Magnets for International and Domestic Migrants" (Washington: Brookings Institution, 2003).

.... "Melting Pot Suburbs: A Study of Suburban Diversity." In B. Katz and R. Lang, eds., *Redefining Urban and Suburban America: Evidence from Census 2000, Volume I* (Washington: Brookings Institution, 2003)

.... "Boomers and Seniors in the Suburbs: Aging Patterns in Census 2000" (Washington: Brookings Institution, 2003).

.... "The New Great Migration: Black Americans' Return to the South, 1965–2000." In A. Berube, B. Katz, and R. Lang, eds., *Redefining Urban and Suburban America: Evidence from Census 2000, Volume II* (Washington: Brookings Institution, 2005).

Frey, William and Berube, Alan, "City Families, Suburban Singles: An Emerging Household Story." In B. Katz and R. Lang, eds. *Redefining Urban and Suburban America: Evidence from Census 2000, Volume I* (Washington: Brookings Institution, 2003).

Frey, William et al, "Tracking Metropolitan America into the 21st Century: A Field Guide to the New Metropolitan and Micropolitan Definitions" (Washington: Brookings Institution, 2004).

Glaeser, Edward et al, "Growth in Cities." *Journal of Political Economy* 100 (6) (1992): 1126–1152.

Glaeser, Edward, Kolko, Jed and Saiz, Albert, "Consumer City." NBER Working Paper 7790 (2000).

Glaeser, E. and Kahn, Matthe, "Job Sprawl: Employment Location in U.S. Metropolitan Areas" (Washington: Brookings Institution, 2001).

Glaeser, Ed and Shapiro, Jesse, "City Growth: Which Places Grew, and Why" (Washington: Brookings Institution, 2001).

Glaeser, Edward and Maré, David C., "Cities and Skills." *Journal of Labor Economics* 19 (2) (2001): 316–342.

Glaeser, Edward L. and Vigdor, Jacob L., "Racial Segregation: Promising News." In B. Katz and R. Lang, eds., *Redefining Urban and Suburban America: Evidence from Census 2000, Volume I* (Washington: Brookings Institution, 2003).

Gottlieb, Paul, "Economy Versus Lifestyle in the Inter-metropolitan Migration of the Young: A Preliminary Look at the 2000 Census." *International Journal of Economic Development* 5 (3) (2003) (June).

Grieco, Elizabeth M. and Cassidy, Rachel C., "Overview of Race and Hispanic Origin." Census 2000 Brief 01-1 (2001).

Hall, Sir Peter *Cities in Civilization: Culture, Innovation, and Urban Order.* New York: Pantheon.

Hanson, Royce and Wolman, Hal, "Corporate Citizenship and Urban Problem Solving: The Changing Civic Role of Business Leaders in America's Cities" (Washington: Brookings Institution, forthcoming 2005).

Haub, Carl , "The U.S. Birth Rate Falls Further" (Washington: Population Reference Bureau, 2003).

Hills, John, *Inequality and the State* (Oxford University Press, 2004).

Himes, Christine L. , "Elderly Americans." *Population Bulletin* 56 (4) (December 2001).

Holtz Kay, Jane, *Asphalt Nation* (London: University of California Press, Ltd, 1997).

Jacobs, Jane, *The Economy of Cities.* New York: Vintage Books.

Jargowsky, Paul, "Stunning Progress, Hidden Problems: The Dramatic Decline of Concentrated Poverty in the 1990s." In A. Berube, B. Katz, and R. Lang, eds., *Redefining Urban and Suburban America: Evidence from Census 2000, Volume II* (Washington: Brookings Institution, 2005).

Katz, Bruce, "Neighbourhoods of Choice and Connection: The Evolution of American Neighbourhood Policy and What It Means for the United Kingdom" (Washington: Brookings Institution, 2004).

Kent, Mary M. et al "First Glimpses from the 2000 U.S. Census." *Population Bulletin* 56 (2) (June 2001).

Lang, Robert, *Edgeless Cities: Exploring the Elusive Metropolis* (Washington: Brookings Institution, 2003).

Lang, Robert E. and Dhavale, Dawn , "Beyond Megalopolis: Exploring America's New 'Megapolitan' Geography" (Alexandria, VA: Metropolitan Institute at Virginia Tech, 2005).

Lang, Robert and Sohmer, Rebecca, "Downtown Rebound." In Bruce Katz and Robert E. Lang, eds. *Redefining Urban and Suburban America: Evidence from Census 2000, Volume I* (Washington: Brookings Institution, 2003).

Lang, Robert and Simmons, Patrick, "Boomburbs:' The Emergence of Large, Fast-Growing Suburban Cities." In B. Katz and R. Lang, eds., *Redefining Urban and Suburban America: Evidence from Census 2000, Volume I* (Washington: Brookings Institution, 2003).

Lang, Robert and Zimmerman Gough, Meghan, "Growth Counties: Home to America's New Suburban Metropolis." In A. Berube, B. Katz, and R. Lang, *Redefining Urban and Suburban America: Evidence from Census 2000, Volume III* (Washington: Brookings Institution, 2005).

Leinberger, Chris, "Financing Progressive Development" (Washington: Brookings Institution, 2001); "Turning Around Downtown: Twelve Steps to Revitalization" (Washington: Brookings, 2005)

McConville, Shannon and Ong, Paul, "The Trajectory of Poor Neighbourhoods in Southern California, 1970–2000." In A. Berube, B. Katz, and R. Lang, *Redefining Urban and Suburban America: Evidence from Census 2000, Volume II* (Washington: Brookings Institution, 2005)

Martin, Philip and Midgley, Elizabeth, "Immigration: Shaping and Reshaping America." *Population Bulletin* 58 (2) (June 2003).

Mishel, Lawrence, Bernstein, Jared and Boushey, Heather, *The State of Working America 2002–03* (Cornell University Press, 2002).

Mishel, Lawrence, Bernstein, Jared and Allegretto, Sylvia, *The State of Working America 2004-05* (Cornell University Press, 2005).

Myers, Dowell and Gearin, Elizabeth, "Current Preferences and Future Demand for Denser Residential Environments." *Housing Policy Debate* 12 (4) (2001): 633–659.

Myers, Dowell and Painter, Gary, "Homeownership and Younger Households: Progress Among African Americans and Latinos." In A. Berube, B. Katz, and R. Lang, eds., *Redefining Urban and Suburban America: Evidence from Census 2000, Volume II* (Washington: Brookings Institution, 2005).

Nelson, Arthur C., "Toward a New Metropolis: The Opportunity to Rebuild America" (Washington: Brookings Institution, 2004).

Orfield, Myron, *American Metropolitics* (Washington: Brookings Institution, 2002).

Pagano, Michael and Bowman, Ann O'M., "Vacant Land in Cities: An Urban Resource" (Washington: Brookings Institution, 2000).

Parsons, Craig and Smeeding, Timothy, "L'Immigration au Luxembourg, et Après?" Luxembourg Income Study Working Paper 396 (Syracuse University, 2004).

Pastor, Manuel et al, *Regions That Work: How Cities and Suburbs Can Grow Together* (University of Minnesota Press, 2000).

Paytas, Jerry, "Does Governance Matter? The Dynamics of Metropolitan Governance and Competitiveness" (Pittsburgh: Carnegie Mellon University Center for Economic Development, 2002).

Pollard, Kelvin M. and O'Hare, William P., "America's Racial and Ethnic Minorities." *Population Bulletin* 54 (3) (September 1999).

Puentes, Robert and Warren, David, "One Fifth of the Nation: A Profile of Change in America's First Suburbs" (Washington: Brookings Institution, forthcoming 2005).

Raphael, Steven and Stoll, Michael, "Modest Progress: The Narrowing Spatial Mismatch Between Blacks and Jobs in the 1990s" (Washington: Brookings Institution, 2002).

Real Estate Research Corporation, *The Costs of Sprawl: Environmental and Economic Costs of Alternative Residential Development Patterns at the Urban Fringe* (1974). As discussed in Robert Burchell and others, "The Costs of Sprawl—Revisited" (Washington: National Academy Press, 1998).

Riche, Martha, "The Implications of Changing U.S. Demographics for Housing Choice and Location in U.S. Cities" (Washington: Brookings Institution, 2001)

Sanders, Heywood, "Space Available: The Realities of Convention Centers as Economic Development Strategy" (Washington: Brookings Institution, 2005).

Singer, Audrey , "The Rise of New Immigrant Gateways." In A. Berube, B. Katz, and R. Lang, *Redefining Urban and Suburban America: Evidence from Census 2000, Volume II* (Washington: Brookings Institution, 2005).

Suro, Robert and Singer, Audrey , "Latino Growth in Metropolitan America: Changing Patterns, New Locations." In B. Katz and R. Lang, eds., *Redefining Urban and Suburban America: Evidence from Census 2000, Volume I* (Washington: Brookings Institution, 2003).

Swanstrom, Todd et al, "Pulling Apart: Economic Segregation among Suburbs and Central Cities in Major Metropolitan Areas" (Washington: Brookings Institution, 2004).

Tunstall, Rebecca, "Using the U.S. and U.K. Censuses for Comparative Research" (Washington: Brookings Institution, 2005).

U.S. Census Bureau, "U.S. Interim Projections by Age, Sex, Race, and Hispanic Origin" (March 18, 2004).

U.S. Census Bureau, Historical Poverty Tables, Table 8: Poverty of People, by Residence.

Vey, Jennifer and Forman, Benjamin, "Demographic Change in Medium-Sized Cities: Evidence from the 2000 Census" (Washington: Brookings Institution, 2002).

Weissbourd, Robert and Berry, Christopher , "Grads and Fads: The Dynamics of Human Capital Location." Draft paper, 2004.

Glossary

A/AS	GCE/VCE A/AS Examinations
ABC	Anti-Social Behaviour Contract
ABI	Area Based Initiative
ACE	Annual Census of Employment
ALMO	Arm's Length Management Organisation
AMION	Amion Consulting
ASB	Anti-Social Behaviour
ASBO	Anti-Social Behaviour Order
AWM	Advantage West Midlands
BCS	British Crime Survey
BL	Business Link
BMEB	Black Minority Ethnic Businesses
BV	Best Value
BVCA	British Venture Capital Association
BVPI	Best Value Performance Indicator
CABE	Commission for Architecture & the Built Environment
CAG	CAG consultants
CC	Community Chest
CCWG	Core Cities Working Group
CDFI	Community Development Finance Institutions
CDRP	Crime and Disorder Reduction Partnership
CEA	Cambridge Economic Associates
CEEDR	Centre for Enterprise & Economic Development Research
CEF	Community Empowerment Fund
CEN	Community Empowerment Network
CIS	Community Innovation Survey
CLC	Community Learning Chest
COVE	Centres of Vocational Excellence
CPA	Comprehensive Performance Assessment
CPO	Compulsory Purchase Order
CPP	Community Participation Programme
CPRE	Council for the Preservation of Rural England
CS	Community Chest
CSGC	Cleaner Safer Greener Communities
CSO	Central Statistical Office
DCMS	Department for Culture, Media and Sport
DEFRA	Department for Environment Food and Rural Affairs
DETR	Department for the Environment, Transport and Regions
DfEE	Department for Education and Employment
DfES	Department for Education and Science
DfT	Department for Transport

DOE	Department of the Environment
DoH	Department of Health
DoT	Department of Transport
DTI	Department for Trade and Industry
DTLR	Department for Transport, Local Government and Regions
DWP	Department for Work and Pensions
EAS	Enterprise Allowance Scheme
EAZ	Education Action Zones
EC	European Commission
EHCS	English Housing Conditions Survey
EiC	Excellence in Cities
ENCAMS	Environmental Campaigns
EP	English Partnerships
EPO	European Patent Office
ESF	European Social Fund
ESOL	English for Speakers of Other Languages
EtFSfE	Entitlement to Foundation Skills for Employability
EZ	Enterprise Zone
FTE	Full-time Equivalent
GCSE	General Certificate of Secondary Education
GDHI	Gross Domestic Household Income
GDP	Gross Domestic Product
GHK	GHK Consulting Limited
GIS	Geographical Information Systems
GLA	Greater London Authority
GNVQ	General National Vocational Qualification
GO	Government Office
GONW	Government Office for North West
GOR	Government Office for the Regions
GOWM	Government Office for West Midlands
GSE	Greater South East
GVA	Gross Added Value
HAT	Housing Action Trust
HAZ	Health Action Zone
HC	Housing Corporation
HE	Higher Education
HEFC	Higher Education Funding Council
HEFCE	Higher Education Funding Council for England
HEI	Higher Education Institutions
HEIF	Higher Education Innovation Fund
HEROBAC	Higher Education Reach-Out to Business and the Community
HLF	Heritage Lottery Fund
HMRP	Housing Market Renewal Pathfinder

HMT	Her Majesty's Treasury
IC	Inner City
ICIC	Initiative for a Competitive Inner City
ICT	Information Communication Technology
ID	Index of Dissimilarity
IDeA	Improvement and Development Agency
IMD	Index of Multiple Deprivation
IPD	Investment Property Data Bank
IS	Income Support
ISCED	International Standard Classification of Education
JSA	Job-Seekers Allowance
KIBS	Knowledge Intensive Business Sector
KS	Key Stage
KTF	Knowledge Transfer Partnerships
LA	Local Authority
LAA	Local Area Agreement
LEA	Local Education Authority
LFS	Labour Force Survey
LGA	Local Government Association
LGMA	Local Government Modernisation Agenda
LIFT	Local Improvement Finance Trust
LLSC	Local Learning and Skills Council
LNRS	Local Neighbourhood Renewal Strategy
LPC	Low Pay Commission
LPSA	Local Public Service Agreements
LSC	Learning Skills Council
LSP	Local Strategic Partnership
LSVT	Large Scale Voluntary Transfers
MORI	Market and Opinion Research International
NACRO	National Association for the Care and Rehabilitation of Offenders
NAO	National Audit Office
NAPO	National Association for Probation Officers
NDC	New Deal for the Community
ND50	New Deal for 50+
NDLP	New Deal for Lone Parents
NDYP	New Deal for Young People
NEF	New Economics Foundation
NESS	National Evaluation of Sure Start
NFER	National Foundation for Educational Research
NHF	National Housing Foundation
NHS	National Health Service
NIC	National Insurance Contribution
NLUD	National Land Use Database

NM	Neighbourhood Management
NMP	Neighbourhood Management Pathfinder
NOF	New Opportunities Fund
NOMIS	Web-based database for Official Labour Market Statistics
NRA	Neighbourhood Renewal Area
NRF	Neighbourhood Renewal Fund
NRU	Neighbourhood Renewal Unit
NSNR	National Strategy For Neighbourhood Renewal
NVQ	National Vocational Qualification
NWDA	North West Development Agency
NWRA	North West Regional Assembly
OECD	Organisation for Economic Co-operation and Development
ODPM	Office of the Deputy Prime Minister
OFSTED	Office for Standards and Training in Education
OPM	Office of Public Management
ONS	Office for National Statistics
PACEC	PA Cambridge Economic Consultants
PAT	Policy Action Team
PCT	Primary Care Trust
PDG	Planning Delivery Grant
PDL	Previously Developed Land
PIU	Performance and Innovation Unit
PPG	Planning Policy Guidance
PSA	Public Service Agreement
PTA	Parent Teacher Association
PUA	Primary Urban Area
RCE	Regional Centres of Excellence
RCU	Regional Co-ordination Unit
R&D	Research and Development
RDA	Regional Development Agency
RSA	Regional Selective Assistance
RSL	Registered Social Landlords
RSP	Regional Spatial Plan
SBS	Small Business Service
SCI	Street Crime Initiative
SCP	Sustainable Cities Programme
SEM	Street Environment Management
SEU	Social Exclusion Unit
SEH	Survey of English Housing
SfBN	Skills for Business Network
SIGOMA	Special Interest Group of Municipal Authorities
SLMC	Single Local Management Centre
SMART	SMART – DTI scheme for Small and Medium-Sized Enterprises

SME	Small and Medium-Sized Enterprises
SOA	Super Output Area
SOC	State of the Cities
SOCD	State of the Cities Database
SOCR	State of the Cities English Report
SQW	SQW Consultants
SRB	Single Regeneration Budget
SS	Sure Start
SSLP	Sure Start Local Parnterships
TCPA	Town & County Planning Association
TEC	Training and Enterprise Council
TFL	Transport for London
TGV	Train Grand Vitesse
TTWAs	Travel to Work Areas
URBIS	Museum of Urban Life, Manchester
UA	Urban Authority
UDC	Urban Development Corporation
UPD	Urban Policy Directorate
URC	Urban Regeneration Company
WBLA	Work Based Learning for Adults
WFTC	Working Family Tax Credit

Not included :	CCTV
	EU
	HMSO
	US
	VAT

Notes

Notes

Notes

Notes

Notes